XQUERY FROM THE EXPERTS

XQuery from the Experts

A Guide to the W3C XML Query Language

Howard Katz, Editor

Don Chamberlin, Denise Draper, Mary Fernández,
Michael Kay, Jonathan Robie, Michael Rys,
Jérôme Siméon, Jim Tivy, Philip Wadler

✦✦ Addison-Wesley

Boston • San Francisco • New York • Toronto • Montreal
London • Munich • Paris • Madrid
Capetown • Sydney • Tokyo • Singapore • Mexico City

The publisher offers discounts on this book when ordered in quantity for bulk purchases and special sales. For more information, please contact:

U.S. Corporate and Government Sales
(800) 382-3419
corpsales@pearsontechgroup.com

For sales outside of the U.S., please contact:

International Sales
(317) 581-3793
international@pearsontechgroup.com

Visit Addison-Wesley on the Web: www.awprofessional.com

Library of Congress Cataloging-in-Publication Data

XQuery from the experts : a guide to the W3C XML query language /
editor: Howard Katz ; authors Don Chamberlin ... [et al.]..
    p. cm.
  ISBN 0-321-18060-7 (alk. paper)
  1. Query languages (computer science) I. Katz, Howard. II.
Chamberlin, D. D. (Donald Dean)
    QA76.7.X64 2003
    005.13—dc21   2003012521

ISBN: 0-321-18060-7
Text printed on recycled paper
1 2 3 4 5 6 7 8 9 10—CRS—0706050403
First printing, August 2003

CONTENTS

PREFACE

Extensible Markup Language (XML) is everywhere. In an astonishingly short period of time, XML has worked itself into the nooks and crannies of corporate IT departments, academic research institutions, and small-shop programming operations everywhere. As one of the authors of this book points out, XML now encodes a bewildering array of datatypes scattered across a large number of diverse application domains.

Where there's information, there are people who are going to need to query that information. Happily, XQuery has come along to provide a powerful and standardized way of searching through all that XML-encapsulated data. Going beyond Google, XQuery provides a flexible and easy-to-use mechanism for querying not only content, but structure as well. Drawing from XSLT, XQuery doesn't content itself with simply providing a query capability; it does transformations too. I believe that it will increasingly replace XSLT in a number of application areas (though XSLT aficionados needn't fear—there are plenty of things to do for both technologies). Most interestingly, some of the data that XQuery will manipulate won't even have started life as XML: A large portion of the data that XQuery deals with will have started life in the form of rows and columns in corporate relational databases.

This Book

Most technical books are either tutorials or reference works. You turn to the former if you're looking for a gentle introduction to a new subject; you look to the latter if you already know something about the subject and want a minimum of hand-holding while you seek out the information you need. This book is unusual in that it shares some of the characteristics of each. It consists of a series of technical essays and perspectives, some of them tutorial-like, on various facets of XQuery from members of the World Wide Web Consortium's (W3C) Query working group, the standards body that has been hard at work creating and crafting the formal definition of the language since the fall of 1999. Their intimate knowledge sheds a lot of light on a technical topic that some find daunting, given the weight and density of the formal spec.

Members of the working group would probably be embarrassed to hear themselves referred to here as "experts," as the title implies, but that's what they are. Nobody knows the material better than this group—after all, they created it! In this case you could say (pun intended) that they "wrote the book." And not just the one you're reading: They also wrote most of the specification itself, since nearly every one of the authors is also an editor of one or more of the numerous documents that comprise the formal specification.

In addition to being intimately involved in the creation of XQuery and the specification documents that define it (twelve at this point and counting), the credentials shared by the collective authorship of this book is impressive. They are researchers and theoreticians, software architects, product managers, educators, and database implementers. They are the designers of no less than six influential computer languages, including Haskell, Quilt, XML-QL, YATL, XQL, and SQL. Their views on query languages and XML are helping to shape the technology strategies of some of the most influential computer companies in the world. All in all, an impressive group! The "Contributors" section gives the bona fides of all our experts. It's worth perusing.

This book provides an opportunity for these people to write individually about the XQuery topics they know best and about which they are most passionate. It allows each of them to write with a personal voice and perspective in a way that's not possible within the carefully and consensually crafted framework of a formal standards specification.

Who Should Read This Book?

You should read this book if you're interested in XQuery—a statement that describes numerous technophiles these days. The members of two programming disciplines in particular, however, will find this volume especially valuable. XSLT developers will be interested in these essays. As noted above, XQuery shares a number of capabilities with XSLT and is likely to replace it in some areas. Michael Kay's chapter on "XQuery, XPath, and XSLT" (Chapter 3) examines the commonalities and differences between the two languages in some detail.

This book will also interest those who are corporately or otherwise involved with SQL and relational databases. XQuery has often been called SQL for XML, and that's no accident, given that several members of the working group come from a relational database background. XQuery was designed from the ground up to work with relational data. Two of the chapters in Part IV, "Databases," examine the connections between XQuery and relational data.

Whatever your specific background, you should be comfortable and familiar with XML basics to benefit most fully from this book. You'll do best if you have some prior exposure to XQuery, although it needn't be extensive. At a minimum, the book assumes that you understand the fundamentals of XPath and know what a location path is. Jonathan Robie's introductory guided tour provides a good overview of XQuery for those who aren't already familiar with the technology.

Organization and Roadmap

Your approach to this material will depend on your specific experience and interests. Here's a quick roadmap to the four parts of the book and a look at the individual chapters to help you figure out where to dive in first.

- Part I: Basics
- Part II: Background
- Part III: Formal Underpinnings
- Part IV: Databases

Part I: Basics

Jonathan Robie's "XQuery: A Guided Tour" provides a good starting point if you're new or relatively new to XQuery. Its easy, tutorial-like style invites you to read it straight through. Jonathan provides a compact and convenient reference to XQuery's key features that newcomers and experts alike can return to periodically for a quick refresher on the basics while working through the detail in the other chapters. Jonathan's coverage is extensive; most of the entries in the glossary (a useful resource when you're stumbling across new terminology) are introduced in this chapter. (Note that glossary entries are **bolded** the first time they appear within the text.)

Part II: Background

The two chapters in Part II provide historical context and a detailed rationale for many of the complex technical decisions the Query working group has had to make as the language has evolved.

As Don Chamberlin explains in Chapter 2, "Influences on the Design of XQuery," the process of designing XQuery has been one of resolving the tensions between conflicting goals, and his chapter provides a historical and technical description of that dialectic in action. This chapter also places XQuery in the context of the other related languages and standards with which it coexists. The second half of the chapter deals in cogent detail with the intricacies of what Don calls "watershed issues": eight complex and often controversial issues that have had a major impact on the design of the language. Don goes a long way to teasing apart the complexities.

As Michael Kay notes in Chapter 3, "XQuery, XPath, and XSLT," the fact that both these languages share a common data model, as well as a common sublanguage in XPath, is a major achievement of the W3C. His chapter explores that commonality and the overlap in functionality between the two languages, as well as their differences. This chapter describes where each language might be employed to best advantage. Mike addresses some of the same issues discussed by Don Chamberlin in the previous chapter but from the particular perspectives of XPath and XSLT.

Part III: Formal Underpinnings

Both chapters in Part III were written by Mary Fernández, Jérôme Siméon, and Philip Wadler. Chapter 4, "Static Typing in XQuery," is a gentle tutorial that explores the ramifications of static typing in a language dealing with XML data. Despite the term *formal* in the title of this part, this chapter fits naturally here because it provides such a great lead-in to the chapter on the formal semantics—the topic isn't difficult or particularly heavy. Static typing is important to XQuery developers because it helps to guarantee program correctness, and it helps significantly to speed up the development cycle, as this chapter attests. Users need to understand the concept of static typing in order to better understand the error messages returned by the query system they're working with.

Chapter 5, "Introduction to the Formal Semantics," is a tutorial-like introduction to the formal semantics, the formal mathematical system on which XQuery is built. This is the most challenging technical component of XQuery. This chapter should appeal to implementers, language theoreticians, and those just terminally curious about this aspect of the language. They will find here a much less daunting approach to the formal semantics than that provided by the specification.

Part IV: Databases

Most major relational database vendors already have or will shortly provide support for XQuery as a front end for relational data, and interest in XQuery from this market sector was one of the driving forces behind its development. Chapters 6 and 7 deal with the topic of XQuery and relational data. The authors collaborated on the content so that the chapters would fit seamlessly together. The last chapter in this part describes the features of what its author refers to as an XML database management system.

XQuery was designed to query XML, and using it to query and pull data out of relational databases that store information in tabular format poses a number of interesting challenges. Denise Draper explores these issues in "Mapping between XML and Relational Data."

Michael Rys's chapter, "Integrating XQuery and Relational Database Systems," builds on the foundation laid in Chapter 6. Michael shows two methods of accessing XML stored in a relational database. One approach uses the XML datatype to store XML into the database as an LOB (large object) and accesses that data using a combination of both XQuery and SQL. He also describes a so-called "top-level XQuery" approach that obviates the need to use SQL altogether.

Jim Tivy's concluding chapter, "A Native XML DBMS," rounds out the offerings in this part. Jim describes the key features of what he calls an XML database management system and explores what that means. He looks at the use of the XQuery data model in that context and explores other XML DBMS features such as command languages and APIs, drawing on his experience with XStreamDB (his own native XML database product), Tamino, and the XML:DB Initiative.

Software

Let's not close without mentioning an extremely valuable resource if you're tracking what's going on with XQuery, `http://www.w3.org/XML/Query`, the W3C XML Query website. This is the official website of the working group, and just about everything relevant to XQuery gets posted here sooner or later, whether it's pointers to the latest specifications, news and articles on XQuery in the trade and technical press, information on the various discussion groups you can join or monitor, and an ever-growing list of real-life XQuery implementations.

Some of these are free, some are open-source (not always the same thing), some are full-strength, industrial products, and some come in the form of online demos. All the authors in this book are involved either directly or indirectly in XQuery-related software efforts at their various companies and research institutions (which shouldn't surprise anybody if you think about it, since most companies on the working group have XQuery projects under way), and a number of the authors of this book have been involved in the development of the software on this list.

Just to mention a few of these author/software connections: Mary Fernández, Jérôme Siméon, and Phil Wadler have all been involved in Lucent's implementation of Galax (which lets you make queries directly in the syntax of the formal semantics). Jim Tivy has already been mentioned in connection with XStreamDB. Jonathan Robie was active in Software AG's development of QuiP (which is a great reference implementation for hands-on exploration of XQuery syntax and semantics, although I'm told it's no longer being maintained), and even I have an open-source, Java-based implementation called XQEngine. Please visit the XML Query website for an up-to-date listing of all the XQuery software that's currently available. The list is growing daily.

Cover Photograph

The photograph on the cover was taken by Don Chamberlin on a visit to the Bronx Botanical Garden in 1972. The tulips are reminiscent of XQuery's FLWOR expression, one of its central and most powerful constructs.

Ongoing

XQuery is alive and still under development, and some of the information in this book is accordingly subject to change. Current information on the status of the specification, as well as corrections to the inevitable typos in the book, will be posted on an ongoing basis at `http:www.fatdog.com/experts.html`.

CONTRIBUTORS

Don Chamberlin

Don Chamberlin is one of IBM's representatives in the W3C XML Query Working Group. He is also a co-author of the Quilt language proposal, which formed the basis for the XQuery design. Don is best known as co-inventor of the SQL database language and as author of two books on the DB2 database system. He holds a Ph.D. from Stanford University and is an IBM Fellow at IBM's Almaden Research Center. He is also an ACM Fellow and a member of the National Academy of Engineering. Don is an editor of the working drafts of *XML Query Use Cases* [XQ-UC], *XQuery 1.0: An XML Query Language* [XQ-LANG], and *XML Path Language (XPath) 2.0* [XPATH2].

Denise Draper

Denise Draper is Chief Technology Officer for Nimble Technology, developer of an XML-based data integration platform for web services. Denise is the designer and visionary behind the development of the product and holds several patents for its XML-based technology. Prior to joining Nimble in 1999, Denise was the lead researcher for several research projects at Rockwell's Palo Alto Research Lab. She earned her B.S. degree in Engineering from Caltech, followed by a Ph.D. in Computer Science from the University of Washington. Denise is an editor of the working draft of *XQuery 1.0 Formal Semantics* [XQ-FS].

Mary Fernández

Mary Fernández is a Principal Technical Staff Member in Large-Scale Programming Research at AT&T Labs—Research. Mary has been at AT&T Labs since she received her Ph.D. in Computer Science from Princeton University in 1995. Her research focuses on improving software development through the design of domain-specific languages and the development of tools for their efficient implementation. She has developed small languages for a variety of domains, including retargetable compilers and linkers, web-site management systems, and database applications. Mary is an editor of the working drafts of *XQuery 1.0 and XPath 2.0 Data Model* [XQ-DM], *XML Path Language (XPath) 2.0* [XPATH2], and *XQuery 1.0 Formal Semantics* [XQ-FS].

Howard Katz

Howard Katz lives in Roberts Creek, British Columbia, Canada, where he runs Fatdog Software, a company that specializes in software for searching XML documents. He's been an active programmer for more than thirty-five years (with time off for good behavior) and is a long-time contributor of technical articles to the computer trade press. He is the author of XQEngine, an open-source, Java-based, full-text XQuery engine hosted at SourceForge. He's lived and traveled extensively in Japan, can order sushi in reasonably good Japanese, co-hosts the Vancouver XML Developer's Association, and does backcountry skiing and ocean kayaking in his spare time with his wife Peg.

Michael Kay

Michael Kay is best known for his work on XSLT, as the developer of the open-source XSLT processor Saxon, and as author of a popular XSLT reference book, *XSLT Programmer's Reference*, now in its second edition. In the course of a long career with the U.K. computer manufacturer ICL, he successively led the design teams for Codasyl, relational, object-oriented, and text database products. He joined Software AG as a member of the architecture team in February 2001 and has recently been appointed as Software AG's representative on the W3C XML Query working group.

His background (and Ph.D.) is in database technology. Michael is an editor of the working drafts of *XSL Transformations (XSLT) Version 1.0* [XSLT], *XSLT 2.0 and XQuery 1.0 Serialization* [SERIAL], and *XML Path Language (XPath) 2.0* [XPATH2].

Jonathan Robie

Jonathan Robie is the XML Product Architect at DataDirect Technologies, working on products that integrate XML and traditional data sources. He has been on the architectural team for XML databases or repositories at three different companies: Software AG, Texcel Research, and POET Software. Jonathan has been a regular speaker at SGML and XML conferences since 1996, and was a regular speaker at object-oriented developer's conferences from 1991 to 1995.

Jonathan was a co-author of two earlier XML query languages: Quilt, the direct ancestor of XQuery, and XQL, a precursor of XPath. Prior to his work with XML, he was an object database specialist at POET Software, where he implemented transactions in the kernel, designed and presented workshops on object database programming, and provided key-customer support. Before that, he worked as a freelance consultant for five years. He has an M.S. in Computer Science from Michigan State University.

Jonathan is an editor of the working drafts of *XQuery 1.0: An XML Query Language* [XQ-LANG], *XML Query Requirements* [XQ-REQ], *XML Syntax for XQuery 1.0 (XQueryX)* [XQ-X], and *XML Path Language (XPath) 2.0* [XPATH2]. He is also a member of the XML Schema Working Group, an editor of the Schema Formalization document, and a former editor of the W3C Document Object Model for both Level 1 and Level 2. He is also one of the authors of the Schema Adjunct Framework.

Michael Rys

After finishing his Ph.D. at the Swiss Federal Institute of Technology in Zurich in the area of database systems, Michael went to Stanford University for postdoctoral work, where he worked on semi-structured databases and distributed heterogeneous information integration. In late 1998, he joined Microsoft Corporation in Redmond, where he is now a Program Manager for SQL Server's XML Technologies. Michael is a member of the ACM and IEEE. He is an editor of the working drafts of *XQuery 1.0 Formal Semantics* [XQ-FS], *XML Syntax for XQuery 1.0 (XQueryX)* [XQ-X], *XML Query Requirements* [XQ-REQ], and *XML Query and XPath Full-Text Requirements* [XQ-FULL-REQ].

Jérôme Siméon

Jérôme Siméon is a member of the Technical Staff at Bell Labs, a division of Lucent Technologies. He graduated from École Polytechnique in France, then spent several years at INRIA, and obtained his Ph.D. in Computer Science from Université D'Orsay. His research interests and expertise are in XML technology, XML query and schema languages, data integration, optimization, and formal methods. He is also one of the implementers of Galax, one of the first XQuery 1.0 implementations. Jérôme is an editor of the working drafts of *XQuery 1.0: An XML Query Language* [XQ-LANG], *XML Path Language (XPath) 2.0* [XPATH2], and *XQuery 1.0 Formal Semantics* [XQ-FS].

Jim Tivy

Jim has spent over ten years working with database technology. He was the system architect of the ODBC 1.0 SQL Engine project for Microsoft Corporation, designing and developing a database engine capable of accessing Microsoft Access, BTrieve, DBase, FoxPro, and text format databases. He was the architect and designer of a multimedia database engine for Adobe. Jim is currently the System Architect at BlueStream Database Software Corporation, where he has designed and overseen implementation of the XStreamDB native XML database, a pure Java, multi-transactional, multi-threaded database engine with an XQuery front-end. He currently represents XML Global Technologies on the W3C XML Query Languages working group.

Philip Wadler

Philip is a researcher at Avaya Labs. He likes to introduce theory into practice, and practice into theory. An example of the former is GJ, the basis for Sun's new version of Java with generics, which derives from quantifiers in second-order logic. An example of the latter is Featherweight Java, a simplification of Java comparable in power and simplicity to lambda calculus (the theory underlying functional languages). Phil is a principal designer of the Haskell programming language, and he co-authored *Introduction to Functional Programming*, which has been translated into Dutch, German, and Japanese.

In previous incarnations, Phil has worked or studied at Bell Labs, Glasgow, Oxford, Carnegie Mellon, Xerox Parc, and Stanford, and has served as guest professor in Sydney and Copenhagen. He edits the *Journal of Functional Programming* for Cambridge University Press and has been invited to give talks all around the world.

Phil is an editor of the working drafts of W3C's *XQuery 1.0 and XPath 2.0 Formal Semantics* [XQ-FS] and *XML Schema: Formal Description*, two efforts to shine the light of mathematics into the murk of industrial standards.

Acknowledgments

Howard wants to thank all the authors for their hard work on this book, on top of already punishing schedules. He wants in particular to acknowledge Michael Kay for going above and beyond the call of duty with his editing work on Jim Tivy's chapter. He wants to thank all the Addison-Wesley staff, including Mary O'Brien, Brenda Mulligan, Alicia Carey, Patrick Cash-Peterson, and Amy Fleischer, for their unfailing and courteous help. He'd like to thank the reviewers for their always useful feedback, and in particular wants to acknowledge Mike Champion for his good humor, his encyclopedic knowledge of XML, and the exquisite sensitivity with which he's always able to point out better ways of doing things. Lastly, Howard wants to thank his loving wife, Peg, for her near-infinite patience and for almost single-handedly building their dream house in the woods while Howard worked on this project.

The authors as a group want to acknowledge their appreciation for the work of all the members of the W3C XML Query and XSLT working groups, who are responsible for the design of XQuery and XPath, and especially for the leadership of Paul Cotton and Sharon Adler, chairs of the two working groups.

Don Chamberlin would like to thank his family and his colleagues at IBM for their support of his work on XQuery.

Mary Fernández thanks her husband Adam Buchsbaum and daughters Elena and Shira for their good cheer and patience during more than three years of travel for XQuery and for making everything that matters in life possible.

Michael Rys would like to thank Howard for encouraging the authors to write this book and the members of the XQuery and XSLT working groups for their relentless work on getting XPath and XQuery defined. He would also like to thank the people at Microsoft with whom he works for their inspiration and influence, especially Istvan Cseri, Michael Brundage, Shankar Pal, Gideon Schaller, Oliver Seeliger, and Joe Xavier, as well as the people working on SQL and XML standardization, especially Fred Zemke, Jim Melton, Andrew Eisenberg, Krishna Kulkarni, and Berthold Reinwald. Last but not least, he would like to express his gratitude to the joys of his life: Ursula, Janine, and Nils.

Jim Tivy would like to thank his family for their support and understanding.

Jonathan Robie would like to thank his wife, Esther, whose support has made it possible for him to participate in the work on XQuery, and his daughters Marissa, Emily, and Bethany, who missed out on time with their father while he was writing his chapter. He is also grateful to the members of the XML Query working group, from whom he has learned much and with whom he's grown, both as a computer scientist and as a person. He dedicates his chapter to the late Nigel Hutchison, who had an unusual gift for finding and appreciating the good in people and helping them to develop it and put it to use.

Mary Fernández, Jérôme Siméon, and Philip Wadler, the co-authors of Chapters 4 and 5, thank their colleagues in the XML Query working group, especially the co-editors of the XQuery Formal Semantics. They'd like to acknowledge the particularly important contributions made by Denise Draper, Peter Fankhauser, and Kristoffer Rose. Kristoffer Rose also provided invaluable help in typesetting.

Part I

Basics

Chapter 1
XQUERY:
A GUIDED TOUR

Jonathan Robie

XML (**Extensible Markup Language**) is an extremely versatile data format that has been used to represent many different kinds of data, including web pages, web messages, books, business and accounting data, XML representations of **relational database** tables, programming interfaces, objects, financial transactions, chess games, vector graphics, multimedia presentations, credit applications, system logs, and textual variants in ancient Greek manuscripts.

In addition, some systems offer XML views of non-XML data sources such as relational databases, allowing XML-based processing of data that is not physically represented as XML. An XML document can represent almost anything, and users of an XML **query language** expect it to perform useful queries on whatever they have stored in XML. Examples illustrating the variety of XML documents and queries that operate on them appear in [XQ-UC].

However complex the data stored in XML may be, the structure of XML itself is simple. An XML document is essentially an outline in which order and hierarchy are the two main structural units. XQuery is based on the structure of XML and leverages this structure to provide query capabilities for the same range of data that XML stores. To be more precise, XQuery is defined in terms of the XQuery 1.0 and **XPath** 2.0 Data Model [XQ-DM], which represents the parsed structure of an XML document as an ordered, labeled tree in which **nodes** have **identity** and may be associated with simple or **complex types.** XQuery can be used to query XML data that has no **schema** at all, or that is governed by a **World Wide Web Consortium** (W3C) **XML Schema** or by a **Document Type Definition** (DTD). Note that the **data model** used by XQuery is quite different from the classical relational model, which has no hierarchy, treats order as insignificant, and does not support identity. XQuery is a **functional language**—instead of executing commands as procedural languages do, every query is an expression to be evaluated, and expressions can be combined quite flexibly with other expressions to create new expressions.

This chapter gives a high-level introduction to the XQuery language by presenting a series of examples, each of which illustrates an important feature of the language and shows how it is used in practice. Some of the examples are drawn from [XQ-UC]. We cover most of the language features of XQuery, but also focus on teaching the idioms used to solve specific kinds of problems with XQuery. We start with a discussion of the structure of XML documents as input and output to queries and then present basic operations on XML—locating nodes in XML structures using **path expressions,** constructing XML structures with **element constructors,** and combining and restructuring information from XML documents using **FLWOR expressions,** sorting, conditional expressions, and quantified expressions. After that, we explore operators and functions, discussing arithmetic operators, comparisons, some of the common functions in the XQuery function library, and how to write and call user-defined functions. Finally, we discuss how to import and use XML Schema **types** in queries.

Many users will learn best if they have access to a working implementation of XQuery. Several good implementations can be downloaded for free from the Internet; a list of these appears on the W3C XML Query Working Group home page, which is found at `http://www.w3.org/xml/Query.html`.

This chapter is based on the May 2003 Working Draft of the XQuery language. XQuery is still under development, and some aspects of the language discussed in this chapter may change.

Sample Data: A Bibliography

This chapter uses bibliography data to illustrate the basic features of XQuery. The data used is taken from the XML Query Use Cases, Use Case "XMP," and originally appeared in [EXEMPLARS]. We have modified the data slightly to illustrate some of the points to be made. The data used appears in Listing 1.1.

Listing 1.1   Bibliography Data for Use Case "XMP"

```
<bib>
    <book year="1994">
        <title>TCP/IP Illustrated</title>
        <author><last>Stevens</last><first>W.</first></author>
        <publisher>Addison-Wesley</publisher>
        <price>65.95</price>
    </book>

    <book year="1992">
        <title>Advanced Programming in the UNIX Environment</title>
        <author><last>Stevens</last><first>W.</first></author>
        <publisher>Addison-Wesley</publisher>
        <price>65.95</price>
        </book>

    <book year="2000">
        <title>Data on the Web</title>
        <author><last>Abiteboul</last><first>Serge</first></author>
        <author><last>Buneman</last><first>Peter</first></author>
        <author><last>Suciu</last><first>Dan</first></author>
        <publisher>Morgan Kaufmann Publishers</publisher>
        <price>65.95</price>
    </book>

    <book year="1999">
        <title>The Economics of Technology and Content
            for Digital TV</title>
        <editor>
           <last>Gerbarg</last>
           <first>Darcy</first>
           <affiliation>CITI</affiliation>
        </editor>
        <publisher>Kluwer Academic Publishers</publisher>
        <price>129.95</price>
    </book>

</bib>
```

The data for this example was created using a DTD, which specifies that a bibliography is a sequence of books, each book has a title, publication year (as an **attribute**), an author or an editor, a publisher, and a price, and each author or editor has a first and a last name, and an editor has an affiliation. Listing 1.2 provides the DTD for our example.

Listing 1.2   DTD for the Bibliography Data

```
<!ELEMENT bib   (book* )>
<!ELEMENT book   (title,  (author+ | editor+ ), publisher, price )>
<!ATTLIST book  year CDATA  #REQUIRED >
<!ELEMENT author  (last, first )>
<!ELEMENT editor  (last, first, affiliation )>
<!ELEMENT title   (#PCDATA )>
<!ELEMENT last   (#PCDATA )>
<!ELEMENT first   (#PCDATA )>
<!ELEMENT affiliation   (#PCDATA )>
<!ELEMENT publisher   (#PCDATA )>
<!ELEMENT price   (#PCDATA )>
```

Data Model

XQuery is defined in terms of a formal data model, not in terms of XML text. Every input to a query is an instance of the data model, and the output of every query is an instance of the data model. In the XQuery data model, every document is represented as a tree of nodes. The kinds of nodes that may occur are: document, **element,** attribute, text, **namespace,** processing instruction, and comment. Every node has a unique node identity that distinguishes it from other nodes—even from other nodes that are otherwise identical.

In addition to nodes, the data model allows **atomic values,** which are single values that correspond to the **simple types** defined in the W3C Recommendation, "XML Schema, Part 2" [SCHEMA], such as strings, Booleans, decimals, integers, floats and doubles, and dates. These simple types may occur in any document associated with a W3C XML Schema. As we will see later, we can also represent several simple types directly as literals in the XQuery language, including strings, integers, doubles, and decimals.

An **item** is a single node or atomic value. A series of items is known as a sequence. In XQuery, every value is a sequence, and there is no distinction between a single item and a sequence of length one. Sequences can only contain nodes or atomic values; they cannot contain other sequences.

The first node in any document is the document node, which contains the entire document. The document node does not correspond to anything visible in the document; it represents the document itself. Element nodes, comment nodes, and processing instruction nodes occur in the order in which they are found in the XML (after expansion of entities). Element nodes occur before their children—the element nodes, text nodes, comment nodes, and processing instructions they contain. Attributes are not considered children of an element, but they have a defined position in **document order:** They occur after the element in which they are found, before the children of the element. The relative order of attribute nodes is implementation-dependent. In document order, each node occurs precisely once, so sorting nodes in document order removes duplicates.

An easy way to understand document order is to look at the text of an XML document and mark the first character of each element **start tag,** attribute name, processing instruction, comment, or text node. If the first character of one node occurs before the first character of another node, it will precede that node in document order. Let's explore this using the following small XML document:

```
<!— document order —>
<book year="1994">
    <title>TCP/IP Illustrated</title>
    <author><last>Stevens</last><first>W.</first></author>
</book>
```

The first node of any document is the document node. After that, we can identify the sequence of nodes by looking at the sequence of start characters found in the original document—these are identified by underlines in the example. The second node is the comment, followed by the book element, the year attribute, the title element, the text node containing `TCP/IP Illustrated`, the author element, the last element, the text node containing `Stevens`, the first element, and the text node containing `W`.

Literals and Comments

XQuery uses "smiley faces" to begin and end comments. This cheerful notation was originally suggested by Jeni Tennison. Here is an example of a comment:

```
(: Thanks, Jeni! :)
```

Note that XQuery comments are comments found in a query. XML documents may also have comments, like the comment found in an earlier example:

```
<!- document order ->
```

XQuery comments do not create XML comments—XQuery has a constructor for this purpose, which is discussed later in the section on constructors.

XQuery supports three kinds of numeric literals. Any number may begin with an optional + or – sign. A number that has only digits is an integer, a number containing only digits and a single decimal point is a decimal, and any valid floating-point literal containing an e or E is a double. These correspond to the XML Schema simple types `xs:integer`, `xs:decimal`, and `xs:double`.

```
1        (: An integer :)
-2       (: An integer :)
+2       (: An integer :)
1.23     (: A decimal  :)
-1.23    (: A decimal  :)
1.2e5    (: A double   :)
-1.2E5   (: A double   :)
```

String literals are delimited by quotation marks or apostrophes. If a string is delimited by quotation marks, it may contain apostrophes; if a string is delimited by apostrophes, it may contain quotation marks:

```
"a string"
'a string'
"This is a string, isn't it?"
'This is a "string"'
```

If the literal is delimited by apostrophes, two adjacent apostrophes within the literal are interpreted as a single apostrophe. Similarly, if the literal is delimited by quotation marks, two adjacent quotation marks within the literal are interpreted as one quotation mark. The following two string literals are identical:

```
"a "" or a ' delimits a string literal"
'a " or a '' delimits a string literal'
```

A string literal may contain predefined entity references. The entity references shown in Table 1.1 are predefined in XQuery.

Here is a string literal that contains two predefined entity references:

```
'&lt;bold&gt;A sample element.&lt;/bold&gt;'
```

Input Functions

XQuery uses input functions to identify the data to be queried. There are two input functions:

1. `doc()` returns an entire document, identifying the document by a **Universal Resource Identifier** (URI). To be more precise, it returns the document node.
2. `collection()` returns a **collection**, which is any sequence of nodes that is associated with a URI. This is often used to identify a database to be used in a query.

TABLE 1.1 Entity References Predefined in XQuery

Entity Reference	Character Represented
`&lt;`	<
`&gt;`	>
`&amp;`	&
`&quot;`	"
`&apos;`	'

If our sample data is in a file named `books.xml`, then the following query returns the entire document:

```
doc("books.xml")
```

A **dynamic error** is raised if the `doc()` function is not able to locate the specified document or the `collection()` function is not able to locate the specified collection.

Locating Nodes: Path Expressions

In XQuery, path expressions are used to locate nodes in XML data. XQuery's path expressions are derived from XPath 1.0 and are identical to the path expressions of XPath 2.0. The functionality of path expressions is closely related to the underlying data model. We start with a few examples that convey the intuition behind path expressions, then define how they operate in terms of the data model.

The most commonly used operators in path expressions locate nodes by identifying their location in the hierarchy of the tree. A path expression consists of a series of one or more **steps,** separated by a slash, `/`, or double slash, `//`. Every step evaluates to a sequence of nodes. For instance, consider the following expression:

```
doc("books.xml")/bib/book
```

This expression opens `books.xml` using the `doc()` function and returns its document node, uses `/bib` to select the `bib` element at the top of the document, and uses `/book` to select the `book` elements within the bib element. This path expression contains three steps. The same books could have been found by the following query, which uses the double slash, `//`, to select all of the `book` elements contained in the document, regardless of the level at which they are found:

```
doc("books.xml")//book
```

Predicates are `Boolean` conditions that select a subset of the nodes computed by a step expression. XQuery uses square brackets around predicates. For instance, the following query returns only authors for which `last="Stevens"` is true:

```
doc("books.xml")/bib/book/author[last="Stevens"]
```

If a predicate contains a single numeric value, it is treated like a subscript. For instance, the following expression returns the first author of each book:

```
doc("books.xml")/bib/book/author[1]
```

Note that the expression `author[1]` will be evaluated for each book. If you want the first author in the entire document, you can use parentheses to force the desired precedence:

```
(doc("books.xml")/bib/book/author)[1]
```

Now let's explore how path expressions are evaluated in terms of the data model. The steps in a path expression are evaluated from left to right. The first step identifies a sequence of nodes using an input function, a variable that has been bound to a sequence of nodes, or a function that returns a sequence of nodes. Some XQuery implementations also allow a path expression to start with a / or //.

Such paths start with the root node of a document, but how this node is identified is implementation-defined. For each / in a path expression, XQuery evaluates the expression on the left-hand side and returns the resulting nodes in document order; if the result contains anything that is not a node, a **type error** is raised. After that, XQuery evaluates the expression on the right-hand side of the / once for each left-hand node, merging the results to produce a sequence of nodes in document order; if the result contains anything that is not a node, a type error is raised. When the right-hand expression is evaluated, the left-hand node for which it is being evaluated is known as the context node.

The step expressions that may occur on the right-hand side of a / are the following:

- A *NameTest*, which selects element or attribute nodes based on their names. A simple string is interpreted as an element name; we have already seen the *NameTest* `bib`, which evaluates to the `bib` elements that are children of the context node. If the name is prefixed by the @ character (pronounced "at"), then the *NameTest* evaluates to the attributes of the context node that have the specified name. For instance, `doc("books.xml")/bib/book/@year` returns the `year` attribute of each book. *NameTest* supports both namespaces and wildcards, which are discussed later in this section.

■ A *KindTest*, which selects processing instructions, comments, text nodes, or any node based on the type of the node. The *KindTest* used to select a given kind of node looks like a function with the same name as the type of the node: `processing-instruction()`, `comment()`, `text()`, and `node()`.

■ An expression that uses an explicit "axis" together with a *NameTest* or *KindTest* to choose nodes with a specific structural relationship to the context node. If the *NameTest* `book` selects `book` elements, then `child::book` selects book elements that are children of the context node; `descendant::book` selects book elements that are descendants of the context node; `attribute::book` selects book attributes of the context node; `self::book` selects the context node if it is a book element, `descendant-or-self::book` selects the context node or any of its descendants if they are book elements, and `parent::book` selects the parent of the context node if it is a book element. Explicit axes are not frequently used in XQuery.

■ A *PrimaryExpression*, which may be a literal, a function call, a variable name, or a parenthetical expression. These are discussed in the next section of this tutorial.

Now let's apply what we have learned to the following expression:

```
doc("books.xml")/bib/book[1]
```

Working from left to right, XQuery first evaluates the input function, `doc("books.xml")`, returning the document node, which becomes the context node for evaluating the expression on the right side of the first slash. This right-hand expression is `bib`, a *NameTest* that returns all elements named `bib` that are children of the context node. There is only one `bib` element, and it becomes the context node for evaluating the expression `book`, which first selects all `book` elements that are children of the context node and then filters them to return only the first book element.

Up to now, we have not defined the `//` operator in terms of the data model. The formal definition of this operator is somewhat complex; intuitively, the `//` operator is used to give access to all attributes and all descendants of the nodes in the left-hand expression, in document order. The expression `doc("books.xml")//bib` matches the `bib` element at the root of our sample document, `doc("books.xml")//book` matches all the `book` elements in the document, and `doc("books.xml")//@year` matches all the `year` attributes in the document. The `//` is formally defined using full axis notation: `//` is equivalent to `/descendant-or-self::node()/`.

For each node from the left-hand expression, the `//` operator takes the node itself, each attribute node, and each descendant node as a context node, then evaluates the right-hand expression. For instance, consider the following expression:

```
doc("books.xml")/bib//author[1]
```

The first step returns the document node, the second step returns the `bib` element, the third step—which is not visible in the original query— evaluates `descendant-or-self::node()` to return the `bib` element and all nodes descended from it, and the fourth step selects the first `author` element for each context node from the third step. Since only `book` elements contain `author` elements, this means that the first author of each book will be returned.

In the examples we have shown so far, *NameTest* uses simple strings to represent names. *NameTest* also supports namespaces, which distinguish names from different vocabularies. Suppose we modify our sample data so that it represents titles with the `title` element from the Dublin Core, a standard set of elements for bibliographical data [DC]. The namespace URI for the Dublin Core is http://purl.org/dc/elements/1.1/. Here is an XML document containing one simple book, in which the `title` element is taken from Dublin Core:

```
<book year="1994" xmlns:dcx="http://purl.org/dc/elements/1.1/">
    <dcx:title>TCP/IP Illustrated</dcx:title>
    <author><last>Stevens</last><first>W.</first></author>
</book>
```

In this data, `xmlns:dcx="http://purl.org/dc/elements/1.1/"` declares the prefix `"dcx"` as a synonym for the full namespace, and the element name `dcx:title` uses the prefix to indicate this is a `title` element as defined in the Dublin Core. The following query finds Dublin Core titles:

```
declare namespace dc="http://purl.org/dc/elements/1.1/"
doc("books.xml")//dc:title
```

The first line declares the namespace `dc` as a synonym for the Dublin Core namespace. Note that the prefix used in the document differs from the prefix used in the query. In XQuery, the name used for comparisons consists of the namespace URI and the "local part," which is `title` for this element.

Wildcards allow queries to select elements or attributes without specifying their entire names. For instance, a query might want to return all the elements of a given book, without specifying each possible element by name. In XQuery, this can be done with the following query:

```
doc("books.xml")//book[1]/*
```

The `*` wildcard matches any element, whether or not it is in a namespace. To match any attribute, use `@*`. To match any name in the namespace associated with the `dc` prefix, use `dc:*`. To match any `title` element, regardless of namespace, use `*:title`.

Creating Nodes: Element, Attribute, and Document Constructors

In the last section, we learned how to locate nodes in XML documents. Now we will learn how to create nodes. Elements, attributes, text nodes, processing instructions, and comments can all be created using the same syntax as XML. For instance, here is an element constructor that creates a book:

```
<book year="1977">
    <title>Harold and the Purple Crayon</title>
    <author><last>Johnson</last><first>Crockett</first></author>
    <publisher>HarperCollins Juvenile Books</publisher>
    <price>14.95</price>
</book>
```

As we have mentioned previously, the document node does not have explicit syntax in XML, but XQuery provides an explicit document node **constructor.** The query `document { }` creates an empty document node. Let's use a document node constructor together with other constructors to create an entire document, including the document node, a processing instruction for stylesheet linking, and an XML comment:

```
document {
  <?xml-stylesheet type="text/xsl"
                   href="c:\temp\double-slash.xslt"?>,
  <!—I love this book! —>,
  <book year="1977">
    <title>Harold and the Purple Crayon</title>
    <author><last>Johnson</last><first>Crockett</first></author>
    <publisher>HarperCollins Juvenile Books</publisher>
    <price>14.95</price>
  </book>
}
```

Constructors can be combined with other XQuery expressions to generate content dynamically. In an element constructor, curly braces, { }, delimit enclosed expressions, which are evaluated to create open content. Enclosed expressions may occur in the content of an element or the value of an attribute. For instance, the following query might be used in an interactive XQuery tutorial to teach how element constructors work:

```
<example>
   <p> Here is a query. </p>
   <eg> doc("books.xml")//book[1]/title </eg>
   <p> Here is the result of the above query.</p>
   <eg>{ doc("books.xml")//book[1]/title }</eg>
</example>
```

Here is the result of executing the above query for our sample data:

```
<example>
   <p> Here is a query. </p>
   <eg> doc("books.xml")//book[1]/title </eg>
   <p> Here is the result of the above query.</p>
   <eg><title>TCP/IP Illustrated</title></eg>
</example>
```

Enclosed expressions in element constructors permit new XML values to be created by restructuring existing XML values. Here is a query that creates a list of book titles from the bibliography:

```
<titles count="{ count(doc('books.xml')//title) }">
 {
  doc("books.xml")//title
 }
</titles>
```

The output of this query follows:

```
<titles count = "4">
   <title>TCP/IP Illustrated</title>
   <title>Advanced Programming in the Unix Environment</title>
   <title>Data on the Web</title>
   <title>The Economics of Technology and Content for
   Digital TV</title>
</titles>
```

Namespace declaration attributes in element constructors have the same meaning they have in XML. We previously showed the following Dublin Core example as XML text—but it is equally valid as an XQuery element constructor, and it treats the namespace declaration the same way:

```
<book year="1994" xmlns:dcx="http://purl.org/dc/elements/1.1/">
    <dcx:title>TCP/IP Illustrated</dcx:title>
    <author><last>Stevens</last><first>W.</first></author>
</book>
```

Computed element and attribute constructors are an alternative syntax that can be used as the XML-style constructors are, but they offer additional functionality that is discussed in this section. Here is a computed element constructor that creates an element named title, with the content "Harold and the Purple Crayon". Inside the curly braces, constants are represented using XQuery's native syntax, in which strings are delimited by double or single quotes.

```
element title {
    "Harold and the Purple Crayon"
}
```

Here is a slightly more complex constructor that creates nested elements and attributes using the computed constructor syntax:

```
element book
{
    attribute year { 1977 },
    element author
    {
        element first { "Crockett" },
        element last { "Johnson" }
    },
        element publisher {"HarperCollins Juvenile Books"},
        element price { 14.95 }
}
```

The preceding example uses literals for the names of elements. In a computed element or attribute constructor, the name can also be an enclosed expression that must have the type *QName*, which represents an element or attribute name. For instance, suppose the user has written a function that takes two parameters, an element name in English and a language, and returns a *QName* that has been translated to the desired language. This function could be used in a computed element constructor as follows:

```
element { translate-element-name("publisher", "German") }
        { "HarperCollins Juvenile Books" }
```

The result of the above query is

```
<Verlag>HarperCollins Juvenile Books</Verlag>
```

In constructors, if sequences of **whitespace** characters occur in the boundaries between **tags** or enclosed expressions, with no intervening non-whitespace characters, then the whitespace is known as boundary whitespace. Implementations may discard boundary whitespace unless the query specifically declares that space must be preserved using the xmlspace declaration, a declaration that can occur in the **prolog.** The following query declares that all whitespace in element constructors must be preserved:

```
declare xmlspace = preserve

<author>
    <last>Stevens</last>
    <first>W.</first>
</author>
```

The output of the above query is

```
<author>
    <last>Stevens</last>
    <first>W.</first>
</author>
```

If the `xmlspace` declaration is absent, or is set to `strip`, then boundary whitespace is stripped:

```
<author><last>Stevens</last><first>W.</first></author>
```

Combining and Restructuring Nodes

Queries in XQuery often combine information from one or more sources and restructure it to create a new result. This section focuses on the expressions and functions most commonly used for combining and restructuring XML data.

FLWOR Expressions

FLWOR expressions, pronounced "flower expressions," are one of the most powerful and common expressions in XQuery. They are similar to the SELECT-FROM-WHERE statements in **SQL.** However, a FLWOR expression is not defined in terms of tables, rows, and columns; instead, a FLWOR expression binds variables to values in `for` and `let` clauses, and uses these variable bindings to create new results. A combination of variable bindings created by the `for` and `let` clauses of a FLWOR expression is called a tuple.

For instance, here is a simple FLWOR expression that returns the title and price of each book that was published in the year 2000:

```
for $b in doc("books.xml")//book
where $b/@year = "2000"
return $b/title
```

This query binds the variable $b to each book, one at a time, to create a series of tuples. Each tuple contains one variable binding in which $b is bound to a single book. The `where` clause tests each tuple to see if `$b/@year` is equal to "2000," and the `return` clause is evaluated for each tuple that satisfies the conditions expressed in the `where` clause. In our sample data, only *Data on the Web* was written in 2000, so the result of this query is

```
<title>Data on the Web</title>
```

The name FLWOR is an acronym, standing for the first letter of the clauses that may occur in a FLWOR expression:

- `for` clauses: associate one or more variables to expressions, creating a tuple stream in which each tuple binds a given variable to one of the items to which its associated expression evaluates
- `let` clauses: bind variables to the entire result of an expression, adding these bindings to the tuples generated by a `for` clause, or creating a single tuple to contain these bindings if there is no `for` clause
- `where` clauses: filter tuples, retaining only those tuples that satisfy a condition
- `order by` clauses: sort the tuples in a tuple stream
- `return` clauses: build the result of the FLWOR expression for a given tuple

The acronym FLWOR roughly follows the order in which the clauses occur. A FLWOR expression starts with one or more `for` or `let` clauses in any order, followed by an optional `where` clause, an optional `order by` clause, and a required `return` clause.

The `for` and `let` Clauses

Every clause in a FLWOR expression is defined in terms of tuples, and the `for` and `let` clauses create the tuples. Therefore, every FLWOR expression must have at least one `for` or `let` clause. It is extremely important to understand how tuples are generated in FLWOR expressions, so we will start with a series of artificial queries that show this in detail for various combinations of `for` clauses and `let` clauses.

We have already shown an example that binds one variable in a `for` clause. The following query creates an element named `tuple` in its `return` clause to show the tuples generated by such a query:

```
for $i in (1, 2, 3)
return
   <tuple><i>{ $i }</i></tuple>
```

In this example, we bind `$i` to the expression `(1, 2, 3)`, which constructs a sequence of integers. XQuery has a very general syntax, and `for` clauses or `let` clauses can be bound to any XQuery expression. Here is the result of the above query, showing how the variable `$i` is bound in each tuple:

```
<tuple><i>1</i></tuple>
<tuple><i>2</i></tuple>
<tuple><i>3</i></tuple>
```

Note that the order of the items bound in the tuple is the same as the order of the items in the original expression `(1, 2, 3)`. A `for` clause preserves order when it creates tuples.

A `let` clause binds a variable to the entire result of an expression. If there are no `for` clauses in the FLWOR expression, then a single tuple is created, containing the variable bindings from the `let` clauses. The following query is like the previous query, but it uses a `let` clause rather than a `for`:

```
let $i := (1, 2, 3)
return
   <tuple><i>{ $i }</i></tuple>
```

The result of this query contains only one tuple, in which the variable `$i` is bound to the entire sequence of integers:

```
<tuple><i>1 2 3</i></tuple>
```

If a `let` clause is used in a FLWOR expression that has one or more `for` clauses, the variable bindings of `let` clauses are added to the tuples generated by the `for` clauses. This is demonstrated by the following query:

```
for $i in (1, 2, 3)
let $j := (1, 2, 3)
return
   <tuple><i>{ $i }</i><j>{ $j }</j></tuple>
```

If a `let` clause is used in a FLWOR expression that has one or more `for` clauses, the variable bindings from `let` clauses are added to the tuples generated by the `for` clauses:

```
<tuple><i>1</i><j>1 2 3</j></tuple>
<tuple><i>2</i><j>1 2 3</j></tuple>
<tuple><i>3</i><j>1 2 3</j></tuple>
```

Here is a query that combines `for` and `let` clauses in the same way as the previous query:

```
for $b in doc("books.xml")//book
let $c := $b/author
return <book>{ $b/title, <count>{ count($c) }</count>}</book>
```

This query lists the title of each book together with the number of authors. Listing 1.3 shows the result when we apply it to our bibliography data.

Listing 1.3   Query Results

```
<book>
  <title>TCP/IP Illustrated</title>
  <count>1</count>
</book>
<book>
  <title>Advanced Programming in the UNIX Environment</title>
  <count>1</count>
</book>
<book>
  <title>Data on the Web</title>
  <count>3</count>
</book>
<book>
  <title>The Economics of Technology and Content for
  Digital TV</title>
  <count>0</count>
</book>
```

If more than one variable is bound in the `for` clauses of a FLWOR expression, then the tuples contain all possible combinations of the items to which these variables are bound. For instance, the following query shows all combinations that include 1, 2, or 3 combined with 4, 5, or 6:

```
for $i in (1, 2, 3),
    $j in (4, 5, 6)
return
  <tuple><i>{ $i }</i><j>{ $j }</j></tuple>
```

Here is the result of the above query:

```
<tuple><i>1</i><j>4</j></tuple>
<tuple><i>1</i><j>5</j></tuple>
<tuple><i>1</i><j>6</j></tuple>
<tuple><i>2</i><j>4</j></tuple>
<tuple><i>2</i><j>5</j></tuple>
<tuple><i>2</i><j>6</j></tuple>
<tuple><i>3</i><j>4</j></tuple>
<tuple><i>3</i><j>5</j></tuple>
<tuple><i>3</i><j>6</j></tuple>
```

A combination of all possible combinations of sets of values is called a Cartesian cross-product. The tuples preserve the order of the original sequences, in the order in which they are bound. In the previous example, note that the tuples reflect the values of each $i in the original order; for a given value of $i, the values of $j occur in the original order. In mathematical terms, the tuples generated in a FLWOR expression are drawn from the ordered Cartesian cross-product of the items to which the for variables are bound.

The ability to create tuples that reflect combinations becomes particularly interesting when combined with where clauses to perform **joins.** The following sections illustrate this in depth. But first we must introduce the where and return clauses.

The where *Clause*

A where clause eliminates tuples that do not satisfy a particular condition. A return clause is only evaluated for tuples that survive the where clause. The following query returns only books whose prices are less than $50.00:

```
for $b in doc("books.xml")//book
where $b/price < 50.00
return $b/title
```

Here is the result of this query:

```
  <title>Data on the Web</title>
```

A where clause can contain any expression that evaluates to a Boolean value. In SQL, a WHERE clause can only test single values, but there is no such restriction on `where` clauses in XQuery. The following query returns the title of books that have more than two authors:

```
for $b in doc("books.xml")//book
let $c := $b//author
where count($c) > 2
return $b/title
```

Here is the result of the above query:

```
<title>Data on the Web</title>
```

The `order` `by` *Clause*

The `order` `by` clause sorts the tuples before the `return` clause is evaluated in order to change the order of results. For instance, the following query lists the titles of books in alphabetical order:

```
for $t in doc("books.xml")//title
order by $t
return $t
```

The `for` clause generates a sequence of tuples, with one `title` node in each tuple. The `order` `by` clause sorts these tuples according to the value of the `title` elements in the tuples, and the `return` clause returns the `title` elements in the same order as the sorted tuples. The result of this query is

```
<title>Advanced Programming in the Unix Environment</title>
<title>Data on the Web</title>
<title>TCP/IP Illustrated</title>
<title>The Economics of Technology and Content for Digital TV</title>
```

The `order` `by` clause allows one or more orderspecs, each of which specifies one expression used to sort the tuples. An **orderspec** may also specify whether to sort in ascending or descending order, how expressions that evaluate to empty sequences should be sorted, a specific collation to be used, and whether stable sorting should be used (stable sorting preserves the relative order of two items if their values are equal). Here is a query that returns authors, sorting in reverse order by the last name, then the first name:

```
for $a in doc("books.xml")//author
order by $a/last descending, $a/first descending
return $a
```

The result of this query is shown in Listing 1.4.

Listing 1.4   Results of Query for Authors Sorted by Last Name

```
<author>
    <last>Suciu</last>
    <first>Dan</first>
</author>
<author>
    <last>Stevens</last>
    <first>W.</first>
</author>
<author>
    <last>Stevens</last>
    <first>W.</first>
</author>
<author>
    <last>Buneman</last>
    <first>Peter</first>
</author>
<author>
    <last>Abiteboul</last>
    <first>Serge</first>
</author>
```

The `order by` clause may specify conditions based on data that is not used in the `return` clause, so there is no need for an expression to return data in order to use it to sort. Here is an example that returns the titles of books, sorted by the name of the first author:

```
let $b := doc("books.xml")//book
for $t in distinct-values($b/title)
let $a1 := $b[title=$t]/author[1]
order by $a1/last, $a1/first
return $b/title
```

The result of this query is

```
<title>The Economics of Technology and Content for Digital TV</title>
<title>Data on the Web</title>
<title>Advanced Programming in the UNIX Environment</title>
<title>TCP/IP Illustrated</title>
```

The first book in this list has editors, but no authors. For this book, `$a1/last` and `$a1/first` will both return empty sequences. Some XQuery implementations always sort empty sequences as the greatest possible value; others always sort empty sequences as the least possible value. The XML Query Working Group decided to allow vendors to choose which of these orders to implement because many XQuery implementations present views of relational data, and relational databases differ in their sorting of **nulls**. To guarantee that an XQuery uses the same sort order across implementations, specify "empty greatest" or "empty least" in an orderspec if its expression can evaluate to an empty sequence.

Two books in our data are written by the same author, and we may want to ensure that the original order of these two books is maintained. We can do this by specifying a stable sort, which maintains the relative order of two items if the comparison expressions consider them equal. The following query specifies a stable sort, and requires empty sequences to be sorted as least:

```
let $b := doc("books.xml")//book
for $t in distinct-values($b/title)
let $a1 := $b[title=$t]/author[1]
stable order by $a1/last empty least, $a1/first empty least
return $b/title
```

This query returns the same result as the previous one, but is guaranteed to do so across all implementations.

Collations may also be specified in an `order by` clause. The following query sorts titles using a U.S. English collation:

```
for $t in doc("books.xml")//title
order by $t collation "http://www.example.com/collations/eng-us"
return $t
```

Most queries use the same collation for all comparisons, and it is generally too tedious to specify a collation for every orderspec. XQuery allows a default collation to be specified in the prolog. The default collation is used when the orderspec does not specify a collation. Here is a query that sets http://www.example.com/collations/eng-us as the default collation; it returns the same results as the previous query:

```
default collation = "http://www.example.com/collations/eng-us"

for $t in doc("books.xml")//title
order by $t
return $t
```

When sorting expressions in queries, it is important to remember that the / and // operators sort in document order. That means that an order established with an `order by` clause can be changed by expressions that use these operators. For instance, consider the following query:

```
let $authors := for $a in doc("books.xml")//author
                order by $a/last, $a/first
                return $a
return $authors/last
```

This query does not return the author's last names in alphabetical order, because the `/` in `$authors/last` sorts the last elements in document order. This kind of error generally occurs with `let` bindings, not with `for` bindings, because a `for` clause binds each variable to a single value in a given tuple, and returning children or descendents of a single node does not lead to surprises. The following query returns author's last names in alphabetical order:

```
for $a in doc("books.xml")//author
order by $a/last, $a/first
return $a/last
```

The `return` *Clause*

We have already seen that a `for` clause or a `let` clause may be bound to any expression, and a `where` clause may contain any Boolean expression. Similary, any XQuery expression may occur in a `return` clause. Element constructors are an extremely common expression in `return` clauses; for instance, the following query uses an element constructor to create price quotes:

```
for $b in doc("books.xml")//book
return
  <quote>{ $b/title, $b/price }</quote>
```

Listing 1.5 shows the result of the above query.

Listing 1.5   Results of Query for Price Quotes

```
<quote>
    <title>TCP/IP Illustrated</title>
    <price>65.95</price>
</quote>
<quote>
    <title>Advanced Programming in the UNIX Environment</title>
    <price>65.95</price>
</quote>
```

Listing 1.5   Results of Query for Price Quotes *(continued)*

```
<quote>
    <title>Data on the Web</title>
    <price>39.95</price>
</quote>
<quote>
    <title>The Economics of Technology and Content for Digital
TV</title>
    <price>129.95</price>
</quote>
```

Element constructors can be used in a `return` clause to change the hierarchy of data. For instance, we might want to represent an author's name as a string in a single element, which we can do with the following query:

```
for $a in doc("books.xml")//author
return
  <author>{ string($a/first), " ", string($a/last) }</author>
```

Here is the result of the above query:

```
<author>W. Stevens</author>
<author>W. Stevens</author>
<author>Serge Abiteboul</author>
<author>Peter Buneman</author>
<author>Dan Suciu</author>
```

Another application might want to insert a name element to hold the first and last name of the author—after all, an author does not consist of a first and a last! Here is a query that adds a level to the hierarchy for names:

```
for $a in doc("books.xml")//author
return
<author>
    <name>{ $a/first, $a/last }</name>
  </author>
```

Here is one author's name taken from the output of the above query:

```
<author>
    <name>
    <first>Serge</first>
    <last>Abiteboul</last>
    </name>
</author>
```

This section has discussed the most straightforward use of `for` and `return` clauses, and it has shown how to combine FLWOR expressions with other expressions to perform common tasks. More complex uses of `for` clauses are explored later in separate sections on joins and positional variables.

The Positional Variable at

The `for` clause supports positional variables, which identify the position of a given item in the expression that generated it. For instance, the following query returns the titles of books, with an attribute that numbers the books:

```
for $t at $i in doc("books.xml")//title
return <title pos="{$i}">{string($t)}</title>
```

Here is the result of this query:

```
<title pos="1">TCP/IP Illustrated</title>
<title pos="2">Advanced Programming in the Unix Environment</title>
<title pos="3">Data on the Web</title>
<title pos="4">The Economics of Technology and Content for Digital
TV</title>
```

In some data, position conveys meaning. In tables, for instance, the row and column in which an item is found often determine its meaning. For instance, suppose we wanted to create data from an XHTML web page that contains the table shown in Table 1.2.

TABLE 1.2   Table from an XHTML Web Page

Title	Publisher	Price	Year
TCP/IP Illustrated	Addison-Wesley	65.95	1994
Advanced Programming in the UNIX Environment	Addison-Wesley	65.95	1992
Data on the Web	Morgan Kaufmann Publishers	39.95	2000
The Economics of Technology and Content for Digital TV	Kluwer Academic Publishers	129.95	1999

The XHTML source for this table is shown in Listing 1.2.

Listing 1.6   XHTML Source for Table 1.2

```
<table border="1">
    <thead>
      <tr>
            <td>Title</td>
            <td>Publisher</td>
            <td>Price</td>
            <td>Year</td>
      </tr>
    </thead>
    <tbody>
      <tr>
            <td>TCP/IP Illustrated</td>
            <td>Addison-Wesley</td>
            <td>65.95</td>
            <td>1994</td>
      </tr>
      <tr>
            <td>Advanced Programming in the UNIX
            Environment</td>
            <td>Addison-Wesley</td>
            <td>65.95</td>
            <td>1992</td>
      </tr>
   <!- Additional rows omitted to save space ->
    </tbody>
</table>
```

In this table, every entry in the same column as the `Title` header is a title, every entry in the same column as the `Publisher` header is a publisher, and so forth. In other words, we can determine the purpose of an entry if we can determine its position as a column of the table, and relate it to the position of a column header. Positional variables make this possible. Since XHTML is XML, it can be queried using XQuery. Listing 1.7 shows a query that produces meaningful XML from the above data, generating the names of elements from the column headers.

Listing 1.7   Query to Generate Names of Elements from Column Headers

```
let $t := doc("bib.xhtml")//table[1]
for $r in $t/tbody/tr
return
  <book>
```

Listing 1.7 Query to Generate Names of Elements from Column Headers *(continued)*

```
  {
    for $c at $i in $r/td
    return element{ lower-case(data($t/thead/tr/td[$i])) }
                  { string( $c ) }
  }
</book>
```

Note the use of a computed element constructor that uses the column header to determine the name of the element. Listing 1.8 shows the portion of the output this query generates for the partial data shown in Table 1.2.

Listing 1.8 Output Generated by the Query of Listing 1.7

```
<book>
   <title>TCP/IP Illustrated</title>
   <publisher>Addison-Wesley</publisher>
   <price>65.95</price>
   <year>1994</year>
</book>
<book>
   <title>Advanced Programming in the Unix Environment</title>
   <publisher>Addison-Wesley</publisher>
   <price>65.95</price>
   <year>1992</year>
</book>
```

Eliminating Duplicate Subtrees with `distinct-values()` *and FLWOR Expressions*

Data often contains duplicate values, and FLWOR expressions are often combined with the `distinct-values()` function to remove duplicates from subtrees. Let's start with the following query, which returns the last name of each author:

```
doc("books.xml")//author/last
```

Since one of our authors wrote two of the books in the bibliography, the result of this query contains a duplicate:

```
<last>Stevens</last>
<last>Stevens</last>
<last>Abiteboul</last>
<last>Buneman</last>
<last>Suciu</last>
```

The `distinct-values()` function extracts the values of a sequence of nodes and creates a sequence of unique values, eliminating duplicates. Here is a query that uses `distinct-values()` to eliminate duplicate last names:

```
distinct-values(doc("books.xml")//author/last)
```

Here is the output of the above query:

```
Stevens Abiteboul Buneman Suciu
```

The `distinct-values()` function eliminates duplicates, but in order to do so, it extracts values from nodes. FLWOR expressions are often used together with `distinct-values()` to create subtrees that correspond to sets of one or more unique values. For the preceding query, we can use an element constructor to create a last element containing each value:

```
for $l in distinct-values(doc("books.xml")//author/last)
return <last>{ $l }</last>
```

Here is the output of the above query:

```
<last>Stevens</last>
<last>Abiteboul</last>
<last>Buneman</last>
<last>Suciu</last>
```

The same problem arises for complex subtrees. For instance, the following query returns authors, and one of the authors is a duplicate by both first and last name:

```
doc("books.xml")//author
```

The output of the above query appears in Listing 1.9.

Listing 1.9 Output of the Query for Authors

```
<authors>
    <author>
      <last>Stevens</last>
      <first>W.</first>
    </author>
    <author>
      <last>Stevens</last>
      <first>W.</first>
    </author>
```

Listing 1.9   Output of the Query for Authors *(continued)*

```
  <author>
    <last>Abiteboul</last>
    <first>Serge</first>
  </author>
  <author>
    <last>Buneman</last>
    <first>Peter</first>
  </author>
  <author>
    <last>Suciu</last>
    <first>Dan</first>
  </author>
</authors>
```

To eliminate duplicates from complex subtrees, we have to decide what criterion to use for detecting a duplicate. In this case, let's say that an author is a duplicate if there is another author who has the same first and last names. Now let's write a query that returns one author for each first and last name that occur together within an author element in our dataset:

```
let $a := doc("books.xml")//author
for $l in distinct-values($a/last),
    $f in distinct-values($a[last=$l]/first)
return
    <author>
      <last>{ $l }</last>
      <first>{ $f }</first>
    </author>
```

In the output of the above query (Listing 1.10), each author's name appears only once.

Listing 1.10   Output of Query to Avoid Duplicate Author Names

```
<authors>
    <author>
      <last>Stevens</last>
      <first>W.</first>
    </author>
    <author>
      <last>Abiteboul</last>
      <first>Serge</first>
    </author>
    <author>
      <last>Buneman</last>
      <first>Peter</first>
    </author>
```

Listing 1.10   Output of Query to Avoid Duplicate Author Names *(continued)*

```
  <author>
    <last>Suciu</last>
    <first>Dan</first>
  </author>
</authors>
```

Joins: Combining Data Sources with `for` *and* `where` *Clauses*

A query may bind multiple variables in a `for` clause in order to combine information from different expressions. This is often done to bring together information from different data sources. For instance, suppose we have a file named `reviews.xml` that contains book reviews:

```
<reviews>
  <entry>
   <title>TCP/IP Illustrated</title>
   <rating>5</rating>
   <remarks>Excellent technical content. Not much plot.</remarks>
  </entry>
</reviews>
```

A FLWOR expression can bind one variable to our bibliography data and another to the reviews, making it possible to compare data from both files and to create results that combine their information. For instance, a query could return the title of a book and any remarks found in a review.

As we have discussed earlier, the Cartesian cross-product of two sequences contains all possible combinations of the items in those sequences. When a `where` clause is used to select interesting combinations from the Cartesian cross-product, this is known as a join. The following query performs a join to combine data from a bibliography with data from a set of reviews:

```
for $t in doc("books.xml")//title,
    $e in doc("reviews.xml")//entry
where $t = $e/title
return <review>{ $t, $e/remarks }</review>
```

The result of this query is as follows:

```
<review>
    <title>TCP/IP Illustrated</title>
    <remarks>Excellent technical content. Not much plot.</remarks>
</review>
```

In this query, the `for` clauses create tuples from the Cartesian cross-product of titles and entries, the `where` clause filters out tuples where the title of the review does not match the title of the book, and the `return` clause constructs the result from the remaining tuples. Note that only books with reviews are shown. SQL programmers will recognize the preceding query as an inner join, returning combinations of data that satisfy a condition.

The tuples generated for a FLWOR expression include all expressions bound in variable bindings in `for` clauses. A FLWOR expression with multiple `for` clauses has the same meaning as a FLWOR expression that binds multiple variables in a single `for` clause. The following query is precisely equivalent to the previous one:

```
for $t in doc("books.xml")//title
for $e in doc("reviews.xml")//entry
where $t = $e/title
return <review>{ $t, $e/remarks }</review>
```

The query shown in Listing 1.11 returns the title of each book regardless of whether it has a review; if a book does have a review, the remarks found in the review are also included. SQL programmers will recognize this as a **left outer join**.

Listing 1.11   Query to Return Titles with or without Reviews

```
for $t in doc("books.xml")//title
return
  <review>
   { $t }
   {
     for $e in doc("reviews.xml")//entry
     where $e/title = $t
     return $e/remarks
   }
  </review>
```

Inverting Hierarchies

XQuery can be used to do quite general transformations. One transformation that is used in many applications is colloquially referred to as "inverting a hierarchy"—creating a new document in which the top nodes represent information which was found in the lower nodes of the original document. For instance, in our sample data, publishers are found at the bottom of the hierarchy, and books are found near the top. Listing 1.12 shows a query that creates a list of titles published by each publisher, placing the publisher at the top of the hierarchy and listing the titles of books at the bottom.

Listing 1.12   Query to List Titles by Publisher

```
<listings>
  {
    for $p in distinct-values(doc("books.xml")//publisher)
    order by $p
    return
        <result>
            { $p }
            {
                for $b in doc("books.xml")/bib/book
                where $b/publisher = $p
                order by $b/title
                return $b/title
            }
        </result>
  }
</listings>

The results of this query are as follows:

<listings>
 <result>
    <publisher>Addison-Wesley</publisher>
   <title>Advanced Programming in the Unix Environment</title>
   <title>TCP/IP Illustrated</title>
   </result>
   <result>
   <publisher>Kluwer Academic Publishers</publisher>
   <title>The Economics of Technology and Content for
   Digital TV</title>
   </result>
   <result>
   <publisher>Morgan Kaufmann Publishers</publisher>
   <title>Data on the Web</title>
   </result>
</listings>
```

A more complex example of inverting a hierarchy is discussed in the following section on quantifiers.

Quantifiers

Some queries need to determine whether at least one item in a sequence satisfies a condition, or whether every item in a sequence satisfies a condition. This is done using quantifiers. An existential quantifier tests whether at least one item satisfies a condition. The following query shows an existential quantifier in XQuery:

```
for $b in doc("books.xml")//book
where some $a in $b/author
      satisfies ($a/last="Stevens" and $a/first="W.")
return $b/title
```

The some quantifier in the where clause tests to see if there is at least one author that satisfies the conditions given inside the parentheses. Here is the result of the above query:

```
<title>TCP/IP Illustrated</title>
<title>Advanced Programming in the Unix Environment</title>
```

A universal quantifier tests whether every node in a sequence satisfies a condition. The following query tests to see if every author of a book is named W. Stevens:

```
for $b in doc("books.xml")//book
where every $a in $b/author
      satisfies ($a/last="Stevens" and $a/first="W.")
return $b/title
```

Here is the result of the above query:

```
<title>TCP/IP Illustrated</title>
<title>Advanced Programming in the Unix Environment</title>
<title>The Economics of Technology and Content for Digital TV</title>
```

The last title returned, *The Economics of Technology and Content for Digital TV,* is the title of a book that has editors but no authors. For this book, the expression $b/author evaluates to an empty sequence. If a universal quantifier is applied to an empty sequence, it always returns true, because every item in that (empty) sequence satisfies the condition—even though there are no items.

Quantifiers sometimes make complex queries much easier to write and understand. For instance, they are often useful in queries that invert hierarchies. Listing 1.13 shows a query that creates a list of books written by each author in our bibliography.

Listing 1.13   Query to List Books by Author

```
<author-list>
  {
    let $a := doc("books.xml")//author
    for $l in distinct-values($a/last),
        $f in distinct-values($a[last=$l]/first)
    order by $l, $f
    return
        <author>
          <name>{ $l, ", ", $f }</name>
          {
              for $b in doc("books.xml")/bib/book
              where some $ba in $b/author satisfies
                    ($ba/last=$l and $ba/first=$f)
              order by $b/title
              return $b/title
          }
        </author>
  }
</author-list>
```

The result of the above query is shown in Listing 1.14.

Listing 1.14   Results of Query to List Books by Author

```
<author-list>
    <author>
        <name>Stevens, W.</name>
        <title>Advanced Programming in the Unix Environment</title>
        <title>TCP/IP Illustrated</title>
    </author>
    <author>
        <name>Abiteboul, Serge</name>
        <title>Data on the Web</title>
    </author>
    <author>
        <name>Buneman, Peter</name>
        <title>Data on the Web</title>
    </author>
    <author>
        <name>Suciu, Dan</name>
        <title>Data on the Web</title>
    </author>
</author-list>
```

Conditional Expressions

XQuery's conditional expressions are used in the same way as conditional expressions in other languages. Listing 1.15 shows a query that uses a conditional expression to list the first two authors' names for each book and a dummy name containing "et al." to represent any remaining authors.

Listing 1.15   Query to List Author's Names with "et al."

```
for $b in doc("books.xml")//book
return
  <book>
    { $b/title }
    {
      for $a at $i in $b/author
      where $i <= 2
      return <author>{string($a/last), ", ",
                     string($a/first)}</author>
    }
    {
      if (count($b/author) > 2)
      then <author>et al.</author>
      else ()
    }
  </book>
```

In XQuery, both the `then` clause and the `if` clause are required. Note that the empty sequence `()` can be used to specify that a clause should return nothing. The output of this query is shown in Listing 1.16.

Listing 1.16   Result of Query from Listing 1.15

```
<book>
    <title>TCP/IP Illustrated</title>
    <author>Stevens, W.</author>
</book>
<book>
    <title>Advanced Programming in the Unix Environment</title>
    <author>Stevens, W.</author>
</book>
<book>
    <title>Data on the Web</title>
    <author>Abiteboul, Serge</author>
    <author>Buneman, Peter</author>
    <author>et al.</author>
</book>
```

Listing 1.16   Result of Query from Listing 1.15 *(continued)*

```
<book>
    <title>The Economics of Technology and Content for
    Digital TV</title>
</book>
```

Operators

The queries we have shown up to now all contain operators, which we have not yet covered. Like most languages, XQuery has arithmetic operators and comparison operators, and because sequences of nodes are a fundamental datatype in XQuery, it is not surprising that XQuery also has node sequence operators. This section describes these operators in some detail. In particular, it describes how XQuery treats some of the cases that arise quite easily when processing XML; for instance, consider the following expression: `1 * $b`. How is this interpreted if `$b` is an empty sequence, untyped character data, an element, or a sequence of five nodes? Given the flexible structure of XML, it is imperative that cases like this be well defined in the language. (Chapter 2, "Influences on the Design of XQuery," provides additional background on the technical complexities that the working group had to deal with to resolve these and similar issues.)

Two basic operations are central to the use of operators and functions in XQuery. The first is called **typed value** extraction. We have already used typed value extraction in many of our queries, without commenting on it. For instance, we have seen this query:

```
doc("books.xml")/bib/book/author[last='Stevens']
```

Consider the expression `last='Stevens'`. If `last` is an element, and `'Stevens'` is a string, how can an element and a string be equal? The answer is that the = operator extracts the typed value of the element, resulting in a **string value** that is then compared to the string `Stevens`. If the document is governed by a W3C XML Schema, then it may be associated with a simple type, such as `xs:integer`. If so, the typed value will have whatever type has been assigned to the node by the schema. XQuery has a function called `data()` that extracts the typed value of a function. Assuming the following element has been validated by a schema processor, the result of this query is the integer 4:

```
data( <e xsi:type="xs:integer">4</e> )
```

A query may import a schema. We will discuss **schema imports** later, but schema imports have one effect that should be understood now. If typed value extraction is applied to an element, and the query has imported a schema definition for that element specifying that the element may have other elements as children, then typed value extraction raises an error.

Typed value extraction is defined for a single item. The more general form of typed value extraction is called **atomization,** which defines how typed value extraction is done for any sequence of items. For instance, atomization would be performed for the following query:

```
avg( 1, <e>2</e>, <e xsi:type="xs:integer">3</e> )
```

Atomization simply returns the typed value of every item in the sequence. The preceding query returns 2, which is the average of 1, 2, and 3. In XQuery, atomization is used for the operands of arithmetic expressions and comparison expressions. It is also used for the parameters and return values of functions and for cast expressions, which are discussed in other sections.

Arithmetic Operators

XQuery supports the arithmetic operators +, -, *, div, idiv, and mod. The div operator performs division on any numeric type. The idiv operator requires integer arguments, and returns an integer as a result, rounding toward 0. All other arithmetic operators have their conventional meanings. If an operand of an arithmetic operator is a node, atomization is applied. For instance, the following query returns the integer 4:

```
2 + <int>{ 2 }</int>
```

If an operand is an empty sequence, the result of an arithmetic operator is an empty sequence. Empty sequences in XQuery frequently operate like nulls in SQL. The result of the following query is an empty sequence:

```
2 + ()
```

If an operand is **untyped data,** it is cast to a double, raising an error if the cast fails. This implicit cast is important, because a great deal of XML data is found in documents that do not use W3C XML Schema, and therefore do not have simple or complex types. Many of these documents however contain data that is to be interpreted as numeric. The prices in our sample document are one example of this. The following query adds the first and second prices, returning the result as a double:

```
let $p := doc("books.xml")//price
return $p[1] + $p[2]
```

Comparison Operators

XQuery has several sets of comparison operators, including value comparisons, general comparisons, node comparisons, and order comparisons. Value comparisons and general comparisons are closely related; in fact, each **general comparison operator** combines an existential quantifier with a corresponding a **value comparison operator.** Table 1.3 shows the value comparison operator to which each general comparison operator corresponds.

The value comparisons compare two atomic values. If either operand is a node, atomization is used to convert it to an atomic value. For the comparison, if either operand is untyped, it is treated as a string. Here is a query that uses the eq operator:

```
for $b in doc("books.xml")//book
where $b/title eq "Data on the Web"
return $b/price
```

TABLE 1.3   Value Comparison Operators vs. General Comparison Operators

Value Comparison Operator	General Comparison Operator
eq	=
ne	!=
lt	<
le	<=
gt	>
ge	>=

Using value comparisons, strings can only be compared to other strings, which means that value comparisons are fairly strict about typing. If our data is governed by a DTD, then it does not use the W3C XML Schema simple types, so the price is untyped. Therefore, a cast is needed to cast `price` to a `decimal` in the following query:

```
for $b in doc("books.xml")//book
where xs:decimal($b/price) gt 100.00
return $b/title
```

If the data were governed by a W3C XML Schema that declared `price` to be a `decimal`, this cast would not have been necessary. In general, if the data you are querying is meant to be interpreted as typed data, but there are no types in the XML, value comparisons force your query to cast when doing comparisons—general comparisons are more loosely typed and do not require such casts. This problem does not arise if the data is meant to be interpreted as string data, or if it contains the appropriate types.

Like arithmetic operators, value comparisons treat empty sequences much like SQL nulls. If either operand is an empty sequence, a value comparison evaluates to the empty sequence. If an operand contains more than one item, then a value comparison raises an error. Here is an example of a query that raises an error:

```
for $b in doc("books.xml")//book
where $b/author/last eq "Stevens"
return $b/title
```

The reason for the error is that many books have multiple authors, so the expression `$b/author/last` returns multiple nodes. The following query uses `=`, the general comparison that corresponds to `eq`, to return books for which *any* author's last name is equal to Stevens:

```
for $b in doc("books.xml")//book
where $b/author/last = "Stevens"
return $b/title
```

There are two significant differences between value comparisons and general comparisons. The first is illustrated in the previous query. Like value comparisons, general comparisons apply atomization to both operands, but instead of requiring each operand to be a single atomic value, the result of this atomization may be a sequence of atomic values. The general comparison returns true if *any* value on the left matches *any* value on the right, using the appropriate comparison.

The second difference involves the treatment of untyped data—general comparisons try to cast to an appropriate "required type" to make the comparison work. This is illustrated by the following query:

```
for $b in doc("books.xml")//book
where $b/price = 100.00
return $b/title
```

In this query, 100.00 is a decimal, and the = operator casts the price to decimal as well. When a general comparison tests a pair of atomic values and one of these values is untyped, it examines the other atomic value to determine the required type to which it casts the untyped operand:

- If the other atomic value has a numeric type, the required type is xs:double.
- If the other atomic value is also untyped, the required type is xs:string.
- Otherwise, the required type is the **dynamic type** of the other atomic value. If the cast to the required type fails, a dynamic error is raised.

These conversion rules mean that comparisons done with general comparisons rarely need to cast when working with data that does not contain W3C XML Schema simple types. On the other hand, when working with strongly typed data, value comparisons offer greater type safety.

You should be careful when using the = operator when an operand has more than one step, because it can lead to confusing results. Consider the following query:

```
for $b in doc("books.xml")//book
where $b/author/first = "Serge"
  and $b/author/last = "Suciu"
return $b
```

The result of this query may be somewhat surprising, as Listing 1.17 shows.

Listing 1.17   Surprising Results

```
<book year = "2000">
  <title>Data on the Web</title>
  <author>
    <last>Abiteboul</last>
    <first>Serge</first>
  </author>
  <author>
    <last>Buneman</last>
    <first>Peter</first>
  </author>
  <author>
    <last>Suciu</last>
    <first>Dan</first>
  </author>
  <publisher>Morgan Kaufmann Publishers</publisher>
  <price>39.95</price>
</book>
```

Since this book does have an author whose first name is "Serge" and an author whose last name is "Suciu," the result of the query is correct, but it is surprising. The following query expresses what the author of the previous query probably intended:

```
for $b in doc("books.xml")//book,
    $a in $b/author
where $a/first="Serge"
  and $a/last="Suciu"
return $b
```

Comparisons using the = operator are not transitive. Consider the following query:

```
let $a := ( <first>Jonathan</first>, <last>Robie</last> ),
    $b := ( <first>Jonathan</first>, <last>Marsh</last> ),
    $c := ( <first>Rodney</first>, <last>Marsh</last> )
return
<out>
  <equals>{ $a = $b }</equals>
  <equals>{ $b = $c }</equals>
  <equals>{ $a = $c }</equals>
</out>
```

Remember that = returns `true` if there is a value on the left that matches a value on the right. The output of this query is as follows:

```
<out>
  <equals>True</equals>
  <equals>True</equals>
  <equals>False</equals>
</out>
```

Node comparisons determine whether two expressions evaluate to the same node. There are two node comparisons in XQuery, `is` and `is not`. The following query tests whether the most expensive book is also the book with the greatest number of authors and editors:

```
let $b1 := for $b in doc("books.xml")//book
           order by count($b/author) + count($b/editor)
           return $b
let $b2 := for $b in doc("books.xml")//book
           order by $b/price
           return $b
return $b1[last()] is $b2[last()]
```

This query also illustrates the `last()` function, which determines whether a node is the last node in the sequence; in other words, `$b1[last()]` returns the last node in `$b1`.

XQuery provides two operators that can be used to determine whether one node comes before or after another node in document order. These operators are generally most useful for data in which the order of elements is meaningful, as it is in many documents or tables. The operator `$a <<` `$b` returns true if `$a` precedes `$b` in document order; `$a >> $b` returns true if `$a` follows `$b` in document order. For instance, the following query returns books where Abiteboul is an author, but is not listed as the first author:

```
for $b in doc("books.xml")//book
let $a := ($b/author)[1],
    $sa := ($b/author)[last="Abiteboul"]
where $a << $sa
return $b
```

In our sample data, there are no such books.

Sequence Operators

XQuery provides the `union`, `intersect`, and `except` operators for combining sequences of nodes. Each of these operators combines two sequences, returning a result sequence in document order. As we have discussed earlier, a sequence of nodes that is in document order, never contains the same node twice. If an operand contains an item that is not a node, an error is raised.

The `union` operator takes two node sequences and returns a sequence with all nodes found in the two input sequences. This operator has two lexical forms: | and `union`. Here is a query that uses the | operator to return a sorted list of last names for all authors or editors:

```
let $1 := distinct-values(doc("books.xml")//(author | editor)/last)
order by $1
return <last>{ $1 }</last>
```

Here is the result of the above query:

```
<last>Abiteboul</last>
<last>Buneman</last>
<last>Gerbarg</last>
<last>Stevens</last>
<last>Suciu</last>
```

The fact that the `union` operator always returns nodes in document order is sometimes quite useful. For instance, the following query sorts books based on the name of the first author or editor listed for the book:

```
for $b in doc("books.xml")//book
let $a1 := ($b/author union $b/editor)[1]
order by $a1/last, $a1/first
return $b
```

The `intersect` operator takes two node sequences as operands and returns a sequence containing all the nodes that occur in both operands. The `except` operator takes two node sequences as operands and returns a sequence containing all the nodes that occur in the first operand but not in the second operand. For instance, the following query returns a book with all of its children except for the price:

```
for $b in doc("books.xml")//book
where $b/title = "TCP/IP Illustrated"
return
    <book>
     { $b/@* }
     { $b/* except $b/price }
    </book>
```

The result of this query contains all attributes of the original book and all elements—in document order—except for the `price` element, which is omitted:

```
<book year = "1994">
<title>TCP/IP Illustrated</title>
<author>
    <last>Stevens</last>
    <first>W.</first>
</author>
<publisher>Addison-Wesley</publisher>
</book>
```

Built-in Functions

XQuery has a set of built-in functions and operators, including many that are familiar from other languages, and some that are used for customized XML processing. The complete list of built-in functions is found in [XQ-FO]. This section focuses on the most commonly used functions, some of which must be understood to follow what is said in the rest of the chapter.

SQL programmers will be familiar with the `min()`, `max()`, `count()`, `sum()`, and `avg()` functions. The following query returns the titles of books that are more expensive than the average book:

```
let $b := doc("books.xml")//book
let $avg := average( $b//price )
return $b[price > $avg]
```

For our sample data, Listing 1.18 shows the result of this query.

Listing 1.18   Result of Query for Books More Expensive Than Average

```
<book year = "1999">
  <title>The Economics of Technology and Content for
  Digital TV</title>
  <editor>
    <last>Gerbarg</last>
    <first>Darcy</first>
    <affiliation>CITI</affiliation>
  </editor>
  <publisher>Kluwer Academic Publishers</publisher>
  <price>129.95</price>
</book>
```

Note that price is the name of an element, but `max()` is defined for atomic values, not for elements. In XQuery, if the type of a function argument is an **atomic type,** then the following conversion rules are applied. If the argument is a node, its typed value is extracted, resulting in a sequence of values. If any value in the argument sequence is untyped, XQuery attempts to convert it to the required type and raises an error if it fails. A value is accepted if it has the expected type.

Other familiar functions in XQuery include numeric functions like `round()`, `floor()`, and `ceiling()`; string functions like `concat()`, `string-length()`, `starts-with()`, `ends-with()`, `substring()`, `upper-case()`, `lower-case()`; and casts for the various simple types. These are all covered in [XQ-FO], which defines the standard function library for XQuery; they need no further coverage here since they are straightforward.

XQuery also has a number of functions that are not found in most other languages. We have already covered `distinct-values()`, the input functions `doc()` and `collection()`. Two other frequently used functions are `not()` and `empty()`. The `not()` function is used in Boolean conditions; for instance, the following returns books where no author's last name is Stevens:

```
for $b in doc("books.xml")//book
where not(some $a in $b/author satisfies $a/last="Stevens")
return $b
```

The `empty()` function reports whether a sequence is empty. For instance, the following query returns books that have authors, but does not return the one book that has only editors:

```
for $b in doc("books.xml")//book
where not(empty($b/author))
return $b
```

The opposite of `empty()` is `exists()`, which reports whether a sequence contains at least one item. The preceding query could also be written as follows:

```
for $b in doc("books.xml")//book
where exists($b/author)
return $b
```

XQuery also has functions that access various kinds of information associated with a node. The most common accessor functions are `string()`, which returns the string value of a node, and `data()`, which returns the typed value of a node. These functions require some explanation. The string value of a node includes the string representation of the text found in the node and its descendants, concatenated in document order. For instance, consider the following query:

```
string((doc("books.xml")//author)[1])
```

The result of this query is the string `"Stevens W."` (The exact result depends on the whitespace found in the original document—we have made some assumptions about what whitespace is present.)

User-Defined Functions

When a query becomes large and complex, it is often much easier to understand if it is divided into functions, and these functions can be reused in other parts of the query. For instance, we have seen a query that inverts a hierarchy to create a list of books by each author in a bibliography. It contained the following code:

```
for $b in doc("books.xml")/bib/book
where some $ba in $b/author satisfies
        ($ba/last=$l and $ba/first=$f)
order by $b/title
return $b/title
```

This code returns the titles of books written by a given author whose first name is bound to $f and whose last name is bound to $1. But you have to read all of the code in the query to understand that. Placing it in a named function makes its purpose clearer:

```
define function books-by-author($last, $first)
  as element()*
{
  for $b in doc("books.xml")/bib/book
  where some $ba in $b/author satisfies
        ($ba/last=$last and $ba/first=$first)
  order by $b/title
  return $b/title
}
```

XQuery allows functions to be recursive, which is often important for processing the recursive structure of XML. One common reason for using **recursive functions** is that XML allows recursive structures. For instance, suppose a book chapter may consist of sections, which may be nested. The query in Listing 1.19 creates a table of contents, containing only the sections and the titles, and reflecting the structure of the original document in the table of contents.

Listing 1.19   Query to Create a Table of Contents

```
define function toc($book-or-section as element())
  as element()*
{
  for $section in $book-or-section/section
  return
    <section>
      { $section/@* , $section/title , toc($section) }
    </section>
}

<toc>
   {
     for $s in doc("xquery-book.xml")/book
     return toc($s)
   }
</toc>
```

If two functions call each other, they are mutually recursive. Mutually recursive functions are allowed in XQuery.

Variable Definitions

A query can define a variable in the prolog. Such a variable is available at any point after it is declared. For instance, if access to the titles of books is used several times in a query, it can be provided in a variable definition:

```
define variable $titles { doc("books.xml")//title }
```

To avoid circular references, a variable definition may not call functions that are defined prior to the variable definition.

Library Modules

Functions can be put in library modules, which can be imported by any query. Every module in XQuery is either a main module, which contains a query body to be evaluated, or a library module, which has a module declaration but no query body. A library module begins with a module declaration, which provides a URI that identifies the module for imports, as shown in Listing 1.20.

Listing 1.20   Module Declaration for a Library Module

```
module "http://example.com/xquery/library/book"

define function toc($book-or-section as element())
  as element()*
{
  for $section in $book-or-section/section
  return
    <section>
      { $section/@* , $section/title , toc($section) }
    </section>
}
```

Functions and variable definitions in library modules are namespace-qualified. Any module can import another module using a module import, which specifies the URI of the module to be imported. It may also specify the location where the module can be found:

```
import module "http://example.com/xquery/library/book"
       at "file:///c:/xquery/lib/book.xq"
```

The location is not required in an import, since some implementations can locate modules without it. Implementations are free to ignore the location if they have another way to find modules.

A **namespace prefix** can be assigned in a module import, which is convenient since the functions in a module can only be called if a prefix has been assigned. The following query imports a module, assigns a prefix, and calls the function:

```
import module namespace b = "http://example.com/xquery/library/book"
    at "file:///c:/xquery/lib/book.xq"

<toc>
 {
   for $s in doc("xquery-book.xml")/book
   return b:toc($s)
 }
</toc>
```

When a module is imported, both its functions and its variables are made available to the importing module.

External Functions and Variables

XQuery implementations are often embedded in an environment such as a Java or C# program or a relational database. The environment can provide external functions and variables to XQuery. To access these, a query must declare them in the prolog:

```
define function outtie($v as xs:integer) as xs:integer external

define variable $v as xs:integer external
```

XQuery does not specify how such functions and variables are made available by the external environment, or how function parameters and arguments are converted between the external environment and XQuery.

Types in XQuery

Up to now, we have not spent much time discussing types, but the **type system** of XQuery is one of the most eclectic, unusual, and useful aspects of the language. XML documents contain a wide range of type information, from very loosely typed information without even a DTD, to rigidly structured data corresponding to relational data or objects. A language designed for processing XML must be able to deal with this fact gracefully; it must avoid imposing assumptions on what is allowed that conflict with what is actually found in the data, allow data to be managed without forcing the programmer to cast values frequently, and allow the programmer to focus on the documents being processed and the task to be performed rather than the quirks of the type system.

Consider the range of XML documents that XQuery must be able to process gracefully:

- XML may be strongly typed and governed by a W3C XML Schema, and a strongly typed query language with static typing can prevent many errors for this kind of data.

- XML may be governed by another schema language, such as DTDs or RELAX-NG.

- XML may have an *ad hoc* structure and no schema, and the whole reason for performing a query may be to discover the structure found in a document. For this kind of data, the query language should be able to process whatever data exists, with no preconceived notions of what should be there.

- XML may be used as a view of another system, such as a relational database. These systems are typically strongly typed, but do not use W3C XML Schema as the basis for their type system. Fortunately, standard mappings are emerging for some systems, such as SQL's mappings from relational schemas to W3C XML Schema. These are defined in the **SQL/XML** proposal, which provides standard XML extensions to SQL [SQLXML].

- XML data sources may have very complex structure, and expressions in XQuery must be well defined in terms of all the structures to which the operands can evaluate.

To meet these requirements, XQuery allows programmers to write queries that rely on very little type information, that take advantage of type information at run-time, or that take advantage of type information to detect potential errors before a query is ever executed. Chapter 4 provides a tutorial-like look at the topic of static typing in XQuery. Chapter 2, "Influences on the Design of XQuery," looks at the intricacies of some of the typing-related issues that members of the Work Group had to resolve.

Introduction to XQuery Types

The type system of XQuery is based on [SCHEMA]. There are two sets of types in XQuery: the built-in types that are available in any query, and types imported into a query from a specific schema. We will illustrate this with a series of functions that use increasing amounts of type information. XQuery specifies a conformance level called **Basic XQuery,** which is required for all implementations and allows two extensions: the schema import feature allows a W3C XML Schema to be imported in order to make its definitions available to the query, and the static typing feature allows a query to be compared to the imported schemas in order to catch errors without needing to access data. We will start with uses of types that are compatible with Basic XQuery. As we explore functions that require more type information, we will point out the points at which schema import and static typing are needed.

The first function returns a sequence of items in reverse order. The function definition does not specify the type of the parameter or the return type, which means that they may be any sequence of items:

```
define function reverse($items)
{
    let $count := count($items)
    for $i in 0 to $count
    return $items[$count - $i]
}
reverse( 1 to 5)
```

This function uses the to operator, which generates sequences of integers. For instance, the expression 1 to 5 generates the sequence 1, 2, 3, 4, 5. The reverse function takes this sequence and returns the sequence 5, 4, 3, 2, 1. Because this function does not specify a particular type for its parameter or return, it could also be used to return a sequence of some other type, such as a sequence of elements. Specifying more type information would make this function less useful.

Some functions take advantage of the known structures in XML or the built-in types of W3C XML Schema but need no advanced knowledge of any particular schema. The following function tests an element to see if it is the top-level element found in a document. If it is, then its parent node will be the document node, and the expression `$e/..` `instance` `of document` will be true when evaluated for that node. The parameter type is `element`, since this is only defined for elements, and the return type is `xs:boolean`, which is a predefined type in XQuery and is the type of Boolean values:

```
define function is-document-element($e as element())
  as xs:boolean
{
  if ($e/.. instance of document-node())
    then true()
    else false()
}
```

All the built-in XML Schema types are predefined in XQuery, and these can be used to write **function signatures** similar to those found in conventional programming languages. For instance, the query in Listing 1.21 defines a function that computes the *n*th Fibonacci number and calls that function to create the first ten values of the Fibonacci sequence.

Listing 1.21   Query to Create the First Ten Fibonacci Numbers

```
define function fibo($n as xs:integer)
{
 if ($n = 0)
 then 0
 else if ($n = 1)
 then 1
 else (fibo($n - 1) + fibo($n - 2))
}

let $seq := 1 to 10
for $n in $seq
return <fibo n="{$n}">{ fibo($n) }</fibo>
```

Listing 1.22 shows the output of that query.

Listing 1.22 Results of the Query in Listing 1.21

```
<fibo n = "1">1</fibo>
<fibo n = "2">1</fibo>
<fibo n = "3">2</fibo>
<fibo n = "4">3</fibo>
<fibo n = "5">5</fibo>
<fibo n = "6">8</fibo>
<fibo n = "7">13</fibo>
<fibo n = "8">21</fibo>
<fibo n = "9">34</fibo>
<fibo n = "10">55</fibo>
```

Schemas and Types

On several occasions, we have mentioned that XQuery can work with untyped data, strongly typed data, or mixtures of the two. If a document is governed by a DTD or has no schema at all, then documents contain very little type information, and queries rely on a set of rules to infer an appropriate type when they encounter values at run-time. For instance, the following query computes the average price of a book in our bibliography data:

```
avg( doc("books.xml")/bib/book/price )
```

Since the bibliography does not have a schema, each price element is untyped. The avg() function requires a numeric argument, so it converts each price to a double and then computes the average. The conversion rules are discussed in detail in a later section. The implicit conversion is useful when dealing with untyped data, but prices are generally best represented as decimals rather than floating-point numbers. Later in this chapter we will present a schema for the bibliography in order to add appropriate type information. The schema declares price to be a decimal, so the average would be computed using decimal numbers.

Queries do not need to import schemas to be able to use built-in types found in data—if a document contains built-in types, the data model preserves type information and allows queries to access it. If we use the same query we used before to compute the average price, it will now compute the price as a decimal. This means that even Basic XQuery implementations, which are not able to import a schema, are able to use simple types found in the data. However, if a query uses logic that is related to the meaning of a schema, it is generally best to import the schema. This can only be done if an implementation supports the schema import feature. Consider the following function, which is similar to one discussed earlier:

```
define function books-by-author($author)
{
  for $b in doc("books.xml")/bib/book
  where some $ba in $b/author satisfies
        ($ba/last=$author/last and $ba/first=$author/first)
  order by $b/title
  return $b/title
}
```

Because this function does not specify what kind of element the parameter should be, it can be called with any element at all. For instance, a book element could be passed to this function. Worse yet, the query would not return an error, but would simply search for books containing an author element that exactly matches the book. Since such a match never occurs, this function always returns the empty sequence if called with a book element.

If an XQuery implementation supports the schema import feature, we can ensure that an attempt to call this function with anything but an author element would raise a type error. Let's assume that the namespace of this schema is "urn:examples:xmp:bib". We can import this schema into a query and then use the element and attribute declarations and type definitions of the schema in our query, as shown in Listing 1.23.

Listing 1.23 Schema Import and Type Checking

```
import schema "urn:examples:xmp:bib" at "c:/dev/schemas/eg/bib.xsd"
default element namespace = "urn:examples:xmp:bib"
define function books-by-author($a as element(b:author))
  as element(b:title)*
{
  for $b in doc("books.xml")/bib/book
  where some $ba in $b/author satisfies
        ($ba/last=$a/last and $ba/first=$a/first)
  order by $b/title
  return $b/title
}
```

In XQuery, a type error is raised when the type of an expression does not match the type required by the context in which it appears. For instance, given the previous function definition, the function call in the following expression raises a type error, since an element named book can never be a valid author element:

```
for $b in doc("books.xml")/bib/book
return books-by-author($b)
```

All XQuery implementations are required to detect type errors, but some implementations detect them before a query is executed, and others detect them at run-time when query expressions are evaluated. The process of analyzing a query for type errors before a query is executed is called static typing, and it can be done using only the imported schema information and the query itself—there is no need for data to do static typing. In XQuery, static typing is an optional feature, but an implementation that supports static typing must always detect type errors statically, before a query is executed.

The previous example sets the default namespace for elements to the namespace defined by the schema. This allows the function to be written without namespace prefixes for the names in the paths. Another way to write this query is to assign a namespace prefix as part of the import and use it explicitly for element names. The query in Listing 1.24 is equivalent to the previous one.

Listing 1.24   Assigning a Namespace Prefix in Schema Imports

```
import schema namespace b = "urn:examples:xmp:bib"
  at "c:/dev/schemas/eg/bib.xsd"

define function books-by-author($a as element(b:author))
  as element(b:title)*
{
  for $b in doc("books.xml")/b:bib/b:book
  where some $ba in $b/b:author satisfies
        ($ba/b:last=$l and $ba/b:first=$f)
  order by $b/b:title
  return $b/b:title
}
```

When an element is created, it is immediately validated if there is a schema definition for its name. For instance, the following query raises an error because the schema definition says that a book must have a price:

```
import schema "urn:examples:xmp:bib" at "c:/dev/schemas/eg/bib.xsd"
default element namespace = "urn:examples:xmp:bib"

<book year="1994">
  <title>Catamaran Racing from Start to Finish</title>
  <author><last>Berman</last><first>Phil</first></author>
  <publisher>W.W. Norton & Company</publisher>
</book>
```

The schema import feature reduces errors by allowing queries to specify type information, but these errors are not caught until data with the wrong type information is actually encountered when executing a query. A query processor that implements the static typing feature can detect some kinds of errors by comparing a query to the imported schemas, which means that no data is required to find these errors. Let's modify our query somewhat and introduce a spelling error—$a/first is misspelled as $a/firt in Listing 1.25.

Listing 1.25   Query with a Spelling Error

```
import schema "urn:examples:xmp:bib" at "c:/dev/schemas/eg/bib.xsd"
default element namespace = "urn:examples:xmp:bib"

define function books-by-author($a as element(author))
  as element(title)*
{
  for $b in doc("books.xml")/bib/book
  where some $ba in $b/author satisfies
          ($ba/last=$a/last and $ba/first=$a/firt)
  order by $b/title
  return $b/title
}
```

An XQuery implementation that supports static typing can detect this error, because it has the definition for an author element, the function parameter is identified as such, and the schema says that an author element does not have a `firt` element. In an implementation that has schema import but not static typing, this function would actually have to call the function before the error would be raised.

However, in the following path expression, only the names of elements are stated:

```
doc("books.xml")/bib/book
```

XQuery allows element tests and attribute tests, node tests that are similar to the type declaration used for function parameters. In a path expression, the node test `element(book)` finds only elements with the same type as the globally declared `book` element, which must be found in the schemas that have been imported into the query. By using this instead of the name test `book` in the path expression, we can tell the query processor the element definition that will be associated with $b, which means that the **static type** system can guarantee us that a $b will contain title elements; see Listing 1.26.

Listing 1.26   Type Tests in Path Expressions

```
import schema "urn:examples:xmp:bib" at "c:/dev/schemas/eg/bib.xsd"
default element namespace = "urn:examples:xmp:bib"

define function books-by-author($a as element(author))
  as element(title)*
{
  for $b in doc("books.xml")/bib/element(book)
  where some $ba in $b/author satisfies
          ($ba/last=$a/last and $ba/first=$a/first)
  order by $b/title
  return $b/title
}
```

Sequence Types

The preceding examples include several queries in which the names of types use a notation that can describe the types that arise in XML documents. Now we need to learn that syntax in some detail. Values in XQuery, in general, are sequences, so the types used to describe them are called **sequence types.** Some types are built in and may be used in any query without importing a schema into the query. Other types are defined in W3C XML Schemas and must be imported into a query before they can be used.

Built-in Types

If a query has not imported a W3C XML Schema, it still understands the structure of XML documents, including types like document, element, attribute, node, text node, processing instruction, comment, ID, IDREF, IDREFS, etc. In addition to these, it understands the built-in W3C XML Schema simple types.

Table 1.4 lists the built-in types that can be used as sequence types.

In the notation for sequence types, **occurrence indicators** may be used to indicate the number of items in a sequence. The character ? indicates zero or one items, * indicates zero or more items, and + indicates one or more items. Here are some examples of sequence types with occurrence indicators:

```
element()+              One or more elements
xs:integer?             Zero or one integers
document-node()*        Zero or more document nodes
```

TABLE 1.4   Built-in Types That Can Be Used as Sequence Types

Sequence Type Declaration	What It Matches
element()	Any element node
attribute()	Any attribute node
document-node()	Any document node
node()	Any node
text()	Any text node
processing-instruction()	Any processing instruction node
processing-instruction("xml-stylesheet")	Any processing instruction node whose target is xml-stylesheet
comment()	Any comment node
empty()	An empty sequence
item()	Any node or atomic value
QName	An instance of a specific XML Schema built-in type, identified by the name of the type; e.g., xs:string, xs:boolean, xs:decimal, xs:float, xs:double, xs:anyType, xs:anySimpleType

When mapping XML documents to the XQuery data model, any element that is not explicitly given a simple or complex type by **schema validation** has the type xs:anyType. Any attribute that is not explicitly given a simple or complex type by schema validation has the type xdt:untypedAtomic. If a document uses simple or complex types assigned by W3C XML Schema, these are preserved in the data model.

Types from Imported Schemas

Importing a schema makes its types available to the query, including the definitions of elements and attributes and the declarations of complex types and simple types. We now present a schema for bibliographies, defining types that can be leveraged in the queries we use in the rest of this chapter. To support some of the examples, we have added an attribute that contains the ISBN number for each book, and have moved the publication year to an element. Listing 1.27 shows this schema—its relevant portions are explained carefully later in this section.

Listing 1.27   An Imported Schema for Bibliographies

```xml
<?xml version="1.0"?>
<xs:schema xmlns:xs="http://www.w3.org/2001/XMLSchema"
    xmlns:bib="urn:examples:xmp:bib"
    targetNamespace="urn:examples:xmp:bib"
    elementFormDefault="qualified">

<xs:element name="bib">
  <xs:complexType>
    <xs:sequence>
      <xs:element ref="bib:book" minOccurs="0"
                  maxOccurs="unbounded" />
    </xs:sequence>
  </xs:complexType>
</xs:element>

<xs:element name="book">
  <xs:complexType>
    <xs:sequence>
      <xs:element name="title" type="xs:string"/>
      <xs:element ref="bib:creator" minOccurs="1"
            maxOccurs="unbounded"/>
      <xs:element name="publisher" type="xs:string"/>
      <xs:element name="price" type="currency"/>
      <xs:element name="year" type="xs:gYear"/>
    </xs:sequence>
    <xs:attribute name="isbn" type="bib:isbn"/>
  </xs:complexType>
</xs:element>
```

Listing 1.27   An Imported Schema for Bibliographies *(continued)*

```
<xs:element name="creator" type="person" abstract="true" />
<xs:element name="author" type="person"
substitutionGroup="bib:creator"/>
<xs:element name="editor" type="personWithAffiliation"
substitutionGroup="bib:creator"/>

<xs:complexType name="person">
  <xs:sequence>
    <xs:element name="last" type="xs:string"/>
    <xs:element name="first" type="xs:string"/>
  </xs:sequence>
</xs:complexType>

<xs:complexType name="personWithAffiliation">
  <xs:complexContent>
    <xs:extension base="person">
     <xs:sequence>
       <xs:element name="affiliation" type="xs:string"/>
     </xs:sequence>
    </xs:extension>
  </xs:complexContent>
</xs:complexType>

<xs:simpleType name="isbn">
  <xs:restriction base="xs:string">
    <xs:pattern value="[0-9]{9}[0-9X]"/>
  </xs:restriction>
</xs:simpleType>

<xs:simpleType name="currency">
  <xs:restriction base="xs:decimal">
     <xs:pattern value="\d+.\d{2}"/>
  </xs:restriction>
</xs:simpleType>

</xs:schema>
```

Here is an example of a bibliography element that conforms to this new definition:

```
<bib xmlns="urn:examples:xmp:bib">
  <book isbn="0201563177">
    <title>Advanced Programming in the Unix Environment</title>
    <author><last>Stevens</last><first>W.</first></author>
    <publisher>Addison-Wesley</publisher>
    <price>65.95</price>
    <year>1992</year>
  </book>
</bib>
```

We do not teach the basics of XML Schema here—those who do not know XML Schema should look at XML Schema primer [SCHEMA]. However, to understand how XQuery leverages the type information found in a schema, we need to know what the schema says. Here are some aspects of the previous schema that affect the behavior of examples used in the rest of this chapter:

- All elements and types in this schema are in the namespace `urn:examples:xmp:bib` (for local elements, this was accomplished by using the `elementFormDefault` attribute at the top level of the schema). All attributes are in the null namespace.

- The following declaration says that the `isbn` type is a user-defined type derived from the `string` type by restriction and consists of nine digits followed either by a digit or by the character x:

```
<xs:simpleType name="isbn">
  <xs:restriction base="xs:string">
    <xs:pattern value="[0-9]{9}[0-9X]"/>
  </xs:restriction>
</xs:simpleType>
```

- The following declaration says that the "currency" type is derived from the decimal type by restriction, and must contain two places past the decimal point:

```
<xs:simpleType name="currency">
  <xs:restriction base="xs:decimal">
    <xs:pattern value="\d+.\d{2}"/>
  </xs:restriction>
</xs:simpleType>
```

- The following declarations say that `creator` is an abstract element that can never actually be created, and the `author` and `editor` elements are in the **substitution group** of `creator`:

```
<xs:element name="creator" type="person" abstract="true" />
<xs:element name="author" type="person"
substitutionGroup="bib:creator"/>
<xs:element name="editor" type="personWithAffiliation"
substitutionGroup="bib:creator"/>
```

- The content model for a book specifies a creator, but since creator is an abstract element, it can never be created—it will always match an author or an editor; see Listing 1.28.

Listing 1.28   Content Model for the Book Element

```
<xs:element name="book">
  <xs:complexType>
    <xs:sequence>
      <xs:element name="title" type="xs:string"/>
      <xs:element ref="bib:creator" minOccurs="1"
          maxOccurs="unbounded"/>
      <xs:element name="publisher" type="xs:string"/>
      <xs:element name="price" type="currency"/>
      <xs:element name="year" type="xs:gYear"/>
    </xs:sequence>
    <xs:attribute name="isbn" type="bib:isbn"/>
  </xs:complexType>
</xs:element>
```

- The following elements are globally declared: bib, book, creator, author, editor. The type of the bib and book elements is "anonymous," which means that the schema does not give these types explicit names.

- All of the named types in this schema are global; in fact, in XML Schema, all named types are global.

Now let us explore the sequence type notation used to refer to constructs imported from the above schema. The basic form of an element test has two parameters: the name of the element and the name of the type:

```
element(creator, person)
```

To match an element, both the name and the type must match. The name will match if the element's name is creator or in the substitution group of creator; thus, in the above schema, the names author and editor would also match. The type will match if it is person or any other type derived from person by extension or restriction; thus, in the above schema, personWithAffiliation would also match. The second parameter can be omitted; if it is, the type is taken from the schema definition. Because the schema declares the type of creator to be person, the following declaration matches the same elements as the previous declaration:

```
element(creator)
```

In XML Schema, element and attribute definitions may be local, available only within a specific element or type. A context path may be used to identify a locally declared element or attribute. For instance, the following declaration matches the locally declared `price` element, which is found in the globally declared `book` element:

```
element(book/price)
```

Although this form is generally used to match locally declared elements, it will match any element whose name is `price` and which has the same type as the `price` element found in the globally declared `book` element. A similar form is used to match elements or attributes in globally defined types:

```
element(type(person)/last)
```

The same forms can be used for attributes, except that (1) attributes never have substitution groups in XML Schema; (2) attributes are not nillable in XML Schema; and (3) the element name is preceded by the @ symbol in the XQuery syntax. For instance, the following declaration matches attributes named `price` of type `currency`:

```
attribute(@price, currency)
```

The following declaration matches attributes named `isbn` of the type found for the corresponding attribute in the globally declared `book` element:

```
attribute(book/@isbn)
```

Table 1.5 summarizes the declarations made available by importing the schema shown in Listing 1.27.

A sequence type declaration containing a name that does not match either a built-in type or a type imported from a schema is illegal and always raises an error.

There are no nillable elements in the sample schema. To indicate that an element test will also match a nilled element, the type should be declared nillable:

```
element(n, person nillable)
```

TABLE 1.5 The Effect of Importing the XML Schema in Listing 1.27

Sequence Type Declaration	What It Matches
`element(creator, person)`	An element named `creator` of type `person`
`element(creator)`	Any element named creator of type `xs:string`—the type declared for `creator` in the schema.
`element(*, person)`	Any element of type `person`.
`element(book/price)`	An element named price of type `currency`—the type declared for `price` elements inside a book element.
`element(type(person)/last)`	An element named last of type `xs:string`—the type declared for `last` elements inside the `person` type.
`attribute(@price, currency)`	An attribute named `price` of type `currency`.
`attribute(book/@isbn)`	An attribute named `isbn` of type `isbn`—the type declared for `isbn` attributes in a `book` element.
`attribute(@*, currency)`	Any attribute of type `currency`.
`bib:currency`	A value of the user-defined type `currency`"

The above declaration would match either an n element of type `person` or an n `person` which is nilled, such as this one, which uses `xsi:nil`:

```
<n xsi:nil="true" />
```

Working with Types

This section introduces various language features that are closely related to types, including function signatures, casting functions, typed variables, the `instance of` operator, `typeswitch`, and `treat as`.

Function Signatures

Parameters in a function signature may be declared with a sequence type, and the return type of a function may also be declared. For instance, the following function returns the discounted price of a book:

```
import schema namespace bib="urn:examples:xmp:bib"
define function discount-price($b as element(bib:book))
  as xs:decimal
```

```
{
  0.80 * $b//bib:price
}
```

It might be called in a query as follows:

```
for $b in doc("books.xml")//bib:book
where $b/bib:title = "Data on the Web"
return
  <result>
    {
      $b/bib:title,
      <price>{ discount-price($b/bib:price) }</price>
    }
  </result>
```

In the preceding query, the `price` element passed to the function exactly matches the declared type of the parameter. XQuery also defines some conversion rules that are applied if the argument does not exactly match the type of the parameter. If the type of the argument does not match and cannot be converted, a type error is raised. One important conversion rule is that the value of an element can be extracted if the expected type is an atomic type and an element is encountered. This is known as atomization. For instance, consider the query in Listing 1.29.

Listing 1.29   Atomization

```
import schema namespace bib="urn:examples:xmp:bib"

define function discount-price($p as xs:decimal)
  as xs:decimal
{
  0.80 * $p//bib:price
}

for $b in doc("books.xml")//bib:book
where $b/bib:title = "Data on the Web"
return
  <result>
    {
      $b/bib:title,
      <price>{ discount-price($b/bib:price) }</price>
    }
  </result>
```

When the typed value of the `price` element is extracted, its type is `bib:currency`. The function parameter expects a value of type `xs:decimal`, but the schema imported into the query says that the currency type is derived from `xs:decimal`, so it is accepted as a decimal.

In general, the typed value of an element is a sequence. If any value in the argument sequence is untyped, XQuery attempts to convert it to the required type and raises a type error if it fails. For instance, we can call the revised `discount-price()` function as follows:

```
let $w := <foo>12.34</foo>
return discount-price($w)
```

In this example, the `foo` element is not validated, and contains no type information. When this element is passed to the function, which expects a decimal, the function first extracts the value, which is untyped. It then attempts to cast 12.34 to a decimal; because 12.34 is a legitimate lexical representation for a decimal, this cast succeeds. The last conversion rule for function parameters involves **type promotion**: If the parameter type is `xs:double`, an argument whose type is `xs:float` or `xs:decimal` will automatically be cast to the parameter type; if the parameter type is `xs:float`, an argument whose type is `xs:decimal` will automatically be cast to the parameter type.

The parameter type or the return type may be any sequence type declaration. For instance, we can rewrite our function to take a `price` element, which is a locally declared element, by using a context path in the sequence type declaration:

```
import schema namespace bib="urn:examples:xmp:bib"

define function discount-price($p as element(bib:book/bib:price))
  as xs:decimal
{
  0.80 * $p
}
```

If the `price` element had an **anonymous type,** this would be the only way to indicate a `price` element of that type. Since our schema says a `price` element has the type `bib:currency`, the preceding function is equivalent to this one:

```
import schema namespace bib="urn:examples:xmp:bib"

define function discount-price($p as element(bib:price, bib:currency))
```

```
  as xs:decimal
{
  0.80 * $p
}
```

The same conversion rules that are applied to function arguments are also applied to function return values. Consider the following function:

```
define function decimate($p as element(bib:price, bib:currency))
  as xs:decimal
{
    $p
}
```

In this function, $p is an element named bib:price of type bib:currency. When it is returned, the function applies the function conversion rules, extracting the value, which is an atomic value of type bib:currency, then returning it as a valid instance of xs:decimal, from which its type is derived.

Casting and Typed Value Construction

Casting and typed value construction are closely related in XQuery. Constructor functions can be used to do both. In XQuery, any built-in type is associated with a constructor function that is found in the XML Schema namespace and has the same name as the type it constructs. This is the only way to create some types, including most date types. Here is a constructor for a date:

```
xs:date("2000-01-01")
```

Constructor functions check a value to make sure that the argument is a legal value for the given type and raise an error if it is not. For instance, if the month had been 13, the constructor would have raised an error.

Constructor functions are also used to cast values from one type to another. For instance, the following query converts an integer to a string:

```
xs:string( 12345 )
```

Some types can be cast to each other, others cannot. The set of casts that will succeed can be found in [XQ-FO]. Constructor functions are also created for imported simple types—this is discussed in the section on imported schemas.

When a schema is imported and that schema contains definitions for simple types, constructor functions are automatically created for these types. Like the built-in constructor functions, these functions have the same name as the type that is constructed. For instance, the `currency` type in our bibliography schema limits values to two digits past the decimal, and the `isbn` type restricts ISBN numbers to nine digits followed by either another digit or the letter `x`. Importing this schema creates constructor functions for these two types. The following expression creates an atomic value of type `isbn`:

```
import schema namespace bib="urn:examples:xmp:bib"
bib:isbn("012345678X")
```

The constructor functions for types check all the **facets** for those types. For instance, the following query raises an error because the pattern in the type declaration says that an ISBN number may not end with the character `Y`:

```
import schema namespace bib="urn:examples:xmp:bib"
bib:isbn("012345678Y")
```

Typed Variables

Whenever a variable is bound in XQuery, it can be given a type by using an `as` clause directly after the name of the variable. If a value that is bound to a typed variable does not match the declared type, a type error is raised. For instance, in the query shown in Listing 1.30, the `let` clause states that `$authors` must contain one or more `author` elements.

Listing 1.30   Declaring the Type of a Variable

```
import schema namespace bib="urn:examples:xmp:bib"

for $b in doc("books.xml")//bib:book
let $authors as element(bib:author)+ := $b//bib:author
return
  <result>
    {
      $b/bib:title,
      $authors
    }
  </result>
```

Since the schema for a bibliography allows a book to have editors but no authors, this query will raise an error if such a book is encountered. If a programmer simply assumed all books have authors, using a typed variable might identify an error in a query.

The `instance of` *Operator*

The `instance of` operator tests an item for a given type. For instance, the following expression tests the variable `$a` to see if it is an `element` node:

```
$a instance of element()
```

As you recall, literals in XQuery have types. The following expressions each return `true`:

```
<foo/> instance of element()

3.14 instance of xs:decimal

"foo" instance of xs:string

(1, 2, 3) instance of xs:integer*

() instance of xs:integer?
(1, 2, 3) instance of xs:integer+
```

The following expressions each return false:

```
3.14 instance of xdt:untypedAtomic

"3.14" instance of xs:decimal

3.14 instance of xs:integer
```

Type comparisons take type hierarchies into account. For instance, recall that SKU is derived from `xs:string`. The following query returns `true`:

```
import schema namespace bib="urn:examples:xmp:bib"
bib:isbn("012345678X") instance of xs:string
```

The `typeswitch` *Expression*

The `typeswitch` expression chooses an expression to evaluate based on the dynamic type of an input value—it is similar to the CASE statement found in several programming languages, but it branches based on the argument's type, not on its value. For instance, suppose we want to write a function that creates a simple wrapper element around a value, using `xsi:type` to preserve the type of the wrapped element, as shown in Listing 1.31.

Listing 1.31   Function Using the `typeswitch` Expression

```
define function wrapper($x as xs:anySimpleType)
  as element()
{
typeswitch ($x)
     case $i as xs:integer
          return <wrap xsi:type="xs:integer">{ $i }</wrap>
     case $d as xs:decimal
          return <wrap xsi:type="xs:decimal">{ $d }</wrap>
     default
          return error("unknown type!")
}

wrapper( 1 )
```

The case clause tests to see if `$x` has a certain type; if it does, the case clause creates a variable of that type and evaluates the associated return clause. The `error` function is a standard XQuery function that raises an error and aborts execution of the query. Here is the output of the query in Listing 1.31:

```
<wrap xsi:type="xs:integer">1</wrap>
```

The case clauses test to see if `$x` has a certain type; if it does, the case clause creates a variable of that type and evaluates the first return clause that matches the type of `$x`. In this example, 1 is both an integer and a decimal, since `xs:integer` is derived from `xs:decimal` in XML Schema, so the first matching clause is evaluated. The error function is a standard XQuery function that raises an error and aborts execution of the query.

The `typeswitch` expression can be used to implement a primitive form of polymorphism. For instance, suppose authors and editors are paid different percentages of the total price of a book. We could write the function shown in Listing 1.32, which invokes the appropriate function to calculate the payment based on the substitution group hierarchy.

Listing 1.32   Using `typeswitch` to Implement Simple Polymorphism

```
import schema namespace bib="urn:examples:xmp:bib"

define function pay-creator(
    $c as element(bib:creator),
    $p as xs:decimal)
{
  typeswitch ($c)
      case $a as element(bib:author)
          return pay-author($a, $p)
      case $e as element(bib:editor)
          return pay-editor($e, $p)
      default
          return error("unknown creator element!")
}
```

The `treat as` *Expression*

The `treat as` expression asserts that a value has a particular type, and
raises an error if it does not. It is similar to a cast, except that it does not
change the type of its argument, it merely examines it. `Treat as` and
`instance of` could be used together to write the function shown in Listing 1.33, which has the same functionality as the function in Listing 1.32.

Listing 1.33   Using `treat as` and `instance of` to Implement Simple Polymorphism

```
import schema namespace bib="urn:examples:xmp:bib"

define function pay-creator(
  $c as element(bib:creator),
  $p as xs:decimal)
{
if ($c instance of element(bib:author))
then pay-author($a, $p)
else if ($c instance of element(bib:editor))
then pay-editor($e, $p)
else error("unknown creator element!")
}
```

In general, `typeswitch` is preferable for this kind of code, and it also provides better type information for processors that do static typing.

Implicit Validation and Element Constructors

We have already discussed the fact that **validation** of the elements constructed in a query is automatic if the declaration of an element is global and is found in a schema that has been imported into the query. Elements that do not correspond to a global element definition are not validated. In other words, element construction uses XML Schema's **lax validation mode**. The query in Listing 1.34 creates a fully validated `book` element, with all the associated type information.

Listing 1.34   Query That Creates a Fully Validated Book Element

```
import schema namespace bib="urn:examples:xmp:bib"

<bib:book isbn="0201633469">
  <bib:title>TCP/IP Illustrated</bib:title>
  <bib:author>
    <bib:last>Stevens</bib:last>
    <bib:first>W.</bib:first>
  </bib:author>
  <bib:publisher>Addison-Wesley</bib:publisher>
  <bib:price>65.95</bib:price>
  <bib:year>1994</bib:year>
</bib:book>
```

Because element constructors validate implicitly, errors are caught early, and the types of elements may be used appropriately throughout the expressions of a query. If the element constructor in Listing 1.34 had omitted a required element or misspelled the name of an element, an error would be raised.

Relational programmers are used to writing queries that return tables with only some columns from the original tables that were queried. These tables often have the same names as the original tables, but a different structure. Thus, a relational programmer is likely to write a query like the following:

```
import schema namespace bib="urn:examples:xmp:bib"

for $b in doc("books.xml")//bib:book
return
```

```
<bib:book>
  {
    $b/bib:title,
    $b//element(bib:creator)
  }
</bib:book>
```

This query raises an error, because the `bib:book` element that is returned has a structure that does not correspond to the schema definition. Validation can be turned off using a `validate` expression, as shown in Listing 1.35, which uses `skip`.

Listing 1.35   Using `validate` to Disable Validation

```
import schema namespace bib="urn:examples:xmp:bib"

for $b in doc("books.xml")//bib:book
return
 validate skip
  {
   <bib:book>
     {
       $b/bib:title,
       $b//element(bib:creator)
     }
    </bib:book>
  }
```

The `validate` expression can also be used to specify a **validation context** for locally declared elements or attributes. For instance, the `price` element is locally declared:

```
import schema namespace bib="urn:examples:xmp:bib"

validate context bib:book
 {
  <bib:price>49.99</bib:price>
 }
```

If an element's name is not recognized, it is treated as an untyped element unless `xsi:type` is specified. For instance, the following query returns a well-formed element with untyped content, because the `bib:mug` element is not defined in the schema:

```
import schema namespace bib="urn:examples:xmp:bib"
<bib:mug>49.99</bib:mug>
```

A query can specify the type of an element using the `xsi:type` attribute; in this case, the element is validated using the specified type:

```
import schema namespace bib="urn:examples:xmp:bib"
<bib:mug xsi:type="xs:decimal">49.99</bib:mug>
```

If a locally declared element is not wrapped in a `validate` expression that specifies the context, it will generally be treated as a well-formed element with untyped content, as in the following query:

```
import schema namespace bib="urn:examples:xmp:bib"
<bib:price>49.99</bib:price>
```

To prevent errors like this, you can set the default validation mode to `strict`, which means that all elements must be defined in an imported schema, or an error is raised. This is done in the prolog. The following query raises an error because the `bib:price` element is not recognized in the global context:

```
import schema namespace bib="urn:examples:xmp:bib"
validation strict
<bib:price>49.99</bib:price>
```

The validation mode may be set to `lax`, which is the default behavior, `strict`, as shown above, or `skip` if no validation is to be performed in the query.

Summary

XQuery is not only a query language, but also a language that can do fairly general processing of XML. It is a strongly typed language that works well with data that may be strongly or weakly typed. Because the types used in XQuery are the same types used in XML and XML Schema, the type system is a better match for the data that is being processed. If the XML is governed only by a DTD or has no schema, the appropriate types are document, element, attribute, node, text node, processing instruction, comment, ID, IDREF, IDREFS, and so on. A strongly typed language that does not support these types tends to get in the way, because it is a poor match for the data being processed, and the language insists on the wrong things. If W3C XML Schema types are present in the data, these types are observed as well. Implementations and users of XQuery can work at various levels of typing by deciding whether to import schemas, whether to use static typing, and whether to set the validation mode to `strict`, `lax`, or `skip`.

XQuery was designed to be compact and compositional, and to be well suited for views of data that is not physically stored as XML. Both data integration and general purpose XML processing are likely to be important applications of XQuery. In practice, queries written in XQuery tend to be well suited to the kinds of tasks for which XML is generally used.

Part II

BACKGROUND

Chapter 2

INFLUENCES ON THE DESIGN OF XQUERY

Don Chamberlin

The emergence of the World Wide Web in the 1990s was a seminal event in human culture. Suddenly, as if overnight, a significant fraction of the world's computers were connected, not only by a physical network but also by a common protocol for exchanging information. The Web offered an unprecedented opportunity to make information truly ubiquitous. It seemed to promise that people would no longer need to move physically to places and times where information was available, since all information would be everywhere, all the time.

Realizing this promise required some organizing principle for the exchange of information. This principle had to be independent of any particular language or application and easily extensible to new and unanticipated kinds of information. At present, the leading candidate for this organizing principle is the Extensible Markup Language, XML [XML]. XML provides a neutral notation for labeling the parts of a body of information and representing the relationships among these parts. Since XML does not attach any semantic meaning to its labels, applications are free to interpret them as they see fit. Applications that agree on a common vocabulary can use XML for data interchange. Since XML does not mandate any particular storage technique, it can be used as a common interchange format among systems that store data in file systems, relational databases, object repositories, and many other storage formats.

Since XML is emerging as a universal format for data interchange among disparate applications, it is natural for queries that cross application boundaries to be framed in terms of the XML representation of data. In other words, if an application is viewed as a source of information in XML format, it is logical to pose queries against that XML format. This is the basic reason why a query language for XML data is extremely important in a connected world.

Recognizing the importance of an XML query language, the World Wide Web Consortium (W3C) [W3C] organized a query language workshop called QL'98 [QL98], which was held in Boston in December 1998. The workshop attracted nearly a hundred participants and fostered sixty-six papers investigating various aspects of querying XML data. One of the long-term outcomes of the workshop was the creation of a W3C working group for XML Query [XQ-WG]. This working group, chaired by Paul Cotton, met for the first time in September 1999. Its initial charter called for the specification of a formal data model and query language for XML, to be coordinated with existing W3C standards such as XML Schema [SCHEMA], XML Namespaces [NAMESP], XML Information Set [INFOSET], and **XSLT** [XSLT]. The purpose of the new query language was to provide a flexible facility to extract information from real and virtual XML documents. Approximately forty participants became members of the working group, representing about twenty-five different companies, along with a W3C staff member to provide logistical support.

One of the earliest activities of the Query working group was to draw up a formal statement of requirements for an XML query language [XQ-REQ]. This document was quickly followed by a set of **use cases** [XQ-UC] that described diverse usage scenarios for the new language, including specific queries and expected results. The XML Query Working Group undertook to define a language with two alternative syntaxes: a **keyword**-based syntax called XQuery [XQ-LANG], optimized for human reading and writing, and an XML-based syntax called XQueryX [XQ-X], optimized for machine generation. This chapter describes only the keyword-based XQuery syntax, which has been the major focus of the working group.

Creating a new query language is a serious business. Many person-years have been spent in defining XQuery, and many more will be spent on its implementation. If the language is successful, developers of web-based applications will use it for many years to come. A successful query language can enhance productivity and serve as a unifying influence in the growth of an industry. On the other hand, a poorly designed language can inhibit the acceptance of an otherwise promising technology. The designers of XQuery took their responsibilities very seriously, not only in the interest of their individual companies but also in order to make a contribution to the industry as a whole.

The purpose of this chapter is to discuss the major influences on the design of the XQuery language. A tutorial introduction to XQuery appears in Chapter 1. Some of the influences on XQuery were principles of computer language design. Others were related languages, interfaces, and standards. Still others were "watershed issues" that were debated by the working group and resolved in ways that guided the evolution of the language. We discuss several of these watershed issues in detail, including the alternatives that were considered and the reasons for the final resolution.

This chapter is based on the most recent XQuery specification at the time of publication. At this time, the broad outline of the language can be considered to be reasonably stable. However, readers should be cautioned that XQuery is still a work in progress, and the design choices discussed here are subject to change until the language has been approved and published as a W3C recommendation.

The Need for an XML Query Language

Early in its history, the XML Query Working Group confronted the question of whether XML is sufficiently different from other data formats to require a query language of its own. The SQL language [SQL99] is a very well established standard for retrieving information from relational databases and has recently been enhanced with new facilities called "structured types" that support nested structures similar to the **nesting** of elements in XML. If SQL could be further extended to meet XML query requirements, developers could leverage their considerable investment in SQL implementations, and users could apply the features of these robust and mature systems to their XML databases without learning a completely new language.

Given these incentives, the working group conducted a study of the differences between XML data and relational data from the point of view of a query language. Some of the significant differences between the two data models are summarized below.

- Relational data is "flat"—that is, organized in the form of a two-dimensional array of rows and columns. In contrast, XML data is "nested," and its depth of nesting can be irregular and unpredictable. Relational databases can represent nested data structures by using structured types or tables with **foreign keys**, but it is difficult to search these structures for objects at an unknown depth of nesting. In XML, on the other hand, it is very natural to search for objects whose position in a document hierarchy is unknown. An example of such a query might be "Find all the red things," represented in the XPath language [XPATH1] by the expression `//*[@color = "Red"]`. This query would be much more difficult to represent in a relational query language.

- Relational data is regular and homogeneous. Every row of a table has the same columns, with the same names and types. This allows **metadata**—information that describes the structure of the data—to be removed from the data itself and stored in a separate catalog. XML data, on the other hand, is irregular and heterogeneous. Each instance of a web page or a book chapter can have a different structure and must therefore describe its own structure. As a result, the ratio of metadata to data is much higher in XML than in a relational database, and in XML the metadata is distributed throughout the data in the form of tags rather than being separated from the data. In XML, it is natural to ask queries that span both data and metadata, such as "What kinds of things in the 2002 inventory have color attributes," represented in XPath by the expression `/inventory[@year = "2002"]/*[@color]`. In a relational language, such a query would require a join that might span several data tables and system catalog tables.

- Like a stored table, the result of a relational query is flat, regular, and homogeneous. The result of an XML query, on the other hand, has none of these properties. For example, the result of the query "Find all the red things" may contain a cherry, a flag, and a stop sign, each with a different internal structure. In general, the result of an expression in an XML query may consist of a heterogeneous sequence of elements, attributes, and primitive values, all of mixed type. This set of objects might then serve as an intermediate result used in the processing of a higher-level expression. The heterogeneous nature of XML data conflicts with the SQL assumption that every expression inside a query returns an array of rows and columns. It also requires a query language to provide constructors that are capable of creating complex nested structures on the fly—a facility that is not needed in a relational language.

- Because of its regular structure, relational data is "dense"—that is, every row has a value in every column. This gave rise to the need for a "null value" to represent unknown or inapplicable values in relational databases. XML data, on the other hand, may be "sparse." Since all the elements of a given type need not have the same structure, information that is unknown or inapplicable can simply not appear. This gives an XML query language additional degrees of freedom for dealing with missing data. The XQuery approach to representing unknown or inapplicable data is discussed in Issue 2 under "Watershed Issues" below.

- In a relational database, the rows of a table are not considered to have an ordering other than the orderings that can be derived from their values. XML documents, on the other hand, have an intrinsic order that can be important to their meaning and cannot be derived from data values. This has several implications for the design of a query language. It means that queries must at least provide an option in which the original order of elements is preserved in the query result. It means that facilities are needed to search for objects on the basis of their order, as in "Find the fifth red object" or "Find objects that occur after this one and before that one." It also means that we need facilities to impose an order on sequences of objects, possibly at several levels of a hierarchy. The importance of order in XML contrasts sharply with the absence of intrinsic order in the relational data model.

The significant data model differences summarized above led the working group to decide that the objectives of XML queries could best be served by designing a new query language rather than by extending a relational language. Designing a query language for XML, however, is not a small task, precisely because of the complexity of XML data. An XML "value," computed by a query expression, may consist of zero, one, or many items, each of which may be an element, an attribute, or a primitive value. Therefore, each operator in an XML query language must be well defined for all these possible inputs. The result is likely to be a language with a more complex semantic definition than that of a relational language such as SQL.

Basic Principles

The XML Query Working Group did not draw up a formal list of the principles that guided the design of XQuery. Nevertheless, throughout the design process, a reasonably stable consensus existed in the working group about at least some of the principles that should underlie the design of an XML query language. Some of these principles were mandated by the charter of the working group, and others arose from strongly held convictions of its members. The following list is my own attempt to enumerate the basic ideas and principles that were most influential in shaping the XQuery language. Tension exists among some of these principles, and several design decisions were the result of an attempt to find a reasonable compromise among conflicting principles.

- *Compositionality:* Perhaps the longest-standing principle in the design of XQuery is that XQuery should be a functional language incorporating the principle of **compositionality**. This means that XQuery consists of several kinds of expressions, such as path expressions, conditional expressions, and element constructors, that can be composed with full generality. The result of any expression can be used as the operand of another expression. No syntactic constraints are imposed on the ways in which expressions can be composed (though the language does have some **semantic constraints**). Each expression returns a value that depends only on the operands of the expression, and no expression has any side effects. The value returned by the outermost expression in a query is the result of the query.

- *Closure*: XQuery is defined as a transformation on a data model called the **Query data model**. The input and output of every query or subexpression within a query each form an instance of the Query data model. This is what is meant by the statement that XQuery is *closed* under the Query data model. The working group spent considerable time on the definition of the Query data model and on how instances of this model can be constructed from input XML documents and/or serialized in the form of output XML documents.

- *Schema conformance*: Since XML Schema has recently been adopted as a W3C Recommendation, the working group considered it highly desirable for XQuery to be based on the type system of XML Schema. This constraint strongly influenced the design of XQuery by providing a set of **primitive types,** a type-definition facility, and an **inheritance** mechanism. The validation process defined by XML Schema also strongly influenced the XQuery facilities for constructing new elements and assigning their types. Nevertheless, members of the working group attempted to modularize the parts of the language that are related to type definition and validation, so that XQuery could potentially be used with an alternative schema language at some future time.

- *XPath compatibility*: Because of the widespread usage of XPath in the XML community, a strong effort was made to maintain compatibility between XQuery and XPath Version 1.0. Despite the importance of this goal, it was necessary in a few areas to compromise compatibility in order to conform to the type system of XML Schema, because the design of XPath Version 1.0 was based on a much simpler type system.

- *Simplicity*: Many members of the working group considered simplicity of expression and ease of understanding to be primary goals of our language design. These goals were often in conflict with other goals, resulting in some painful compromises.

- *Completeness*: The working group attempted to design a language that would be complete enough to express a broad range of queries. The existence of a well-motivated use case was considered a strong argument for inclusion of a language feature. The expressive power of XQuery is comparable to the criterion of "relational completeness" defined for database query languages [CODD], though no such formal standard has been defined for an XML data model. Informally, XQuery is designed to be able to construct any XML document that can be computed from input XML documents using the power of the first-order predicate calculus. In addition, recursive functions add significant expressive power to the language.

■ *Generality*: XQuery is intended for use in many different environments and with many kinds of input documents. The language should be applicable to documents that are described by a schema, or by a Document Type Definition [XML], or by neither. It should be usable in strongly typed environments where input and output types are well known and rigorously enforced, as well as in more dynamic environments where input and output types may be discovered at execution time and some data may be untyped. It should accommodate input documents from a variety of sources, including XML files discovered on the Web, repositories of pre-validated XML documents, streaming data sources such as stock tickers, and XML data synthesized from databases.

■ *Conciseness*: In the interest of conciseness, the semantics of the XQuery operators were defined to include certain implicit operations. For example, arithmetic operators such as +, when applied to an element, automatically extract the numeric value of the element. Similarly, comparison operators such as =, when applied to sequences of values, automatically iterate over the sequences, looking for a pair of values that satisfies the comparison (this process is called **existential quantification**). These implicit operations are consistent with XPath Version 1.0 and were preferred over a design that would require each operation to be explicitly specified by the user.

■ *Static analysis*: From the beginning, the processing of a query was assumed to consist of two phases, called *query analysis* and *query evaluation* (roughly corresponding to compilation and execution of a program.) The analysis phase was viewed as an opportunity to perform **optimization** and to detect certain kinds of errors. A great deal of effort went into defining the kinds of checks that could be performed during the analysis phase and in deciding which of these checks should be required and which should be permitted.

The Query Data Model

The first step in designing XQuery was to specify the data model on which the language operates. The Query data model [XQ-DM] represents XML data in the form of nodes and values, which serve as the operands and results of the XQuery operators. XQuery is closed under the Query data model, which means that the result of any valid XQuery expression can be represented in this model. Since all the operators and expressions of XQuery are defined in terms of the Query data model, understanding this model is the key to understanding the language.

In defining the Query data model, the working group did not intend to deviate from existing standards, but to conform to them wherever possible. Therefore, the Query data model draws from several previously existing specifications. The information that results from parsing an XML document is specified by the XML **Information Set** [INFOSET], in the form of a collection of **information items.** The XML Information Set (or Infoset) contains no type information, and it represents data at a very primitive level—for example, every character has its own information item. XML Schema specifies an augmented form of the XML Infoset called the **Post-Schema Validation Infoset,** or PSVI. In the PSVI, information items that represent elements and attributes have type information and normalized values that are derived by a process called *schema validation*. The PSVI contains all the information about an XML document that is needed for processing a query, and the Query data model is based on the information contained in the PSVI.

For reasons described in the next section, the working group decided early to include the existing language XPath [XPATH1] as a subset of XQuery. XPath provides a notation for selecting information within an existing XML document, but it does not provide a way to construct new XML elements. Section 5 of the XPath specification shows how to represent the information in the XML Infoset in terms of a tree structure containing seven kinds of nodes. The operators of XPath are defined in terms of these seven kinds of nodes. In order to retain the original XPath operators and still take advantage of the richer type system of XML Schema, the XQuery designers decided to augment the XPath data model with the additional type information contained in the PSVI. The result of this process is the Query data model. The Query data model can be thought of as representing the PSVI in the form of a **node hierarchy,** much as the XPath data model represents the XML Infoset in the form of a node hierarchy.

In the Query data model, every value is an ordered sequence of zero or more **items.** An item can be either an *atomic value* or a *node*. An atomic value has a *type*, which is one of the atomic types defined by XML Schema or is derived from one of these types by restriction. A node is one of the seven kinds of node defined by XPath, called document, element, attribute, text, comment, processing instruction, and namespace nodes. Nodes have identity, and an ordering called *document order* is defined among all the nodes that are in scope.

An instance of the Query data model may contain one or more XML documents or fragments of documents, each represented by its own tree of nodes. The **root node** of the tree that represents an XML document is a document node. Each element in the document is represented by an element node, which may be connected to attributes (represented by attribute nodes) and content (represented by text nodes and nested element nodes). The primitive data in the document is represented by text nodes, which form the leaves of the node tree.

Figure 2.1 illustrates the Query data model representation of a simple XML document. Nodes are represented by circles labeled *D* for document nodes, *E* for element nodes, *A* for attribute nodes, and *T* for text nodes. The XML document represented by Figure 2.1 is shown in Listing 2.1:

Listing 2.1   XML Document Represented by Figure 2.1

```
<?xml version="1.0" ?>
<procedure title="Removing a light bulb">
   <time unit="sec">15</time>
   <step>Grip bulb.</step>
   <step>
      Rotate it
      <warning>slowly</warning>
      counterclockwise.
   </step>
</procedure>
```

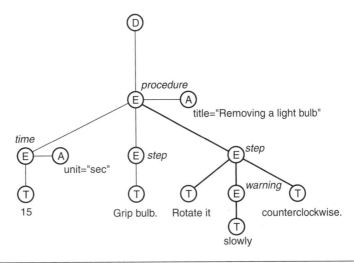

Figure 2.1   Example of the Query Data Model

In the Query data model, each element or attribute node has a name, a string value, a **type annotation,** and a typed value. These properties are not independent. The type annotation of an element represents its type as determined by the schema validation process. An element that has not been validated, or for which no more specific type is known, has the type annotation xs:anyType, where xs: is a prefix representing the namespace of XML Schema. If an element has no descendant elements, then its typed value can be derived from its string value and its type annotation.

Bear in mind that the type of an element describes the potential content of the element and does not depend on the name of the element. For example, two elements named cost and price could both have the type annotation decimal because they both require decimal content. Similarly, two elements named shipto and billto could both have the type annotation address, which might be a complex type defined in a schema that describes the potential content of the elements.

XQuery is defined as a transformation from one instance of the Query data model to another instance of the Query data model. This simplifies the definition of XQuery but leaves open the issues of where input data comes from and how output data is delivered to applications. A query gains access to input data by calling an XQuery input function such as `doc` or `collection`, or by referencing some part of the external context (such as a prebound variable or "current node"). Each of these input methods is defined to return a Query data model instance in the form of one or more node hierarchies. One way in which a node hierarchy could be created is by parsing an XML document, validating it against a known or default schema, and converting the resulting PSVI into the Query data model as described in [XQ-DM]. Another way is for a system to store XML documents in a pre-validated form so that their Query data model representation can be materialized quickly on demand. A third way is for the Query data model to be synthesized directly from some data source such as a relational database, deriving its type information from "metadata" in the database catalog.

The process of serializing a Query data model instance as a linear XML document remains unspecified at present. All XML documents can be represented using the Query data model, but not all instances of the Query data model are valid XML documents. For example, the result of a query might be a sequence of atomic values, or an attribute that is not attached to any element. Mechanisms for serializing these values and for binding them to variables in a host programming language remain to be specified.

Related Languages and Standards

The designers of XQuery did not begin with a completely blank slate. The design of XQuery was strongly constrained by the requirement for compatibility with established standards and was also influenced by the design of other query languages with which the members of the working group were familiar. This section describes some of the ways in which XQuery was influenced by related languages and standards.

XML and Namespaces

Since XQuery is a query language for XML data sources, it is obvious that the language must be strongly influenced by the structure of XML itself

[XML]. From XML comes the notion that information is represented as a hierarchy of elements that have names, optional attributes, and optional content. The content of an element may consist of text, nested elements, or some mixture of these. The content of an XML document has an intrinsic order, and it is often important to preserve this order.

XQuery was also influenced by some of the lexical conventions of XML. Since XML is a **case-sensitive** language, it was decided that XQuery should be case-sensitive also. Since XML allows a hyphen to be used as part of a name, XQuery adopted the same convention. A consequence of this convention is that whitespace is sometimes significant in XQuery expressions. For example, spaces are used to distinguish the arithmetic expression `a - b` from the name `a-b`.

One important feature of an XML query language is the ability to construct an element with a given name and content. One of the ways in which XQuery supports element construction is by using XML notation. An XQuery element constructor can consist of a start tag and an **end tag,** enclosing character data that is interpreted as the content of the element, as illustrated in the following example:

```
<price>15.99</price>
```

Within an element constructor, curly braces are used to enclose expressions that are to be evaluated rather than treated as text, as in the following example, which computes a price from two variables named `$regprice` and `$discount`:

```
<price>{$regprice - $discount}</price>
```

Namespaces are very important to XML because they define the structure of an XML name. Namespaces provide a way for XML applications to be developed independently while avoiding the risk of name collisions. **Qualified names** (*QNames*), as defined in the XML Namespaces specification [NAMESP], are used as the names of XML elements and attributes. XQuery also uses *QNames* as the names of functions, types, and variables. A *QName* consists of two identifiers, called the *namespace prefix* and the *local part*, separated by a colon. The namespace prefix and colon are optional. If present, the namespace prefix must be bound to a Uniform Resource Identifier (URI) that uniquely identifies a namespace.

As an example, suppose that the namespace prefix `student` is bound to the URI `http://example.org/student`, and the namespace prefix `investment` is bound to the URI `http://example.org/investment`. Then the *QNames* `student:interest` and `investment:interest` are recognized as distinct names even though their local parts are the same.

XQuery provides two ways of binding a namespace prefix to a URI. The first of these is by a declaration in the **prolog,** a part of a query that sets up the environment for query execution. Namespace prefixes declared in the prolog remain in scope throughout the query. This method of declaring a namespace prefix is illustrated by the following example:

```
declare namespace student = "http://example.org/student"
```

The second way to bind a namespace prefix to a URI in XQuery can be used when an element is constructed and defines a namespace prefix for use within the scope of the element. This method relies on an attribute with the prefix `xmlns`, which indicates that the attribute is binding a namespace prefix. For example, in the following start tag, the attribute named `xmlns:student` binds the namespace prefix `student` to a given URI within the scope of a constructed element named `school`:

```
<school xmlns:student = "http://example.org/student">
```

XQuery allows a user to specify, in the prolog, default namespace URIs to be associated with *QNames* that have no namespace prefix. Separate default namespaces can be specified for names of functions and for names of elements and types.

XQuery also provides a set of predefined namespace prefixes that can be used in any query without an explicit declaration. For example, the prefix `xs` is automatically bound to the namespace of XML Schema, so it is easy to refer to the names of built-in schema types such as `xs:integer`. Similarly, the prefix `fn` is automatically bound to the namespace of the XQuery core function library [XQ-FO], so it is easy to refer to the names of built-in XQuery functions such as `fn:max` and `fn:string`. If a query does not declare otherwise, the default namespace for function names is the namespace of the XQuery core function library (also bound to the prefix `fn`.)

XML Schema

As noted earlier, one of the major goals of the XML Query Working Group has been to define a query language based on the type system of XML Schema. This goal was made more difficult by the fact that XML Schema was designed to support validation of documents rather than to serve as the type system for a query language.

XML Schema has had a strong impact on XQuery because its type system is quite complex and includes some unusual features. The influences of XML Schema on the design of XQuery include the following:

- In XQuery, there is no distinction between a single value and a sequence of length one. To state this rule in another way, all XQuery values are sequences of length zero, one, or more. This rule arises from the XML Schema "facets" named `minOccurs` and `maxOccurs`, which can be attached to a part of a schema in order to constrain its number of occurrences. For example, in a schema, an **element declaration** without any occurrence constraints is considered identical to an element declaration with the facets `minOccurs="1"` and `maxOccurs="1"`; both declarations specify a sequence of elements of length one. Since all XQuery values are sequences, each parameter of a function can potentially accept a sequence of multiple items. For example, the function call `foo(1, (2, 3), ( ))` invokes a function with three arguments: the first argument is a sequence of length one, the second argument is a sequence of length two, and the third argument is a sequence of length zero.

- In XQuery, there is no notion of nested sequences—that is, a sequence directly containing another sequence as one of its members. The members of an XQuery sequence are always nodes or atomic values. A node, however, may in turn have another sequence as its content. These rules are derived from XML Schema, in which the content of an element is always a "flat" sequence of atomic values and other elements (which may, in turn, have content of their own).

- In XQuery, sequences may be heterogeneous—that is, a sequence may contain mixtures of nodes and atomic values, and may contain atomic values of different types. Again, these rules are derived from XML Schema, in which the content of an element can be declared to be "mixed" (that is, consisting of a mixture of text and nested elements), and a sequence can contain values that conform to a "choice" of types.

- The working group chose to rely on the features of XML Schema for defining and naming complex types. As a result, XQuery depends on the conventions of XML Schema for associating names with types. Unfortunately, in XML Schema, some types have no name, and many types may have the same name. XML Schema does not, in general, provide a unique way to refer to a user-defined type. The impact on XQuery of the XML Schema naming system is discussed under Issue 3 ("What Is a Type?") in the "Watershed Issues" part of this chapter.

- XML Schema defines two different forms of type inheritance, called **derivation by extension** and **derivation by restriction,** and also introduces the concept of a *substitution group*, which can allow one kind of element to substitute for another kind of element based on its name. This combination of features has added a considerable amount of complexity to the syntax of XQuery. For example, as a step in a path expression, the name `frog` refers to an element whose name is exactly `frog`, but the notation `element(frog)` refers to an element that is either named `frog` or is in the same substitution group as the element named `frog`.

XML Schema defines a large set of built-in primitive types and an additional set of built-in **derived types.** In general, XQuery operators are defined on the primitive types of XML Schema, and operators on derived types are defined to promote their operands to the nearest primitive type. However, an exception to this rule was made for the type `integer`. Although `integer` is considered by most languages to be a primitive type, XML Schema considers it to be derived from `decimal`. If the general rule of promoting derived types to their primitive base types were applied to integers, arithmetic operations on integers such as `2 + 2` would return decimal results. As a consequence, an expression such as `2 + 2` would raise a type error when used in a function call where an integer is expected. In order to avoid these type errors, operations on integers in XQuery are defined to return integers even though XML Schema considers `integer` to be a derived type.

XML Schema defines a `duration` type, which consists of six components named `year`, `month`, `day`, `hour`, `minute`, and `second`. This definition ignores the experience of the relational database community, which has discovered that neither comparison nor arithmetic operators can be supported by a duration type defined in this way. The following questions illustrate the problems encountered by operations on the `duration` type of XML Schema: Which is greater, one month or thirty days? What is the result of dividing one month by two? To deal with these problems, the SQL Standard in 1992 [SQL92] introduced two datatypes called a "year-month interval" and a "day-time interval." Each of these supports a well-defined set of arithmetic and comparison operators, but they cannot be mixed in a single expression. In order to facilitate arithmetic and comparison operations on dates, times, and durations, XQuery followed the practice of SQL in defining subtypes of `duration` called `xdt:yearMonthDuration` and `xdt:dayTimeDuration` (`xdt` is a predefined namespace prefix that represents the namespace containing all new datatypes defined by the XQuery specification).

Following the mandate of its charter, the working group designed XQuery to be fully compatible with XML Schema. At the same time, the group attempted to design XQuery in a way that would not preclude its adaptation to alternative schema definition languages. XQuery might be viewed as relying on an external schema facility for defining types and type hierarchies and for determining the type of a given element (in XML Schema, this process is called *validation*). To the extent that a schema facility meets these requirements, it can be considered compatible with XQuery.

XPath

Comparable to XML Schema in its influence on the design of XQuery is XPath [XPATH1], which has been a W3C Recommendation since November 1999. XPath is widely used in the XML community as a compact notation for navigating inside XML documents, and it is an integral part of other standards, including XSLT [XSLT] and XPointer [XPTR].

The functionality of XPath is clearly needed as part of an XML query language, and there is a clear precedent that this functionality should be expressed using the syntax of XPath Version 1. Therefore, from the beginning, compatibility with XPath Version 1 was a major objective and constraint on the design of XQuery.

Initially, the Query working group considered using the path expression of XPath as a "leaf expression" in the XQuery syntax—that is, as a primitive form of expression that could be used as an operand in higher-level XQuery expressions but could not in turn contain other XQuery operators. However, at the same time that XQuery was being designed, the XSLT working group had collected a set of requirements for new functionality in XPath [XPATH2REQ], and these requirements overlapped substantially with the functionality proposed for XQuery. As a result, it was decided that a new version of XPath would be developed jointly by the XSLT and Query working groups. The new version, to be called XPath Version 2 [XPATH2], would be a syntactic subset of XQuery, would be backward-compatible with XPath Version 1, and would be available for use in XSLT and other standards. XPath Version 2 would include many of the features of XQuery and would be fully integrated with the rest of the XQuery syntax rather than serving as a non-decomposable "leaf expression."

Types in XPath

For XPath to be used in a query language based on the type system of XML Schema, its own type system had to be revised. XPath Version 1 recognized only four types: Boolean, string, "number" (a double-precision, floating numeric type), and "node-set" (an unordered collection of nodes). XPath Version 1 was designed with a very permissive view of types, in which conversions of one type to another could be done with very few limitations. For example, if a node-set is encountered where a number is expected, the string value of the first node in the node-set (in document order) is extracted and cast into a number. These permissive rules were deliberately designed to minimize the likelihood of non-recoverable errors during the processing of path expressions, which are often used in rendering web pages by a browser or in other contexts where run-time errors are unwelcome.

From a type system based on only four types, XPath had to be adapted to the type system of XML Schema, which included forty-four built-in types and a complex set of rules for defining additional types, encompassing atomic, simple, complex, primitive, derived, list, union, and anonymous types, as well as two forms of inheritance, twelve "constraining facets," substitution groups, and various other features. Also, from a very permissive set of type-conversion rules, XPath had to be adapted to a philosophy of strict typing, including both static and dynamic type-checking. Users of XPath were assured that these changes constituted an improvement. Adaptation of XPath to the XML Schema type system also provided an opportunity to make a very small number of incompatible changes to the semantics of the language.

Syntax and Semantics

The adoption of XPath as a subset had significant effects on both the syntax and semantics of XQuery, including the following:

- Since XPath uses the symbol / in path expressions, it is not available for use as a division operator. XQuery adopted the XPath operator `div` for division, supplemented by a new `idiv` operator for division of integers, returning an integer.

- XPath has a few keywords, such as `and`, `or`, `div`, and `mod`, but none of these keywords are **reserved words.** This means that the XPath grammar is defined in such a way that an XPath expression can search for an element named (for example) `mod`, without confusing the element name with the keyword. It is obviously desirable to avoid any limitation on names that can be searched for in documents. One way to accomplish this would be to require a special "escape" syntax to be used with names that are the same as keywords (one alternative that was considered was to prefix these names with a colon). But for compatibility with XPath Version 1, it was decided that XQuery should have no reserved keywords and no special syntax for names. This was accomplished by careful grammar design and by defining some rules for "lookahead" during the process of converting a query from a stream of characters into grammatical tokens.

■ The concept of *document order* is very important to the definition of several XPath operators, and as a result it also plays an important role in XQuery semantics, as described below.

Document order is an ordering that is defined among all the nodes in the Query data model representation of a document. As defined in XPath, document order corresponds to the order in which the XML representations of the various nodes would be encountered if the document were to be serialized in XML format. In other words, each element node is followed by its namespace nodes, its attribute nodes, and its children (text, element, comment, and processing instruction nodes) in the order in which they naturally appear in the document. Reverse document order is defined as the reverse of document order.

One of the defining features of XPath is the *path expression*, which consists of a series of *steps*, each of which selects a set of nodes. In the set of nodes selected by a step, each node has a *position* based on its relationship to the other nodes in (forward or reverse) document order. In effect, the set of nodes resulting from each step must be sorted on the basis of document order, a potentially expensive process. The idea of sorting intermediate results was particularly unfamiliar to people with a background in relational databases, in which sets of data values have no intrinsic order. The working group briefly considered relaxing this requirement and allowing the nodes selected by each step to remain in the order in which they were generated (based on iterating over the nodes selected by the previous step). This idea was put to rest by an example suggested by Michael Kay. The example is based on the following input document:

```
<warning>
<p>
Do <emph>not </emph> touch the switch.
The computer will <emph>explode!</emph>
</p>
</warning>
```

The representation of this input document in the Query data model is shown in Figure 2.2, in which element nodes are represented as circles labeled *E*, and text nodes are represented as circles labeled *T*.

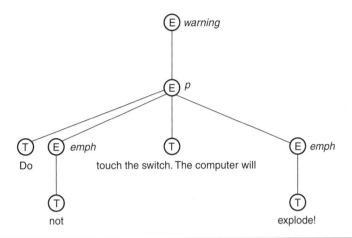

Figure 2.2   Query Data Model Representation of "Warning" Document

Against this input document we wish to execute the following path expression:

```
/warning//text()
```

In XPath Version 1, this path expression would return all the text nodes that are descendants of the `warning` element, in document order. The concatenated content of these nodes is as follows:

```
Do not touch the switch. The computer will explode!
```

It is interesting to consider how the result of this path expression would change if each step in the path preserved the order of nodes generated by the previous step rather than sorting its results in document order. Under these rules, the path expression would be executed as follows:

1. The first step, `/warning`, returns the top-level element node, which has the name `warning`.
2. The notation `//` is an abbreviation for a second step, which in fully expanded form might be written as `/descendant-or-self::node()/`. This step returns the `warning` element node

returned by the previous step, and all its descendants—in other words, all eight of the nodes shown in Figure 2.2, in document order.

3. The third step, `text()`, uses the default child axis of XPath to return text nodes that are children of the nodes returned by the previous step. Only element nodes have children that are text nodes. Processing the element nodes returned by the previous step, in order, leads to the following result (ignoring some subtle issues relating to the handling of whitespace):

The first element node to be processed is named `p` and has two text node children, containing the strings `"Do"` and `"touch the switch. The computer will"`.

The second element node to be processed is named `emph` and has one text node child, containing the string `"not"`.

The third element node to be processed is named `emph` and has one text node child, containing the string `"explode!"`.

The concatenated contents of the text nodes returned by the final step is as follows:

```
Do touch the switch. The computer will not explode!
```

This example is a good illustration of how processing documents places some requirements on a query language that are beyond the scope of a traditional database query language. The Query working group included representatives from both the database and document processing communities, and these individuals had much to learn from each other during the process of designing XQuery.

Predicates

XPath has several kinds of *predicates*, which are tests that are used to filter sequences of nodes. All of these predicates have the general form `E1[E2]`, in which the expression `E2` is used to filter the items in the sequence generated by expression `E1`. The different kinds of XPath predicates are illustrated by the following examples:

- `/employee[salary > 1000]` selects `employee` elements that have a `salary` **subelement** with value greater than 1000.
- `/employee[5]` selects the fifth `employee` element in a sequence.
- `/employee[secretary]` selects `employee` elements that have a `secretary` subelement.

For XQuery, it was necessary to preserve all these kinds of predicates, but to generalize their definitions so that the value of an expression (either `E1` or `E2` in the above format) could be a heterogeneous sequence of nodes and atomic values. In XQuery, `E1[E2]` is defined as follows: For each item `e1` in the sequence returned by `E1`, the expression `E2` is evaluated with `e1` as the **context item** (the context item serves as the "starting point" for a path expression). For a given `e1`, if `E2` returns a number n, the value `e1` is retained only if its ordinal position in the `E1`-sequence is equal to n. Otherwise, `e1` is retained only if the **Effective Boolean Value** of `E2` is `true`. Effective Boolean Value is defined to be `false` for an empty sequence and for the following single atomic values: the Boolean value `false`, a numeric or binary zero, a zero-length string, or the special float value `NaN`. Any other sequence has an Effective Boolean Value of `true`. Note especially that the Effective Boolean Value of any node is `true`, regardless of its content, and the Effective Boolean Value of any sequence of length greater than one is `true`, regardless of its content.

This definition of Effective Boolean Value is used not only in predicates but also in other parts of XQuery where it is necessary to reduce a general sequence to a Boolean value (for example, in conditional expressions and quantified expressions). The definition was arrived at by considerations of XPath Version 1 compatibility, logical consistency, and performance. This definition has the desirable property that the Effective Boolean Value of a sequence of arbitrary length depends only on the value of the first item in the sequence and the existence (but not the values) of additional items. It also has the surprising property that an element with the Boolean content `false` has an Effective Boolean Value of `true` (as required for compatibility with XPath Version 1). Another surprising property of this definition is that a sequence of atomic values, all of which are `false`, has the Effective Boolean Value of `true` (because it contains more than one item).

Implicit Operations and Transitivity

XPath Version 1 is defined to perform many implicit conversions during the processing of an expression. Some of these conversions are illustrated by the following example:

```
//book[author = "Mark Twain"]
```

On the left side of the = operator, we find `author`, which denotes a sequence of zero or more element nodes. On the right side of the = operator, we find `"Mark Twain"`, which is a string. Since a sequence of zero or more nodes is not the same thing as a string, these expressions are made comparable by the following implicit actions:

- The values of the `author` nodes are extracted and treated as atomic values.
- Since these atomic values are being compared with a string, they are treated as strings.
- If there is more than one `author` value, an implied existential quantifier is inserted, so the predicate is considered to be true if any `author` value is equal to the string `"Mark Twain"`.

These implicit actions make the above expression equivalent to the following expression in which the same actions are represented explicitly:

```
//book[some $a in ./author satisfies string(data($a)) = "Mark Twain"]
```

In keeping with the basic principle of conciseness as well as the principle of backward compatibility, XQuery preserved these implicit XPath conversions and in fact extended them in a uniform way to apply to other parts of the XQuery language. The extraction of atomic values from nodes is called *atomization* in XQuery, and is applied to sequences as well as to individual nodes. For example, the expression `avg(/employee/salary)` extracts numeric values from a sequence of `salary` nodes before applying the `avg` function.

The implicit conversions described above led to a serious concern for the designers of XQuery: They caused the comparison operators such as = and > to lack the **transitivity** property. Thus, if `$book1/author = $book2/author` is true, and `$book2/author = $book3/author` is true, it is not possible to conclude that `$book1/author = $book3/author` is true. For example, this inference would fail if `$book1/author` has the value ("Billy", "Bonnie"), `$book2/author` has the value ("Bonnie", "Barry"), and `$book3/author` has the value ("Barry", "Benny").

Transitivity is a useful property for comparison operators. For example, transitivity of equality comparisons is required for certain kinds of query transforms that are useful in optimization. Transitivity of a comparison operator is also required if the operator is to serve as the basis for imposing a global ordering on a sequence of values. Since the six *general comparison* operators (`=`, `!=`, `>`, `>=`, `<`, and `<=`) lack transitivity, the designers of XQuery decided to supplement them with six more primitive *value comparison* operators (`eq`, `ne`, `gt`, `ge`, `lt`, and `le`) that have the transitivity property. These primitive comparison operators can be used to compare single atomic values, but they raise an error if either of the operands to be compared is not a single value. The value comparison operators always treat an untyped operand as a string.

Incompatible Changes

Despite the general objective of backward compatibility, a small number of XPath Version 1 features remained unacceptable to the designers of XQuery. Some of these features were considered important for other usages of XPath, such as XSLT style sheets that had been written to exploit these features. To deal with this problem, an "XPath Version 1 compatibility mode" was defined for XPath Version 2. When embedded in XQuery, XPath Version 2 will not run in compatibility mode, and the semantics of certain operators will be different from those of XPath Version 1. Other host environments of XPath Version 2, such as XSLT, are free to interpret XPath Version 2 in compatibility mode to preserve the semantics expected by existing applications. The cases in which compatibility mode influences the semantics of XPath Version 2 include the following:

- In XPath Version 1, if an operand of an arithmetic operator such as + is a sequence containing more than one node, the numeric value of the first node in the sequence is extracted and used as the operand. In XQuery, this case is treated as an error.
- In XPath Version 1, inequality operators on strings cast their operands to `double`, but the equality operator on two strings performs a string comparison. This leads to the surprising result that

`"4"` `<=` `"4.0"` and `"4"` `>=` `"4.0"` are both `true`, but `"4"` `=` `"4.0"` is `false`. In XQuery, all comparison operators on strings perform string comparisons without attempting to convert their operands to numbers.

- In XPath Version 1, arithmetic operators can be applied to strings and implicitly convert their operands to `double`. For example, the expression `"1"` `+` `"2"` returns `3.0E0`. In XQuery, arithmetic on strings is treated as an error.

- In XPath Version 1, the `=` operator on two elements compares their string values, ignoring nested markup. For example, a book with title `"Tom Sawyer"` and author `"Mark Twain"` is considered to be equal (by the `=` operator) to a book with author `"Tom Sawyer"` and title `"Mark Twain"`. In XQuery, applying the `=` operator to two elements whose content consists entirely of subelements is treated as an error. However, XQuery provides several functions, such as `fn:deep-equal`, that can be used to perform various kinds of comparisons between element nodes. Comparison of the string values of two element nodes can be done by extracting their string values, using the `fn:string` function, as in `fn:string($node1)` `=` `fn:string($node2)`.

Other Query Languages

The influence of other languages on XQuery is not limited to directly related standards such as XPath and XML Schema. XQuery has also been strongly influenced by other query languages used in both the database and information retrieval communities. In several cases, designers of these precursor languages have also contributed to the design of XQuery.

The immediate ancestor of XQuery is **Quilt** [QUILT], a language proposal submitted to the XML Query Working Group by three of its participants in June 2000. Quilt provided the basic framework of XQuery as a functional language based on several types of composable expressions, including an iterative expression and an element constructor. The FLWOR expression, one of the most important of the XQuery expression types, was adopted from Quilt (though the original Quilt version did not have an `order-by` clause). From its origin in the Quilt proposal, XQuery has evolved by changing the syntax for element constructors, adding a more complex syntax for declaring the types of function parameters, and adding some new kinds of expressions, such as `validate`, `instance-of`, and `typeswitch`. The XQuery specification is also much more complete and rigorous than the original Quilt proposal in formally specifying the semantics of various kinds of expressions, as described in Chapter 4.

The Quilt proposal, in turn, reflects the influence of several other query languages. In fact, the name "Quilt" was intended to suggest that features had been patched together from a variety of sources to form a new language.

From SQL [SQL99] and from the relational database community in general, XQuery adopted an English-keyword notation and a rich collection of use cases. Many SQL facilities such as **grouping** and outer join have their counterparts in XQuery, though they are often expressed in different ways. The `select-from-where` query block of SQL has a rough analogy in the `for-let-where-order-return` (FLWOR) expression of XQuery, in the sense that both kinds of expression are used for both *selection* (retaining certain items while discarding others) and *projection* (retaining certain properties of the selected items while discarding others.) Some features of SQL, however, such as a special null value and three-valued logic for the `and` and `or` operators, were considered unnecessary in the XML context and were not duplicated in XQuery.

From XML-QL [XML-QL], Quilt (and hence XQuery) adopted the approach of binding variables to sequences of values and then constructing new output elements based on the bound variables. An XML-QL query consists of a WHERE clause followed by a CONSTRUCT clause. The result of the WHERE clause is a stream of tuples of bound variables. The CONSTRUCT clause is executed once for each of these tuples, generating a stream of output elements. As in XQuery, the combination of WHERE and CONSTRUCT is a nestable unit from which queries can be constructed. The creation of an ordered stream of tuples, and iteration over these tuples to generate output, have direct counterparts in the FLWOR expression of XQuery. XQuery also adopted from XML-QL the convention of prefixing variable names with a $ sign.

From OQL [OQL], Quilt (and hence XQuery) adopted the approach of designing the language around a fully composable set of expressions, all of which use a common data model for their operands and results. The `select-from-where` expression of OQL, rather than providing a framework for the whole language, as in SQL, is simply one of several independent expressions that include arithmetic and set operators, function calls, and universal and existential quantifiers. Similarly, in XQuery, the FLWOR expression is simply one of many types of expressions that can be combined in various ways. The atoms, structures, and collections in the OQL data model are suggestive of the atomic values, elements, and sequences in the Query data model (though the Query data model supports only one kind of collection). Interestingly, OQL (like Quilt) has a fully independent `sort-by` operator that can be applied to any sequence of values, whereas in XQuery the sorting facility is supported only as a clause inside the FLWOR expression, for reasons described under Issue 8 ("Ordering Operators") in the following section.

Watershed Issues

A large fraction of the total effort invested in the design of XQuery by the working group has been focused on a relatively small number of "watershed issues." These are issues whose resolution had a significant global impact on the language by influencing a number of related decisions. All of these issues are complex, and some of them were quite contentious. Eight of these watershed issues are discussed here; they are listed below.

1. *Handling of untyped data.* This issue deals with the kinds of operations that can be applied to data whose type is not known.

2. *Unknown and inapplicable data.* This issue deals with how unknown values can be encoded in XML and how various operators should be defined on these values.

3. *What is a type?* This issue deals with how a datatype is specified in XQuery.

4. *Element constructors.* This issue deals with the details of how to construct a new XML element by using a query expression.

5. *Static typing.* This issue deals with the kinds of type-checking that can be performed on a query independently of any input data.

6. *Function resolution.* This issue deals with how functions are defined and how function calls are processed.

7. *Error handling.* This issue deals with the kinds of errors that can be encountered in queries, and whether query expressions are

deterministic (that is, whether they always return the same result for a given input).

8. *Ordering operators.* This issue deals with the kinds of operators that are provided in the language for controlling the order of results.

Issue 1: Handling of Untyped Data

Despite publication of XML Schema as a W3C Recommendation in May 2001, a great many XML documents exist that are not described by a schema. Some of these documents have Document Type Definitions (DTDs), and some do not have a formal description of any kind. In the absence of a schema, the character data in an XML document does not have a well-defined type. A DTD might describe this data as CDATA ("character data") or PCDATA ("parsed character data"), but in fact it might represent either text or numeric data.

Many of the operators of XQuery require data of a particular type—for example, the arithmetic operators are defined on numeric data. It is highly desirable that these operators be usable for querying schema-less documents, even though the data in these documents is not explicitly declared to be of any particular type. The approach of requiring all untyped data to be explicitly cast into a specific type whenever it is referred to in a query was rejected as putting an unreasonable burden on the query writer. Instead, the designers of XQuery attempted to define a set of rules that allow types to be inferred for input data based on the context in which the data is used.

Consider the following fragment of an input document:

```
<employee>
    <name>Fred</name>
    <salary>5000</salary>
    <bonus>2000</bonus>
</employee>
```

The process of representing this input data in the Query data model causes each element node to receive a type annotation. If the input document is validated against a schema, the `employee` node might receive a type annotation of `employee-type`, and the `salary` and `bonus` nodes might receive a type annotation of `xs:decimal`.

Suppose that a query binds a variable named $fred to the employee element, and evaluates the expression $fred/salary + $fred/bonus. Each of the operands of the + operator evaluates to an element node whose type annotation is xs:decimal. The + operator extracts the decimal values from the nodes and adds them together. The result of the expression is an atomic value of type xs:decimal.

Now consider the following similar fragment from an input document that has no schema:

```
<a>
   <b>5</b>
   <c>17</c>
</a>
```

Syntactically, this fragment consists of an element containing two nested elements. In the absence of a schema, the elements are given the generic type annotation xs:anyType, which indicates that no type information is available. An atomic value occurring inside an untyped element, such as 5 or 17 in the above example, is given the type annotation xdt:untypedAtomic,[1] which denotes an atomic value for which no type is available.

In the above example, suppose that a query binds a variable named $a to the outer element, and executes the expression $a/b + $a/c. Looking at the input document, we see that the nested elements b and c contain numbers, and it seems reasonable that these numbers should be added together. But it is necessary to define the rules under which this operation is performed. As in the earlier example, the + operator extracts the typed values from the b and c nodes. The value of the b node is 5, and the value of the c node is 17, and the type of both values is xdt:untypedAtomic. Each operator in XQuery has a rule for how it handles values of type xdt:untypedAtomic. In the case of arithmetic operators such as +, the rule states that any operand of type xdt:untypedAtomic is cast to the

---

[1] The type xdt:untypedAtomic is closely related to the type xs:anySimpleType, which is the root of the simple type hierarchy in XML Schema [SCHEMA]. The type xdt:untypedAtomic is different from xs:anySimpleType in two ways: (1) xs:anySimpleType includes non-atomic values such as lists that are considered to be "simple" by XML Schema, whereas xdt:untypedAtomic includes only atomic values; and (2) xs:anySimpleType includes primitive types such as xs:string and xs:decimal as subtypes, whereas xdt:untypedAtomic has no subtypes. In general, an atomic value in a PSVI whose type property is xs:anySimpleType is represented in the Query data model with the type annotation xdt:untypedAtomic.

type `xs:double` before the addition is performed. If a value of type `xdt:untypedAtomic` cannot be successfully cast to the type `xs:double`, the arithmetic operator raises an error. In our example expression, the operands are successfully cast to the double-precision values `5.0E0` and `1.7E1`, and the result of the expression is `2.2E1`.

Various operators in XQuery have different rules for handling of values of type `xdt:untypedAtomic`. As we have seen, arithmetic operators cast `xdt:untypedAtomic` values to `xs:double`. General comparison operators such as `=` and `>`, on the other hand, cast operands of type `xdt:untypedAtomic` to the type of the other operand, and if both operands are of type `xdt:untypedAtomic`, they are both cast to the type `xs:string`. These rules reflect the facts that addition is defined only for numbers, but comparison can be defined for any string value. Casting `xdt:untypedAtomic` values into numbers before comparing them would preclude comparison of non-numeric strings.

Suppose that, instead of `$a/b + $a/c`, our example expression had been `$a/b > $a/c`. Since the type of both operands is `xdt:untypedAtomic`, `$a/b` is cast to the string `"5"` and `$a/c` is cast to the string `"17"`, and the strings are compared using a default collation order. The result depends on the default collation, but the expression is likely to return the value `true` since in most collations the string `"5"` is greater than the string `"17"`.

Each XQuery operator has its own rule for processing operands based on their types. For some operators, such as the general comparison operators, the rule depends on the **dynamic types** of both operands. These rules make XQuery by definition a dynamically dispatched language, meaning that, in general, the semantics of an operation are determined at run-time. However, the rules are such that, when operating on well-typed data that is described by a schema, static analysis can often determine the semantics of an operation at compile type and can use this information to execute the query efficiently (avoiding run-time branching).

The working group considered the alternative of treating all untyped data as strings. In the example `$a/b + $a/c` above, this design would have resulted in the `+` operator having strings as its operands. In order for this useful example to work, it would have been necessary for arithmetic operators to cast their string operands into a numeric type (say, `double`). Then `5 + "7"` would no longer be a type error, even though it adds a number to a string.

Similarly, if untyped data were to be treated as strings, comparison operators between numbers and strings would need to be defined. For example, consider the expression `age > 40`. In the absence of a schema, `age` is untyped. If untyped data is treated as a string, `age > 40` will give the expected result only if its string operand is cast to a number. But then `5 = "5"` and `5 = "05"` would be true rather than type errors (but `"5" = "05"` would be false). Also, then `5 > 17` and `"5" > 17` would be false but `"5" > "17"` would be true. It was felt that these rules would generate confusion and would compromise the strong typing of the language. Therefore, the working group chose to treat untyped data according to its context rather than always treating it as a string.

Issue 2: Unknown and Inapplicable Data

In the real world, data is sometimes unknown or inapplicable. Any data model needs to have a way to represent these states of knowledge.

In the relational data model, data is represented in a uniform way using rows and columns. Every row in a given table has the same columns, and there is exactly one value in every column. For example, if a table describing cars has a `mileage` column containing information about the expected miles per gallon of each car, then every row in that table must have some value in the `mileage` column, including rows that describe cars whose mileage is unknown and rows that describe electric cars for which the concept of mileage is inapplicable. This requirement gave rise to the "null" value in relational databases, an "out-of-range" value that is used to represent unknown or inapplicable data. In the relational query language SQL, arithmetic and comparison operators always return the null value if any of their operands is null. Since logical operators such as `and` and `or` must deal with the null value as well as the Boolean values `true` and `false`, SQL is said to use **three-valued logic.**

XML is considerably more flexible than the relational model when it comes to representing unknown or inapplicable data. In an XML Schema, a `car` element might be defined to contain `make` and `year` elements and an optional `mileage` element. The `mileage` element in turn might be defined to contain an optional decimal value. Then, any of the following is a valid XML representation of a `car` element:

The `mileage` element could be present and have a value:

```
<car><make>Toyota</make><year>2002</year><mileage>26</mileage></car>
```

The `mileage` element could be present but empty:

```
<car><make>Ford</make><year>2002</year><mileage/></car>
```

The `mileage` element could be absent:

```
<car><make>Porsche</make><year>2002</year></car>
```

XQuery leaves it up to the application to define the mapping of states of knowledge about cars onto various XML representations. For example, the absence of a `mileage` element might be used to represent the absence of any knowledge about mileage, whereas the presence of an empty `mileage` element might be used to represent the knowledge that mileage is inapplicable for the given car.

Because XML already provides a way to represent various states of knowledge about data, including unknown and inapplicable data, the designers of XQuery saw no need to introduce a special "out-of-range" value (which, in any case, would not have been consistent with XML Schema). Instead, XQuery focuses on defining the operators of the language in such a way that they return a reasonable and useful result for all of the possible syntactic states of their operands. This approach provides application developers with the tools they need to represent various knowledge states as they see fit.

The main operators of XQuery that operate on scalar values are arithmetic, comparison, and logical operators. These operators are also defined on nodes, but always begin by reducing their operands to scalar values by a process called *atomization*. The result of atomization on an absent or empty element is an empty sequence.

If arithmetic is performed on unknown or inapplicable data (for example, `mileage div cost` where `mileage` is unknown), the result should be unknown or inapplicable. Therefore, the arithmetic operators of XQuery are defined in such a way that if either of their operands (after atomization) is an empty sequence, the operator returns an empty sequence.

XQuery provides two sets of comparison operators. The general comparison operators, =, ! =, >, >=, <, and <=, which are inherited from XPath Version 1, have an implied existential quantifier on both operands. For example, the expression A = B, if A and B are sequences of multiple values, returns true if some item in sequence A is equal to some item in sequence B. If either of their operands is an empty sequence, the general comparison operators return false. These operators (as in XPath Version 1) have the interesting property that the predicates length > width, length < width, and length = width can all be simultaneously true (if length or width contains multiple values), and can also all be simultaneously false (if length or width contains no values).

As noted earlier, XQuery also provides a set of value comparison operators, eq, ne, gt, ge, lt, and le, which require both of their operands to consist of exactly one atomic value. These operators raise an error if either of their operands is an empty sequence. These operators are designed to be "building blocks" with well-defined mathematical properties that can serve as the basis for defining more complex logical operations.

Some consideration was given to defining three-valued comparison operators that return an empty sequence (representing the unknown truth value) if either of their operands is an empty sequence. This approach was rejected because such operators would not be transitive. For example, consider the expression salary eq 5 and bonus eq salary. A query optimizer might wish to transform this expression by adding an additional predicate bonus eq 5, deduced by the transitivity property. This transformation is valid under **two-valued logic** but not under three-valued logic. For example, under three-valued logic, if salary is empty (unknown) and bonus has the value 7, then the truth value of salary eq 5 and bonus eq salary would be unknown, but the truth value of bonus eq 5 would be false. Since transitive comparisons were considered necessary for defining other operations, such as sorting and grouping, the value comparison operators were defined using two-valued logic.

The semantics of the logical operations and, or, and not in the presence of empty sequences are constrained by compatibility with XPath Version 1. In XPath, a predicate expression that returns an empty sequence is interpreted as false (as a failed test for the existence of something). For example, the query `//employee[secretary]` searches for `employee` elements that have a `secretary` subelement; if the predicate expression `secretary` returns an empty sequence, the predicate is considered to be `false`. For compatibility with XPath Version 1, the `and` and `or` operators of XQuery (and the `not` function) treat the empty sequence as having a Boolean value of `false`.

In languages such as SQL that are based on three-valued logic, queries do not generally return data for which the search-condition evaluates to the unknown truth value. Therefore, the distinction between two-valued and three-valued logic is somewhat subtle. The difference can be illustrated by a query that performs negation on an intermediate result. Consider how the following two queries would operate on a `car` element that has no `mileage` subelement:

Query: Find cars whose mileage is less than or equal to 25.

```
//car[mileage <= 25]
```

Query: Find cars for which it is not true that mileage is greater than 25.

```
//car[not(mileage > 25)]
```

In SQL, if the value of `mileage` is null, the predicates `mileage <= 25` and `mileage > 25` both return the unknown truth value. The inverted predicate `not(mileage > 25)` also returns the unknown truth value. According to this logic, the `car` with no `mileage` subelement would not be returned by either query.

In XQuery, if `mileage` is an empty sequence, the predicates `mileage <= 25` and `mileage > 25` both return `false`, and `not(mileage > 25)` is `true`. Therefore the car with no mileage subelement would be returned by the second query above but not by the first query.

A language that wishes to define three-valued `and`, `or`, and `not` operators needs to specify the truth tables for these operators. One approach is to adopt the rule that `and`, `or`, and `not` return the unknown truth value if any of their operands is the unknown truth value. SQL, however, adopts a different approach, represented by the truth tables in Figure 2.3.

AND	T	F	?
T	T	F	?
F	F	F	F
?	?	F	?

OR	T	F	?
T	T	T	T
F	T	F	?
?	T	?	?

NOT		
T	F
F	T
?	?

Figure 2.3   Truth Tables in SQL

If an XQuery application needs three-valued logic, it can easily be simulated by writing functions that use the built-in XQuery operators. The value comparison operator eq can be supplemented by a function, possibly named eq3, that returns the empty sequence if either of its operands is empty. This function, and functions that implement the SQL truth tables of Figure 2.3, are illustrated in Listing 2.2.

Listing 2.2   Defined Function eq3 and Others Implementing the Truth Tables of Figure 2.3

```
define function eq3($a as xdt:anyAtomicType?, $b as
xdt:anyAtomicType?)
   as xs:boolean?
   {
    if (empty($a) or empty($b)) then ()
    else ($a eq $b)
   }

define function not3($a as xs:boolean?)
   as xs:boolean?
   {
    if (empty($a)) then ()
    else not($a)
   }

define function and3($a as xs:boolean?, $b as xs:boolean?)
   as xs:boolean?
   {
    if ($a and $b) then true()
    else if (not3($a) or not3($b)) then false()
    else ()
   }

define function or3($a as xs:boolean?, $b as xs:boolean?)
   as xs:boolean?
   {
    if ($a or $b) then true()
    else if (not3($a) and not3($b)) then false()
    else ()
   }
```

It is worth mentioning that XML Schema defines a special attribute named `xsi:nil`. This attribute affects only the process of Schema validation. It permits an element to be accepted as valid with no content, even though the element has a declared type that requires content. The `xsi:nil` attribute is treated by XQuery as an ordinary attribute. Its presence or absence does not affect the semantics of XQuery operators.

Issue 3: What Is a Type?

Query languages use types to check the correctness of queries and to ensure that operations are being applied to data in appropriate ways. The specification and handling of types has been one of the most complex and contentious parts of the XQuery design.

XML Schema provides a set of built-in types and a facility for defining and naming new types. In XML Schema, the name of an element or attribute is distinguished from the name of its type. For example, a schema might define an element named `shipto` with the type `address`. This means that the content of the `shipto` element is determined by the declaration of the `address` type—possibly consisting of subelements such as `street`, `city`, `state`, and `zipcode`. However, not all elements have a named type. For example, a schema might define an element named `offering` to contain subelements named `product` and `price` without giving a name to the type of the `offering` element. In this case, the `offering` element is said to have an *anonymous* type. Furthermore, an `offering` element might be defined to have different types in different contexts—for example, an `offering` in a `university` might be different from an `offering` in a `catalog`. XML Schema also allows an element, an attribute, and a type all to have the same name, so it is necessary to distinguish somehow among different usages of a name (for example, to distinguish an element named `price` from an attribute named `price`). All the names defined in a schema belong to an XML namespace called the *target namespace* of the schema.

XQuery allows the names of elements, attributes, and types that are defined in a schema to be used in queries. The prolog of a query explicitly lists the schemas to be imported by the query, identifying each schema by its target namespace. Importing a schema makes all the names defined in that schema available for use in the query. An error results if two or more imported schemas define the same name with conflicting meanings. The prolog of a query can also bind a namespace prefix to the target namespace of an imported schema. For example, the following statement imports a schema and assigns the namespace prefix `po` to its target namespace:

```
import schema namespace po = "http://example.org/purchaseOrder"
```

As noted earlier, each element or attribute node in the Query data model has a type annotation that identifies the type of its content. For example, a `salary` element might have the type annotation `xs:decimal`, indicating that it contains a decimal number. A type annotation identifies either a built-in Schema type, such as `xs:decimal`, or a type that is defined in some imported schema. For example, a schema might define the type `hatsize` to be derived from `xs:integer` by restricting its values to a certain range. Element and attribute nodes acquire their type annotation through a process called *schema validation*, which involves comparing the content of the node to the schema declaration for nodes with that name. For example, the element named `hat` might be declared in a schema to have the type `hatsize`. If the content of a given element node with the name `hat` conforms to the definition of the type `hatsize`, the element node receives the type annotation `hatsize` during schema validation; otherwise, schema validation fails, and an error is reported. Schema validation may be performed on input documents before query processing, and on newly constructed elements and attributes during query processing. Validation of nodes against user-provided schemas is an optional feature of an XQuery implementation. In an implementation that does not support this feature, all element nodes have the generic type annotation `xs:anyType`.

Several places in the XQuery syntax call for a reference to a type. One of these is a function definition, which specifies the types of the function parameters and result. Other XQuery expressions that require type references include `instance-of`, `typeswitch`, and `cast` expressions. In these expressions, it is not always sufficient to refer to a type simply by its name. For example, when declaring the type of a function parameter, the user may wish to specify an element with a particular name, or with a particular type annotation, or both. Alternatively, the type of a function parameter might be an unrestricted element node, or some other kind of node such as an attribute or text node, or an unrestricted atomic value. Furthermore, since all XQuery values are sequences, we may want a type reference to indicate a permissible number of occurrences, such as exactly one, zero or one, zero or more, or one or more.

Specifying the syntax of a type reference in XQuery was a difficult and important part of the language design. Although XML Schema itself has all the necessary features, embedding fragments of XML Schema language in a query was not considered appropriate, because Schema syntax is quite verbose and is inconsistent in style with XQuery. The working group considered inventing a new type-definition syntax with power comparable to that of XML Schema, but rejected this approach because it would have added a great deal of complexity to XQuery and would have duplicated the features of an existing W3C recommendation.

In the end, the working group defined a type reference syntax containing a few keywords and symbols to give users a limited degree of flexibility in defining types. The main features of this type reference syntax are listed below:

- An atomic type is referred to simply by its *QName*, such as `xs:integer` or `po:price`. The generic name `xdt:anyAtomicType` refers to a value of any atomic type.
- Element nodes can be referred to in any of the following ways:
  - `element($N$, $T$)` denotes an element with name N and type annotation T. For example, `element(shipto, address)` denotes an element named `shipto` whose type annotation is `address`.
  - `element($N$, *)` denotes an element with name N, regardless of its type annotation.
  - `element(*, $T$)` denotes an element with type annotation T, regardless of its name.
  - `element($N$)` denotes an element whose name is N and whose type annotation is the (possibly anonymous) type declared in the imported schema for elements named N.
  - `element($P$)`, where P is a valid schema "path" beginning with the name of a global element or type and ending with one of its component elements, denotes an element whose name and type annotation conform to that schema path. For example, `element (order/shipto/zipcode)` denotes an element named `zipcode`

that has been validated against the type definition in the schema context `order/shipto`.

- `element()` denotes any element, regardless of its name or type annotation.

■ Attribute nodes can be referred to in a similar way to element nodes, except that attribute names are prefixed by an `@` sign. For example, `attribute(@N, T)` denotes an attribute node with name *N* and type annotation *T*, and `attribute()` denotes any attribute node, regardless of its name or type annotation.

■ Other kinds of nodes can be referred to by keywords that indicate the kind of node, followed by empty parentheses. For example, `text()`, `document()`, `comment()`, and `processing-instruction()` refer to any node of the named kind; `node()` refers to a node of any kind; and `item()` refers to either a node or an atomic value.

■ Any type reference may be followed by one of the following *occurrence indicators:* `*` denotes a sequence of zero or more occurrences of the given type; `+` represents one or more occurrences; and `?` represents zero or one occurrence. The absence of an occurrence indicator denotes exactly one occurrence of the given type. For example, `xs:integer?` denotes an optional integer value, and `element(hatsize)*` denotes a sequence of zero or more elements named `hatsize`.

Occurrence indicators are often useful in defining the parameter types of functions. For example, consider a function that classifies jobs into categories such as "Professional," "Clerical," and "Sales," based on criteria such as job title and salary. The definition of this function might be written as follows, indicating that the function accepts an element named `job` and returns a string:

```
define function job-category($j as element(job)) as xs:string
```

The `job-category` function defined above will raise an error if its argument is anything other than exactly one `job` element. This error might be encountered by the following query:

```
for $p in //person return $p/name, job-category($p/job)
```

For any `person` in the input stream that has no `job` or more than one `job`, this query will invoke the `job-category` function with an invalid argument. This error could be avoided by making the `job-category` function more flexible. The following definition uses the occurrence indicator `*` on the function parameter, allowing the function to accept a sequence of zero or more `job` elements:

```
define function job-category($j as element(job)*) as xs:string
```

Of course, the body of the `job-category` function must be written in such a way that it returns an appropriate result for any argument that matches the declared parameter type in the function definition.

If a function parameter is specified as an element node with a particular name, such as `element(shipto)`, the actual argument passed to the function can be an element that is in the substitution group of the named element. Similarly, if a function parameter is specified as an element node with a particular type, such as `element(*, address)`, the actual argument passed to the function can be an element whose type is derived (by restriction or by extension) from the named type.

Type references in XQuery are designed to be compatible extensions of the node tests that are defined in XPath Version 1. For example, in XPath Version 1, `text()` and `comment()` are valid node tests that can be used in path expressions to select text nodes or comment nodes. The following path expression, valid in XPath Version 1, finds all text nodes that are descendants of a particular `contract` element node:

```
/contract[id="123"]//text()
```

In XQuery, the following path expression uses an extended node test to find all element nodes of type `address` that are descendants of a particular `contract` element node. Note that the type reference syntax in XQuery is an extension of the node test syntax of XPath Version 1, and that XQuery allows a type reference to serve as a node test in a path expression.

```
/contract[id="123"]//element(*, address)
```

Issue 4: Element Constructors

One of the strengths of XQuery is its ability to construct new XML objects such as elements and attributes. The syntax used to do this has evolved considerably during the design of the language.

In the original Quilt proposal, a constructed element was denoted simply by an XML start tag and end tag, enclosing an expression that represented the content of the element. The expression enclosed between the tags was evaluated in the same way as any other Quilt expression. This design was criticized because it resembled XML notation but was not interpreted in the same way as XML notation, as illustrated by the following examples:

- `<greeting>Hello</greeting>`. In XML this is an element containing character content. But in Quilt, `Hello` would be interpreted as a path expression and evaluated, unless it were denoted as a string by enclosing it in quotes as follows:
`<greeting>"Hello"</greeting>`
- `<animal>A <color>black</color> cat</animal>`. In XML this is an element with mixed content. But in Quilt it would be a syntax error because the sequence of values inside the `animal` element is not separated by commas. The Quilt equivalent of the given XML expression would be as follows:
`<animal>"A ", <color>"black"</color>, " cat"</animal>`.

The working group decided that XQuery should provide a form of element constructor that conforms more closely to XML notation. However, in the content of an element, it is necessary to distinguish literal text from an expression to be evaluated. Therefore, in an XQuery element constructor, an expression to be evaluated must be enclosed in curly braces. For example:

- `<price>123.45</price>` is a constructed element named `price`, containing a literal value.
- `<price>{$retail * 0.85}</price>` is a constructed element whose content is computed by evaluating an expression.

The syntax described above is not identical to XML notation because it uses the left-curly-brace character { to denote the beginning of an evaluated expression, whereas in XML { is an ordinary character. If a left-curly-brace is intended to be interpreted as an ordinary character in the content of a constructed element, XQuery requires it to be doubled ({{).

In addition to an XML-like syntax for constructing elements, XQuery provides an alternative syntax called a *computed constructor* that can be used to construct elements with computed names as well as other kinds of nodes. The use of computed constructors is illustrated by the following examples:

- `element {$name} {$content}` constructs an element node with a given name and content (of course, `$name` and `$content` can be replaced by any valid XQuery expression).
- `attribute {$name} {$content}` constructs an attribute node with a given name and content.
- `document {$content}` constructs a document node with a given content.
- `text {$content}` constructs a text node with a given content.

The most complex and difficult issue in the design of XQuery constructors turned out to be determining the type of a constructed element. Since every node in the Query data model has a type annotation, it is necessary to attach a type annotation to the node produced by an element constructor. Since the type annotation of an element node indicates the type of the element's content, the first approach investigated by the working group was to derive the type annotation of the constructed node from the type of its content. For example, the following element constructor contains an integer-valued expression, so it seems natural to annotate the resulting element node with the type `xs:integer`:

```
<a>{8}</a>
```

The problem with this approach is that, by definition, elements are assigned their type annotations by the process of schema validation. The type assigned by schema validation may not be the same as the type of the data from which the element was constructed. For example, if the element in the above example were validated against a schema, it might receive an annotation that is more specific than `xs:integer`, such as `hatsize`.

In some cases, the type assigned to an element by schema validation is guaranteed to be different from the original type of its content. As an example, consider the following element constructor:

```
<a>{1, "2"}</a>
```

This element constructor contains an expression whose value is a sequence of an integer followed by a string. However, XML provides no way to represent this element in such a way that, after validation, its content is typed as an integer followed by a string. The XML representation of this element is as follows:

```
<a>1 2</a>
```

Depending on its definition in the relevant schema, this XML element might be validated as containing one string, or two integers, or possibly a more specific user-defined type such as two hatsizes. But there is no possible schema definition that will cause this element to be validated as containing an integer followed by a string.

The designers of XQuery were confronted with the fact that a type annotation based on the content of a constructed element is never guaranteed to be correct after validation of the element, and in some cases is guaranteed to be incorrect. The working group tried hard to find a reasonable rule by which the type of a constructed element could be derived from its content in "safe and obvious" cases. After much study and debate, the group found it impossible to define such a rule that satisfied everyone. As a result, they decided that each constructed element in XQuery should be automatically schema-validated as part of the construction process.

In order to perform schema validation on a constructed element, a *validation mode* must be specified. Validation mode can have one of the following three values:

- ▪ `strict` requires that the given element name must be declared in an imported schema and that the content of the element must comply with its schema declaration.

- `skip` indicates that no validation is attempted for the given element. In this mode, constructed elements are given the type annotation `xs:anyType`, and constructed attributes are given the type annotation `xs:anySimpleType`.

- `lax` behaves like `strict` if the element name is declared in an imported schema, and like `skip` otherwise.

XQuery allows a query writer to specify the validation mode for a whole query or for any expression nested within a query. By specifying `lax` validation, a user can allow the construction of *ad hoc* elements that are not declared in any schema, and by specifying `skip` validation, a user can avoid the performance overhead of validating constructed elements entirely.

In addition to a validation mode, the process of schema validation for an element requires a *validation context*. Validation context controls how the name of the given element is matched against declarations in the imported schemas. If the context is `global`, the element name is matched against global (topmost) schema declarations. Alternatively, the context may specify a path, beginning with a global element or type declaration, within which the given element name is to be interpreted. For example, the element `zipcode` might not match a global schema declaration, but might match an element declaration within the context `PurchaseOrder/customer/shipto`.

The outermost element constructor in a query is validated in the global context unless the user specifies a different context. Each element constructor then adds the name of its element to the validation context for nested elements. For example, if the outermost constructed element in a query is named `PurchaseOrder`, then the immediate children of this element have a validation context of `PurchaseOrder`.

Issue 5: Static Typing

As noted earlier, one of the basic principles of XQuery design is that the processing of a query can include a static analysis phase in which some error checking and optimization can be performed. By definition, static analysis is performed on the query only and is independent of input data. Some kinds of static analysis are clearly essential, such as parsing and finding syntax errors. In addition, the working group saw some value in taking advantage of schema information to infer the types of query expressions at query analysis time. This kind of type inference is called *static typing.* Chapter 4, "Static Typing in XQuery," looks at this subject in some depth.

Static typing offers the following advantages: (1) It can guarantee in some cases that a query, if given valid input data, will generate a result that conforms to a given output schema; (2) It can be helpful in early detection of certain kinds of errors such as calling a function with the wrong type of parameter; (3) It can produce information that may be helpful in optimizing the execution of a query—for example, it may be possible to prove by static analysis that the result of some expression is an empty sequence.

The *static type* of an expression is defined as the most specific type that can be deduced for that expression by examining the query only, in the absence of input data. The *dynamic type* of a value is the most specific type assigned to that value as the query is executed. Note that static type is a compile-time property of an expression, whereas dynamic type is a runtime property of a value.

Static typing in XQuery is based on a set of *inference rules* that are used to infer the static type of each expression, based on the static types of its operands. Some kinds of expressions have requirements for the types of their operands (for example, arithmetic operators are defined for numeric operands but not for strings). Static analysis starts with the static types of the "leaves" of the expression tree (simple constants and input data whose type can be inferred from the schema of the input document). It then uses inference rules to infer the static types of more complex expressions in the query, including the query itself. If, during this process, it is discovered that the static type of some expression is not appropriate for the context where it is used, a type error is raised.

Type-inference rules are written in such a way that any value that can be returned by an expression is guaranteed to conform to the static type inferred for the expression. This property of a type system is called **type soundness.** A consequence of this property is that a query that raises no type errors during static analysis will also raise no type errors during execution on valid input data. The importance of type soundness depends somewhat on which errors are classified as "type errors," as we will see below.

$$statEnv \vdash Expr_0 : Type_0$$
$$\frac{statEnv + varType(Var : Type_0) \vdash Expr_1 : Type_1}{statEnv \vdash \texttt{let } \$Var := Expr_0 \texttt{ return } Expr_1 : Type_1} \quad \text{(LET-STATIC)}$$

Figure 2.4   A Typical Type-Inference Rule

Figure 2.4 illustrates a type-inference rule used in XQuery.

Some inference rules use a notation (`Type1 | Type2`) to denote a type that includes all the instances of type `Type1` as well as all the instances of type `Type2`. This inferred type has no name. It is an example of the fact that, in many cases, the inferred static type of an expression can be given only a structural description. *XQuery 1.0 Formal Semantics* [XQ-FS] uses its own notation for the structural description of types, using operators such as | (or), & (and), " , " (sequence), and ? (optional).

XML Schema also includes a notation for structural description of types. The working group decided not to use the notation of XML Schema in the type-inference rules in the XQuery formal semantic specification because XML Schema notation is very verbose, and because not all types inferred by the XQuery type inference rules are expressible in XML Schema notation. For example, the rule named "Schema Component Constraint: Element Declarations Consistent" [SCHEMA] prevents an XML Schema type from containing two subelements with the same name but different types. Similarly, the rule named "Schema Component Constraint: Unique Particle Attribution" prevents the definition of an XML Schema type that cannot be validated without lookahead. The XQuery type system does not have these constraints. As a result, unlike XML Schema, the XQuery type system has the **closure** property (any type inferred by the XQuery type inference rules is a valid type).

The structural type notation used in [XQ-FS] is used only in the formal semantic specification and is not part of the syntax of XQuery as seen by users. This decision was made to avoid adding complexity to the query language, and because the working group did not wish to introduce a user-level syntax that duplicated the facilities of XML Schema.

The working group spent considerable time on the issue of whether static typing should be based on validated type annotations or on structural comparison. As an illustration of this issue, consider a function named `surgery` that expects as one of its parameters an element of type `surgeon`. Suppose the type `surgeon` is defined to consist of a `name` and a `schedule`. Is it an error if the `surgery` function is invoked on an element that contains a `name` and a `schedule` but has not been schema-validated as a `surgeon`? The working group decided that this should be a type error. In addition to assigning a specific type annotation to an element, schema validation may perform processing steps that are not otherwise supported in the XQuery type system, such as checking pattern facets and providing default attribute values.

Another question closely related to the preceding one is this: Is it a type error if the `surgery` function is invoked on an element that has been schema-validated as having the type `brainSurgeon`? In XQuery, this function call is valid if the type `brainSurgeon` is declared in an imported schema to be a subtype of (derived from) the type `surgeon`. In other words, **static type-checking** in XQuery is based on validated type names and on the type hierarchy declared in imported schemas.

Although the benefits of static typing are well understood in the world of programming languages, extending this technology to the very complex world of XML Schema proved to be a challenging task. Many of the features of XML Schema, such as ordered sequences, **union types,** substitution groups, minimum and maximum cardinalities, pattern facets, and two different kinds of inheritance, were difficult to assimilate into a system of type-inference rules. Even after some simplifying approximations (such as limiting cardinalities to zero, one, or multiple), the resulting set of rules is quite complex.

XQuery is designed to be used in a variety of environments. Static typing of a query is of greatest benefit when the expected type of the query result is known in advance, the input documents and expected output are both described by schemas, and the query is to be executed repeatedly. This represents one usage scenario for XQuery, but not the only one. Some queries may be exploratory in nature, searching loosely structured data sources such as web pages for information of unknown types. Many XML documents are described by a DTD rather than by a schema, and many have neither a DTD nor a schema. Some XML documents may be described by structural notations other than XML Schema, such as

RELAX-NG [RELAXNG]. In some cases, query inputs may be synthesized directly from information sources such as relational databases rather than from serialized XML documents.

To make XQuery adaptable for many usage environments, the language was organized as a required subset called Basic XQuery and two optional features called Schema Import and Static Typing. This approach keeps Basic XQuery relatively simple and lowers the implementation cost of the language in environments where the optional features are of limited benefit.

Basic XQuery includes all the kinds of expressions in the full language. However, a Basic XQuery implementation is not required to deal with user-defined types and is not required to raise static type errors. In Basic XQuery, the only types that are recognized are the built-in atomic types of XML Schema, such as `xs:string`, `xs:integer`, and `xs:date`; the derived duration types `xdt:yearMonthDuration` and `xdt:dayTimeDuration`; and predefined generic types such as `xdt:untypedAtomic` and `xs:anyType`. Basic XQuery might be used, for example, to query data that is exported in XML format from a relational database whose datatypes can be mapped into built-in XML types. When a Basic XQuery implementation is used to query a document that has been validated against an XML schema, the type annotations in the PSVI are mapped into their nearest built-in supertypes (complex types are mapped into `xs:anyType`, and derived atomic types such as `hatsize` are mapped into their built-in base types such as `xs:integer`).

The first optional feature, Schema Import, provides a way for a query to import a schema and to take advantage of type definitions in the imported schema. For example, a query might import a schema containing the definition of the user-defined type `hatsize`, derived from `xs:integer`. This query could then define a function that accepts a parameter of type `hatsize`. Under the Schema Import feature, an attempt to call this function with an argument that has not been schema-validated as a `hatsize` is an error.

The second optional feature, Static Typing, defines a specific set of type errors and requires conforming implementations to detect and report these errors during query analysis. An XQuery implementation that does not claim conformance to this feature can still do static query analysis in its own way, for optimization or for error detection. Also, an implementation that does not claim conformance to Static Typing is still responsible for detecting and reporting dynamic type errors. Any condition that will necessarily lead to a run-time error can be reported as a static error at the discretion of the implementation.

It is important to understand that an expression that raises a static type error may nevertheless execute successfully on a given input document. This is because the rules for static type inference are conservative and require a static type error to be raised whenever it cannot be proven that no possibility of a type error exists. For example, consider the following function definition:

```
define function pay($e as element(employee)) as xs:decimal?
   { $e/salary + $e/bonus }
```

A user may want to execute this query against an XML document containing records from a department in which every `employee` has at most one `bonus`. However, the only schema available may be a company-wide schema in which the declaration of the `employee` element allows multiple (zero or more) `bonus` subelements. In this case, a system that conforms to the Static Typing feature would be required to raise a static error, although execution of the query on the given input data would have been successful.

Conversely, a query that passes static analysis without error may still raise an error at run-time. For example, consider the following expression, where the variable `$c` is bound to a `customer` element:

```
$c/balance + $c/address
```

If the `customer` element has no schema declaration, the typed values of the `balance` and `address` subelements of a given `customer` will be of type `xdt:untypedAtomic`. Addition of two values of type `xdt:untypedAtomic` does not raise a static type error—instead, at execution time the values are converted to the type `xs:double`. If, at run-time, the value of `$c/balance` or `$c/address` cannot be converted to `xs:double`, a dynamic error is raised. In order to preserve the claim of "type soundness," this kind of error is not classified as a type error.

Before leaving the subject of static typing, it is worth discussing the influence that static typing has had on the syntax of the XQuery language. Two kinds of XQuery expressions are present in the language solely in order to support better static type inference. The first kind is the `type-switch` expression, which is illustrated by the example below. The expression in this example branches on the type of a variable named `$employee`, computing total pay in one of three ways depending on whether the employee is a salesperson, a manager, or a generic employee.

```
typeswitch ($employee)
  case $s as element(*, salesperson)
    return $s/salary + $s/commission
  case $m as element(*, manager)
    return $m/salary + $m/bonus
  default $d
    return $d/salary
```

The dynamic behavior of a `typeswitch` expression can always be obtained by using two other kinds of expression called an `if-then-else` expression and an `instance-of` expression. For example, the `typeswitch` expression in the preceding example might have been expressed as follows:

```
if ($employee instance of element(*, salesperson))
then $employee/salary + $employee/commission
else if ($employee instance of element(*, manager))
then $employee/salary + $employee/bonus
else $employee/salary
```

The dynamic (run-time) behavior of the two expressions above is identical. However, the first example will pass static type-checking because it can be proven statically that the variable `$s` can only be bound to an element of type `salesperson`, and therefore `$s/commission` will always return a valid result. The second example, on the other hand, is considered to be a static type error because static analysis cannot predict which branch of the conditional expression will be executed, nor can it prove that the subexpression `$employee/commission` will not be evaluated for some `employee` element that is not of type `salesperson`.

The second type of expression that was added to XQuery solely in support of static typing is the `treat` expression. To understand the use of `treat`, consider the following expression, in which the variable `$a` is bound to an element whose static type is `Address`:

```
$a/zipcode
```

Suppose that only an element of type USAddress, a subtype of Address, is guaranteed to have a zipcode. In this case, the above expression is a static error, since static analysis cannot guarantee that the element bound to $a has the type USAddress. To avoid this static error, the Static Typing feature requires this expression to be written as follows:

```
($a treat as element(*, USAddress))/zipcode
```

At query analysis time, the static type of the treat expression is element(*, USAddress), which enables the zipcode to be extracted without a static type error. The treat expression serves as a "promise" that the variable $a will be bound to an element of type USAddress at execution time. At execution time, if $a is not in fact bound to an element of type USAddress, a dynamic error is raised.

As in the case of typeswitch, the dynamic behavior of treat can be simulated by using a combination of an if-then-else expression and an instance-of expression. For example, the dynamic behavior of the preceding expression can be simulated as follows:

```
if ($a instance of element(*, USAddress))
then $a/zipcode
else error("Not a USAddress")
```

Although this expression simulates the dynamic behavior of the preceding treat expression, it is nevertheless considered to be a static error because the compiler cannot predict which branch of the if-then-else expression will be executed. (Chapter 4 provides more details about static type-checking in XQuery.)

Issue 6: Function Resolution

The *signature* of a function is defined by its expected number of parameters and by the respective types of those parameters. Many modern query and programming languages support **function overloading,** which permits multiple functions to be defined with the same name but with different signatures. The process of choosing the best function for a given function call based on static analysis of the argument types is called **function resolution.** Some languages also support *polymorphism,* a form of function overloading in which static analysis of a function call does not necessarily choose a single function—instead, it can result in a list of applicable functions from which the most specific function is selected at execution time on the basis of the dynamic types of the actual arguments.

The designers of XQuery made an early decision not to support function overloading. The reasons for this decision were as follows:

- Despite the advent of schemas, much XML data is untyped. For the convenience of the user, XQuery automatically coerces untyped data to a specific type based on the context where it is used. In order for this feature to work, each function-name must correspond to a single, well-defined signature. For example, consider the untyped element `<a>47</a>`. If this element is passed to a function that expects an element, it retains its character as an element; if it is passed to a function that expects a decimal, the value `47` is extracted and treated as a decimal value; if it is passed to a function that expects a string, the value `47` is extracted and treated as a string. This flexibility in treatment of untyped data would not be possible if three functions could have the same name while one takes an element parameter, one takes a decimal parameter, and one takes a string parameter.

- The type system of XQuery is based on XML Schema and is quite complex. It has two different kinds of type inheritance: derivation by restriction and derivation by extension. In addition, it has the concept of substitution groups, which allow one kind of element to be substituted for another on the basis of its name. The rules for casting one type into another and for promotion of numeric arguments are also complex. They are made even more complex by XPath Version 1 compatibility rules, which come into play when XPath Version 2 (a subset of XQuery) is used in "XPath Version 1 Compatibility Mode" (as it is when embedded in XSLT). The designers of XQuery were not eager to add another increment of complexity on top of the rules they inherited from XML Schema and XPath. In the end, it was decided that the added complexity of function overloading outweighed its benefit, at least for the first version of XQuery.

Despite the decision not to support function overloading, it was necessary for XQuery to support the XPath Version 1 core function library, which already contained some overloaded functions. Support for these functions was reconciled with the XQuery design in the following ways:

- Some XPath Version 1 functions take an optional parameter. For example, the `name` function returns the name of a node, but if called with no argument, it returns the name of the context node. In XQuery, this kind of function is treated as two functions with the same name but with different *arity* (number of parameters). The built-in function library of XQuery contains several sets of functions that differ only in their arity. This form of overloading is permitted in the built-in function library but not among user-defined functions. It does not complicate the rules for function resolution, since a function is always uniquely identified by its name and its arity.

- Some XPath Version 1 functions can accept several different parameter types. For example, the `string` function of XPath Version 1 can turn almost any kind of argument into a string. In XQuery, functions like `string` have a generic signature that encompasses all their possible parameter types. For example, the signature of the XQuery `string` function is `string($s as item?)`. The type `item?` denotes an optional occurrence of a node or atomic value. The description of the `string` function specifies how it operates on arguments of various types that satisfy its signature. The technique of creating a function with a generic signature is also available to users for creating user-defined functions. The body of such a function can branch on the dynamic type of the actual argument.

One painful consequence of the decision not to support function overloading was the loss of polymorphism. Polymorphism is convenient because it facilitates introducing new subtypes of existing types that inherit the behavior of their supertypes where appropriate and specialize it where necessary. A polymorphic language allows a query to iterate over a heterogeneous sequence of items, dispatching the appropriate function for each item based on its dynamic type. For example, in a polymorphic language, a generic function named `postage` might be defined for elements of type `Address`, with specialized `postage` functions for elements of type `USAddress` and `UKAddress` that are derived from `Address`.

Although XQuery does not support true polymorphism, the designers wished to make it possible and reasonably convenient for users to simulate a form of polymorphism. This was accomplished by the following rule: Any function can be invoked with an argument whose dynamic type is a subtype of the expected parameter type. When this occurs, the argument retains its original dynamic type within the body of the function.

This rule makes it possible for a user to write functions such as the `postage` function shown in Listing 2.3, which invokes one of several more specialized functions depending on the dynamic type of its argument:

Listing 2.3   Function Simulating a Form of Polymorphism

```
define function postage($a as element(*, Address)) as xs:decimal
{
typeswitch($a)
   case $usa as element(*, USAddress)
      return us-postage($usa)
   case $uka as element(*, UKAddress)
      return uk-postage($uka)
   default
      return error("Unknown address type")
}
```

The `postage` function can be used in a query that iterates over a set of addresses of mixed type. However, if a new type named `GermanAddress` is introduced that is also derived from the `Address` type, it is necessary to add a new case to the body of the `postage` function, since XQuery will not automatically dispatch a specialized function for the new type.

It is worth considering whether function overloading could be introduced in a later version of XQuery. The main barrier to the introduction of this feature would be the implicit coercions of function parameters that are defined in XQuery. As noted above, untyped data can be coerced into either a string or a number, depending on context. If it were possible to define two functions with the same name that respectively take a string parameter and a numeric parameter, it would be necessary to define a priority order among the possible coercions, in order to resolve an ambiguous function call. This could certainly be done. If function overloading is introduced in a future version of XQuery, users will need to exercise care in the evolution of their function libraries to ensure that existing queries continue to run successfully.

Issue 7: Error Handling

In general, XQuery expressions return values and have no side effects. However, some special consideration is needed for error cases. For example, what should be the value of an expression that contains a division by zero?

One approach that the working group considered was to define a special *error value* in the Query data model, to be returned by all expressions that encounter an error. The error value would have its own *error type* that is different from all other types. In this approach, for example, the static type of a double-precision arithmetic expression would be (`double | error`) rather than simply `double`. After some study, the group decided that including a special error value (and error type) in the Query data model complicated the semantics of the language and made it difficult to distinguish one kind of error from another.

The approach finally adopted for handling dynamic errors in XQuery is to allow an expression either to return a value or to raise a dynamic error. An expression that raises an error is not considered to return a value in the normal sense. Therefore dynamic errors are handled outside the scope of the type system. An error carries with it an ordinary value (of any type) that describes the error. A function named `error` is provided that raises an error and attaches the argument of the function to the error as a descriptive value.

Propagation of dynamic errors through XQuery expressions is handled by a general rule and some special rules that apply to specific kinds of expressions. The general rule is that if the operands of an expression raise one or more dynamic errors, the expression itself must also raise a dynamic error. Which of several operand errors is propagated by an expression is not specified. If one operand of an expression raises an error, the expression is permitted, but is not required, to evaluate its other operands. For example, in evaluating the expression `"Hello" + (length * width * height)`, an XQuery implementation can raise an error as soon as it discovers that `"Hello"` is not a number.

The special error-handling rules for certain kinds of expressions are intended to make these expressions easier to optimize and more efficient to implement. These rules have the effect of making the result of an

XQuery expression non-deterministic in a certain limited sense. In some cases, an expression may either return a result or raise an error. However, if an expression returns a result, the result is always well defined by the semantics of the language. The circumstances in which non-deterministic handling of errors is permitted are as follows:

- If one operand of `and` is `false` and the other operand raises an error, the `and` operator may either return `false` or raise an error.

- If one operand of `or` is `true` and the other operand raises an error, the `or` operator may either return `true` or raise an error.

- The result of a quantified expression may depend on the order of evaluation of its operands, which may vary from one implementation to another. As an example, consider the expression `some` *variable* `in` *range-expr* `satisfies` *test-expr*. If *range-expr* contains a value for which *test-expr* is `true` and another value for which *test-expr* raises an error, the quantified expression may either return `true` or raise an error. Similarly, in the universally quantified expression `every` *variable* `in` *range-expr* `satisfies` *test-expr*, if *range-expr* contains a value for which *test-expr* is `false` and another value for which *test-expr* raises an error, the quantified expression may either return `false` or raise an error.

- Since some comparison operators, such as `=`, are defined to include an implicit existential quantifier, these operators are made non-deterministic by the above rules. For example, the expression `(47, 3 div 0) = 47`, which compares a sequence of two values to a single value, might either return `true` or raise an error.

- The Effective Boolean Value of an expression is defined to be `true` if the expression returns a sequence containing more than one item. But if an error is raised during evaluation of the items in such a sequence, the Effective Boolean Value computation may either return `true` or raise an error.

- If a function can evaluate its body expression without evaluating one of its arguments, the function is allowed, but not required, to evaluate that argument. If such an argument contains an error, the function may either raise an error or return the value of its body expression.

An ideal language would be both deterministic and efficient in execution. As illustrated by some of the preceding examples, the presence of sequences in the Query data model leads to some tension between the goals of determinism and efficiency in XQuery. In general, this tension has been resolved in favor of efficiency for queries that contain errors; however, a query that contains no errors must always return a deterministic result.

Users can protect themselves against some kinds of errors by using an `if-then-else` expression, which evaluates one of two subexpressions (called "branches" here) depending on the Boolean value of a test expression. The `if-then-else` expression is defined in such a way that it evaluates only the branch that is selected by the test expression; therefore errors in the other branch are ignored. By using an `if-then-else` expression, a query can control the value that is returned when an error condition is encountered. For example, a user could guard against division by zero by the following expression, which returns an empty sequence rather than raising an error if the divisor is zero:

```
if ($divisor ne 0) then $dividend div $divisor else ( )
```

The working group discussed a proposal for a "try/catch" mechanism similar to that used in the Java language, which would have allowed expressions at various levels of the query hierarchy to "catch" errors raised by nested expressions. An expression might specify "handlers" for various kinds of errors encountered in its operands, and in some cases might be able to recover from these errors rather than propagating them. In the end, this approach was considered to be too complex for the first version of XQuery. The working group may revisit this proposal in a future version of the language.

Issue 8: Ordering Operators

Since all values in XQuery are ordered sequences, operators for controlling the order of a sequence are of considerable importance to the language. All of the operators of XQuery return their results in a well-defined order. For example, path expressions and the `union` and `intersect` operators always return sequences of nodes in document order. Of course, the ordering of the sequences returned by various expressions in a query is not always essential to the meaning of the query. The cost of evaluating a sequence may depend strongly on the order in which it is evaluated, due to the organization of physical storage or the availability of access aids such as indexes. If the order of some result is not important, the query writer should have some way to say so, thus giving the implementation the flexibility to generate the result in the fastest or least expensive way.

For a time, the working group experimented with "unordered" versions of various operators. In the end, it was decided that the XQuery function library should include a general-purpose function named `unordered`. The `unordered` function can be applied to any sequence, and it returns the same sequence in a non-deterministic order. In effect, the `unordered` function signals an optimizing compiler that its argument expression can be materialized in any order that the optimizer finds convenient. Obviously, applying the `unordered` function to an expression E can have implications for the ordering properties of expressions that are nested inside E or that use E as an operand, and XQuery implementations are free to take advantage of these implications.

XQuery also needs to provide a way for users to specify a particular order for the items in a sequence. In fact, the result of a query may be a hierarchy of elements in which an ordering needs to be specified at several levels of the hierarchy. The working group explored two alternative approaches to this problem.

The first approach was to provide a general-purpose operator called `sort by` that could be applied to any expression to specify an order for the result of the expression. This might be called the "independent sorting" approach because `sort by` is an operator that can be applied to any sequence, and is independent of any other operator. In this approach, the meaning of `E1 sort by E2` is defined as follows: For each item in the result of expression `E1`, the expression `E2` is evaluated with that item as the context item. The resulting values are called **sort keys.** The items returned by `E1` are then arranged in an order that is controlled by their respective sort keys. Options are provided that allow the user to specify primary and secondary sort keys, ascending or descending order, placement of items whose sort key is empty, and other details.

The independent sorting approach is illustrated by the following example, in which a query searches its input for employees in a particular department, and returns them in alphabetical order by their names. In this example, the `sort by` operator is applied to a path expression.

```
//employee[dept = "K55"] sort by name
```

The independent sorting approach has two important disadvantages. First, it can only specify an ordering for a sequence based on sort keys that are actually present in the sequence. Suppose, for example, that a query is intended to return the names of all employees in a particular department, in the order of their salaries, but not to return the actual salaries. This query, while not impossible under the independent sorting approach, is not as straightforward as the previous example. It might be expressed as follows:

```
for $e in //employee[dept = "K55"] sort by salary
return $e/name
```

The difficulty of expressing an ordering by the independent sorting approach becomes greater if the sort key is computed from two or more bound variables but is not included in the query result. As an example of this problem, a query might need to join `employee` elements with their respective `department` elements, and sort the result according to the ratio between the employee's salary and the department's budget, but not include this ratio in the final output. Such a query is difficult (but not impossible) to express with an independent `sort by` operator.

The second disadvantage of the independent sorting approach is that it separates iteration and ordering into two separate syntactic constructs. The result of an iteration might be processed in various ways, combined with other results, given a new name, and finally sorted. The most efficient way to process such a query might be to perform the initial iteration in the order required for the final result. However, the specification of this ordering may be syntactically distant from the iteration, and it may not be expressed in a way that is easy for an implementation to use in optimizing the iteration.

Another ordering approach that the working group investigated and ultimately adopted consists of combining the ordering expression with the expression that controls iteration. The iteration expression in XQuery was originally called a "FLWR" expression because of its keywords `for`, `let`, `where`, and `return`. An `order by` clause was added to this expression between the `where` and `return` clauses, changing the name of the expression to "FLWOR." Positioning the `order by` clause inside the FLWOR expression gives it access to the bound variables that control the iteration, even though the values bound to these variables may not ultimately be returned. Associating the ordering directly with the iteration also makes it easier for a system to implement the iteration efficiently. The disadvantage of this approach is that an ordering must always be expressed in the form of a FLWOR expression, even though it would not otherwise require an explicit iteration.

The advantages and disadvantages of the "ordered FLWOR" approach can be illustrated by repeating the two preceding example queries. The query that returns all the employees in a given department, sorted by name, can be expressed as follows (note that it now requires an explicit iteration, which was not needed in the "independent sorting" approach):

```
for $e in //employee[dept = "K55"]
order by $e/name
return $e
```

Similarly, the query that returns names of employees in a given department, ordered by their salaries but without returning the salaries, can be expressed as follows:

```
for $e in //employee[dept = "K55"]
order by $e/salary
return $e/name
```

The choice between the "independent sorting" approach and the "ordered FLWOR" approach is not obvious. The working group considered including both approaches, but decided not to do this on the grounds that the two alternatives are redundant and potentially confusing. In the end, the working group decided to include only the "ordered FLWOR" approach to control ordering of results in XQuery.

Conclusion

The design of XQuery has been a process of resolving the tensions between conflicting goals. It has been a slow process, and compromise has frequently been necessary.

The designers of XQuery did not begin with a blank slate. The Query data model was largely dictated by XML itself and by related W3C Recommendations such as XML Namespaces. The design of the language was also constrained by compatibility with existing standards such as XPath and XML Schema. Reconciling these constraints was not straightforward—for example, XPath Version 1 has only four types and a rather loose set of rules for type conversions, whereas XML Schema has forty-four built-in atomic types, a complex syntax for defining new types, and a strict set of rules for type validation.

As a general-purpose query language, XQuery needs to support a variety of usage modes. It needs to operate on untyped documents as well as on documents that are described by schemas and by DTDs. It needs to operate on individual XML files, on large repositories of pre-validated documents, on XML data synthesized from sources such as relational databases, and on streaming XML data. It needs to support applications in which all types are known and static typing guarantees are important, as well as exploratory queries in which the expected type of the result is not known in advance. It needs to support precise and reproducible queries as well as approximate searches, such as searches for synonyms of a given word. In order to span these modes of use while keeping the entry cost of an implementation as low as possible, the working group organized XQuery as a basic language and a set of optional features.

The Query working group did not conduct its work in isolation. All changes to XPath were discussed and approved jointly by the Query working group and the XSLT working group, since XPath is embedded in both the XQuery and XSLT languages. The Query working group consulted frequently with the Schema working group on issues such as date/time arithmetic, which required two new subtypes to be derived from the `duration` type. Internationalization aspects of XQuery were designed in cooperation with the Internationalization (I18N) working group. Suggestions on XQuery requirements and features were received from other working groups and individuals from time to time.

During the design of XQuery, the working group typically had a membership of between thirty and forty members, representing around twenty-five companies. These representatives formed a diverse group, with backgrounds ranging from relational database management to library science, and included the designers of several query languages.

Some were theoretical in their orientation, and others were more prag-matic. Some represented software vendors and some represented the user community. The world's largest software companies were represented, as were several new startup companies.

The working group conducted weekly conference calls and held a face-to-face meeting about every six weeks. Subgroups were formed to deal with specialized topics such as full-text search and the core function library. As is customary in the W3C, the working group operated by a process of consensus building, in which design alternatives were explored and decisions were made only after a consensus was reached (as deter-mined by the chair). Design progress was documented in a series of work-ing drafts that described the language in general, the data model, the function library, the formal semantics of the language, and a set of use cases. Each of these working drafts was republished on the working group web page about every three months. Throughout this process, public feedback was invited, and the members of the working group responded to public comments in online forums. At all times, the work-ing group maintained a prototype parser based on the latest XQuery grammar.

At the time of this writing, the broad outline of XQuery Version 1 is rea-sonably stable, and the working group is engaged in editing the details of the language specification. Because of a strong desire to publish a stable recommendation as soon as possible, it is likely that several important features will not be included in XQuery Version 1. Examples include an update facility, text search features such as stem-matching and relevance ranking, a view definition facility, and bindings to specific host languages such as Java. These features are strong candidates for inclusion in a future version of XQuery.

The design process used by the Query working group is probably not the fastest way to design a query language, and languages designed by large committees are not often noted for elegance and simplicity. Nevertheless, the members of the working group hope that their diverse backgrounds and interests have contributed to making XQuery robust for a broad spectrum of usage environments. Time and experience will provide a measure of their success.

Chapter 3

XQUERY, XPATH, AND XSLT

Michael Kay

This chapter explores the relationships between XSLT, XPath, and XQuery. It explains why we need three languages rather than one and the way in which they are interrelated. For readers who might be familiar with XSLT, it explains the areas in which XQuery is similar to XSLT, and the areas in which it is necessarily different. It also explores some of the differences between transformation and query that affect the implementation architecture—in particular, the relationship to schemas and type definitions, and the differences in the way optimization is carried out in the two environments.

XSLT: A Quick Introduction

XSLT is a language for describing XML transformations—that is, operations that take one or more XML documents as input and produce one or more XML documents as output. The language was developed within W3C as part of a wider exercise concerned with styling, or rendition, of XML: hence the name "eXtensible Stylesheet Language—Transformations."

XSLT 1.0 was published as a W3C Recommendation on 16 November 1999. During the first three years of its life it has attracted a substantial number of implementations (probably as many as twenty), including implementations built into the two main web browsers, Internet Explorer and Netscape, and a number of open-source implementations, one of these being Saxon, distributed by the author of this chapter. Most of the implementations achieve an excellent level of conformance to the W3C specification, although the existence of vendor extensions means that portability is not always as easy to achieve across implementations as one might like. The language has been widely adopted by the user community, despite having a reputation in some quarters for being difficult to learn and sluggish in performance.

Probably 80 percent of the actual usage of XSLT today is for transforming XML to HTML. This is handled by treating the result document as a well-formed XML tree, with the transformation being followed by a serialization phase that translates this tree into an HTML output file. Another 10 percent of XSLT usage performs the function of rendering XML into other display formats, such as SVG, WML, or PDF (via the other part of XSL, the formatting objects vocabulary). The remaining 10 percent of usage is in XML-to-XML applications, notably the transformation of messages sent between applications in an enterprise integration infrastructure, either within an organization or across organization boundaries. But although small today, this segment of the market is probably the one that is growing fastest, and the one that offers the greatest commercial returns for suppliers.

Some of the key characteristics of XSLT as a language are listed below:

- *XML-based syntax:* An XSLT transformation program (referred to, for historic reasons, as a stylesheet) is itself an XML document. This feature is particularly useful when large parts of the stylesheet contain fixed, or relatively fixed, XML elements and attributes to be written directly to the output, because then we can regard the stylesheet as a template for the result document. Another useful consequence of this design decision is that we can use XSLT stylesheets as the source or target of further transformations. Although this appears at first sight to be a rather exotic idea, it is actually common in large-scale applications for stylesheets to be generated or adapted using "meta-stylesheets," which are themselves written in XSLT.

- *Declarative, functional programming model:* The basic programming paradigm of XSLT is functional programming. A stylesheet describes a transformation of a source tree to a result tree. The result tree is a function of the source, and individual subtrees of the result are functions of the source information from which they are derived. Although a stylesheet contains constructs such as conditionals and iterations that are familiar from procedural programming, nothing in the language prescribes a certain order of execution. In particular, there are no assignment statements and no updateable variables. This feature probably accounts for the reputation of the language as being hard to learn, because web authors accustomed to languages like JavaScript find that it can require a considerable mental readjustment. It also accounts for the poor performance that is sometimes reported, because without a simple imperative model of what the machine is actually doing, it is easy for programmers to write extremely inefficient code. (For further discussion, see the section on optimization later in this chapter.)

■ *Rule-based:* An XSLT stylesheet is expressed as a collection of rules, in the tradition of text-processing languages like *awk* and *sed*. The rules consist of a pattern to be matched in the input, and instructions for generating nodes in the result tree (a template) when the pattern is matched. Unlike the rules in text-processing languages, however, the rules are not applied sequentially to each line of input text in turn; instead, they perform a traversal of the input tree. In most simple transformations, each template rule for a parent node triggers the activation of the rules for its children, which results in a recursive, depth-first traversal of the source tree. But this is entirely under the control of the stylesheet author, and it is possible to traverse the input tree in any way the author chooses.

The advantage of this rule-based approach is that the stylesheet can be made very resilient to changes in the details of the structure of the input document. It is particularly good at handling the recursive structures that occur in "document-oriented" XML, which often have very liberal rules for the nesting of one tag within another. For "data-oriented" XML transformations, where the structures are more rigid, this style of processing has fewer advantages, and in fact there is no need to write every stylesheet in this way.

■ *Tree-to-tree transformation:* The input and output of a transformation are modeled as trees, not as serial XML. The construction of a source tree (using an XML parser) and the serialization of a final result tree are separate operations from the transformation itself, and in many applications they are not actually performed; for example, it is common to build a pipeline of transformations, so that the output of one is used directly as the input to the next, without intermediate serialization. This means that incidental details of the source XML (for example, the distinction between single and double quotes around attributes) are not visible to the application, and in general are not preserved through a transformation. Sometimes this can cause usability problems; for example, a transformation will always expand entity references and attribute defaults defined in a DTD, which is not ideal if the result document is intended to be further edited by the user.

▪ *Two-language model:* XSLT uses XPath as a sublanguage. We examine the relationship of XSLT and XPath in more detail in the following section. Roughly speaking, XSLT instructions are used to produce nodes in the result tree and to control the sequence of processing. XPath expressions are used to select data from the source tree. XPath expressions are always invoked from XSLT instructions; there is no capability (in XSLT 1.0) of any callback in the opposite direction. This means that the language is not fully composable in the sense that any expression can be nested inside any other.

The segment of XSLT code in Listing 3.1 illustrates these features.

Listing 3.1   Code Illustrating Key Features of XSLT

```
<xslt:template match="appendix">
    <h2>
        Appendix <xslt:number format="A">
        <xslt:text> </xslt:text>
        <a name="{@id}"/>
        <xslt:value-of select="@title"/>
    </h2>
    <xslt:apply-templates/>
</xslt:template>
```

This shows a single template rule. The pattern is very simple: `match="appendix"` indicates that the template rule matches elements named `appendix`. The body of the template rule defines nodes to be written to the output tree. Here `xslt:number` is an instruction for generating a sequence number; `xslt:text` indicates literal text to be written to the output tree; `xslt:value-of` computes the result of an XPath expression and writes that as text to the output tree; and `xslt:apply-templates` selects further nodes from the source tree (by default, the children of the current node), and causes them to be processed by firing the appropriate template rule for each one. The elements `a` and `h2`, which are not in the XSLT namespace, are copied directly to the output. The curly brackets in the name attribute of the `a` element indicate an *attribute value template:* They enclose an XPath expression that computes a string value to be inserted in the content of the attribute. This construct is used because the constraints of XML syntax make it impossible to nest instructions inside an attribute value.

Suppose that the input document looks like this:

```
<appendix id="bibl" title="Bibliography">
    <para>A reference</para>
</appendix>
```

We haven't shown the template rule that processes the `para` elements, but assuming it outputs an HTML `p` element and copies the textual content, the result of applying this stylesheet is likely to be:

```
<h2>Appendix C <a name="bibl"/>Bibliography</h2>
<p>A reference</p>
```

XPath 1.0

XPath 1.0 was published as a W3C Recommendation on the same day as XSLT 1.0: 16 November 1999. The two specifications were necessarily closely related because of the intimate way in which XPath expressions are embedded in XSLT stylesheets. However, XPath was deliberately published as a free-standing document, with the expectation that it could be used in many contexts other than XSLT. In fact, the original decision to make XPath separate from XSLT was motivated by the fact that XSLT and XPointer (the hyperlink format used by the XLink specification for document linking) were developing different languages that had a high degree of functional overlap, and everyone agreed that it would be better if W3C defined a single basic language for addressing into XML documents.

The decision to make XPath separate has been justified by subsequent events. Many implementers have provided XPath implementations that are either free-standing or coupled with an implementation of either the Document Object Model (DOM)[1] or one of the other tree-based XML models, such as JDOM.[2] Subsets of XPath have been adopted by other specifications in the XML family, such as XML Schema. And, of course, XPath now forms a core subset of XQuery.

The central construct of XPath, which gave the language its name, is the path expression, which uses a sequence of steps, separated by / characters, to address nodes within the tree representation of an XML document. The syntax is derived from the syntax of UNIX filenames or URIs, but this is deceptive, because the detailed semantics are much more powerful. Semantically, each step in a path expression actually has three parts:

- *An axis*, which describes the relationship to be traversed: For example, it selects the children of the context node, the parent of the context node, or the ancestors, descendants, or siblings. Because the child axis is the one used most frequently, it is the default when no other axis is named.

- *A node test*, which places constraints on the names or kinds of nodes to be selected: For example, it might select all elements, or attributes called `code`.

- Optionally, *one or more predicates*, which place further restrictions on the sequence of nodes to be selected. These restrictions may depend on the content of the nodes, or on their position in the sequence of nodes. They may also contain further path expressions, so that the condition for selecting nodes depends on a further complex traversal of the tree.

---

[1] DOM: the Document Object Model, see http://www.w3.org/TR/DOM.

[2] JDOM: a variant of the DOM, designed more specifically for Java. See http://www.jdom.org/.

Thus a path expression such as

```
/book/*[1]/@id
```

consists of three steps: the first step implicitly uses the child axis to select elements named `book`; the second selects the first child element regardless of its name; and the third uses the attribute axis (denoted by `@`) to select attribute nodes named `id`.

Like filenames and URIs, path expressions may be absolute or relative. Relative path expressions select nodes starting at a point (the *context node*) that is, in effect, an implicit parameter to the path expression. Absolute path expressions select from the document root node (though it is rather misleading to call them "absolute," since there may be several documents around, and the selection of a particular document is again an implicit parameter).

The biggest difference between XPath path expressions and the file-names or URIs that they resemble is that each step selects a set of nodes, not a single node. Each step is applied to all the nodes selected by the previous step. XPath therefore shares with SQL the characteristic that it is always processing *sets* (of nodes in the case of XPath, of tuples in the case of SQL), never individual nodes one at a time.

As well as path expressions that select nodes, XPath 1.0 also has a range of operators and functions for computing values. For example, `count(/book/chapter)` returns a number giving the number of nodes selected by the path expression `/book/chapter`, while `substring(@desc, 1, 1)` selects the first character of the `desc` attribute of the context node. These operators and functions use just three datatypes in addition to the node-sets that are manipulated by path expressions: strings, Booleans, and numbers. Numeric arithmetic is all based on double-precision floating point. When operations are applied to values of the wrong type, implicit conversions take place; for example, using a string as input to an addition causes no problem, so long as the string actually contains a number. This aspect of the language is very familiar to JavaScript programmers, who are accustomed to using functions and operators with very little regard to datatypes.

Why Was a New Query Language Needed?

Historically, the work that led to the development of XQuery started long before XSLT 1.0 and XPath 1.0 were published. At first there was little contact between the two groups. During 1998 and 1999 there was some cross-influence between XQL, one of the precursors of XQuery, and the emerging XPath language (probably each language influenced the other, though this is hard to verify). But neither group would have seen the other language as being directly relevant to the requirements they were addressing—the degree of overlap only became apparent later.

The differences between XSLT and XQuery are of two kinds. First, they have different requirements, and therefore a design decision that was appropriate for XSLT would not necessarily be right for XQuery, and vice versa. The second kind of difference results from their being designed by different people from different communities and computing traditions, with different beliefs about what constitutes good design, and different experiences as to what works well and what doesn't.

Differing Requirements

As we have seen, XSLT was produced as a spin-off from the XSL (eXtensible Stylesheet Language) activity, whose primary focus was the rendition (for human consumption) of information contained in XML documents. Although the concept of transformation was seen as having much more general applicability, and the language was clearly designed to be capable of performing a wide variety of transformation tasks, styling of XML remained the primary use case. The fact that the working group chose to concentrate on this requirement is evident in a statement right at the start of the XSLT 1.0 specification: "XSLT is not intended as a completely general-purpose transformation language. Rather, it is designed primarily for the kinds of transformation that are needed when XSLT is used as part of XSL" [XSLT, p. 1]

I was not a member of the working group at the time, but I find it easy to imagine the members agreeing on this statement as a matter of policy, and then using it to reject the inclusion of features that were considered outside this scope; for example, the inclusion of advanced mathematical or text-manipulation operators. But it is also easy to imagine that some members of the group knew in their hearts that a general-purpose transformation language was needed and were determined that XSLT should be capable of fulfilling this role; indeed, if there had not been people who believed this, it is hard to see why the policy statement reproduced above would have been inserted.

The concept of a transformation language implies certain assumptions about the processing environment. Transformation essentially takes one document (or a few documents) as input, and produces one document (or a few documents) as output. The documents, although processed as trees, will typically be parsed from serial files immediately before they are transformed; they will not have been preloaded into a database providing specialized indexing or access methods. The source document is not modified by the transformation process, and it generally fits in main memory.[3]

The fact that the working group focused on the transformations that occur during document styling added further assumptions. Document-oriented XML would be encountered more often than data-oriented XML. The source documents might or might not be valid according to a DTD. Stylesheets would typically be written to process a variety of source documents with differences in structure. The processing would most often be serial in nature: The order of elements in the result tree would usually be the same as the order of corresponding elements in the source. The language should probably be permissive in its error handling: Errors in the stylesheet should result in as much of the source document as possible being displayed, rather than causing a run-time error message that would mean nothing to the end user.

The intended role and purpose of the language also created expectations about the user who would be writing the transformations. The user would probably be authoring XML documents as well as stylesheets, so use of common XML editing tools, as well as the ability to copy and paste

---

[3] Actually, this assumption is not always true, but XSLT is essentially designed to handle those cases where it is true. There is no widely used implementation of XSLT that avoids the need to build the source tree in memory

chunks of XML into a stylesheet, would be convenient. Stylesheets would typically exist as free-standing documents, accessible by URL, and compiled on demand; sometimes they might be embedded in the source documents themselves.

The scenario addressed by XQuery was very different. As a database query language, XQuery was concerned with the extraction of information from large collections of documents (or large individual documents), which would normally be held on disk, in databases with physical storage structures, such as indexes, designed to enable rapid retrieval. Such collections of documents would often be subject to some kind of central design control, which means they would usually have a uniform schema, and they would typically be validated against this schema before being loaded into the database. Indeed, some vendors see XQuery being used essentially to query an XML view of a conventional relational database.

This different scenario leads to different requirements, or at least to differing emphasis among the requirements. Documents were more likely to be data-oriented than document-oriented, although the query language was supposed to be able to handle both. Optimization of queries was essential if performance was to be acceptable, and this optimization would involve an analysis of the query against the schema of the target database, if only to discover what indexes might be available. Because the documents would often be data-oriented, preserving order was less important, and would in many cases be unnecessary. Error handling would probably need to be strict: If a query was incorrect, it would be better to produce an error message as early as possible, rather than to execute a perhaps lengthy query and produce results to a question that the user did not mean to ask.

The expected usage scenario for XQuery would be similar to that for other database query languages like SQL. Occasionally, expert users might use the query language directly from a terminal; but much more frequently, queries would be embedded in programs written in a host language such as Java or C#, delivering their results into host language variables for further processing by the application. Some people even see XQuery being embedded within SQL, as a sublanguage for querying XML held within relational databases. Serializing the query results as an XML document might be one option for delivering the results, but by no means the only option.

Thus, although there is a considerable overlap in what XSLT and XQuery actually need to do (they both select data from input XML documents and construct new XML documents from this data), substantial differences exist in the usage scenarios where the two languages were primarily targeted, and these have led to some genuine differences in the optimum design parameters for the two languages.

Differing Cultures

At the beginning of this section I described two reasons for the differences between XSLT and XQuery. We have looked at the differences in technical requirements for the two languages; now let's examine the differences resulting from differing cultures. These are no less valid: Just as an architect designing a building in Tokyo has to take into account the fact that the lifestyle is not the same as that in Los Angeles, so the designers of a computer language have to work within a tradition that sets implicit criteria for what is good design and what is not acceptable. The design of software, as with music or physical architecture, is essentially a creative intellectual activity, and the outcome depends a great deal on the experiences and creative preferences of the people doing the design and the peer group who provide them with feedback.

The designers of XSLT came predominantly from an SGML (Standard Generalized Markup Language) background. They were familiar with document processing, with the abstractions of the formal model underlying SGML and its stylesheet language DSSSL (Document Style Semantics and Specification Language), itself heavily based on functional programming languages such as Scheme. They understood the complexities of pagination, wordwrap, and hyphenation algorithms, and the way in which these varied depending on the natural language of the text and local typographical traditions. But few of them had any background in database technology. They were not experts in the optimization of relational algebra, nor were they immersed in the traditions of database report writers or the calculations involved in data visualization.

By contrast, the designers of XQuery came solidly from the database world. Several of the leading figures in the XQuery working group (including several authors represented in this book) have also played a significant role in the development of SQL and of object database languages such as OQL. These people brought with them the knowledge gained from thirty years of progress in database technology—progress primarily in the design of query languages and the associated optimization strategies, together with the gradual evolution of data models to handle richer structures than the traditional "punched card" model of the 1970s relational database. Few of these people, however, had much previous exposure to the SGML or XML culture, with its very different way of thinking about structural constraints and validation, or to the kind of structural manipulations required to handle the trees that result from markup of a linear text.

There's another difference in the culture behind the two languages that is worth mentioning. The group that developed XSLT 1.0 was much smaller, in terms of active participants, than the XQuery group, and one individual, James Clark, had the unofficial role of chief designer, with the rest of the group essentially acting as a steering group and review body. The XQuery group never had a single individual who could be identified as the chief architect in the same kind of way. It had (and has still) a much broader base of talented individuals, each of them highly capable, who do not always share the same vision. The result is that while the group is less exposed to the mistakes that can be made by one individual, it is much harder for the team to maintain a consistency of approach across the whole language, to ensure that different decisions in different areas are made on the same criteria, and above all to keep the language small and simple. In short, XQuery is a language designed by committee in a way that XSLT is not.

Convergence: XPath 2.0

During the twelve months after XSLT 1.0 and XPath 1.0 were published, it became increasingly clear that XQuery could not ignore them. All the major vendors were shipping implementations, and there was a high level of uptake by the user community. Unlike some other standards organizations, W3C likes to keep its specifications consistent and coherent: It does not like overlaps and duplications between different recommendations that offer multiple solutions to the same problem. So XQuery quickly aligned itself with XPath, adopting path expressions as part of the XQuery language that were strongly aligned with the XPath specification, though initially there were many differences in the detailed syntax and semantics (as well as many gaps, where the syntax and semantics were not fully defined).

For the management of W3C, however, a superficial similarity between the languages was not enough. If XQuery used the same syntax as XPath, but with different detailed semantics, there would be few benefits for users, indeed, there would be a great deal of confusion. However, XQuery could not easily take XPath 1.0 on board without changes, because there were fundamental differences in the data model and the type system.

At the same time, XML Schema was starting to make itself felt. XQuery and XML Schema have always had a close relationship and mutual dependency, of the same kind that data-description languages and data-manipulation languages have had since the earliest days of database technology in the mid 1960s. In the early days of XQuery development, the language had its own type system that was separate from that of XML Schema. But this clearly wasn't tenable, and the working group decided that XQuery would use XML Schema as its type system (despite the objections of language theorists like Phil Wadler, who argued cogently that it was technically incorrect to describe XML Schema as a type system).

There was also pressure, though less intense, for XSLT to align itself more closely with XML Schema. This move has aroused some fairly vocal opposition in some quarters, especially from those whose primary interest is in document processing. But many of the large corporations using XML increasingly see XML Schema as a key tool in the way they plan to manage integration of applications within and beyond the corporation, and XSLT as a key tool in handling the diversity and evolution of those applications. Although initially no one was quite sure what it meant in detail, some degree of integration of XSLT (and therefore XPath) with XML Schema was therefore seen as an important strategic goal.

The result of these pressures was the decision that the XQuery and XSL working groups would work together on the development of XPath 2.0, which would have a type system aligned with that of XML Schema, and that XQuery would be a superset of XPath 2.0. The two groups set up a joint task force to develop XPath 2.0. They decided that XSLT and XQuery meetings would in future be co-located, and they set up joint meetings to promote consistency between XSLT and XQuery in other areas, such as the formalization of the shared data model and the rules for tree construction.

As some members predicted, creation of the XPath 2.0 language was tough. There was a natural tendency for the XSLT representatives to fight for backwards compatibility with XPath 1.0, while the XQuery people argued that there were aspects of the XPath 1.0 specification that they could not live with. Gradually mechanisms were devised that encompassed both objectives, for example, by retaining the implicit type conversions of XPath 1.0 as a "fallback mode" that would be supported in XSLT but not in XQuery, and in some cases by providing new functions and operators that overlapped the old but had cleaner semantics. Some of the semantics of XPath 1.0 that had initially seemed unacceptable—for example, the fact that the results of path expressions were always in document order—were found to be acceptable after all, as XQuery people gradually became familiar with the strange properties of text markup structures. In some other areas, particularly where the XPath 1.0 specification had led to usability problems, compromises affecting backwards compatibility were made— though generally only in areas where very few users were likely to be adversely affected. There was a great deal of debate over how much of the XQuery language should be included in the XPath subset, with some wanting to keep XPath extremely small, and others arguing for the inclusion of any feature that might be useful in an XSLT context.

The result is inevitably a compromise. XPath 2.0 is a substantially bigger language than XPath 1.0. Most of the growth is due to the definition of a vastly extended library of core functions, which is a good way of adding capability without increasing complexity. Aside from the growth in functions (and in operators that merely provide convenient syntax for an underlying function call), the syntax of the language has grown by a relatively modest 40 percent, and in fact some of the increased power (in particular, the generalization of path expressions) has been achieved by eliminating restrictions present in XPath 1.0, so it has actually made the language smaller.[4]

---

[4] The number of productions in the XPath grammar has grown from 39 to 71, but only 16 of the new productions introduce basic syntactic constructs: The rest merely expand the range of binary operators available. The number of functions, however, has grown from 28 to more than 100.

XSLT and XQuery Compared

We've looked at the factors that caused XSLT and XQuery to differ. In this section we examine the differences between the two languages in detail. Wherever possible, I try to explain why the differences exist, though in many cases, the only real explanation is that two different design teams inevitably come up with different answers to the same problem.

As we have seen, XSLT and XQuery share XPath as a common core. In contrasting the languages, therefore, we mainly need to look at the parts outside XPath. However, although there is a single XPath definition, this definition allows some flexibility to the host language, so in practice there are some differences even at the XPath level.

It's worth pointing out that the similarities between the two languages are considerable:

- Both languages have facilities for constructing new nodes in an XML result tree. In fact, both languages have two flavors of this: a direct XML-like syntax in which the elements to be constructed are written directly in their XML form, and an indirect syntax in which the names of elements or attributes need to be computed at run-time.

- Both languages allow the definition of user-written functions, which can be called using the XPath function call mechanism. In the case of XSLT, this is a new facility in XSLT 2.0. (XSLT 1.0 allowed functions to be simulated using named templates, but these could not be called directly from within XPath expressions.)

- Both languages provide control structures for nested iterations or joins: the FLWOR expression in the case of XQuery, and nested `xslt:for-each` instructions in the case of XSLT. (In XSLT 2.0, this is supplemented by a `for` expression in XPath 2.0, which is a subset of the XQuery FLWOR expression.)

- Both languages allow variables to be defined. In both cases the variables are read-only. Both are declarative functional languages with no assignment statements.

XML-Based Syntax

The syntax for XSLT is based on XML. A stylesheet is an XML document. As we saw earlier, there are two main reasons for this: It makes it easy to write stylesheets that contain large chunks of HTML to be copied directly into the result document, and it makes it possible to use XSLT to transform stylesheets.

XQuery chose not to take this route (there is an XML representation of queries called XQueryX, but it is not really suitable for human consumption, as it represents a very low-level view of the XQuery parse tree). Instead, XQuery has a syntax that mimics XML where necessary, particularly when constructing target elements. Sometimes the syntax is very close to XSLT; for example, the following snippet could be written in either language:

```
<a href="{@href}">see below</a>
```

The difference is that in XSLT, this really is XML (it is parsed by an XML parser, and must follow all the XML rules), whereas in XQuery it merely mimics XML. This makes it possible to nest expressions in XQuery in a way that is not possible in XSLT; for example, it is possible (though not very useful) in XQuery to write

```
<item size="{ count((<b/>, <c/>, <d/>)) }"/>
```

which would be quite impossible in XSLT because it is not legal XML (attributes cannot contain elements). XQuery thus achieves better composability than XSLT, but at a price: Because it is not pure XML, there are new rules to learn regarding how whitespace and character references are handled, and standard XML tools (such as editors) cannot be used to manipulate the query text. There's a good reason for this choice: XQuery is likely to be often used as an embedded language with programming languages such as Java and C#, or even within SQL, where XML tools would not be much use anyway.

Semantics of Element Construction

Behind the superficially similar facilities for constructing elements and attributes in a result tree, there has until recently been a significant difference in the semantics of the processing model. In the latest working drafts, however, XSLT 2.0 has moved closer to the XQuery model.

XSLT 1.0 insists that an entire tree be constructed before any part of it can be accessed using XPath expressions. In XSLT 1.0, it was not even possible to access a constructed tree—known as a result tree fragment—without using the `node-set()` extension function, which, while widely implemented, is not actually part of the standard. This restriction has disappeared in XSLT 2.0, but it remained true until the May 2003 draft that XPath operations could only operate on trees representing a complete document (that is, a tree with a document node at its root). This is a natural consequence of the two-language model, whereby XSLT instructions can call XPath expressions but not vice versa. A temporary tree is always constructed by means of a variable declaration, and the nodes within the tree can only be accessed by an XPath expression that references this variable: The scope rules on variables ensure that the tree can always be fully constructed before any of its nodes are referenced. This is illustrated in Listing 3.2.

Listing 3.2   Constructing a Temporary Tree in XSLT

```
<xslt:variable name="tree">
  <calendar>
    <month number="1" length="31"/>
    <month number="2" length="{if ($leap-year) then 29 else 28}"/>
    <month number="3" length="31"/>
    <month number="4" length="30"/>
    . . .
    <month number="12" length="31"/>
  </calendar>
</xslt:variable>
. . .
<xslt:value-of select="sum($tree/calendar/month/@length)"/>
. . .
```

The fact that trees were not accessible while they were incomplete means that it was possible to describe tree construction in XSLT using a top-down model, in which parent nodes were constructed conceptually before their children. Of course, in a functional language the actual order of execution is not defined, so this was merely a way of describing the effect of the language and not necessarily a description of how an actual implementation works. In practice, though, most XSLT 1.0 processors probably followed this model fairly closely.

In XQuery, by contrast, an element constructor is just an expression and can be used in any place where other kinds of expressions may appear. For example, it is quite legitimate to write the following:

```
sum(
<calendar>
  <month number="1" length="31"/>
  <month number="2" length="if ($leap-year) then 29 else 28"/>
  <month number="3" length="31"/>
  <month number="4" length="30"/>
  . . .
  <month number="12" length="31"/>
</calendar> / month / @length )
```

In this example, although the difference looks fairly superficial, it has considerable implications for the detailed semantics of the model. XQuery treats an expression that constructs an element or attribute node in the same way as any other expression. This means that the semantics are described in a bottom-up way. Just as in the expression x * (y - 1) the subtraction is evaluated first, and then the multiplication, so in the expression `<a>{$x+1}</a>`, we first do the addition, then we create a text node containing the result, then we construct an element node as the parent of this text node.

This means that in XQuery it is possible to manipulate partially constructed trees (trees that do not have a document node as their root). For example, a path expression may reference an attribute node that is not connected to any element. The attribute can then be attached to an element "later," as shown below:

```
let $att1 := attribute code { "23" },
    $att2 := attribute desc { "24" } return

if ($condition)
  then <a> {$att1} </a>
  else <a> {$att2} </a>
```

This also means, of course, that the attribute node represented by $att1 or $att2 can be added to several different elements. Because an attribute cannot actually have two parents, the semantics require an identical copy to be made each time the attribute is attached to an element. In the formal model, this copying happens all the way up the tree: Each time a child node is added to a parent node, the child node is copied. In practice,

XQuery processors will usually be able to avoid this copying, and in the vast majority of cases will use the same top-down implementation that an XSLT 1.0 processor uses; but the formal model is completely different, to allow for the increased generality of the language.

Because XQuery copies subtrees implicitly when they are attached to a new parent, it does not require an explicit instruction to do the copying. By contrast, XSLT 1.0 built an entire tree first, and then allowed it to be copied explicitly using the `xslt:copy-of` instruction if required. In the most recent XSLT 2.0 drafts, the processing model has changed so that it is now very close to the XQuery model. Tree construction is described bottom up, and nodes are accessible before they have been attached to a parent node. Most users will not notice the change, but the difference affects many minor details, such as the way in which new nodes are validated against schema types and the way that namespaces work. It also means that some care is needed with absolute path expressions. For example, if the root of a tree is an "a" element with "b" children, then to select the "b" elements, you need to write `/b`, rather than `/a/b` as you might expect. The syntax `/a/b` (which is short for `root(.)/child::a/child::b`) only works where the element named "a" is the child of the root node.

Functions and Named Templates

XQuery and XSLT 2.0 both offer the ability to define functions. Again, at first sight the facilities are not very different. In XQuery we can reverse a sequence with the recursive function:

```
define function reverse ($seq as item()*) as item()* {
  if (count($seq) < 2)
  then $seq
  else (reverse(subsequence($seq, 2)), $seq[1])
}
```

In XSLT 2.0 we can write the same function as follows:

```
<xslt:function name="reverse" as="item()*">
  <xslt:param name="seq" as="item()*"/>
  <xslt:sequence as="item()*" select="
      if (count($seq) &lt; 2)
      then $seq
      else (reverse(subsequence($seq, 2)), $seq[1])"/>
</xslt:function>
```

Not a big difference. However, the fact that XSLT is a two-language system again creates differences. Because XSLT has one language for constructing nodes in the result tree and a different language (XPath) for selecting nodes from the source tree, it effectively has two mechanisms for defining what logically are functions: `xslt:function` for functions that can be called from XPath expressions and that return values; `xslt:template` for subroutines that can be called from the XSLT level and that write nodes to the result tree. XQuery only has a single language, so its expressions are more composable, which means that it gets by with a single function mechanism.

FLWOR Expressions

In the same way as the core construct of XPath is the path expression, at the center of the XQuery language lies the FLWOR expression. FLWOR expressions perform the same role in XQuery as the SELECT statement in SQL; and indeed, the SQL SELECT statement and its successors in various post-relational languages had a powerful influence on this language construct.

Nevertheless, a FLWOR expression contains nothing that does not translate directly into XSLT. The `for` part translates directly into `xslt:for-each`, the `let` part into `xslt:variable`, the `where` part into `xslt:if`, and the `order by` clause into `xslt:sort`.

FLWOR expressions are generally understood in very declarative terms, being based on the operations of the relational calculus such as Cartesian products, selection, and projection. By contrast, the equivalent XSLT constructs are often understood in procedural terms: People think of `xslt:for-each` as the analog of a loop in a procedural programming language. But beneath the surface, after cutting through the formal language used in explaining the semantics, there is very little real difference in functionality.

It's probably true that most XSLT processors actually evaluate `xslt:for-each` instructions using a procedural approach very similar to the surface model: Certainly, Saxon does so. Where two `xslt:for-each` instructions are nested, they are likely to be implemented by means of a nested loop.

With FLWOR expressions, the implementation is much more likely to use the repertoire of optimization techniques developed for relational databases, which can involve considerable rearrangement of the order of execution.

But these are not differences caused by the semantics of the language. They arise because XQuery is used in a different environment: that of searching large persistent databases. In this environment, the efficiency of a query depends on finding preconstructed indexes that give fast access to particular selections appearing in a query. The thrust of XQuery optimization is therefore to rewrite the query to make optimum use of indexes. XSLT processors don't generally have this luxury: There are no preconstructed indexes. The range of access paths available is much more limited; consequently, the opportunities for performance advantages from rewriting the query are also limited.

The difference in approach also arises because of XSLT's focus on handling document-oriented XML, whereas XQuery emphasizes data-oriented XML. When handling documents, the order of both the source document and the result document are significant, and they are often the same. Sequential processing is therefore usually the best strategy. When handling data, order (certainly in the relational tradition) is often unimportant, and strategies that change the order of execution can have a high payoff.

Template Rules

One of the few really significant differences between XSLT and XQuery is XSLT's use of template rules: an event-driven approach that decouples the description of how to process individual elements in the source tree from any assumptions about the context in which these elements appear. XQuery has no corresponding facility, although it is possible to prove that this does not reduce the expressive capability of the language: Any `xslt:apply-templates` instruction can in principle be translated into a conditional expression that makes direct calls on an explicit template depending on the properties of the selected node.

What template rules provide is not extra functionality, but modularity and potential for change. They enable the stylesheet to make fewer assumptions about the structure of the source document, and therefore to be more resilient to changes in this structure. This, of course, is very important for handling document-oriented XML and much less significant for data-oriented XML.

The very strength of the event-driven approach of template rules is also the cause of its difficulties: It makes optimization difficult. While XSLT processors use all kinds of tricks to limit the number of patterns that each node is tested against, and may in the future use schema information to limit this choice still further, it is hard to optimize the stylesheet as a whole, as distinct from optimizing individual template rules, because so little is known statically about which rules will call which others. XSLT processors can afford the cost of matching template rules, because the most common action of a stylesheet is to process each node exactly once, in sequential order. XQuery cannot afford this cost, because the very feasibility of executing a query in a reasonable length of time depends on static analysis of the query to devise an execution strategy that only visits the minimum number of nodes. There is a real difference in requirements here, and in the application areas that the two languages are addressing, that leads to a genuine difference in design philosophy.

Axes

XQuery does not offer the full set of axes used in XPath path expressions: This is the only part of XPath that is not incorporated directly into XQuery. Specifically, XQuery does not offer the `following` and `preceding` axes, the `following-sibling` and `preceding-sibling` axes, or the `ancestor` axis. Why was this decision made? I find it difficult to explain this decision, because I argued against it, but the arguments on both sides are credible, and I will try to do them justice.

XPath approaches the selection of nodes in a tree in a way that some regard as navigational. I prefer to think of it as functional, because the word *navigational* has connotations of procedural algorithms, but the essence is that nodes are found by virtue of their relationship to other nodes: go up three, then left two, then down one. This approach is traditionally difficult to optimize. In databases, following the relational tradition, the approach is to select objects based on their properties, not by describing a route by which they can be reached. This makes some people from the relational tradition deeply suspicious of path expressions, and anxious about the difficulty of optimizing them.

Some XQuery implementers are also using database engines whose storage and indexing structures are finely tuned to relational data and relational queries. Adapting these engines to hierarchic data structures and recursive path expressions is not an easy task, and queries that fit well into the relational pattern are often likely to execute far more efficiently than those that do not.

It is true that any expression involving the axes that XQuery has omitted can be rewritten to avoid these axes. Take, for example, the query "find a figure element that is immediately followed by another figure without any intervening text or elements." In XPath we would write:

```
//figure[following-sibling::node()[1][self::figure]]
```

XQuery does not offer the following-sibling axis, so how can this query be expressed? One way is the following:

```
for $p in //*
  for $f at $i in $p/figure
  where $p/node()[$i+1][self::figure]
  return $f
```

While this seems highly convoluted to someone familiar with XPath, I am told it comes very naturally to people who think in SQL terms. Is it any easier to optimize than the XPath version? Not for a processor that is working on a tree model implemented in terms of a fully connected object model either in memory or in persistent storage (typically a native XML database such as Software AG's Tamino).[5] But for implementers who have flattened the tree into a tuple structure held in tabular storage, who knows?

Perhaps it comes down to different views as to the importance of such queries. In document-oriented XML, ordering is essential, and objects are much more likely to be identified by their relationships to other objects than by their properties. In data-oriented XML, objects are most

---

[5] See http://www.softwareag.com/tamino.

usually identified by their content. So I strongly suspect that the real underlying reason for this decision is the natural bias in the XQuery group towards data-oriented XML.

Type Strictness

In XSLT 1.0 and XPath 1.0, the type system was very weak, in the sense that very few types were defined, and most operations accepted arguments of any type. As with scripting languages like JavaScript, if you supplied the wrong kind of object, the system did its best to convert it to the required type. So you could add strings, and you could concatenate numbers, and you could compare a set of nodes to a number, and get an answer. Not always the answer you might have expected, but an answer. Very few operations would ever cause a run-time error.

There was a reason behind this. The primary purpose of XSLT was for translating XML into display formats such as HTML or PDF. It was originally expected that the work would usually be done client-side, in the browser. And the last thing you want to happen when rendering a document on a browser is to put up a message saying "error in stylesheet." If the stylesheet is totaling a set of numbers, and it finds that one of the fields in the source document is not numeric after all, it should put something on the screen, even if it's only asterisks, rather than falling over in a heap.

Another reason for this was the awareness that in the XML world, all data is ultimately text. XML is basically (as we often tend to forget) a way of adding markup to text to indicate its structure. Other datatypes such as integers and Booleans exist only insofar as we decide to carve them out of the raw text: They are abstractions, whereas the text is real. With this world view, it is very natural that any operations on data should implicitly convert what they are given into the datatype that they are designed to process.

The developers of XQuery, by contrast, always believed firmly that a rich type system should be at the core of the language. There are many excellent reasons why languages in general, and query languages in particular, have tended to adopt strong type systems. Since the early days of databases, there has been the idea of separating the data description, or schema, from the data-manipulation, or query language. The data description reflects the common understanding of the data that is shared by the user community, even though each user is constructing different queries. It defines the types of objects that can be found in the database, and as such it naturally forms the type system for the query language, because a query that isn't expressed in terms of these types of objects doesn't make sense.

A query processor makes use of type information from the database schema in two significant ways. One use is for error detection. It is helpful to detect errors as early as possible, and it is certainly desirable to detect an error rather than returning wrong data. Every SQL user has had the experience of getting an answer to a query that is not actually the answer to the query they thought they were asking. This can never be completely prevented, but a good type system can detect many of the sillier mistakes in advance. The second reason is optimization. The more knowledge that the system has at compile-time, the more clever it can be in devising an efficient execution plan for the query, and knowing about the types of the objects handled by the query is a key part of the picture.

As it happens, the thinking in the XSL group on typing has evolved considerably since XSLT 1.0. This is partly because XSLT has proved to be of significance in a great many roles other than client-side web browsing, and partly because of the emergence of XML Schema as a powerful influence on the adoption of XML by big business, even if it is fiercely resisted by the SGML cognoscenti. The thinking in the XQuery camp has also evolved, with an increasing recognition that there is a legitimate need to handle **semi-structured** data. The process has been one of gradual convergence and of increasing recognition on both sides that there is a wide spectrum of requirements. But XSLT still has more of a foot in the "loose typing" camp than XQuery does, because there is still more interest in processing schema-less documents, and also because the design of the language, with its event-based template rules, makes it much harder to use static type information effectively, either for error reporting or for optimization. So it can be said that XQuery has been making tentative steps towards looser typing, while XSLT has been making tentative steps in the opposite direction.

The range of views in both working groups ensured that discussions of the type system accounted for a great deal of the time and effort spent in developing the two languages. Many users may fail to notice this, because the bottom line is that in both XSLT and XQuery, most users can safely ignore most of the complexities of the type system. For example, both languages have elaborate facilities for validating the output documents against a schema. Some XQuery designers have always aspired to make it possible to report a compile-time error when a query is incapable of producing output that conforms to the required schema, or even—a stronger test—to report an error when it *is* capable of producing output that does not conform to the required schema. I suspect, however, that many users will simply output untyped XML, and if they need to validate it, they will do this as a separate process once the query or transformation is complete.

Optimization Techniques

In the three years since XSLT became a W3C Recommendation, a considerable number of implementations have appeared and have had some time to mature. Competitive comparisons of their performance have occasionally been published, which, although they suffer the same problems as all such benchmarks, have certainly spurred vendors to improve their ratings. Implementers will also have had feedback from their own users highlighting performance problems. All the products have improved significantly since their first appearance.

It is reasonable to expect, therefore, that the performance of XSLT processing is by now a fairly widely understood subject, and that the lessons learned by XSLT suppliers will be available for XQuery vendors to study, giving them a head start. Unfortunately, though, very little has been published on XSLT implementation techniques. Several of the products are open-source, so one can study the techiques they use by reading the source code, but that's a far cry from having published articles written by their designers. Apart from anything else, the source code doesn't tell you what techniques were tried but failed, or what ideas are still present in the product even though they actually made little impact.

The notes here come mainly from my experiences with Saxon.[6] The ideas in Saxon were influenced by ideas used in the xt and Xalan products.[7] One of the interesting features of the XSLT world is that there are multiple open-source products all competing with each other, but without the benefit of being able to hide their secrets. Of course there are other products, notably Microsoft's MSXML,[8] that have not revealed the secrets of their design, so it's quite possible that the account given here misses some important ideas.

The reason for writing this section is because I think there are likely to be many similarities between the challenges of XSLT optimization and XQuery optimization. There are also many differences, which I return to at the end of the section; but I think the similarities are important, and many of the experiences with XSLT will prove also to be relevant to XQuery.

Where Does the Time Go?

It's useful to start the discussion with a breakdown of how an XSLT processor spends its time. Of course, this depends on the particular problem under discussion. The charts in Figures 3.1 and 3.2 show the breakdown for two particular transformation tasks. One is the job of rendering the XML version of the XSLT specification itself as HTML; the second one uses the same stylesheet but applies it to a much smaller document. The figures were obtained using Saxon 6.5.2.

Figure 3.1 shows the breakdown of time spent on the four key activities in applying a stylesheet to a large document: compiling the stylesheet, building the source document tree, performing the actual transformation, and serializing the result tree as HTML. In this case the stylesheet is around 1,350 lines long, divided into three modules; the source document is 600KB, and the result document 860KB. The total transformation time on my machine was about 8.3 seconds. In Saxon, there are three phases

---

[6] Saxon: see http://saxon.sf.net/.

[7] On xt, see http://www.blnz.com/xt/index.html. On Xalan, see http://xml.apache.org/.

[8] MSXML: see http://www.microsoft.com/xml.

executed serially: compiling, tree-building, and transformation/serialization. The division of time between transformation and serialization is calculated by comparing the effect of not doing the HTML serialization (just feeding the result to a user-written content handler that does nothing with it).

This kind of transformation is generally done as a one-off. There are few benefits to be obtained by compiling the stylesheet in advance and amortizing the compilation cost over multiple transformations of different source documents, since the saving this would achieve is 15 percent at best. The total elapsed time of 8.3 seconds also includes a heavy overhead for "warming up" the Java VM—loading and initializing all the required classes, and getting to the point where the just-in-time Java compilation has reached steady state. The actual stylesheet is performing four or five passes over the source document (one to render the main text, additional passes to build the table of contents, the glossary, and various appendices), and is also doing a considerable amount of keyed access to construct extensive cross-references in the form of hyperlinks. It is striking, therefore, that the cost of parsing the source document and building it into a tree structure is almost as great as the transformation cost proper.

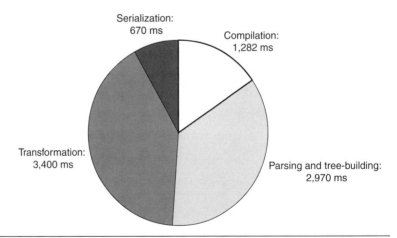

Figure 3.1   Time Breakdown for Rendering a Large Document

For contrast, Figure 3.2 shows a transformation that is more typical of the "on-demand" XML-to-HTML transformation performed on a web site where the data is stored in XML and rendered each time the content is requested by a user. The stylesheet used is the same; the only difference is that the source document is much smaller—only 8KB this time. This reduces the total transformation time to 1.6 seconds, of which 79 percent is the cost of compiling the stylesheet. The obvious message from this is the vital importance of compiling stylesheets once and reusing them in this scenario.

Another interesting point is that although the stylesheet is the same as in the example of Figure 3.1, the ratio of transformation time to parsing and tree-building is much higher in this case. A possible explanation for this is that the tree-building phase is responsible for acquiring all the memory used for the transformation, and the cost of allocating the required memory increases more than linearly with the size of the source document, because of paging or memory fragmentation. It might also be the case that the transformation phase includes a one-time startup cost that is independent of document size.

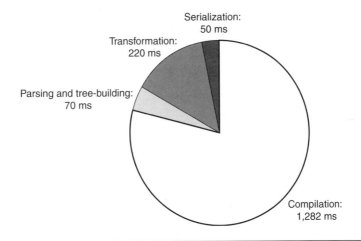

Figure 3.2   Time Breakdown for Rendering a Small Document

What messages are there here for XQuery? Many XQuery systems will work on databases where the data has been preloaded into a database structure. The database structure performs the same role as the in-memory tree used by XSLT processors, but it is only built once, when a document is loaded or replaced in the database; it is not done on each query. This doesn't mean that the time taken to build the tree can be ignored—on the contrary, data loading and updating time has always been a critical factor for databases supporting efficient hierarchic access paths, and this is easy to forget after twenty years in which the relational database with its flat storage structures has dominated the scene. XQuery systems need to make exactly the same trade-off as XSLT processors between the time taken to build and index the tree, and the speed of the access paths offered by the tree once it has been built. In many ways they have tougher decisions to make, because whereas an XSLT processor can build the tree with knowledge of the transformation that will take place, the trees built by an XQuery processor will have to support many different kinds of queries.

The observations about compilation time are also relevant to a query processor. Although 1,000-line queries will probably be less common than 1,000-line stylesheets, complex queries will occur, and the complexities of compiling them will probably be proportionately greater than with XSLT stylesheets because of the crucial importance of finding the optimum access path to the data when dealing with gigabytes of source rather than mere kilobytes. But as with XSLT, there will be one-off queries where nothing can be gained by reusing the compiled query, and there will be transactional queries where this is essential.

Having put the actual execution time of a query or transformation into some kind of perspective, we turn now to the various optimizing techniques that can be used.

Internal Coding Efficiency

Books on relational databases don't go out of their way to tell you something that every implementer of a database system knows: The most important way of getting good performance out of the system is simply to write fast code. Most queries in a database system, and most XSLT transformations, are quite simple, and the smartest optimizer in the world can do very little to improve the performance of a simple query. If xt processes the same stylesheet five times faster than Xalan (and it sometimes does), this isn't because it has a better optimizer; it's mainly because James Clark writes very slick code.

Associated with this is the design of efficient data structures. The design of the source tree structure is critical to XSLT performance. The trade-off between time and space is important (people want to transform documents as large as 100MB), as is the trade-off between the time taken to build the tree and the time taken to navigate it. A simplistic tree representation, using one Java object for each node in the tree, would be hopelessly inadequate on both counts. Saxon uses an adaptive approach in which many of the access paths (for example, pointers from nodes to their preceding siblings) are built only if and when these access paths are actually used.

But this book isn't about how to write good code or design efficient data structures in Java or any other programming language. Having made this point, therefore, I'll move on to other factors more specific to XSLT and XQuery processing.

Pipelining and Lazy Evaluation

The world of functional programming languages such as Scheme and Haskell and the world of database management systems often seem to have little in common. But the theory in both areas has one thing in common: the idea of pipelining. The terminology may be different, but the essential idea is the same.

In the relational model, an SQL query can be translated into an expression in the relational algebra using operations such as restriction, projection, union, sort, and join. These are set-at-a-time operations: each operation takes sets of tuples as its input and produces sets (or sometimes, sequences) of tuples as its output. It would be hideously expensive if all these sets of tuples were actually materialized in memory. Allocating memory dynamically is an expensive operation, and memory is a finite resource: use more of it for intermediate results, and less is available for other purposes such as caching. The same factors apply to functional programming languages based on list manipulation, and equally to XPath, whose semantics are defined in terms of sets of nodes. Materializing these sets is expensive.

The technique used to avoid allocating memory to these intermediate results is called *pipelining*. The way pipelining works is that an operation such as restriction is implemented to deliver one object at a time, on request from another operation, and it in turn requests one object at a time from its subordinate operators. The tree of operators that makes up an SQL or XPath expression is thus represented at run-time by a sequence of so-called *iterators*, each of which supports a *get-next* operation to deliver the next object in a stream. In a relational system, the objects are tuples, and the pipeline is described in terms of the flow of a stream of tuples delivered by one node in the expression tree to its parent node in the expression tree.

Not all XPath operations can be pipelined. An obvious example is the `last()` function: to find out the value of the `last()` function in an expression such as `$x[last() idiv 2]`, (which returns the item in the middle of a sequence), you need to know how many objects the current operation is going to return, and the only way of finding out is to read them all. This breaks the pipeline, and is therefore a costly operation. There are actually two strategies for implementing the `last()` function. One is to evaluate the containing expression once (in this case, `$x`) and save the results in memory. The other is to evaluate the containing expression twice, once to count the nodes and once to feed them to the next operator in the pipeline. Sometimes one technique is better, sometimes the other: this is the kind of decision where a good optimizer can make a difference.

The other common operation that breaks a pipeline is sorting. One technique often used by optimizers is to rewrite expressions so that sorting is done last. This can often reduce the number of objects to be sorted, and it can eliminate the need for multiple sorts. With XPath expressions of the form `a/b/c`, for example, the results are guaranteed by the semantics of the language to be in document order. But there is no need to sort the intermediate result `a/b` (or `b/c`, depending on the evaluation strategy). The entire path expression can be evaluated in a single pipeline and sorted at the last possible moment.

A path expression may often be evaluated without performing a sort at all. XSLT processors such as Saxon have at least three techniques available to avoid sorting:

- Performing static analysis of the path expression to determine that the results are "naturally sorted": that is, that when evaluated using the "obvious" evaluation strategy, the results will automatically be in document order. The rules for this are quite subtle; it's not immediately obvious, for example, that while `a//b` and `a/b/c` are both naturally sorted, `a//b/c` is not.

- Evaluating reverse axes in forward order to make the expression naturally sorted where it would otherwise not be.

- Detecting the context in which a path expression is used, in order to recognize that although the language semantics require the results to be sorted, in some contexts it makes no difference to the result. The obvious examples are where the path expression is used as an argument to functions such as `count()`, `sum()`, or `boolean()`. In XQuery this also arises when a path expression is used within a FLWOR expression that has an ORDER BY clause to specify the order of the results. However, there is a further subtlety here: some functions such as `count()` require duplicate nodes to be eliminated from the result, whereas others such as `boolean()` do not.

Although eliminating sorts is useful in its own right, because sorting is expensive, the chief benefit of eliminating sorts is that it improves pipelining.

Closely associated with pipelining is another technique well known in the functional programming literature: lazy evaluation. The principle of lazy evaluation is to avoid doing work until the results are actually needed. There are two benefits. First, you don't need any memory to hold the results. Second, you might discover that the results aren't actually needed anyway.

Listing 3.3 shows a simple example of lazy evaluation at work in XSLT.

Listing 3.3   Example of Lazy Evaluation in XSLT

```
<xslt:param name="account-nr"/>
<xslt:template match="/">
  <xslt:variable name="transactions"
              select="/*/transaction[account=$account-nr]"/>
  <xslt:choose>
  <xslt:when test="starts-with($account-nr, 'Z')">
     <xslt:value-of select="closing-balance"/>
  </xslt:when>
  <xslt:otherwise>
     <xslt:value-of select="opening-balance +
                          sum($transactions/value)"/>
  </xslt:otherwise>
  </xslt:choose>
</xslt:template>
```

The `xslt:variable` instruction is potentially expensive to evaluate: It involves selecting all the transactions for a given account, which probably means scanning the whole source document. But now look at how the result is used. In one branch of the conditional `xslt:choose`, the variable isn't used at all. In the other branch, it is only used as the argument to the `sum()` function. This means that by delaying the evaluation of the variable until it is actually used, we might avoid evaluating it at all; and even if we do need it, we can incorporate it in a pipeline so that the list of `transaction` elements never needs to be held in memory, and we can certainly avoid sorting the results.

The tricky part of lazy evaluation is that the value of an XPath expression depends on the context in which it appears (the current node, the values of other variables, the namespaces that are in scope), so as well as saving the expression, the relevant parts of the context also need to be saved. This means that an important role of an XPath optimizer is to determine the *dependencies* of an expression—the parts of the context on which it depends, which need to be saved when doing lazy evaluation.

Pipelining and lazy evaluation are likely to be just as important to an XQuery processor as to an XSLT/XPath processor.

Expression Rewriting

In relational database theory, the term *optimization* is used almost synonymously with query rewriting. The job of an optimizer is to take a tree-representation of a query, as produced by the query language parser from the original query text as written, and rearrange it into a different (but equivalent) tree that can be evaluated more efficiently. Many standard techniques are used, such as pushing down restrictions closer to the leaves of the tree. The selection of different operators to implement the relational join functionality has been the staple diet of the research journals for nearly thirty years.

Expression rewriting is also a powerful technique used in an XPath optimizer. There are two variants of the approach. The first rewrites the expression in terms of another valid XPath expression. For example, the expression

```
a/b/c | a/b/d
```

can be rewritten as

```
a/b/(c|d)
```

(which is a valid XPath 2.0 expression, though not valid in XPath 1.0).

Another example of such a rewrite is `count($x)>10`, which can be rewritten as `exists($x[11])`. The latter expression is likely to be more efficient, because (with the benefit of pipelining and lazy evaluation) items beyond the eleventh are likely never to be read. Rewrites that move subexpressions out of a loop can also be regarded as falling into this category. For example, the expression

```
items[value > $customer/credit-limit]
```

can be rewritten as

```
let $x := $customer/credit-limit
return items[value > $x]
```

Again this relies on dependency analysis, that is, knowing that the subexpression `$customer/credit-limit` has no dependency on the context item or context position, which would make the value vary for different items.

The second variant of the technique rewrites expressions in terms of internal operators that are not available in the surface language. One of the most powerful examples is the expression

```
$x[position() != last()]
```

which can be rewritten as

```
$x[hasNext()]
```

where `hasNext()` is an internal function that tests whether there are any more items in the pipeline. The beauty of this rewrite is that it avoids breaking the pipeline. In the expression as written, when the first item is read, its position `(1)` needs to be compared with the number of nodes in the pipeline (perhaps thousands), which means that these nodes have to be counted. In the rewritten expression, each node is simply tested to see whether it is the last, which only requires a single-item lookahead.

In the relational database tradition, the most significant rewrites (those with the highest payoff) are those concerned with optimizing joins that occur in the SQL SELECT expression. It is quite likely, therefore, that XQuery vendors will put a lot of emphasis into optimizing the joins that arise in FLWOR expressions, which are the XQuery equivalent of SQL SELECT expressions. There is a risk that this effort could be misplaced, depending on the way users decide to write their queries. In the relational model, all relationships are modeled using primary keys and foreign keys, and equijoins between primary keys and foreign keys are ubiquitous in queries. In the hierarchic world of XML, many relationships are modeled instead by means of the containment relationship: Instead of order-lines holding an order number to indicate the purchase order that they relate to, the order-lines are represented as subelements within an element representing the purchase order. The join that is therefore inevitable in the SQL query is replaced in the XQuery formulation by a path expression. Instead of

```
SELECT customer.name, order.date, order-line.value
FROM customer, order, order-line
WHERE customer.id = order.customer-id AND order-line.order-no =
order.order-no
```

we are likely to see

```
for $c in /customers/customer,
    $o in $c/order, $ol in $o/order-line
    return $c/name, $ol/date, $o/value
```

Now, of course, some query systems are likely to use tabular storage underneath the covers, and will implement this query as a value-based join even though there are no explicit join keys in the user query. Processors that use a tree-based representation of the data, however, will evaluate the query in exactly the same way as an XSLT processor would—by means of a depth-first traversal of the tree.

Of course, join optimization has a role to play in XQuery, especially where multiple indexes are available at different levels of a hierarchy, giving a wide choice of access paths to implement the same query. Joins that relate data held in different documents can also be very important. But I suspect that the join operation will be a lot less important than it is in relational databases, and that optimizing the hierarchic access paths—effectively, the XPath expressions—will be at least as significant, and perhaps more so.

As far as I'm aware, XSLT processors have until now done little to optimize joins. I think there are several reasons for this. The language design (with its nested `xslt:for-each` and `xslt:apply-templates` instructions) does not make join queries easy to detect. At the same time, the fact that the tree is built anew for each transformation means that there isn't a wide choice of access paths to select from. But the biggest reason, I suspect, is that the stylesheets that XSLT implementers have studied to look for optimization opportunities simply don't do many joins. Their access paths predominantly follow the hierarchic relationships intrinsic to the XML model. XQuery implementers are coming to the game armed with a formidable array of optimization tools that proved useful in the relational world. Only time will tell how effective these tools are in an XML world.

Using Type Information

As we have seen, XSLT 1.0 and XPath 1.0 work without a schema for either the source or the result document. The stylesheet authors need to know what the constraints are on the structure of these documents, but they do not need to tell the system what these constraints are.

This changes in XQuery (and indeed in XSLT 2.0 and XPath 2.0), with the ability to import schemas and make assertions about the types of expressions and function arguments: XQuery is a much more strongly typed language than its predecessors. Or at any rate, it has the potential to be, if users decide to take advantage of these capabilities.

One of the arguments made in favor of stronger typing is that knowledge of types will make much more powerful optimizations possible. There is good theoretical justification for this view. Achieving the results in practice, though, is not easy. Here's a simple case. A very common construct in stylesheets is to use an expression such as `//item`, whose value is the set of all `item` elements in the document. Evaluating this expression is expensive in most XSLT processors because it involves a full scan of the source tree. With knowledge of the schema, it becomes possible to limit the search to those branches of the tree where `item` elements can validly appear.

In XSLT, it's debatable whether this is worth doing. There are some practical problems, because it's not at present possible to know statically that the document to be searched using the `//item` expression is valid against a particular schema. It's also arguable that other approaches to optimizing this expression may be more powerful. For example, the information about which element types appear on which branches of the tree is not only available from the schema, it can also be collected (with greater precision) during parsing of the source document. In XQuery, this kind of schema-based optimization is much more important, because one of the most important tasks of the query optimizer is to identify access paths that take advantage of prebuilt indexes.

An XSLT or XQuery processor that performs static analysis of the types of expressions can make many decisions at compile-time that would otherwise be made at run-time. Saxon does this even with the loosely typed XPath 1.0 language. For example, it can usually distinguish at compile-time whether the predicate in a filter expression such as `$x[FILTER]` is a Boolean filter or a numeric subscript. Having schema knowledge available at compile-time will certainly increase the ability to make early decisions about the access path. However, many of these optimizations have only a small payoff. In relation to the overall execution cost of a query, for example, deciding at compile-time to do integer arithmetic rather than floating-point is not a big win.

So in my view the jury is still out on the importance of schema-based optimization. We will have to wait for real implementation experience before we know the answers. Extrapolating the relational experience is not necessarily going to give the right predictions. My own guess is that strong typing will prove less useful in practice than some of its advocates hope, especially because I think many users will take the easy road of not declaring the expected types of variables, function parameters, and constructed nodes when they can get away without it.

Conclusion

In this chapter we have looked at the relation between XQuery and XSLT (and their common subset, XPath) from a number of perspectives. We began with an analysis of the areas of similarity and difference between the two languages and the reasons why the differences occur. We saw that although there are large areas of overlapping functionality, significant differences exist in the requirements that the two languages were designed to meet, and that we can trace many of the design differences to the fact that the two languages were intended to be used in different environments. Other differences, however, reflect the different cultures of the document world, with its SGML history, and the database world, with its traditions based on SQL. Perhaps the most significant difference is that XSLT is stronger at handling loosely structured data, while XQuery is strongest at handling data that is highly regular. This in turn accounts for the different emphasis in the two communities on schemas and type systems—though as we saw, the languages are converging here, with better facilities in XSLT to handle strongly typed data, and better facilities in XQuery to handle semi-structured information.

Then we looked at the state of the art in XSLT optimization, with the aim of understanding the extent to which the lessons learned from three years of XSLT experience are applicable to XQuery. In my view, many of the techniques that are used by XSLT optimizers will be equally applicable to XQuery processors, in particular techniques such as pipelining, lazy evaluation, expression rewriting, and avoiding sorts in path expressions. XQuery environments, however, will present additional challenges and additional opportunities for their optimizers, because they will generally be working on databases that have a choice of indexed access paths available. In database work, the key task of an optimizer is to identify the indexes that enable the query to be evaluated without sequential searching. XQuery implementers will bring a wide range of experience to this task from the relational world. But we saw that one risk in this is that the heavy emphasis on join optimization may prove less important in the XML world. This depends greatly on the types of applications that XML databases end up being used for, which is difficult to predict at this stage in the game.

The fact that XQuery and XSLT share a common data model, and in XPath a common sublanguage, is a major achievement by the W3C, given the diverse backgrounds of the two working groups. I believe that it will also be a major benefit to users. It will reduce learning curves because so much is common to the two languages. It will also enable the two technologies to be used in complementary roles; for example, it becomes very easy to present the result of an XQuery using an XSLT stylesheet. And I suspect—only time will tell if I am right—that many implementers will be able to reuse the same run-time engines to implement both languages, which will obviously benefit both user communities.[9]

---

[9] Since writing this, I have fulfilled my own prediction. The latest release of Saxon does just this.

Part III

FORMAL
UNDERPINNINGS

Chapter 4
STATIC TYPING IN XQUERY

Mary Fernández, Jérôme Siméon, and Philip Wadler

XQuery is a strongly typed language, meaning that the types of values and expressions must be compatible with the context in which the value or expression is used. All implementations of XQuery must support dynamic typing, which checks during dynamic evaluation that the type of a value is compatible with the context in which it is used and raises a type error if an incompatibility is detected. XQuery implementations may optionally support static typing, which checks during static analysis that the type of an expression is compatible with the context in which it is used. Static Typing can shorten the development cycle by detecting common type errors before a query is evaluated.

This chapter explains how to use the XQuery type system to write type-safe queries, how to understand and resolve type errors, and how to work around the type system when necessary. Although focused on the XQuery static type system, this chapter is appropriate for all XQuery users, because it explains the relationships between dynamic typing, static typing, and validation.

Before reading this chapter, you should read Chapter 1, "XQuery: A Guided Tour," and you should read this chapter before reading Chapter 5, "Introduction to the Formal Semantics." Most of the typing concepts described by example in this chapter are described formally and completely in Chapter 5. Although informal examples help us learn how to use the XQuery type system, the formal definition of XQuery is necessary to build correct and complete implementations.

All typing concepts are introduced in the context of a realistic programming scenario, in which a programmer is given an input schema and an output schema, and he must write a query that transforms data conforming to the input schema into data conforming to the output schema.

The Benefits of Static Typing

Writing reliable software is hard. It is not difficult to write programs of several dozen or even hundreds of lines of code without bugs. But writing large applications is a difficult job even for the most experienced developer. Although many large applications are written in scripting languages such as Javascript and Perl, programmers debug such applications almost entirely at run-time, because scripting languages provide few compile-time checks. Most modern compiled languages (Java, C++, C#, ML, Haskell, etc.) provide static typing to help build large, reliable applications. Static typing can help by detecting common type errors in a program during static analysis so that they can be handled instead of being discovered only when the program is run.

Static typing helps programmers have confidence in the correctness of their programs. A type-correct program is guaranteed never to raise a type error in *any* evaluation. A type error occurs when the type of an expression is not compatible with the type required by the context in which the expression is used. For example, an expression whose type is a date typically cannot be used in an expression that requires a floating-point number. Because static analysis examines a program's expressions, not the values that those expressions produce, it must be conservative; that is, a type error may be raised during static analysis, even though running the program may raise no type errors. For example, the type system may determine that an expression has type `element(surgeon) | element(plumber)`, meaning that it will return either a `surgeon` or `plumber` element. It will raise a static error if that expression is used in a context requiring a `plumber` element, even though every actual evaluation of the expression may yield a `plumber` element and so would not raise a dynamic error. Further, although static typing allows us to detect all potential *type* errors, it cannot detect all potential errors of other kinds. For example, it cannot detect errors that depend on the values of expressions at run-time, such as divide-by-zero or array-bounds-overflow errors.

To use a statically typed language, the developer must have a basic understanding of the language's type system and what it can express. A developer using Java or C++ must understand the fundamentals of object-oriented programming. The developer also must have a basic understanding of how the type system works, so that she can understand what type errors mean. She must understand how to work around the type system when it is too restrictive. For example, Java developers know how to apply downcasting when the type system cannot infer a precise enough type.

Static typing is most effective for applications that use authoritative and stable schemas to describe their input and output data and that access XML data sources that are valid with respect to those schemas. Most serious applications of XML (electronic commerce, large-scale web publishing, relational data integration, etc.) define and use authoritative schemas and require a high level of reliability that static typing can help to achieve. Not all XML applications, however, consume or produce schema-validated data, so static typing is an optional conformance feature in XQuery.

This chapter explains how to use the XQuery static type system to write type-safe queries, how to understand and resolve type errors, and how to work around the type system when necessary. We start with one example of an application that can benefit from static typing. Then we explain the fundamentals of the XQuery type system and describe the kinds of errors it can detect. Along the way, we show how to work (safely!) around the cases where the type system may be too conservative.

An XQuery Programming Scenario

We present here a scenario of programming in XQuery inspired by the relational use case in [XQ-UC]. We follow the steps of a programmer who is writing a query that transforms data about an auction into an XHTML document. Each step in the scenario reveals an error in the query, explains how the programmer found the error, and explains how to correct the error.

We start with a description of the input data and schema and the output schema. The input data in Listing 4.1 is information about an auction that has been exported from a relational source in XML. The XML data conforms to the XML Schema in Listing 4.2. An auction contains a set of users, articles, and bids. A user has a name, a rating, and a unique identifier. An article is offered by a user, is available for sale between a start and end date, and has a reserve price and description. A bid associates a user with an article and a bid price.

Listing 4.1   Relational Auction Data in XML

```
<auction xmlns="http://www.example.com/auction">
  <users>
    <user id="U01">
      <name><first>Tom</first><last>Jones</last></name>
      <rating>B</rating>
    </user>
    <user id="U02">
      <name><first>Mary</first><last>Doe</last></name>
      <rating>A</rating>
    </user>
    <user id="U03">
      <name><first>Dee</first><last>Linquent</last></name>
      <rating>D</rating>
    </user>
    <user id="U04">
      <name><first>Roger</first><last>Smith</last></name>
      <rating>C</rating>
    </user>
    <user id="U05">
      <name><first>Jack</first><last>Sprat</last></name>
      <rating>B</rating>
    </user>
  </users>
  <articles>
    <article id="1001">
      <name>Red Bicycle</name>
      <seller idref="U01"/>
      <start_date>1999-01-05</start_date>
      <end_date>1999-01-20</end_date>
      <reserve_price>40</reserve_price>
    </article>
    <article id="1002">
      <name>Motorcycle</name>
      <seller idref="U02"/>
      <start_date>1999-02-11</start_date>
      <end_date>1999-03-15</end_date>
      <reserve_price>500</reserve_price>
      <description>In <em>really</em> good condition!</description>
    </article>
```

Listing 4.1   Relational Auction Data in XML *(continued)*

```
  <article id="1003">
    <name>Old Bicycle</name>
    <seller idref="U02"/>
    <start_date>1999-01-10</start_date>
    <end_date>1999-02-20</end_date>
    <reserve-price>10</reserve-price>
    <description>I bought it from Jack last month.</description>
  </article>
</articles>

<bids>
  <bid>
    <userid idref="U02"/>
    <articleno idref="1001"/>
    <amount>45</amount>
    <date>1999-01-11</date>
  </bid>
  <bid>
    <userid idref="U04"/>
    <articleno idref="1001"/>
    <amount>50</amount>
    <date>1999-01-13</date>
  </bid>
  <bid>
    <userid idref="U02"/>
    <articleno idref="1001"/>
    <amount>55</amount>
    <date>1999-01-15</date>
  </bid>
  <bid>
    <userid idref="U01"/>
    <articleno idref="1002"/>
    <amount>400</amount>
    <date>1999-02-14</date>
  </bid>
  <bid>
    <userid idref="U02"/>
    <articleno idref="1002"/>
    <amount>600</amount>
    <date>1999-02-16</date>
  </bid>
  <bid>
    <userid idref="U04"/>
    <articleno idref="1002"/>
    <amount>1000</amount>
    <date>1999-02-25</date>
  </bid>
```

Listing 4.1   Relational Auction Data in XML *(continued)*

```
<bid>
  <userid idref="U02"/>
  <articleno idref="1002"/>
  <amount>1200</amount>
  <date>1999-03-02</date>
</bid>
<bid>
  <userid idref="U05"/>
  <articleno idref="1003"/>
  <amount>20</amount>
  <date>1999-02-03</date>
</bid>
    </bids>
</auction>
```

Listing 4.2   XML Schema for the Relational Auction Data

```
<xs:schema targetNamespace="http://example.com/auction"
           xmlns:xs="http://www.w3.org/2001/XMLSchema"
           xmlns="http://www.example.com/auction">

  <xs:element name="auction">
    <xs:complexType>
      <xs:sequence>
        <xs:element name="users"/>
        <xs:element name="articles"/>
        <xs:element name="bids"/>
      </xs:sequence>
    </xs:complexType>
  </xs:element>

  <xs:element name="users">
    <xs:complexType>
      <xs:element ref="user" maxOccurs="unbounded"/>
    </xs:complexType>
  </xs:element>

  <xs:element name="articles">
    <xs:complexType>
      <xs:element ref="article" maxOccurs="unbounded"/>
    </xs:complexType>
  </xs:element>

  <xs:element name="bids">
    <xs:complexType>
      <xs:element ref="bid" maxOccurs="unbounded"/>
    </xs:complexType>
  </xs:element>
```

Listing 4.2   XML Schema for the Relational Auction Data *(continued)*

```
<xs:element name="rating" type="xs:string"/>

<xs:element name="user" type="User"/>
<xs:complexType name="User">
   <xs:sequence>
      <xs:element name="name">
        <xs:complexType>
           <xs:element name="first" type="xs:string" minOccurs="0"/>
           <xs:element name="last" type="xs:string"/>
        </xs:complexType>
      </xs:element>
      <xs:element ref="rating" minOccurs="0"/>
   </xs:sequence>
   <xs:attribute name="id" type="xs:ID" use="required"/>
</xs:complexType>

<xs:attribute name="idref" type="xs:IDREF"/>

<xs:element name="article" type="Article"/>
<xs:complexType name="Article">
   <xs:sequence>
      <xs:element name="name" type="xs:string"/>
      <xs:element name="seller">
         <xs:complexType>
            <xs:attribute ref="idref" use="required"/>
         </xs:complexType>
      </xs:element>
      <xs:element name="start_date" type="xs:date"/>
      <xs:element name="end_date" type="xs:date"/>
      <xs:element name="reserve_price" type="xs:decimal"/>
      <xs:element name="description" type="Freeform" minOccurs="0"/>
   </xs:sequence>
   <xs:attribute name="id" type="xs:ID" use="required"/>
</xs:complexType>

<xs:complexType name="Freeform" mixed="true">
  <xs:anyAttribute processContents="skip">
  <xs:any processContents="skip" minOccurs="0"
          maxOccurs="unbounded"/>
</xs:complexType>
```

Listing 4.2   XML Schema for the Relational Auction Data *(continued)*

```
<xs:element name="bid" type="Bid"/>
<xs:complexType name="Bid">
  <xs:sequence>
    <xs:element name="userid">
      <xs:complexType>
        <xs:attribute ref="idref" use="required"/>
      </xs:complexType>
    </xs:element>
    <xs:element name="articleno">
      <xs:complexType>
        <xs:attribute ref="idref" use="required"/>
      </xs:complexType>
    </xs:element>
    <xs:element name="amount" type="xs:decimal"/>
  </xs:sequence>
</xs:complexType>

</xs:schema>
```

The output is an XHTML document that can be rendered by a browser. It contains a table of all of the currently active auctions. For each auctioned article, the output table contains the name of the person selling the article, the last (i.e., most recent) bid on the article, and the expiration date for the article. The desired output page is shown in Figure 4.1 in the Mozilla browser. The output XHTML document must conform to the schema in Listing 4.3. This schema is a subset of the complete XHTML schema and includes headings, tables, paragraphs, and links.

Figure 4.1   Desired Result

Listing 4.3   XML Schema for XHTML

```
<xs:schema targetNamespace="http://www.w3.org/1999/xhtml"
           xmlns:xs="http://www.w3.org/2001/XMLSchema"
           xmlns="http://www.w3.org/1999/xhtml">

  <xs:element name="html" type="html.type"/>
  <xs:complexType name="html.type">
    <xs:sequence>
      <xs:element ref="head"/>
      <xs:element ref="body"/>
    </xs:sequence>
  </xs:complexType>

  <xs:element name="head" type="head.type"/>
  <xs:complexType name="head.type">
    <xs:element ref="title"/>
  </xs:complexType>

  <xs:element name="title" type="title.type"/>
  <xs:complexType name="title.type" mixed="true"/>

  <xs:element name="body" type="Block.type"/>

  <xs:complexType name="Block.type" mixed="true">
    <xs:choice minOccurs="0" maxOccurs="unbounded">
      <xs:element ref="h1"/>
      <xs:element ref="p"/>
      <xs:element ref="table"/>
    </xs:choice>
  </xs:complexType>

  <xs:element name="h1" type="heading.type"/>
  <xs:complexType name="heading.type" mixed="true">
    <xs:element ref="a" minOccurs="0" maxOccurs="unbounded"/>
  </xs:complexType>

  <xs:element name="p" type="p.type"/>
  <xs:complexType name="p.type" mixed="true">
    <xs:element ref="a" minOccurs="0" maxOccurs="unbounded"/>
  </xs:complexType>

  <xs:element name="a" type="a.type"/>
  <xs:complexType name="a.type" mixed="true">
    <xs:attribute name="href" type="xs:anyURI"/>
  </xs:complexType>

  <xs:element name="table" type="table.type"/>
  <xs:complexType name="table.type" mixed="true">
    <xs:element ref="tr" maxOccurs="unbounded"/>
  </xs:complexType>
```

Listing 4.3 XML Schema for XHTML *(continued)*

```
<xs:element name="tr" type="tr.type"/>
<xs:complexType name="tr.type">
   <xs:choice maxOccurs="unbounded">
      <xs:element ref="th"/>
      <xs:element ref="td"/>
   </xs:choice>
</xs:complexType>

<xs:element name="th" type="Block.type"/>
<xs:element name="td" type="Block.type"/>
```

```
</xs:schema>
```

The XQuery in Listing 4.4 takes as input the data in Listing 4.1 and generates an XHTML document containing the table of articles available for auction. The external global variable $input is bound to the input document in the query evaluation environment. Line [1] specifies that the auction schema namespace is the default element namespace for elements constructed by the query, and line [2] declares the namespace prefix 'x' for the XHTML output document. Line [3] defines a global variable $base containing the base URI for the output document. Lines [4–6] define the function makeURI, which converts a string to a URI and is called on lines [25] and [28]. Lines [9–18] construct an HTML element that contains the body of the page, which in turn contains a table that contains the headers for each column in the table. Lines [20–34] construct one row in the table for each article that is still available for auction. Each row contains the article's name (with a link to the article's description), the seller's name, the last bid, and the expiration date for the article.

Listing 4.4 XQuery

```
[1] default element namespace = "http://www.example.com/auction"
[2] declare namespace x = "http://www.w3.org/1999/xhtml"
[3] define variable $base :=
                    xs:anyURI("http://www.example.com/auction/")
[4] define function makeURI ($resource as xs:string) as xs:anyURI {
[5]   xs:anyURI(fn:concat(xs:string($base), $resource))
[6] }
[7] let $auction := $input/auction
[8] return
[9] <x:html>
[10]   <x:body>
[11]     <x:h1>Auctions</x:h1>
[12]     <x:table>
```

Listing 4.4   XQuery *(continued)*

```
[13]        <x:td>
[14]          <x:th>Item Name</th>
[15]          <x:th>Seller</x:th>
[16]          <x:th>Last Bid</x:th>
[17]          <x:th>Closes On</x:th>
[18]        </x:td>
[19]        {
[20]        for $article in $auction/articles/article[start_date <=
                                                     date()]
[21]        let $last_bid := $auction/bids/bid[articleno/@idref =
                                            $article/@id][last()]
[22]        return
[23]          <x:td>
[24]            <x:tr>
[25]              <x:a href="{ makeURI($article/@id) }">{
                                   data($article/anme) }</x:a>
[26]            </x:tr>
[27]            <x:tr>
[28]              <x:a href="{ makeURI($article//@idref) }">{
[29]                fn:data($auction/users/user[@id =
                                       $article//@idref]/name)
[30]              }</x:a>
[31]            </x:tr>
[32]            <x:tr>{ fn:data($last_bid/amount) }</x:tr>
[33]            <x:tr>{ fn:data($last_bid/date) }</x:tr>
[34]          </x:td>
[35]        }
[36]      </x:table>
[37]    </x:body>
[38] </x:html>
```

Debugging

Running the query on the input auction document results in the web page in Figure 4.2. As you can see, the table is a mess. The query apparently contains some errors. A closer look at the query reveals that the `tr` and `td` tags are inverted on lines [13–18] and [23–34]. Fixing that problem results in the Web page in Figure 4.3. On our second try, we see that the article names in the first column are missing. This results from an error on line [25], in which the article's element name is misspelled as `anme` instead of `name`. This expression always yields empty content, because an `article` element does not contain any `anme` elements. Fixing this problem results in the Web page in Figure 4.4.

Figure 4.2   First Try

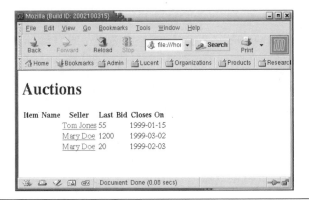

Figure 4.3   Second Try

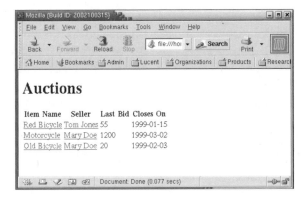

Figure 4.4   Third Try

On our third try, the output looks identical to the desired output in Figure 4.1, so we are almost done. It turns out, however, that the query still has an error that is not tripped by our example input data but might be exercised by other data. The link to the seller is computed by this expression on line [28] of Listing 4.4:

```
<x:a href="{ makeURI($article//@idref) }">
```

This expression accesses the `idref` attribute of some descendant of the article. In Listing 4.2, it appears that the `idref` attribute must be in the `seller` element, but we also see that the `description` element has type `xs:anyType` and, therefore, might contain `idref` attributes. If we apply this query to data in which some description element contains an `idref` attribute, the query will generate a run-time type error because the function `makeURI` expects one value, not multiple values, as input. When we evaluate the query on data of this kind (our fourth try), we get the error message shown below:

```
Line [28]: Run-time type error. Argument to function 'makeURI'
contains more than one value.
```

We can correct the error by replacing `$article//@idref` with `$article/seller/@idref`.

After four cycles of debugging by changing and then running the query, we believe that we have a query that will generate the correct output for any input auction data. Next, we consider how document validation and static typing can help to shorten this debugging cycle.

Validation

The XML community (and before that the SGML community) have long understood the importance of validating the formats of the input and output documents. This was first done using DTDs and more recently using XML Schema. A typical query-processing model validates the input against a specified input DTD or XML Schema, then evaluates the query on the input that generates the output, and finally validates the output against a specified output DTD or XML Schema.

To enable validation in our example, we rewrite the query to explicitly import the schemas of the input and output and to explicitly validate the input data. We do not need to explicitly validate the output, because element constructors implicitly validate the elements that they construct. The following code segment shows the changes to lines [1–2, 7] in the query shown in Listing 4.4 and adds line [2a]. (The other lines are identical to those in Listing 4.4, after correcting for the errors discovered in our first four tries.)

```
[1] import schema default element namespace =
                    "http://www.example.com/auction" at "auction.xsd"
[2] import schema namespace x = "http://www.w3.org/1999/xhtml" at
                                                          "xhtml.xsd"
[2a] default validation strict
    ...
[7] let $auction := validate { $input }
```

XML Schema provides three modes of validation (`strict`, `skip`, and `lax`). Line [2a] defines that the default validation mode for the query is `strict`. This query will raise an error at run-time if the input document does not conform to the auction schema or if the output document does not conform to the XHTML schema.

Validation aids the debugging cycle because it flags errors that we previously had to identify by examining the output. When we run the query, we get the following error message:

```
Validation error:  Missing 'x:head' element in 'x:html' element.
```

This error is raised because the XHTML schema requires a `head` element containing a `title` element. We did not detect this error during our debugging process because browsers try to produce output whenever they can, even if validation would fail. If we look closely, we see that the desired output in Figure 4.1 is not identical to the actual output in Figure 4.4, because the former contains the title "Auctions" in the title bar, whereas the latter contains only the name of the browser.

How would validation affect our earlier debugging cycles? Validation detects the first error in which we inverted the `tr` and `td` elements. But validation fails to detect the second error, in which a misspelled element name leads to empty content, because the XHTML schema permits empty content in the `"a"` (anchor) element. Validation also fails to detect the third error, which occurs for input data in which description elements contain `idref` attributes. This happens because the input data that triggers the bug is perfectly valid against the given input schema, and if the input does trigger the bug, there will be no output data to validate against the output schema, instead the `makeURI` function will raise an error.

Static Typing

So far, our debugging cycle has consisted of running the query, which may raise a validation error or produce output, possibly observing an error in the output, identifying and correcting the bug in the query, and then running the query again. Static typing can help us to shorten this cycle.

Static typing differs from validation in that validation detects the presence of certain kinds of errors in the format of the data, whereas static typing guarantees their absence. In particular, static typing performs a conservative analysis of the query and raises a static type error when the analysis cannot guarantee that the structure of the result conforms to the structure required by the output schema.

Static typing can greatly accelerate the debugging cycle. First, it can spot errors during static analysis rather than at run-time. Second, it can detect many errors at once without requiring multiple runs of the query. Third, it can spot errors without the need for a tester to concoct data that will exercise those errors.

The result of static typing the query in Listing 4.4 (after the revisions above) is shown in Listing 4.5.

Listing 4.5 Static Errors

```
Line [10]: Element 'x:body' encountered where element 'x:head' expected.

Line [13]: Element 'x:td' encountered where element 'x:tr' expected.

Line [23]: Element 'x:td' encountered where element 'x:tr' expected.

Line [25]: Expression '$article/anme' is always empty.

Line [28]: Argument to function 'makeURI' has actual type
           ( attribute(@idref) | attribute(@idref,xs:anySimpleType) )+
           instead of expected type 'xs:string'.
```

The error on line [10] is discovered because the static type inferred for the content of the x:html element does not conform to the static type declared for the content of the html element in the XHTML schema in Listing 4.3. Similarly, the errors on lines [13] and [23] are discovered because the static type inferred for the content of the table element does not conform to the static type declared for the content of the table element in Listing 4.3. The error on line [25] is discovered because the static type inferred for the expression $article/anme is the empty sequence, since the static type of an article element does not contain any anme elements. The error on line [28] is discovered because the static type inferred for the expression $article//@idref is

```
( attribute(@idref) | attribute(@idref,xs:anySimpleType) )+
```

but the static type declared for argument to the function makeURI is xs:string. The type above is a mouthful. Where does it come from? There is one idref attribute declared in $article/seller, and there may be zero or more idref attributes of any simple type in $article/description; hence, there are one or more idref attributes in total.

Correcting all of these type errors yields the query shown in Listing 4.6. (The corrections are in bold italics.) This query passes static type-checking and yields the desired result shown in Figure 4.1. In our example, all of the errors were type errors and were detected by the static type system. This may not always be the case, however; for example, a query may contain other kinds of errors that can only be detected during evaluation.

Listing 4.6   Corrected Query

```
[1] default element namespace = "http://www.example.com/auction"
[2] declare namespace x = "http://www.w3.org/1999/xhtml"
[2a] default validation strict
[3] define variable $base :=
                    xs:anyURI("http://www.example.com/auction/")
[4] define function makeURI ($resource as xs:string) as xs:anyURI {
[5]   xs:anyURI(fn:concat(xs:string($base), $resource))
[6] }
[7] let $auction := $input/auction
[8] return
[9] <x:html>
[9a]    <x:head><x:title>Auctions</x:title></x:head>
[10]    <x:body>
[11]       <x:h1>Auctions</x:h1>
[12]       <x:table>
```

Listing 4.6   Corrected Query *(continued)*

```
[13]      <x:tr>
[14]        <x:th>Item Name</th>
[15]        <x:th>Seller</x:th>
[16]        <x:th>Last Bid</x:th>
[17]        <x:th>Closes On</x:th>
[18]      </x:tr>
[19]      {
[20]        for $article in $auction/articles/article[start_date <=
                                                      date()]
[21]        let $last_bid :=
            $auction/bids/bid[articleno/@idref=$article/@id][last()]
[22]        return
[23]          <x:tr>
[24]            <x:td>
[25]              <x:a href="{xs:anyURI($article/@id)}">{
                                         data($article/name) }</x:a>
[26]            </x:td>
[27]            <x:td>
[28]              <x:a href="{xs:anyURI($article/seller/@idref)}">{
[29]                fn:data($auction/users/user[@id =
                                          $article//@idref]/name)
[30]                }</x:a>
[31]            </x:td>
[32]            <x:td>{ fn:data($last_bid/amount) }</x:td>
[33]            <x:td>{ fn:data($last_bid/date) }</x:td>
[34]          </x:tr>
[35]      }
[36]    </x:table>
[37]  </x:body>
[38] </x:html>
```

Getting Started with Types

We hope by now you are convinced of the value of a static type system. Now that we know what a static type system can do, we will describe how it works. The following sections describe how the type system assigns a type to different kinds of expressions. The expressions described include literals and operators, variables, function calls, conditionals, paths, FLWORs, and element constructors. We begin with a description of XML Schema, XQuery types, and XQuery values, and then explain how they all relate.

XML Schema and XQuery Types

The type system of XQuery is based on XML Schema, so to understand types in XQuery, we must first understand XML Schema. XML Schema has so many features, however, that we can only describe its basic features: simple types and complex types, anonymous types, global and local declarations, and derivation by restriction.

As we describe XML Schema's features, we show how they are represented in the type notation used in the XQuery **formal semantics** [XQ-FS] so that you can understand the type errors that may arise. The formal type notation is simpler and more concise than the XML Schema notation, in part because it serves a different purpose. XML Schema is designed for a user's convenience and provides many alternatives for modeling data and documents, whereas the XQuery type notation is designed for the type system's convenience and provides orthogonal (i.e., nonredundant) features for constructing types. Allowing only one way to construct a particular type, makes it easier for the type system to compare types, which it must do when type-checking a query.

You do not need to learn all of the formal type notation, but you do need to understand that it exists. Later we describe sequence types, the subset of the XQuery type notation for referring to types in XQuery expressions. Chapter 5 describes the relationship between XML Schema and XQuery's type system in more detail.

In XML Schema, element declarations may be *global*, at the top-level, or *local*, nested within a type declaration. The XML Schema for our auction data in Listing 4.2 contains both **global element declarations** (e.g., auction, users) and **local element declarations** (e.g., name, first, last). Local elements with the same name may have different content models. For example, the name element in element user is a complex type containing first and last elements, while the name element in article contains a string.

In the formal type notation, the globally declared elements user and rating are represented by the following declarations:

```
define element user of type User
define element rating of type xs:string
```

An element declaration associates an element name with a type. A type is either a predefined or a user-defined type. The predefined types include the forty-four built-in datatypes defined in [SCHEMA-2] (e.g., `xs:string`, `xs:integer`, etc.) plus the five types: `xdt:yearMonthDuration`, `xdt:dayTimeDuration`, `xdt:untypedAtomic`, `xs:anySimpleType`, and `xs:anyType`.[1] A user-defined type is any type defined in an imported XML Schema document.

In XML Schema, a type may be globally named or may be specified in an element declaration without a name. An unnamed type is called an *anonymous type*. Our auction schema has four named types (`User`, `Article`, `Freeform`, and `Bid`), and four anonymous types associated with the local elements `User/name`, `Article/seller`, `Bid/userid`, and `Bid/articleno`.

For example, here is how declaration of the type `User` is expressed in the formal type notation:

```
define type User {
  attribute id of type xs:ID ,
  element name of type AnonymousType1 ,
  element rating ?
}
define type AnonymousType1 {
  element first of type xs:string ? ,
  element last of type xs:string
}
```

The translation from XML Schema into the formal type notation invents a unique name for each anonymous type; thus, every element has a named type.

A complex type declaration associates a name with a content model. The name `User`, for example, is associated with the content model containing one `id` attribute and one locally declared `name` element followed by an optional global `rating` element. The name `AnonymousType1` is associated with the content model containing an optional `first` element followed by one `last` element. Types can be combined with the operators for sequence (`,`) and union (`|`), in addition to the occurrence indicators zero or one (`?`), one or more (`+`), or zero or more (`*`).

---

[1] The `xdt` namespace is used for special data types required by XPath and XQuery but not defined in XML Schema.

In XML Schema, a simple type declaration associates a name with an atomic type, a list type, or a union type; a simple type may also specify constraining facets. The atomic types include the forty four built-in datatypes defined in [SCHEMA-2]. Here is an example of a list type.

```
<xs:simpleType name="IntegerList">
    <xs:list itemType="xs:integer"/>
</xs:simpleType>
```

In the formal type notation, list types are formed using the occurrence indicators ?, +, and *. Here is the declaration corresponding to the simple type above:

```
define type IntegerList { xs:integer + }
```

Union types are formed using the choice operator |. The XQuery type system does not represent constraining facets, because facets typically constrain values and therefore cannot be checked or enforced statically.

New simple and complex types may be derived by restriction. Listing 4.7 shows a type named NewUser that restricts the type User by requiring that the first and rating elements be present. The element newuser has type NewUser.

Listing 4.7   The NewUser Type Derived by Restriction of the Type User

```
<xs:complexType name="NewUser">
  <xs:complexContent>
    <xs:restriction base="User">
      <xs:sequence>
        <xs:element name="name">
          <xs:complexType>
            <xs:element name="first" type="xs:string"/>
            <xs:element name="last" type="xs:string"/>
          </xs:complexType>
        </xs:element>
        <xs:element name="rating" type="xs:string"/>
      </xs:sequence>
      <xs:attribute name="id" type="xs:ID" use="required"/>
    </xs:complexType>
  </xs:complexContent>
</xs:complexType>
<xs:element name="newuser" type="NewUser"/>
```

Listing 4.8 shows the corresponding type declarations in the formal type notation.

Listing 4.8   Type Declarations for `NewUser` in the Formal Type Notation

```
define type NewUser restricts User {
  attribute id of type xs:ID ,
  element name of type AnonymousType2 ,
  element rating
}
define type AnonymousType2 {
  element first of type xs:string ,
  element last of type xs:string
}
define element newuser of type NewUser
```

Derivation by restriction declares a relationship between two types. This relationship depends on both names and content models, in the sense that one name may be derived by restriction from another name only if every value that matches the content model of the first also matches the content model of the second. When one type is derived from another by restriction, it is fine to pass the restricted type where the base type is expected. For example, here is a function that takes as its argument an element with any name and with type `User`.

```
define function user-name($user as element(*,User)) as xs:string {...}
```

This function can be applied to either a `user` or `newuser` element.

There is a type `xs:anyType` from which all other types are derived. If a type definition does not specify otherwise, it is considered a restriction of `xs:anyType`. There is also a type `xs:anySimpleType` that is derived from `xs:anyType` and from which all other simple types are derived. XML Schema also supports derivation by extension, which we do not discuss here (see the XQuery formal semantics [XQ-FS] and Chapter 5 for details).

Values

Every XQuery expression evaluates to a *value* in the XQuery data model. Every value in XQuery is a sequence of individual *items*. Sequences are central to XQuery's semantics—so much so that one item and a sequence containing that item are indistinguishable. An item is either an atomic value or a node. We have seen many examples of atomic values, including strings and integers. A node is either an element, attribute, document, text, comment, or processing instruction.[2]

Every atomic value, element node, and attribute node has an associated XQuery type. The process of XML Schema validation specifies how elements and attributes are labeled with types. Input data is validated, and elements and attributes created while processing a query may also be validated. Atomic values are labeled with one of the twenty-three XML Schema primitive types (e.g., xs:string, xs:integer, and xs:decimal). Element and attribute nodes are labeled with any of the forty-nine predefined types listed earlier, and any type specified in an XML Schema used for validation.

Here is a document fragment of the input document in Listing 4.1.

```
<user id="U02">
  <name><first>Mary</first><last>Doe</last></name>
  <rating>A</rating>
</user>
```

After validation, this document fragment is represented by the following XQuery values. We use this notation to illustrate the labeling of elements and attributes—it is not a valid XQuery expression, because XQuery does not support the of type notation in element and attribute constructors.

```
element user of type User {
  attribute id of type xs:ID { "U02" } ,
  element name of type AnonymousType1 {
    element first of type xs:string { "Mary" } ,
    element last of type xs:string { "Doe" } ,
  } ,
  element rating of type xs:string { "A" }
}
```

The element user is labeled with type User, and the attribute id is labeled with type xs:ID, etc. We can use the fn:data function to extract the typed data. If we apply fn:data to the first element above, we get the value xs:string("Mary"), which is an atomic value labeled with the type xs:string.

---

[2] Although namespace nodes exist in the XQuery data model, they are not really values; instead, they are used to define the scope of namespace prefixes. They do not contribute to an expression's type, so we do not discuss them here.

Sequence Types

XQuery provides a notation for referring to types in queries, called a *sequence type*, that is a subset of the formal type notation. Sequence types can be used in several XQuery constructs, including function declarations, variable declarations in `let` and `for` expressions, and in `type-switch`, `instance of`, and `treat as` expressions. Table 4.1 provides some examples of sequence types.

A sequence type may contain an optional context for specifying a local element; if no context is given, then the element is global. Some examples are shown in Table 4.2.

TABLE 4.1   Examples of Sequence Types and What They Match

Sequence Type	What It Matches
`xs:decimal`	Atomic value of any type derived from `xs:decimal`
`empty()`	The empty sequence
`item()`	Any item
`node()`	Any node
`document-node()`	Any document node
`text()`	Any text node
`element()`	Any element
`element(x:td)`	Element `x:td` as defined in the imported XHTML Schema
`element(*,x:Block.type)`	Any element of type `x:Block.type`
`element(x:td,x:Block.type)`	Element with name `x:td` of type `x:Block.type`
`attribute()`	Any attribute
`attribute(@href)`	Attribute `href` as defined in the imported XHTML Schema
`attribute(@*,xs:anyURI)`	Any attribute of type `xs:anyURI`
`attribute(@href,xs:anyURI)`	Attribute with name `href` of type `xs:anyURI`
`comment()`	Any comment node
`processing-instruction()`	Any processing-instruction node

TABLE 4.2   Sequence Types for Local Elements

Sequence Type	What It Matches
element(article)	Global element article
element(article/name)	Local element name in global element article
element(user)	Global element user
element(type(User)/context)	Local element name in global type User
element(type(User)/name/first)	Local element first in element name in global type User
element(type(User)/name/last)	Local element last in element name in global type User

Any sequence type (other than empty) may be followed by one of the occurrence indicators zero or one (?), one or more (+), or zero or more (*). Here are some examples:

```
xs:decimal?    Matches the empty sequence or a decimal value
element()+     Matches any sequence of one or more elements
item()*        Matches any sequence
```

We saw earlier that the formal type notation permits us to combine types with the type operators for sequence (,) and union (|), in addition to the occurrence indicators (?, +, and *). This additional expressiveness is necessary to enable us to assign accurate types to expressions. Here are some examples:

```
(1, "two", 3.14e0) has type (xs:integer,xs:string,xs:double)
if ($x<$y) then "three" else 4.00 has type (xs:string | xs:decimal)
```

Even though sequence types do not include the types above, they might appear in an error message. We'll see more examples of such types in the next section.

Schema Import

A sequence type may refer to an element, attribute, or type defined in an XML Schema, if that schema has been imported in the prolog. The earlier section entitled "Validation" presented an example (the first two revised lines of Listing 4.4) with two schema imports.

```
[1] import schema default element namespace =
                    "http://www.example.com/auction" at "auction.xsd"
[2] import schema namespace x =
                    "http://www.w3.org/1999/xhtml" at "xhtml.xsd"
```

This imports two schemas defining two namespaces (as named by the URLs after the equal signs), defined by resources at the specified locations (as given by the `at` clauses). Just as in other uses of XML Schema, the location is a hint: The XQuery processor may use it to locate the schema to import, or it may find the schema to import by some other means. The namespace URL is required if the schema has a namespace; the location is optional unless the schema has no namespace. If both a namespace and a location are given, it is an error if the schema at the given location does not have as its target the given namespace.

The first import specifies that the first namespace is the default, and the second import binds the prefix x to the second namespace. Any reference to an element or type with no prefix refers to the default namespace. Thus, for example, `article` refers to an element in the first namespace, and `x:h1` refers to an element in the second.

Relating Values and Types

Types are used for two related but distinct purposes in XQuery, connected with two phases of executing a query: analysis time (when static type analysis is performed) and evaluation time (when the query is evaluated to yield an answer).

At evaluation time, the value of a query depends upon the types that label values. For example, when comparing two values, the comparison operator used depends on whether the two values are labeled as strings or numbers; if one is labeled as a string and the other as a number, it is a type error. Arithmetic operations also depend upon these labels: The result of adding two integers is an integer, the result of adding two decimals is a decimal, and the result of adding an integer and a decimal is a decimal. It is also possible to explicitly refer to type labels , as in the following example:

```
//element(*,x:Block.type)
```

This returns all elements in an XHTML document labeled with type `x:Block.type`.

At analysis time, each expression is labeled with a type. XQuery queries are compositional, in that each query expression is built from smaller subexpressions. Just as evaluation combines the value of subexpressions to compute the value of the expression as a whole, static typing combines the types assigned to subexpressions to compute the type of the expression as a whole. In other words, both evaluation and type assignment proceed bottom up.

Evaluation-time types and analysis-time types are closely related. The evaluation-time type labeling a value must conform to the analysis-time type assigned to the expression that yields that value. For instance, if an expression is assigned the type `xs:decimal`, the possible values of that expression may be labeled with type `xs:decimal` or `xs:integer` or any other type derived from `xs:decimal`.

The formal semantics of XQuery, introduced in Chapter 5, list the rules for how to compute the value of an expression from the values of its subexpressions and how to compute the type assigned to an expression from the types of its subexpressions. In the remaining sections of this chapter, we explain by example the rules for computing the type of an expression.

Literals and Operators

Now that we know about values and types in XQuery, we describe how the static type system assigns types to expressions. The static type system checks that the type of an expression is compatible with the type required by the context in which the expression is used. If they are not compatible, the static type system raises a type error.

In the remaining sections, the term *type* refers to the static type associated with an XQuery expression. We use the phrase *dynamic type* whenever referring to the type associated with a value.

Literals are the simplest XQuery expressions. Every literal expression has one of the types `xs:string`, `xs:integer`, `xs:decimal`, or `xs:double`. Here are some examples:

`"hello"` **has type** `xs:string`

```
42 has type xs:integer
42.00 has type xs:decimal
4.2e1 has type xs:double
```

(Note: XQuery could have given `42` the more specific type `xs:positive-Integer`, which is derived from `xs:integer`, but for simplicity the language specification does not distinguish between positive and negative integer literals.)

The type of an arithmetic operation depends on the types of its operands. Here are some examples:

```
42 + 69 has type xs:integer
42.00 + 69.00 has type xs:decimal
4.2e1 + 6.9e1 has type xs:double
```

If the arguments are both numeric, but have different types, then one type is *promoted* to match the other (see Glossary, s.v. "type promotion"). The order of promotion follows: `xs:integer`, `xs:decimal`, `xs:float`, `xs:double`. Here are some examples of expressions whose types are promoted:

```
42 + 69.00 has type xs:decimal
4.2e1 + 69 has type xs:double
42.00 + 6.9e1 has type xs:double
```

In the first line, the type of the first argument is promoted from `xs:integer` to match the type of the second argument, `xs:decimal`. These static type rules correspond to exactly the same rules that are used to promote values at evaluation time.

It is also possible to construct dates and durations by applying constructor functions to string literals (e.g., `xs:date("1994-01-18")`) and to perform arithmetic on dates and durations when sensible (for example, one may add a date to a duration, or multiply a duration by a decimal, but not add a date to a date). The details are spelled out in the XQuery specification [XQ-LANG].

A static type error is raised if the operands do not have sensible types. For instance, addition does not apply to strings. Here are some examples:

```
"one" + "two" is a static type error
"42" + 69.00 is a static type error
```

A comparison operation always yields a Boolean. The operation is well typed if the operands have types that can sensibly be compared. Here are some examples:

```
"one" < "two" has type xs:boolean
1 < 2 has type xs:boolean
1 < 2.0 has type xs:boolean
```

A static type error is raised if the operands cannot be sensibly compared. Here is an example that raises a type error because a string cannot be compared to an integer:

```
"one" < 2 is a static type error
```

The sequence operator concatenates two sequences. Here are some examples:

```
(1, "two", 3.14e0) has type (xs:integer, xs:string, xs:double)
(<th>value</th>,<td>1</td>) has type (element(th), element(td))
```

Note that the type of each sequence expression is a sequence type. Even though you cannot use sequence types explicitly in queries, such a type might appear in an error message.

Variables

A variable may be bound by a `let` clause in a FLWOR expression. The type of the variable is the same as the type of its defining expression. Here are some examples:

```
let $z := 1+2 return $z+$z has type xs:integer
let $z := 1e0+1.0 return $z+$z has type xs:double
```

In the first `let` expression, the expression 1+2 has type xs:integer; therefore, the variable $z also has type xs:integer, and the return expression is typed assuming that $z has type xs:integer. Similarly, in the second expression, variable $z has type xs:double. The static type system keeps track of the types of variables in the **static environment;** whenever a variable is bound, the static environment is extended by associating the variable with the computed type.

The type of a variable may also be declared explicitly. In this case, a static type error is raised if the type of the defining expression is not a subtype of the declared type. Here are some examples:

```
let $x as xs:integer := 1+2 return $x+$x has type xs:integer
let $x as xs:decimal := 1+2 return $x+$x has type xs:decimal
```

The second example is well typed, because `xs:integer` is a subtype of `xs:decimal`.

One type is a subtype of another if every value that matches the first type always matches the second type. In particular, whenever one type is derived from a second type by restriction, the first type is a subtype of the second. So `xs:integer`, for example, is a subtype of `xs:decimal`, and the type `NewUser` defined earlier is a subtype of the type `User`.

Subtyping does not include type promotion. So `xs:integer` is not a subtype of `xs:double`, even though it is beneath it in the promotion hierarchy.

```
let $x as xs:double := 1+2 return $x+$x is a static type error
```

One can specify promotion by including an explicit type coercion, with or without a type declaration.

```
let $x := xs:double(1+2) return $x+$x has type xs:double
let $x as xs:double := xs:double(1+2) return $x+$x has type
xs:double
```

The type of an expression depends only on the type of its subexpressions. Thus, a static type error will be raised whenever the type of the defining expression is not a subtype of the declared type, even if the value belongs to the declared type. The `let` expression defining variable `$y` below is an example of such a static type error:

```
let $x as xs:decimal := 1,
    $y as xs:integer := $x+$x
return $y+$y
```

Even though the value of `$x` is an integer at run-time, the type of `$x` is decimal for the purposes of static analysis.

Functions

A function call consists of the name of the function and a list of comma-separated expressions, which are the arguments to the function. Here is an example:

```
fn:concat("http://www.example.com/auction/", "1001")
```

This function call applies the built-in function `fn:concat` to the values of the literal expressions "`http://www.example.com/auction/`" and "`1001`" and returns the concatenation of its arguments.

A function's *signature* specifies the required types of its arguments and the type of its result. The XQuery specifications (see [XQ-FO]) provide the signatures for all built-in XQuery functions. Here is the signature for the function `fn:concat`:

```
fn:concat($op1 as xs:string ?, $op2 as xs:string ?) as xs:string
```

This signature specifies that the first and second argument to `fn:concat` must each be the empty sequence or a string and that the value returned will be a string. The signature serves as a contract between the function call and the function: The function call is required to provide an empty sequence or a string for each argument, and in turn the function guarantees to return a string. (The argument to `fn:concat` may be the empty sequence because the function treats the empty sequence as the zero-length string.)

A function call is well typed if the types of the argument expressions match the required types of the function's arguments declared in its signature. An argument type matches the required type if the argument type is derived from the required type or if the argument type can be promoted to the required type.

In the following examples of function calls, we assume the variable `$resource` is of any type derived from `xs:string`.

```
fn:concat("http://www.example.com/auction/", $resource) has
type xs:string
fn:concat((), "http://www.example.com/auction/") has type
xs:string
fn:concat(10e1, $resource) is a static type error
```

The third example raises a type error because the literal expression `10e1`
has type `xs:double`, which is not derived from or promotable to the
required type `xs:string ?`.

A user-defined function consists of the function's signature and its body,
which is an expression. A function definition is well typed if the type of
the body expression matches the return type. Here is the function
`makeURI` from Listing 4.4:

```
define function makeURI ($resource as xs:string) as xs:anyURI {
  xs:anyURI(fn:concat(xs:string($base), $resource))
}
```

The function `makeURI` takes one string argument and returns one URI
value. The function is well-typed because the type of its body is
`xs:anyURI`, which matches the required return type.

As a convenience to programmers, XQuery permits operators and functions that require sequences of atomic values as arguments to be applied
to any item sequence. Before applying the operator or function, the function `fn:data` is applied to convert the item sequence to a sequence of
atomic values. Each atomic value in the item sequence is returned
unchanged, and each node is converted to its *typed value*. In the XQuery
specification, automatic conversion of arguments is called *atomization*.
For example, an `idref` attribute defined in Listing 4.2 must contain one
IDREF value. In the following examples of atomization, we assume the
variable `$idref` has type `attribute idref`:

```
makeURI($idref) has type xs:anyURI
fn:concat("Item ID is:", $idref) has type xs:string
$idref * 0.07 is a static type error
```

The first and second function calls are both well typed, because the
atomic content of `$idref` is `xs:IDREF`, which is derived from `xs:string`,
and `xs:string` is the required type of `makeURI` and `fn:concat`. The
third call is a static type error, because `xs:idref` is not derived from or
promotable to any numeric type.

Conditionals

A conditional expression consists of a condition and two branch expressions. The condition must be a Boolean. If both branches have the same type, then the type of the conditional expression is also that type. Assume that $x and $y are both integers. Here is an example:

```
if ($x<$y) then 3 else 4 has type xs:integer
```

If the two branches have different types, then the type of the conditional expression is the union of those types. Here is an example:

```
if ($x<$y) then "three" else 4.00 has type (xs:string | xs:decimal)
```

Recall that in the XQuery formal type notation, a vertical bar indicates the union of two types. The union of a type with itself is just the type, so the rule about conditionals with two branches of the same type is just a special case of the rule for two branches with different types.

Unlike arithmetic operators, conditionals involve no notion of promotion. Here is an example:

```
if ($x < $y) then 4.2e1 else 69 has type (xs:double | xs:integer)
```

At run-time, if the `else` branch is taken, then we do not expect the integer `69` to be promoted to a double, and so the type system also does not perform any promotion.

When arithmetic is performed on an operand expression with a union type, promotion is applied to each member of the union separately. Here is an example:

```
(if ($x < $y) then 4.2e1 else 69) + 0.5 has type (xs:double | xs:decimal)
```

For the `then` branch, the promotion rule specifies that adding an `xs:double` and an `xs:decimal` yields an `xs:double`, and for the `else` branch, the promotion rule specifies that adding an `xs:integer` and an `xs:decimal` yields an `xs:decimal`, thus the type of the result is (`xs:double` | `xs:decimal`).

Early in this chapter, we explained that static type analysis is conservative: The type assigned to an expression always contains all possible values of the expression, but often it will contain more values than the expression can yield. We have already seen one example of this, where 42 is assigned the type xs:integer rather than the type xs:positiveInteger. Here is another example. Say that $x, $y, $z, and $n are four integer variables, and say that the function fermat($x, $y, $z, $n) returns true if $n is greater than 2 and $x^{$n} + $y^{$n} = $z^{$n}. Now consider this conditional expression:

```
(if (fermat($x,$y,$z,$n) then 1 else "two") + 3
```

This raises a static type error. After 350 years of uncertainty, mathematicians now know that the else branch of the conditional expression above can never be executed. But we don't expect a query analyzer to be clever enough to know that. So the typing rules presume that either branch of a conditional may be executed, and this is a good enough compromise for practical purposes.

Path Expressions

We saw earlier in the chapter many examples of path expressions. Here are some more:

```
$auction/articles has type element(articles)
$auction/articles/article has type element(article)+
$auction/itesm/article is a static type error
```

These assume that $auction has type element(auction) as defined in Listing 4.2. The first expression has type element(articles) because there is exactly one articles element in an auction element. The second expression has type element(article)+ because there are one or more article elements in an articles element. The third expression is a static type error, because there is no itesm element in an auction element. Here is how the error is caught: the type rules assign to the last path expression the type empty(), which is the type of the empty sequence. Assigning this type to any expression other than () raises a static type error, since it is unlikely someone would intentionally write an expression other than () that always returns the empty sequence.

Another operator on path expressions is union.

```
$auction/(articles | users) has type ( element(articles) |
element(users) )+
```

This path expression selects all `articles` and `users` elements that are children of the `auction` element. The static typing inference rules compute the type in two parts: a choice of items and an occurrence indicator. The `auction` element has one `articles` element as a child, and one `users` element as a child, so the result is a choice of `articles` or `users` elements. The occurrence indicator is one-or-more, which is computed by approximate arithmetic: A union of one item and one item contains one-or-more items.

One might wonder why this expression is not given a more precise type, such as the following:

```
$auction/(articles | users) doesn't have type (element(users) ,
element(articles))
```

From the auction schema, we know that an `auction` element contains exactly one `users` element followed by one `articles` element. So why not give this more precise type? There is a trade-off here: Increased precision of typing requires increased complexity in the typing rules. As an engineering judgment, the designers of XQuery chose simple rules that apply uniformly to all path expressions, and yield types good enough for most practical purposes.

A type consisting of a choice of items and an occurrence indicator is called a **factored type**. There is always a unique, best way to factor a type: Take the union of all items that occur in the type and compute the occurrence indicator by approximate arithmetic (e.g., one plus one is one-or-more).

If the type of a sequence is in factored form, then any reordering of the sequence also has the same factored type. The result of a path expression is always sorted in document order; therefore, the type of a path expression is always in factored form, and any reordering of the sequence to preserve document order does not change its type. For instance, `users` precedes `articles` in the declaration of the `auction` element, but this doesn't affect the type above.

Path expressions may contain wild cards. Here are some examples:

```
$auction/* has type ( element(users) | element(articles) |
element(bids) )+
$auction/*/* has type ( element(user) | element(article) |
element(bid) )+
```

An `auction` element has three children, the `users` and `articles` and `bids` elements. So the first expression's type is a choice of these three element types, and its occurrence indicator is one-or-more (since one plus one plus one is one-or-more). A `users` element has as children one or more `user` elements, and similarly for the other two. So the second expression's type is a choice of the three element types, and its occurrence indicator is one-or-more (since one-or-more plus one-or-more plus one-or-more is one-or-more).

Another operator on path expressions is the descendant operator. Here is an example:

```
$article//@idref has type
(attribute(@idref,xs:string) |
attribute(@idref,xs:anySimpleType))+
```

This example appeared in line [28] of Listing 4.4 and generated the type error reported earlier in the section entitled "Debugging." There is one `idref` attribute of type string in a `seller` element, and there may be zero or more `idref` attributes of any simple type in an `description` element. So the expression's type is a choice of the two attribute types, and its occurrence indicator is one-or-more (since one plus zero-or-more is one-or-more).

The type of a path expression may include a locally declared element. Here's a path expression that selects all `name` elements occurring in `user` or `article` elements:

```
$auction//(user|article)/name has type
( element(type(User)/name) | element(type(Article)/name) )+
```

A `user` element contains one `name` element locally declared in type `User`, and an `article` element contains one `name` element locally declared in type `Article`; therefore, the expression's type contains both locally declared elements.

The expression `$auction//name` selects all `name` elements within `$auction`. Referring back to the schema in Listing 4.2, we see that it explicitly declares `name` elements in the two places already considered (context `User` and context `Article`), but it also allows for `name` elements within the `description` element, which is permitted to contain any content whatsoever. So the type of the expression is

```
( element(type(User)/name) | element(type(Bid)/name) |
element(name,xs:anyType) )+
```

Predicates

A predicate selects nodes in a path expression that satisfy a given expression. Here is an example:

```
$auction/articles/article[start_date <= date()] has type
element(article)*
```

The path extracts one or more articles from the auction, and then selects zero, one, or more of these.

Sometimes, predicates are intended to single out a particular item, but, in general, the type system is not clever enough to know this.

```
$auction/articles/article[@id=$id] has type element(article)*
```

Here the type assigned suggests that there may be zero, one, or many articles. But if the `id` attribute is used as a key, then there will be at most one result, and if `$id` is bound to a valid key, then there will be exactly one result. XQuery provides three functions, `exactly-one`, `zero-or-one`, and `one-or-more` to allow the query writer to provide additional information about the number of items that might be returned by an expression.

```
exactly-one($auction/articles/article[@id=$id]) has type
element(article)
zero-or-one($auction/articles/article[@id=$id]) has type
element(article)?
```

At analysis time, these occurrence functions adjust the type of their result accordingly; at evaluation time, they check that the argument sequence contains a number of items in the specified range and raise an error if it does not.

The designers of XQuery separated errors into two classes: *type errors* are either caught at analysis time (if static typing is in use) or at evaluation time (if static typing is not in use); other errors may be caught at any time. Occurrence functions only raise errors at evaluation time, so the errors they raise are not classed as type errors.

Predicates may be used to pick out elements according to their position. Predicates with numeric type (rather than Boolean) select elements at the current position; and a Boolean predicate may mention the special function `position()`. Here are some examples:

```
$auction/articles/article[1] has type element(article)
$auction/articles/article[2] has type element(article)?
$auction/articles/article[position() > 2] has type element(article)*
```

The first expression selects the first article; since there are one or more articles in an auction, this always yields exactly one article. The second expression selects the second article; since there are one or more articles in an auction, this may yield zero or one articles. The third expression selects all articles after the second article; since there are one or more articles in an auction, this may yield zero or more articles.

More than one predicate may appear in a path expression.

```
$auction/articles/article[start_date <= current_date()]
has type element(article)*
$auction/articles/article[start_date <= current_date()][1]
has type element(article)?
```

The first expression picks out all articles with a start date before the current date; there may be zero or more such articles. The second predicate selects the first of these, if there is a first, and so has a type indicating zero or one article. Sometimes, the query writer will know that there is at least one auction currently in progress, and will want to adjust the type accordingly.

```
exactly-one($auction/articles/article[start_date <= current_date()][1])
has type element(article)
```

This uses the `exactly-one()` function described above.

The following two expressions have the same meaning, but different types.

```
$auction/articles/article[1] has type element(article)
$auction/articles/article[position() = 1] has type element(article)*
```

The designers of XQuery decided to include a special type rule for the case where the predicate is an integer literal, because it is so common. Note, however, if the predicate is an integer-valued expression, then no special rule applies, and the type can be more general than one might expect. Here are four examples:

```
$auction/articles/article[$i] has type element(article)*
$auction/articles/article[last()] has type element(article)*
$auction/articles/article[position()] has type element(article)*
$auction/articles/(let $i := position() return article[$i]) has type
element(article)*
```

These have exactly the same meaning, and the same type, as these examples:

```
$auction/articles/article[position() = $i]
has type element(article)*
$auction/articles/article[position() = last()]
has type element(article)*
$auction/articles/article[position() = position()]
has type element(article)*
$auction/articles/(let $i := position() return article[position() = $i])
has type element(article)*
```

Note that the second-to-last of these will return every article, which shows why, in general, a predicate that has an integer value might still select more than one item.

FLWOR Expressions

The FLWOR expression is the workhorse of XQuery: It allows a user to iterate over sequences of values, compute intermediate results, and conditionally filter values. Like the typing of path expressions, the typing of FLWOR expressions also relies on factored types.

FLWOR expressions iterate over the items in a sequence. Here is an example in which we suppose that $articles has type element(article)+:

```
for $article in $articles
return $article/end_date - $article/start_date
```

has type xdt:dayTimeDuration +. To type the body of the for expression, we strip off the occurrence indicator from element(article)+ and type the body of the for expression assuming that $article has type element(article), yielding type xdt:dayTimeDuration. Then we add back the occurrence indicator, to get the type xdt:dayTimeDuration+. The same rule applies for other occurrence indicators:

```
for $article in $articles[start_date <= current_date()]
return $article/end_date - $article/start_date
```

has type xdt:dayTimeDuration*, and

```
for $article in $articles[start_date <= current_date()][1]
return $article/end_date - $article/start_date
```

has type xdt:dayTimeDuration?.

In general, the type of the input sequence in the FLWOR expression will be factored; recall that a factored type consists of a choice of items and an occurrence indicator. The body of the for expression is typed assuming that the iteration variable has as its type the choice of item types, and the occurrence indicator will be added to the type of the body to give the type of the FLWOR expression.

The effect of a where clause on the type of a FLWOR expression is similar to the effect of a predicate on the type of a path expression:

```
for $article in $articles
where $article/start_date <= current_date()
return $article/end_date - $article/start_date
```

has type xdt:dayTimeDuration*.

A FLWOR expression may also contain an `order` by clause:

```
for $article in $articles
order by $article/end_date - $article/start_date
return $article
```

has type `element(article)+`. Because the type of the input sequence in the FLWOR expression is factored, reordering the sequence returned by the FLWOR does not change its type.

Element Construction

We've seen how to perform operations on data, use path expressions to select data, and iterate over data. Now we look at how to construct data. The simplest way to construct data is to include literal XML data in a query. Here is an example:

```
<article id="1001">
  <name>Red Bicycle</name>
  <seller idref="U01"/>
  <start_date>1999-01-05</start_date>
  <end_date>1999-01-20</end_date>
  <reserve_price>40</reserve_price>
</article>
```

has type `element(article)`.

The type of this expression is the type declared for the `article` element in Listing 4.2. This type states that the element has one attribute (an `id` of type `xs:ID`), and five elements (including `start_date` and `end_date`, both of type `xs:date`). At evaluation time, the element is constructed and then validated. This ensures that the element itself and all the attributes and elements within it are labeled with the correct type. The validation implicit in element construction depends on a mode and context specified by the static environment; details of controlling validations are discussed in the next section.

One may also include computed data within a constructor. The function in Listing 4.9 takes an article that has failed to sell and yields a new article with new dates and a reduced reserve price:

Listing 4.9   Using Computed Data in a Constructor: Definition of the `bargain` Function

```
define function bargain($a as element(article)) as element(article)
{
    <article>{
      $a/@id,
      $a/name,
      $a/seller,
      <start_date>{ fn:current-date() }</start_date>
      <end_date> { fn:current-date() + ($a/end_date - $a/start_date)
                                                     }</end_date>
      <reserve_price>{ $a/reserve_price * 0.80 }</reserve_price>
    }</article>
}
```

This function definition is well typed, because the type of the function's body matches the return type, `element(article)`.

The real value of the type system is for detecting errors. Here is a variant of the `bargain` function that contains several type errors:

```
define function bargain($a as element(article)) as element(article)
{
    <article>{
      $a/name,
      $a/seller,
      <start_date>{ fn:current-date() }</start_date>
      <end_date> { $a/end_date - $a/start_date }</end_date>
      <reserve_price>{ $a/reserve_price * 0.80 }</reserve_price>
    }</article>
}
```

Now the type system detects two errors. First, an `article` element is required to contain an `id` attribute, but none appears in the above constructor expression. Second, the type expected for the `end_date` element is `xs:date`, but the type of the expression `$a/end_date` - `$a/start_date` is `xs:dayTimeDuration`.

Validation Context

Validation makes sense only in a given context. Validating a `name` element inside a `user` element checks that it contains `first` and `last` elements; while validating a `name` element inside an `article` element checks that it contains a string.

In addition to keeping track of the types of variables, the static environment contains a validation context. Initially, this context is set to global. During static analysis, when an element constructor with a given name is entered, the context is extended by that element name within the constructor. For example, consider the query in Listing 4.10, which constructs a `user` element, omitting the first name if it is too long, or the rating if it is too low.

Listing 4.10   Validation Context Specified by Lexical Scope of Constructors

```
let $first := "Mary",
    $last := "Doe",
    $rating := "A"
return
  <user id="U02">
    <name>
       { if (fn:string-length($first) > 10) then () else
                                 <first>{ $first }</first> }
       <last>{ $last }</last>
    </name>
    { if ($rating > "C") then () else <rating>{ $rating }</rating> }
  </user>
```

Here, the `user` element is validated in the global context, the `name` and `rating` elements are validated in the context `user`, and the `first` and `last` elements are validated in the context `user/name`.

It would be impossible to determine static types if the context used to validate an element constructor was not known statically; thus, the validation context is part of the static environment. It is determined by lexical scope, not by the nesting of elements in the final document. When there is a mismatch between the two, this may be fixed by adding an explicit context to a `validate` expression. For example, Listing 4.11 shows a variant of the query in Listing 4.10.

Listing 4.11   Validation Context Specified Explicitly in Validate Expression

```
let $first := validate context user/name { <first>Mary</first> },
    $last := validate context user/name { <last>Doe</last> },
    $rating := validate context user { <rating>A</rating> }
return
```

Listing 4.11   Validation Context Specified Explicitly in Validate Expression *(continued)*

```
<user id="U02">{
  <name>{
    if (string-length($first) > 10) then () else $first,
    $last
  }</name>,
  if ($rating > "C") then () else $rating
}</user>
```

Since the `first`, `last`, and `rating` elements are no longer lexically nested within the `user` and `name` elements, the validation context must be explicitly given when the elements are constructed. This guarantees that validation labels the elements with the appropriate types.

Lexical nesting and evaluation order may also differ in the presence of a function call. Again, an explicit context must be given in this case. The function shown in Listing 4.12 takes the locally declared elements `first` and `last` in the context `user/name`.

Listing 4.12   Validation Context in Function Call and Body

```
define function make_name (
  $first as element(user/name/first),
  $last as element(user/name/last)
) as element(user/name) {
  validate context user {
    <name>{
      if (string-length($first) > 10) then () else $first,
      $last
    }</name>
  }
}

let $rating := "A"
return
  <user>{
    make_name(
      validate context user/name { <first>Mary</first> },
      validate context user/name { <last>Doe</last> }
    ),
    if ($rating > "C") then () else <rating>{ $rating }</rating>
  }</user>
```

The `validate` expressions above are used to supply context for the `name` element in the function body, and the `first` and `last` elements in the function call.

You might conclude from this discussion that it is easiest always to construct elements in the proper context. One way to ensure this is to prefer global declarations to local declarations when designing a schema, since a globally declared element requires no context for validation.

Validation Mode

XML is known as a *semi-structured* data format because it accommodates both valid and well-formed data. Valid data corresponds to a given schema (or DTD). Well-formed data is syntactically correct (all open tags have matching end tags), but is otherwise unconstrained.

XML Schema provides three modes of validation, to allow mixing of valid and well-formed data.

1. `strict` requires that a declaration be available for the element, and the element must validate with respect to that declaration. The element is labeled with the declared type, as are all elements and attributes within the element.
2. `skip` has no constraints; the element must simply be well formed. The element and all elements within it are labeled with type `xs:anyType`, and all attributes within it are labeled with type `xs:anySimpleType`.
3. `lax` behaves as `strict` if there is a declaration available; otherwise, it behaves as `skip`.

In addition to keeping track of the types of variables and the validation context, the static environment also contains a validation mode, which is one of `strict`, `skip`, or `lax`. The initial validation mode may be specified by including a default declaration in the prolog. Our running example in the corrected query of Listing 4.6 includes the following declaration (see line [2a]), so all element constructors in the query perform strict validation:

```
default validation strict
```

Just as with context, it would be impossible to determine static types if the mode used to validate an element constructor was not known statically. Therefore, the validation mode is part of the static environment: It is determined by lexical scope, not by the schema as it traverses the final document. When there is a mismatch between the two, this may be fixed by adding a mode to a `validate` expression. For example, recall that the `description` element defined in Listing 4.2 contains attribute and element wildcards processed with `skip` validation. Previously, we wrote a function `bargain` that takes an article that has failed to sell, and yields a new article with new dates and a reduced reserve price. Listing 4.13 shows a modified function that also inserts a `bargain` element inside the `description` element.

Listing 4.13   Validation Mode Used to Skip Validate Element Content

```
define function bargain($a as element(article)) as element(article)
{
    <article>{
      $a/name,
      $a/seller,
      <start_date>{ fn:current-date() }</start_date>
      <end_date>{ fn:current-date() + ($a/end_date - $a/start_date)
                                                  }</end_date>
      <reserve_price>{ $a/reserve_price * 0.80 }</reserve_price>
      <description>{
        $a/description/(@* | * | text()),
        validate skip { <bargain>Marked down from { $a/reserve_price
                                              }</bargain> }
      }</description>
    } </article>
}
```

Here a `validate` expression is used to set a `skip` validation mode for the `bargain` element. Otherwise, the `bargain` constructor would raise an error. At static-analysis time, it would fail because `strict` mode requires the element to be declared, and the given schema does not define a `bargain` element. If static analysis was turned off, it would fail at evaluation time because validation in `strict` mode requires the element to be declared.

A `strict` validation mode is not appropriate for XML literal data that contains data that is not strictly validated. It is possible to include `skip` or `lax` validated data by wrapping the element constructor in two `validate` expressions. For example, Listing 4.14 shows a call to the function of Listing 4.13 that takes literal data as its argument:

Listing 4.14   Call to the Function of Listing 4.13 That Takes Literal Data as Its Argument

```
bargain(
  validate { validate skip {
    <article id="1001">
      <name>Red Bicycle</name>
      <seller idref="U01"/>
      <start_date>1999-01-05</start_date>
      <end_date>1999-01-20</end_date>
      <reserve_price>40</reserve_price>
      <description>
         A <brand>Schwinn</brand> <make>String-ray</make> with
         <accessory>banana seat</accessory>.
      </description>
    </article>
  } }
)
```

Here, the inner `validate` expression sets the validation mode to `skip`. This is necessary because the validation performed by the construction of the `brand`, `make`, and `accessory` elements would fail in a `strict` validation mode. The outer `validate` revalidates the XML literal data in the `strict` mode specified by the static environment. This is necessary because the `article` element must be labeled as correctly validated in order to match the element type specified by the function signature. Because validation proceeds top-down at evaluation time, the outer validation above uses `skip` mode for the contents of the `description` element, as specified by the schema, and so the `brand`, `make`, and `accessory` elements cause no problem.

These examples show that when the validation mode of the query and the validation mode of a constructed element match, which we expect to be the common case, no extra work is necessary to avoid static type errors. But when the two modes do not match, some care is necessary to avoid static type errors. This extra work is a useful "red flag" to remind users that they are mixing valid and well-formed data.

A Final Example: Grouping

We conclude the chapter with an example that ties together most of the concepts that we've covered. Suppose we wish to display all articles for sale, grouped by seller. Listing 4.15 provides a query to do so.

Listing 4.15   Query to Display Articles for Sale, Grouped by Seller

```
default element namespace = "http://www.example.com/auction"
declare namespace x = "http://www.w3.org/1999/xhtml"
let $auction := $input/auction
return
<x:html>
  <x:head><x:title>Items by Seller</x:title></x:head>
  <x:body>
    <x:h1>Items by seller</x:h1>
    {
      for $id in distinct-values
                        ($auction/articles/article/seller/@idref)
      let $name := exactly-one($auction/users/user[@id = $id]/name)
      order by $name
      return
        <x:p>{ $name }</x:p>
        <x:table>{
          for $article in one-or-more
                    ($auction/articles/article[seller/@idref = $id])
          return
            <x:tr><x:td>{ $article/name }</x:td></x:tr>
          }</x:table>
    }
  </x:body>
</x:html>
```

We use a path expression to find the `idref` of every seller of an article, and apply the function `distinct-values` to eliminate duplicates. For each identifier in this sequence, we find the name of the user with that identifier, order the sequence by the names, and display a paragraph containing the name of the user with that identifier and a table of all articles offered by that user.

Note that we iterate over identifiers extracted from the `articles` element, rather than from the `users` element; this guarantees that there will be at least one article displayed for each seller. This is just as well, because the schema for XHTML requires that a `table` element contain at least one row. Also, because of the integrity constraints on the data, every `idref` that appears in the article will correspond to exactly one user.

However, the static type inference rules are not clever enough to work this out; the types inferred for the articles and the name will both have zero-or-more occurrence indicators. This is fixed by applying the occurrence functions `exactly-one` and `one-or-more` at the appropriate points.

This example illustrates both the strengths and weaknesses of the XQuery static type system. The type system can catch many common errors at analysis time, including misspelled names in path expressions and constructors, and the use of an expression whose type is not compatible with the type required by the context in which the expression is used. Moreover, the type system guarantees that if a query does not raise a type error at analysis time, it will not raise a type error at evaluation time. Catching common errors at analysis time is especially important in applications that access large amounts of data, and it helps a programmer have confidence in the correctness of his program. The type system, however, is not always clever enough to infer the precise cardinality of an expression. This often occurs when a query joins or regroups data based on an unique key value. In these cases, the user must provide extra information to the type system by applying the occurrence functions.

Conclusions

In this chapter we illustrated the benefits of static typing for a small but nontrivial XQuery application and then explained how XQuery infers the type for each expression during static analysis. Along the way, we learned about the many common errors that can be detected by static typing, including misspelled names in path expressions and constructors, and the use of an expression whose type is not compatible with the type required by the context in which the expression is used. We also showed how to compensate for the limitations of static typing, such as refining the cardinality of a type.

We expect that the benefits of static typing will increase with the size of XQuery applications. Like other modern languages, XQuery supports modules, which aid in the development of reusable libraries. XQuery modules most often will be designed for XML data conforming to some XML schema (e.g., SOAP, RDF, BizTalk, etc.). Hundreds of domain-specific DTDs and XML Schemas already exist, and we expect the number and complexity of these schemas to increase as XML data proliferates. Consequently, more XQuery applications will use imported modules and their associated schemas. Static typing can help make these applications more robust by guaranteeing that an application's uses of a module's data and functions are type-safe.

Although specific aspects of static typing, such as error messages, may differ across XQuery implementations, the examples in this chapter should help the users of any XQuery implementation get started with static typing. XQuery implementers, however, need to understand the details of the type system's inference rules. Those rules, and the rules for dynamic evaluation, are the subject of Chapter 5.

Chapter 5

INTRODUCTION TO THE FORMAL SEMANTICS

Mary Fernández, Jérôme Siméon, and Philip Wadler

"When a Mathematical Reasoning can be had it's as great a folly to make use of any other, as to grope for a thing in the dark, when you have a Candle standing by you."

—*John Arbuthnot, The Laws of Form, 1692*

XQuery is described by two documents: the XQuery language document [XQ-LANG], which uses prose, and the XQuery Formal Semantics document [XQ-FS], which uses symbols. Symbols support a degree of precision that prose alone cannot achieve, but they require some training in their use. This chapter provides such training and is intended for XQuery implementers and expert users who need a deeper understanding of XQuery's semantics.

This chapter does not describe the XQuery Formal Semantics in its entirety. Our aim is to teach enough about the notations and techniques used in that document so that you can go off and read it yourself. A basic understanding of XQuery is a prerequisite to this chapter. We suggest reading Chapters 1 and 4 before studying this chapter.

As of this writing, XQuery and its formal specification are still in working draft. The material presented in this chapter is expected to be aligned with the May 2003 working drafts.

The Benefits of a Formal Semantics

In their book *The Definition of Standard ML*, Robin Milner, Mads Tofte, and Robert Harper have the following to say about the value of formally describing a programming language:

> A precise description of a programming language is a prerequisite for its implementation and for its use. The description can take on many forms, each suited to a different purpose. A common form is a reference manual, which is usually a careful narrative description of each construct of the language, often backed up with a formal presentation of the grammar (for example, in Backus-Naur form). This gives the programmer enough understanding for many of his purposes. But it is ill-suited for use by an implementer, or by someone who wants to formulate laws for equivalence of programs, or by a programmer who wants to design programs with mathematical rigor.
>
> This document is a formal description of both the *grammar* and the *meaning* of a language which is both designed for large projects and widely used. As such it aims to serve the whole community of people seriously concerned with the language. At a time when it is increasingly understood that programs must withstand rigorous analysis, particularly for systems where safety is critical, a rigorous language presentation is even important for negotiators and contractors; for a robust program written in an insecure language is like a house built upon sand.

The XML Query working group has taken the unusual step of writing both a prose and a formal description of XQuery.[1] These two descriptions benefit both language designers and implementers. For language designers, two descriptions offer twice as many opportunities to expose inconsistency, errors, or bad design. History has shown that it is useful to formalize a language's semantics before the language goes into widespread use and becomes hard to change. After the Java programming language was released, several formal semantics of aspects of the language

---

1 We thank our colleagues in the XML Query Working Group, especially the coeditors of *XQuery 1.0 Formal Semantics* [XQ-FS]. Particularly important contributions were made by Denise Draper, Peter Fankhauser, and Kristoffer Rose. Kristoffer Rose also provided invaluable help in typesetting. Some material in "Values and Types" and "Matching and Subtyping" in our second main section is taken from Siméon and Wadler's paper *The Essence of XML* [ESSENCE].

were written. Some of these semantics revealed errors in the type system, which in turn could lead to security holes in browsers that run Java programs. In some cases, revisions were then made to the Java release to plug the holes that were discovered.

XQuery has already benefited from its formal semantics. During the design of XQuery, the working group chose to make the type system depend more closely upon the type names assigned to elements and attributes by XML Schema validation. This change was written in prose in the XQuery language document and later written in the formal semantics. The process of formalization revealed ten issues that had not been addressed by the prose description.

For language implementers, a formal description provides more details than a prose description alone, and those details are necessary to develop complete, correct, and conforming implementations. The formal semantics contains the only complete description of the XQuery static type system, so implementers of that feature depend heavily on the formal semantics. Several early implementations of XQuery are actually modeled after the formal semantics. Our own implementation of XQuery, Galax [GALAX], corresponds so closely to the formal semantics that the formal-semantics rules that define an expression and the code that implements those rules often resemble each other.

One reason that XQuery is such an interesting language to us is that implementers are pursuing many alternative implementation strategies. For example, some relational database vendors implement XQuery within relational query engines extended with XML-aware operators, and some data-integration vendors focus on the difficult problem of decomposing XQuery queries into queries that can be implemented by legacy database or business-process systems. We refer you to Chapters 6–8, which investigate the relationship between XQuery and various evaluation environments. These alternatives make the formal semantics even more valuable to implementers, as it codifies XQuery's semantics independently of any particular implementation strategy.

This chapter is divided into two main sections: "Getting Started with the Formal Semantics" and "Learning More about XQuery." The first section introduces the key techniques used in the formal semantics and describes the formal rules and notations used by each technique. We illustrate the techniques on a tiny subset of XQuery—the focus here is on learning how to read and use the formal rules rather than learning the details of the language. The second section applies the techniques introduced in the first section to XQuery itself—the focus here is on specific XQuery expressions and how the formal rules clarify the expression's semantics and enhance the prose description.

Getting Started with the Formal Semantics

The formal semantics of XQuery has three components: a **dynamic semantics**, a **static semantics**, and **normalization rules**. The dynamic semantics specifies precisely the relationship between input data, an XQuery expression, and output data. The static semantics specifies precisely the relationship between the type of the input data, an XQuery expression, and the type of the output data. The dynamic and static semantics are related by the important **type soundness theorem**. The normalization rules transform full XQuery into a small core language, which is easier to define, implement, and optimize. The dynamic and static semantics are defined in terms of the core language.

The XQuery formal semantics describes a processing model that relates query parsing, normalization, static analysis, and dynamic evaluation. This processing model works as an "idealized" implementation of the language. The parsing phase takes as input a query in XQuery's full syntax and either raises a parse error or produces a parse tree of the input query. Normalization implements XQuery's normalization rules—it transforms the parse tree of the input query into an equivalent parse tree in the core language. Static type analysis implements XQuery's static semantics—it takes the parse tree in the core language and assigns types to expressions in the parse tree. Static analysis either raises a static type error or produces a parse tree where each expression has been assigned a type. Dynamic evaluation implements XQuery's dynamic semantics—it takes a parse tree in the core language (which may be the result of normalization or static analysis) and reduces expressions in the parse tree to XML values. Dynamic evaluation either raises a dynamic error or produces an XML value that is the result of the query.

The main technique we use to specify XQuery's static and dynamic semantics is commonly known as an **operational semantics**. An operational semantics is specified using inference rules—you may already be familiar with inference rules from the study of logic. If you want to learn more about the mathematical foundations of semantics and inference rules, the concluding section of this chapter contains references to the foundational literature.

We introduce inference rules by specifying a tiny subset of XQuery, which has only two types (xs:boolean and xs:integer) and just a few constructs, including if and let expressions. We first apply the technique to describe the dynamic semantics of the language, and then the static semantics. We describe normalization last.

Dynamic Semantics

Evaluation is a process that takes an expression and returns a value. Here is how we write it in formal notation:

$$Expr \Rightarrow Value$$

This is read, "Evaluation of expression *Expr* yields value *Value*." We call this an **evaluation judgment**. Recall that dynamic evaluation takes a parse tree in the core language and produces an XML value. So you should read *Expr* as representing such a parse tree and *Value* as representing the resulting value. For the time being, we consider the very simple case of expressions without variables, so we don't need any environment to give the values of the variables; we will consider environments later in this section.

Our first definition of values is simple; it includes just Boolean and integer literals.

Value	::=	*Boolean* | *Integer*
Boolean	::=	fn:true() | fn:false()
Integer	::=	0 | 1 | -1 | 2 | -2 | . . .

To completely specify the integers we would need to use a grammar, but we don't go to that level of detail here. One of the tricks to effective use of formalism is to know when not to formalize!

Our first definition of expressions is also simple: literal values, one comparison operation (less than), one arithmetic operation (sum), and conditionals.

$$
\begin{array}{lll}
Expr & ::= & Value \\
& | & Expr < Expr \\
& | & Expr + Expr \\
& | & \texttt{if } (Expr) \texttt{ then } Expr \texttt{ else } Expr
\end{array}
$$

This grammar is called an **abstract syntax**. Issues like precedence or parenthesis are specified in the grammar of the language's **concrete syntax** and implemented by the parsing phase. We don't concern ourselves with concrete syntax here.

In general, evaluation relates the expression on the left of the arrow and the value on the right. For the simple case described here, every expression evaluates to at most one value. A sensible expression (like `1+2`) yields one value, while a nonsensical expression (like `if (1+2) then 3 else 4`) yields no value.

Evaluation is described by five rules. Each inference rule has zero or more judgments above the line, called **hypotheses**, and one judgment below the line, called the **conclusion**. When all the hypotheses are true, then the conclusion must be true also. The following rules illustrate how literals, comparison, arithmetic, and conditional expressions are evaluated.

$$
\frac{}{Value \Rightarrow Value} \tag{VALUE}
$$

$$
\frac{\begin{array}{c} Expr_0 \Rightarrow Integer_0 \\ Expr_1 \Rightarrow Integer_1 \end{array}}{Expr_0 < Expr_1 \Rightarrow Integer_0 < Integer_1} \tag{LT}
$$

$$\frac{\begin{array}{c} Expr_0 \Rightarrow Integer_0 \\ Expr_1 \Rightarrow Integer_1 \end{array}}{Expr_0 + Expr_1 \Rightarrow Integer_0 + Integer_1} \quad \text{(SUM)}$$

$$\frac{\begin{array}{c} Expr_0 \Rightarrow \texttt{fn:true()} \\ Expr_1 \Rightarrow Value \end{array}}{\texttt{if } (Expr_0) \texttt{ then } Expr_1 \texttt{ else } Expr_2 \Rightarrow Value} \quad \text{(IF-TRUE)}$$

$$\frac{\begin{array}{c} Expr_0 \Rightarrow \texttt{fn:false()} \\ Expr_2 \Rightarrow Value \end{array}}{\texttt{if } (Expr_0) \texttt{ then } Expr_1 \texttt{ else } Expr_2 \Rightarrow Value} \quad \text{(IF-FALSE)}$$

Inference rules can be read as deductions in logic. From some hypothesis (above the line), one can deduce a conclusion (below the line). Another way to read inference rules is as a program—or an algorithm—to compute a result from some input. In our rules, we compute a value from an expression. The inference rule explains how to find the value of a larger expression (below the line) in terms of the values of its subexpressions (above the line).

For example, here is a **proof tree** to evaluate the expression 1+2. The proof tree constrains two instances of the rule (VALUE), with $Value = 1$ in the first instance and $Value = 2$ in the second instance; and one instance of the rule (SUM), with $Expr_0 = 1$, $Expr_1 = 2$, $Integer_0 = 1$, and $Integer_1 = 2$.

$$\cfrac{\cfrac{\rule{2cm}{0.4pt}}{1 \Rightarrow 1}\text{(VALUE)} \quad \cfrac{\rule{2cm}{0.4pt}}{2 \Rightarrow 2}\text{(VALUE)}}{1+2 \Rightarrow 3}\text{(SUM)}$$

With some effort we have proved the obvious: The expression 1 yields the value 1, and the expression 2 yields the value 2, so the expression 1+2 yields their sum, which is the value 3. Each instance of rule (VALUE) has no hypotheses, and so its conclusion follows immediately; and the instance of rule (SUM) has two hypotheses that are proved by the instances of rule (VALUE), and so its conclusion follows.

Another way to read the above is as a trace of an evaluation: To evaluate the expression 1+2, evaluate the subexpression 1 to yield the value 1, and evaluate the subexpression 2 to yield the value 2, then add those values to yield the final value 3.

As a second example, here is a proof tree concluding in an instance of the rule (IF-TRUE), where we choose $Expr_0$ = 1 < 3, $Expr_1$ = 3+4, $Expr_2$ = 5+6, and $Value$ = 7.

$$
\cfrac{
  \cfrac{
    \cfrac{\rule{2cm}{0.4pt}}{1 \Rightarrow 1}\text{(VALUE)} \quad
    \cfrac{\rule{2cm}{0.4pt}}{2 \Rightarrow 2}\text{(VALUE)}
  }{1 < 2 \Rightarrow \texttt{fn:true()}}\text{(LT)} \quad
  \cfrac{
    \cfrac{\rule{2cm}{0.4pt}}{3 \Rightarrow 3}\text{(VALUE)} \quad
    \cfrac{\rule{2cm}{0.4pt}}{4 \Rightarrow 4}\text{(VALUE)}
  }{3+4 \Rightarrow 7}\text{(SUM)}
}{\texttt{if (1 < 2) then 3+4 else 5+6} \Rightarrow 7}\text{(IF-TRUE)}
$$

So evaluation of the expression if (1 < 2) then 3+4 else 5+6 yields the value 7. Note that $Expr_2$ = 5+6 did not appear in the hypotheses, which formalizes the intuition that the else branch is not evaluated when the condition is true.

Inference rules may be applied in any order: as long as the hypotheses are all true, we can draw the corresponding conclusion. Building a proof tree corresponds to a successful evaluation of an expression—if you cannot build a proof tree for an expression, you cannot evaluate it!

We designed the rules so that there is at most one proof tree with a given expression in its conclusion. This means the result of evaluating the expression is deterministic. Later, when we discuss errors and evaluation order, we'll see cases where more than one proof tree exists for a given expression, which means the result of evaluating the expression is non-deterministic.

As language designers, we may write out proof trees to make sure that the semantics of an expression are what we expect them to be, or we may automate this process by building a theorem prover that applies the inference rules automatically. The rules are compact and, once you get used to them, easy to read. It is usually not difficult to convert these rules into executable code—this is exactly what we have done in writing Galax, our implementation of XQuery [GALAX]. On the other hand, using executable code as the formal specification would be unsatisfactory, because such code contains too many low-level details that hinder readability.

Environments

Evaluation is defined as a judgment relating an expression to a value. Typically, the evaluation judgment also has a third component, an **environment**. Here is how we write it:

$$dynEnv \vdash Expr \Rightarrow Value$$

This is read, "In environment *dynEnv*, the evaluation of expression *Expr* yields the value *Value*." Here *dynEnv* represents the dynamic environment, such as the values of variables, which captures the context available at query-evaluation time.

In general, an environment may have many components, each of which is given a name. For now, we require an environment, which we call *dynEnv*, with just one component, a map from variables to their values, which we call *varValue*. Later we will add other components to the environment.

We use the following notations to manipulate environments:

TABLE 5.1   Notations That Manipulate Environments

Notation	Meaning
$\varnothing$	The initial environment with an empty map
$dynEnv.varValue(Var_1 \Rightarrow Value_1, \ldots, Var_n \Rightarrow Value_n)$	The environment that maps Var_i to $Value_i$
$dynEnv + varValue(Var \Rightarrow Value)$	The environment identical to *dynEnv* except that *Var* maps to *Value*
$dynEnv.varValue(Var)$	The value of *Var* in *dynEnv*
$dom(dynEnv.varValue)$	The set of variables mapped in *dynEnv*

Binding a variable in the environment overrides any previous binding for the same variable. For example, consider the following environments:

$$dynEnv_0 = \emptyset$$
$$dynEnv_1 = dynEnv_0 + varValue(\text{x} \Rightarrow 1) = varValue(\text{x} \Rightarrow 1)$$
$$dynEnv_2 = dynEnv_1 + varValue(\text{y} \Rightarrow 2) = varValue(\text{x} \Rightarrow 1, \text{y} \Rightarrow 2)$$
$$dynEnv_3 = dynEnv_2 + varValue(\text{x} \Rightarrow 3) = varValue(\text{x} \Rightarrow 3, \text{y} \Rightarrow 2)$$

Given these environments, we have $dynEnv_2.varValue(\text{x}) = 1$, *dom* $(dynEnv_0.varValue) = \emptyset$, and $dom(dynEnv_3.varValue) = \{\text{x}, \text{y}\}$. Note that x maps to a different value in $dynEnv_2$ and $dynEnv_3$.

If you have ever implemented a compiler or interpreter, you have implemented some kind of environment. Typically, environments are implemented by stacks of dictionaries or associative arrays. But for the purposes of the formal semantics, we need not worry about these implementation details.

With these preliminaries out of the way, we can now formalize variables and `let` expressions. We extend the earlier syntax to include these.

$$Expr ::= \dots \text{previous expressions} \dots$$
$$| \quad \$Var$$
$$| \quad \text{let } \$Var := Expr \text{ return } Expr$$

The five rules we gave before need to be revised to mention the environment. Here is the revision of the first two rules.

$$\frac{}{dynEnv \vdash Value \Rightarrow Value} \quad \text{(VALUE)}$$

$$\frac{dynEnv \vdash Expr_0 \Rightarrow Value_0 \quad dynEnv \vdash Expr_1 \Rightarrow Value_1}{dynEnv \vdash Expr_0 < Expr_1 \Rightarrow Value_0 < Value_1} \quad \text{(LT)}$$

The revisions of the other rules are similar.

There are also two new rules. The first rule illustrates how the value of a variable is retrieved from the dynamic environment.

$$\frac{dynEnv.varValue(Var) = Value}{dynEnv \vdash \$Var \Rightarrow Value} \quad \text{(VAR)}$$

If in *dynEnv* the value bound to *Var* is *Value*, then in *dynEnv* evaluating expression *Var* yields value *Value*. The rule implicitly requires that the variable be in the domain of the dynamic environment, since *dynEnv.varValue(Var)* makes sense only if $Var \in dom(dynEnv.varValue)$. The formalism doesn't specify what happens if the variable is *not* in the dynamic environment. In an implementation, an undefined variable error would typically be caught prior to evaluation, so the dynamic semantics does not even mention it. Again, it is important to know when not to formalize. (Later, when some subtleties about errors arise, we will discuss how to formalize them.)

The second rule illustrates how environments are modified and how the modified environment is used in a `let` expression.

$$\frac{dynEnv \vdash Expr_0 \Rightarrow Value_0 \qquad dynEnv + varValue(Var \Rightarrow Value_0) \vdash Expr_1 \Rightarrow Value_1}{dynEnv \vdash \text{let } \$Var := Expr_0 \text{ return } Expr_1 \Rightarrow Value_1} \quad \text{(LET)}$$

In the first hypothesis, the original environment *dynEnv* is used to evaluate expression $Expr_0$ yielding value $Value_0$. In the second hypothesis, the environment is extended by binding variable *Var* to value $Value_0$, and the extended environment is used to evaluate expression $Expr_1$ yielding value $Value_1$. The conclusion states that evaluating the `let` expression in the original environment *dynEnv* yields value $Value_1$.

A nested `let` expression may rebind variables. It is not always easy for a user to predict the result of a query when the same variable is bound several times. For instance, consider the following expression:

```
let $x := 1 return
  let $y := $x+$x return
    let $x := $x+$y return
      $x+$y
```

Proof Tree 5.1 shows a proof tree in which $dynEnv_0$, $dynEnv_1$, $dynEnv_2$, and $dynEnv_3$ are defined as in the example at the beginning of this section. Applying the inference rules step by step in this proof clarifies the behavior of nested `let` expressions, in particular, that variables defined in inner `let` expressions hide variables of the same name defined in outer `let` expressions.

Proof Tree 5.1   Evaluation of a let Expression

$$
\cfrac{
\cfrac{}{dynEnv_0 \vdash \texttt{1} \Longrightarrow \texttt{1}}\;(\text{VALUE})
\quad
\cfrac{
\cfrac{
\cfrac{
\cfrac{}{dynEnv_1 \vdash \texttt{\$x} \Longrightarrow \texttt{1}}\;(\text{VAR}) \quad
\cfrac{}{dynEnv_1 \vdash \texttt{\$x} \Longrightarrow \texttt{1}}\;(\text{VAR})
}{dynEnv_1 \vdash \texttt{\$x+\$x} \Longrightarrow \texttt{2}}\;(\text{SUM})
\quad
\cfrac{
\cfrac{
\cfrac{
\cfrac{}{dynEnv_2 \vdash \texttt{\$x} \Longrightarrow \texttt{1}}\;(\text{VAR}) \quad
\cfrac{}{dynEnv_2 \vdash \texttt{\$y} \Longrightarrow \texttt{2}}\;(\text{VAR})
}{dynEnv_2 \vdash \texttt{\$x+\$y} \Longrightarrow \texttt{3}}\;(\text{SUM})
\quad
\cfrac{
\cfrac{}{dynEnv_3 \vdash \texttt{\$x} \Longrightarrow \texttt{3}}\;(\text{VAR}) \quad
\cfrac{}{dynEnv_3 \vdash \texttt{\$y} \Longrightarrow \texttt{2}}\;(\text{VAR})
}{dynEnv_3 \vdash \texttt{\$x+\$y} \Longrightarrow \texttt{5}}\;(\text{SUM})
}{dynEnv_2 \vdash \texttt{let \$x := \$x+\$y return \$x+\$y} \Longrightarrow \texttt{5}}\;(\text{LET})
}{dynEnv_1 \vdash \texttt{let \$y := \$x+\$x return let \$x := \$x+\$y return \$x+\$y} \Longrightarrow \texttt{5}}\;(\text{LET})
}{dynEnv_0 \vdash \texttt{let \$x := 1 return let \$y := \$x+\$x return let \$x := \$x+\$y return \$x+\$y} \Longrightarrow \texttt{5}}\;(\text{LET})
$$

(When dealing with large proof trees, such as the one above, some readers prefer to start reading at the top with the first (VALUE) judgment, and some to start reading at the bottom with the final (LET) judgment.)

Now that we have shown a nontrivial proof tree, in what follows we often present just the rules and some example judgments, and omit the detailed proof trees. Regardless of the number or complexity of the rules that we present, however, proof trees can be used to clarify the evaluation of any expression.

Matching Values and Types

The relationship between values and types plays an important role in the formal semantics. This relationship can be illustrated by extending the grammar with a second form of `let` expression, which declares a type for the bound variable. The intention is that a type error is raised if the value does not match the specified type.

$$
\begin{aligned}
\textit{Expr} ::= \quad &\ldots \text{previous expressions} \ldots \\
\mid \quad &\texttt{let } \$\textit{Var} \texttt{ as } \textit{Type} := \textit{Expr} \texttt{ return } \textit{Expr}
\end{aligned}
$$

In addition to `let` expressions, type declarations occur in `for`, `some`, and `every` expressions and in function signatures, so once you understand the semantics of type declarations in `let`, you will understand them in those contexts as well.

For now, we use only two types:

$$
\textit{Type} ::= \texttt{xs:boolean} \mid \texttt{xs:integer}
$$

Type declarations can be checked in two ways: *statically*, when the expression is analyzed, or *dynamically*, when the expression is evaluated. For now, we focus on dynamic checking; static checking is discussed in the section below entitled "Static Semantics."

We need a new **matching judgment** that matches a value against a given type. In what follows, judgments are always written in **bold**. Here is how we write the matching judgment:

Value **matches** *Type*

This is read, "Value *Value* matches the type *Type*."

The inference rules for literal expressions are straightforward. Every literal integer matches the type `xs:integer`, and every literal Boolean matches the type `xs:boolean`.

$$
\frac{\rule{0pt}{0pt}}{\textit{Integer} \textbf{ matches } \texttt{xs:integer}} \qquad \text{(INT-MATCH)}
$$

$$
\frac{\rule{0pt}{0pt}}{\textit{Boolean} \textbf{ matches } \texttt{xs:boolean}} \qquad \text{(BOOL-MATCH)}
$$

The modified evaluation rule for the `let` expression with type declarations shows how to check that the value bound to the variable matches the declared type.

$$dynEnv \vdash Expr_0 \Rightarrow Value_0$$

$$Value_0 \ \textbf{matches} \ Type$$

$$\frac{dynEnv + varValue(Var \Rightarrow Value_0) \vdash Expr_1 \Rightarrow Value_1}{dynEnv \vdash \texttt{let} \ \$Var \ \texttt{as} \ Type := Expr_0 \ \texttt{return} \ Expr_1 \Rightarrow Value_1} \quad \text{(LET-DECL)}$$

The first and third hypotheses are the same as those in the rule for `let` without type declarations. The second hypothesis asserts that $Value_0$ matches the declared type.

Since XQuery is a strongly typed language, matching values to types is central to its dynamic semantics. Later in the chapter, we define additional **matches** judgments relating complex XML values to complex types, but these additions don't affect the use of the **matches** judgment above—the same hypothesis applies. The inference-rule formalism makes it possible to change and test out XQuery's semantics simply by adding (or deleting) rules, which illustrates another advantage of having a formal semantics.

Errors

So far, our semantics associates a value with every expression. Some expressions, however, have no value; instead they raise an error. We have seen one error—the use of an undefined variable—that we chose not to formalize. But the behavior of other errors can be subtle, and the prose XQuery description goes to some lengths to specify what freedom vendors have and do not have to raise errors. So it is worth the effort to formalize errors.

We introduce a new judgment to indicate that evaluation of an expression may raise an error.

$$dynEnv \vdash Expr \ \textbf{raises} \ Error$$

This is read, "In the environment $dynEnv$, the evaluation of expression $Expr$ raises the error $Error$."

We classify errors as either type errors or dynamic errors.

$$Error ::= \texttt{typeErr} \mid \texttt{dynErr}$$

These do not indicate the cause of the error (e.g., "divide by zero" or "value does not match required type"). The formal semantics could make this distinction, but we don't bother with it here.

To illustrate the semantics of errors, we extend our subset of XQuery with an operator for integer division.

$$Expr ::= \ldots \text{previous expressions} \ldots$$
$$\mid Expr \; \texttt{idiv} \; Expr$$

Type errors are triggered if an operand's value does not match the operator's required type. We use the matching judgments from the preceding section, and write the following if none of the **matches** judgments above hold for a particular *Value* and *Type*:

$$\textbf{not}(Value \; \textbf{matches} \; Type)$$

The evaluation rule for division is similar to that for addition. The first two hypotheses are the same as those for addition, and the third hypothesis guarantees that the divisor in $Expr_1$ is not equal to zero:

$$\frac{\begin{array}{c} dynEnv \vdash Expr_0 \Rightarrow Value_0 \\ dynEnv \vdash Expr_1 \Rightarrow Value_1 \\ Value_1 \neq 0 \end{array}}{dynEnv \vdash Expr_0 \; \texttt{idiv} \; Expr_1 \Rightarrow Value_0 \; \texttt{idiv} \; Value_1} \quad \text{(IDIV)}$$

We now add rules that indicate when errors should be raised. The next rule shows how evaluation of the integer division operator raises an error if the divisor is zero.

$$\frac{dynEnv \vdash Expr_1 \Rightarrow 0}{dynEnv \vdash Expr_0 \; \texttt{idiv} \; Expr_1 \; \textbf{raises} \; \texttt{dynErr}} \quad \text{(IDIV-ERR)}$$

Notice that the rule does not require evaluation of the dividend in $Expr_0$ to discover such an error.

The following rules show how type errors may be raised during evaluation of arithmetic and comparison operators. The less-than, sum, and division operators raise a type error if they act on a value that is not an integer. We give the two rules for less than; the other operators are similar.

$$\frac{\begin{array}{c} dynEnv \vdash Expr_0 \Rightarrow Value_0 \\ \textbf{not}\,(Value_0\ \textbf{matches}\ \texttt{xs:integer}) \end{array}}{dynEnv \vdash Expr_0 < Expr_1\ \textbf{raises}\ \texttt{typeErr}} \quad \text{(LT-LEFT-TYPE-ERR)}$$

$$\frac{\begin{array}{c} dynEnv \vdash Expr_1 \Rightarrow Value_1 \\ \textbf{not}\,(Value_1\ \textbf{matches}\ \texttt{xs:integer}) \end{array}}{dynEnv \vdash Expr_0 < Expr_1\ \textbf{raises}\ \texttt{typeErr}} \quad \text{(LT-RIGHT-TYPE-ERR)}$$

The rule for the `if` expression is omitted but similar—it raises a type error when the value of its condition expression is not a Boolean.

The `let` expression with a type declaration raises an error if the value is not of the declared type.

$$\frac{\begin{array}{c} dynEnv \vdash Expr_0 \Rightarrow Value_0 \\ \textbf{not}\,(Value_0\ \textbf{matches}\ Type) \end{array}}{dynEnv \vdash \texttt{let}\ \$Var\ \texttt{as}\ Type := Expr_0\ \texttt{return}\ Expr_1\ \textbf{raises}\ \texttt{typeErr}} \quad \text{(LET-TYPE--ERR)}$$

Recall that in XQuery, type declarations also occur in `for`, `some`, and `every` expressions and in function signatures—the rules for raising type errors in these expressions are similar.

The following rules illustrate how an error is propagated from the sub-expression in which it occurs to the containing expression. In XQuery, there is no expression for catching an error, so typically an error is propagated all the way back to the programming environment in which the query is evaluated. Here are the rules for propagating errors through the less-than operator. If either argument of an operator raises an error, then the operator raises an error. We give the two rules for less than, the rules for the other operators are similar.

$$\frac{dynEnv \vdash Expr_0\ \textbf{raises}\ Error}{dynEnv \vdash Expr_0 < Expr_1\ \textbf{raises}\ Error} \quad \text{(LT-LEFT-ERR)}$$

$$\frac{dynEnv \vdash Expr_1 \textbf{ raises } Error}{dynEnv \vdash Expr_0 < Expr_1 \textbf{ raises } Error} \quad \text{(LT-RIGHT-ERR)}$$

The rules for an `if` expression are omitted, but similar—an error is propagated if it arises in the condition, or if it arises in the branch that is evaluated.

In a `let` expression, an error is propagated if it arises in the first or second expression.

$$\frac{dynEnv \vdash Expr_0 \textbf{ raises } Error}{dynEnv \vdash \texttt{let } \$Var \text{ as } Type := Expr_0 \text{ return } Expr_1 \textbf{ raises } Error} \quad \text{(LET-LEFT)}$$

We bind the variable to its value before checking whether the second expression raises an error:

$$\frac{\begin{array}{c} dynEnv \vdash Expr_0 \Rightarrow Value_0 \\ dynEnv + varValue(Var \Rightarrow Value_0) \vdash Expr_1 \textbf{ raises } Error \end{array}}{dynEnv \vdash \texttt{let } \$Var \text{ as } Type := Expr_0 \text{ return } Expr_1 \textbf{ raises } Error} \quad \text{(LET-RIGHT)}$$

Here is an example of evaluation that raises an error.

$$\cfrac{\cfrac{\quad}{dynEnv_0 \vdash \texttt{0} \Rightarrow \texttt{0}} \text{(VALUE)} \quad \cfrac{\cfrac{\cfrac{\quad}{dynEnv_1 \vdash \texttt{\$x} \Rightarrow \texttt{0}} \text{(VAR)}}{dynEnv_1 \vdash \texttt{1 idiv 0 } \textbf{raises } \texttt{dynErr}} \text{(IDIV-ERR)}}{dynEnv_1 \vdash \texttt{\$x+(1 idiv \$x) } \textbf{raises } \texttt{dynErr}} \text{(SUM-RIGHT-ERR)}}{dynEnv_0 \vdash \texttt{let \$x := 0 return \$x+(1 idiv \$x) } \textbf{raises } \texttt{dynErr}} \text{(LET)}$$

where $dynEnv_0 = \varnothing$, $dynEnv_1 = varValue(x \Rightarrow 0)$.

By the rules above, sometimes an expression may raise two different errors. For example, the expression

```
(1 idiv 0) + (2 < 3)
```

may raise a dynamic error (for division by zero) or a type error (for using a Boolean as a summand). If the static type checking feature is in use, then all type errors are caught in the static analysis phase. But if the static type-checking feature is not in use, then a conforming implementation may raise either error for the expression above.

Note that there exist other kinds of errors in XQuery which are not detected by the type system. For instance, parse errors, which are typically detected even before static typing occurs, or recursive functions going into infinite loops, which are typically never detected by the system.

Static Semantics

The previous sections described the *dynamic semantics*, that is how expressions in core XQuery are evaluated. The next step is to explain the *static semantics*, how static types are associated with expressions in core XQuery. We reuse the inference-rule notation of the previous section to describe the static semantics.

Static typing is a remarkable innovation. If the static analysis phase concludes that an expression has a given type, then one can be sure that expression *always* yields a value that matches the given type. In effect, the static analysis has performed a small proof, ensuring that the expression always returns data that fits a certain format.

Static typing is a process that takes a static environment and an expression and returns a type. Here is how we write it:

$$statEnv \vdash Expr : Type$$

This is read, "In environment *statEnv*, expression *Expr* has type *Type*." We call this a **typing judgment**.

Here *statEnv* represents the static environment that captures the context available at query-analysis time, which includes variables and their types. The notation for the static environment is analogous to the notation for dynamic environments. We write Ø for the initial static environment with an empty map. We write *statEnv* + *varType(Var : Type)* for the environment that is identical to *statEnv* except that *Var* maps to *Type*, and we write *statEnv.varType(Var)* for the type of *Var* in *statEnv*. We write *dom(statEnv.varType)* for the set of variables that are given a type in *statEnv*.

Here is the XQuery grammar that we have built so far:

Value	::=	*Boolean* | *Integer*
Expr	::=	*Value*
	|	*Expr* < *Expr*
	|	*Expr* + *Expr*
	|	*Expr* `idiv` *Expr*
	|	`if` (*Expr*) `then` *Expr* `else` *Expr*
	|	`$`*Var*
	|	`let $` *Var* := *Expr* `return` *Expr*
	|	`let $`*Var* `as` *Type* := *Expr* `return` *Expr*
Type	::=	`xs:boolean` | `xs:integer`

Static typing is defined by the nine rules below, which correspond closely to the rules for dynamic evaluation on page 242–243 and 246–247. We are going to compare the static rules for each expression with the corresponding dynamic rules, because doing so makes crystal clear the meaning of each expression. We encourage you do make the same comparisons when you read the XQuery Formal Semantics [XQ-FS].

The static rules (LT), (SUM), (IDIV), (VAR), and (LET) look like the corresponding dynamic rules; we've replaced judgments of the form *Expr* ⇒ *Value* by judgments of the form *Expr* : *Type*, taking care to ensure that the dynamic value has the static type. In effect, we've replaced concrete evaluation that yields values by abstract evaluation that yields types.

$$\frac{\begin{array}{c} statEnv \vdash Expr_0 : \texttt{xs:integer} \\ statEnv \vdash Expr_1 : \texttt{xs:integer} \end{array}}{statEnv \vdash Expr_0 < Expr_1 : \texttt{xs:boolean}} \quad \text{(LT-STATIC)}$$

$$\frac{\begin{array}{c} statEnv \vdash Expr_0 : \texttt{xs:integer} \\ statEnv \vdash Expr_1 : \texttt{xs:integer} \end{array}}{statEnv \vdash Expr_0 + Expr_1 : \texttt{xs:integer}} \quad \text{(SUM-STATIC)}$$

$$\frac{\begin{array}{c} statEnv \vdash Expr_0 : \texttt{xs:integer} \\ statEnv \vdash Expr_1 : \texttt{xs:integer} \end{array}}{statEnv \vdash Expr_0 \; \texttt{idiv} \; Expr_1 : \texttt{xs:integer}} \quad \text{(IDIV-STATIC)}$$

$$\frac{statEnv.varType(Var) = Type}{statEnv \vdash \$Var : Type} \quad \text{(VAR-STATIC)}$$

$$\frac{\begin{array}{c} statEnv \vdash Expr_0 : Type_0 \\ statEnv + varType(Var : Type_0) \vdash Expr_1 : Type_1 \end{array}}{statEnv \vdash \texttt{let} \; \$Var := Expr_0 \; \texttt{return} \; Expr_1 : Type_1} \quad \text{(LET-STATIC)}$$

The dynamic evaluation rule for literal expressions (VALUE) breaks into one rule for each type, (BOOLEAN) and (INTEGER). We need two rules so we can assign the appropriate type to each literal expression.

$$\frac{}{statEnv \vdash Boolean : \texttt{xs:boolean}} \quad \text{(BOOLEAN-STATIC)}$$

$$\frac{}{statEnv \vdash Integer : \texttt{xs:integer}} \quad \text{(INTEGER-STATIC)}$$

The two dynamic rules for conditionals (IF-TRUE) and (IF-FALSE) coalesce into one static typing rule (IF).

$$\frac{\begin{array}{c} statEnv \vdash Expr_0 : \texttt{xs:boolean} \\ statEnv \vdash Expr_1 : Type \\ statEnv \vdash Expr_2 : Type \end{array}}{statEnv \vdash \texttt{if} \; (Expr_0) \; \texttt{then} \; Expr_1 \; \texttt{else} \; Expr_2 : Type} \quad \text{(IF-STATIC)}$$

Here, the formalism helps us distinguish clearly between the static and dynamic behavior of the language. In the static semantics, we do not examine the *value* of the condition expression as we do in the dynamic semantics, because the value is not known statically. Instead, we only examine the *type* of the condition, which must be Boolean, and we require that the branches have the same type. (XQuery, unlike many other languages, has a sufficiently expressive type system that we don't need to make this restriction; we'll return to this point later in the subsection entitled "Values and Types.")

The static rule for a `let` expression with a type declaration requires that the type of the first expression must match the declared type. The first judgment below ensures that $Expr_0$ has type $Type_0$, and the second judgment extends the environment of variable types by adding a new mapping from the variable Var to its type $Type_0$, and then uses this new environment to type the subexpression $Expr_1$.

$$\frac{\begin{array}{c} statEnv \vdash Expr_0 : Type_0 \\ statEnv + varType(Var : Type_0) \vdash Expr_1 : Type_1 \end{array}}{statEnv \vdash \texttt{let } \$Var \text{ as } Type_0 := Expr_0 \texttt{ return } Expr_1 : Type_1} \text{(LET-DECL-STATIC)}$$

Recall that the two dynamic rules for a `let` expression with a type declaration perform a check at evaluation time to confirm that the value of the first expression matches the declared type; otherwise they raise a type error:

$$\frac{\begin{array}{c} dynEnv \vdash Expr_0 \Rightarrow Value_0 \\ Value_0 \textbf{ matches } Type \\ dynEnv + varValue(Var \Rightarrow Value_0) \vdash Expr_1 \Rightarrow Value_1 \end{array}}{dynEnv \vdash \texttt{let } \$Var \text{ as } Type := Expr_0 \texttt{ return } Expr_1 \Rightarrow Value_1} \text{(LET-DECL)}$$

$$\frac{\begin{array}{c} dynEnv \vdash Expr_0 \Rightarrow Value_0 \\ \textbf{not}(Value_0 \textbf{ matches } Type) \end{array}}{dynEnv \vdash \texttt{let } \$Var \text{ as } Type := Expr_0 \texttt{ return } Expr_1 \text{ \underline{raises} } \texttt{typeErr}} \text{(LET-TYPE-ERR)}$$

As we will see in the next section, an important consequence of static analysis is that we do not need to check for type errors at evaluation time, which means the **matches** judgment in the first dynamic rule above and the entire second rule are redundant when static typing is in effect.

Proof Tree 5.2 shows the static typing of a conditional expression, corresponding to the dynamic evaluation on page 248. Note that the static type computed for the expression is xs:integer and that the dynamic value computed for the expression is 7, which is indeed an integer.

Proof Tree 5.2   Static Typing of a Conditional Expression

$$
\cfrac{
  \cfrac{
    \cfrac{\cfrac{}{statEnv \vdash 1 \; : \; \texttt{xs:integer}}\;(\text{INTEGER})}{\cfrac{}{statEnv \vdash 2 \; : \; \texttt{xs:integer}}\;(\text{INTEGER})}
    \;(\text{LT})
  }{statEnv \vdash \texttt{1<2} \; : \; \texttt{xs:boolean}}
  \quad
  \cfrac{
    \cfrac{\cfrac{}{statEnv \vdash 3 \; : \; \texttt{xs:integer}}\;(\text{INTEGER})}{\cfrac{}{statEnv \vdash 4 \; : \; \texttt{xs:integer}}\;(\text{INTEGER})}
    \;(\text{SUM})
  }{statEnv \vdash \texttt{3+4} \; : \; \texttt{xs:integer}}
  \quad
  \cfrac{
    \cfrac{\cfrac{}{statEnv \vdash 5 \; : \; \texttt{xs:integer}}\;(\text{INTEGER})}{\cfrac{}{statEnv \vdash 6 \; : \; \texttt{xs:integer}}\;(\text{INTEGER})}
    \;(\text{SUM})
  }{statEnv \vdash \texttt{5+6} \; : \; \texttt{xs:integer}}
}{statEnv \vdash \texttt{if (1<2) then 3+4 else 5+6} \; : \; \texttt{xs:integer}} \;(\text{IF})
$$

The XQuery static type rules are written so that the correspondence between an expression's type and its value is *guaranteed* for all expressions—this guarantee is called *type soundness*, which we discuss next.

Type Soundness

Of course, the dynamic semantics and static semantics of an expression should be related. Say that an expression has a given type. Then we expect that the expression either yields a value that has that type or raises a dynamic error. This property is called **type soundness.** A consequence of type soundness is that, when the static typing feature of XQuery is implemented, if a query passes the static-analysis phase, then it cannot raise a type error during the evaluation phase.

Here is an example of successful evaluation.

$$
\cfrac{
  \cfrac{
    \cfrac{\rule{2.5cm}{0.4pt}}{dynEnv_0 \vdash \texttt{1} \Rightarrow \texttt{1}} \text{ (VALUE)}
  }{
    \texttt{1} \underline{\texttt{matches}} \texttt{ xs:integer}
  } \text{ (INT-MATCH)}
  \qquad
  \cfrac{
    \cfrac{\cfrac{\rule{2.5cm}{0.4pt}}{dynEnv_1 \vdash \texttt{\$x} \Rightarrow \texttt{1}} \text{ (VAR)} \quad \cfrac{\rule{2.5cm}{0.4pt}}{dynEnv_1 \vdash \texttt{\$x} \Rightarrow \texttt{1}} \text{ (VAR)}}{dynEnv_1 \vdash \texttt{\$x+\$x} \Rightarrow \texttt{2}}
  }{} \text{ (SUM)}
}{
  dynEnv_0 \vdash \texttt{let \$x as xs:integer := 1 return \$x+\$x} \Rightarrow \texttt{2}
} \text{ (LET-DECL)}
$$

where $dynEnv_0 = \varnothing$, $dynEnv_1 = varValue(\text{x} \Rightarrow 0)$.

As before, we write *Value* **matches** *Type* to indicate that the given value belongs to the given type. To phrase type soundness properly, we need to capture the relationship between a dynamic environment and the corresponding static environment. We write

$$dynEnv \ \textbf{matches} \ statEnv$$

if $dom(dynEnv.varValue) = dom(statEnv.varType)$, that is, the dynamic and static environments contain the same variables, and for every variable x in that domain,

$$dynEnv.varValue(x) \ \textbf{matches} \ statEnv.varType(x).$$

For example, the following two environments match.

$$dynEnv_1 \ := \ varValue(\text{x} \Rightarrow \texttt{1, y} \Rightarrow \texttt{0, z} \Rightarrow \texttt{fn:false()})$$
$$statEnv_1 \ := \ varType(\text{x} : \texttt{xs:integer, y} : \texttt{xs:integer, z} : \texttt{xs:boolean})$$

We can now state two type soundness results, one for evaluation and one for errors. The first result states that dynamic and static evaluation in matching environments yield matching results.

Theorem 5.1   Type Soundness for Values

If

$$dynEnv \textbf{ matches } statEnv$$
$$dynEnv \vdash Expr \Rightarrow Value$$
$$statEnv \vdash Expr : Type$$

then

$$Value \textbf{ matches } Type.$$

For example, assume *statEnv*₁ and *dynEnv*₁ are as above. We have

$$dynEnv_1 \textbf{ matches } statEnv_1$$
$$dynEnv_1 \vdash \texttt{if (\$z) then \$x else \$y} \Rightarrow 0$$
$$statEnv_1 \vdash \texttt{if (\$z) then \$x else \$y : xs:integer}$$

and hence

$$0 \textbf{ matches } \texttt{xs:integer}$$

as we expect.

The type soundness theorem looks a little like an inference rule, in that it has hypotheses and a conclusion. But it differs from an inference rule in that it is not invoked as part of static analysis or dynamic evaluation; instead, it is a statement that relates those two processes.

The second result states that if an expression has a static type, then evaluation will not yield a type error.

Theorem 5.2   Type Soundness for Errors

If

$$dynEnv \textbf{ matches } statEnv$$
$$dynEnv \vdash Expr \textbf{ raises } Error$$
$$statEnv \vdash Expr : Type$$

then

$$Error \neq \texttt{typeErr}.$$

Static checking guarantees the absence of type errors, but of course it cannot guarantee the absence of dynamic errors. For example, the following judgments are consistent with the type soundness for errors theorem, because the error that the expression raises is not a type error:

$$dynEnv_1 \text{ matches } statEnv_1$$
$$dynEnv_1 \vdash \texttt{\$x idiv \$y } \textbf{raises } \texttt{dynErr}$$
$$statEnv_1 \vdash \texttt{\$x idiv \$y } : \texttt{xs:integer}$$

If evaluation of an expression raises a type error, then we know it cannot type check. For example,

$$dynEnv_1 \vdash \texttt{\$x+\$z } \textbf{raises } \texttt{typeErr}.$$

This expression raises a type error when it attempts to apply addition to a Boolean. Hence we know that

$$statEnv_1 \vdash \texttt{\$x+\$z } : \textit{Type}$$

does not hold for any *Type*.

The converse does not hold. An expression that does not raise a type error may still fail to statically type. For example,

$$dynEnv_1 \vdash \texttt{if (\$x < \$y) then \$x+\$z else \$y} \Rightarrow 0$$

does not raise a type error because the ill-typed expression is not evaluated. However, it still fails to type check, since

$$statEnv_1 \vdash \texttt{if (\$x < \$y) then \$x+\$z else \$y} : \textit{Type}$$

does not hold for any *Type*. (Recall $z has type xs:boolean.)

In other words, static typing is a *conservative* analysis—passing static type checking guarantees the absence of type errors, but the absence of dynamic type errors does not guarantee that an expression will pass static type checking.

Type soundness has practical as well as theoretical implications. For implementers, type soundness determines how clever they can be when implementing the dynamic and static rules. If the implementation never performs static typing, then the dynamic-evaluation rules that raise type errors and all the **matches** judgments must be implemented. If the implementation always performs static typing, then the dynamic-evaluation rules that raise type errors and all the **matches** judgments need not be implemented. If the implementation optionally supports static typing, then the implementer may choose to implement the dynamic rules with type errors, knowing they are redundant, or skip evaluation of the type error rules and **matches** judgments when static typing is enabled. These last two implementation strategies are only possible when type soundness is guaranteed. If the type system is not sound, then an expression's type and value might not match, in which case elimination of run-time type checks of values would be disastrous.

XQuery has been carefully designed so that it satisfies these two soundness theorems. Usually, typed languages are designed to satisfy similar theorems. But there have been exceptions, where a language designed by one group of researchers and subsequently formalized by another was found not to satisfy an appropriate soundness theorem; this typically indicates some problem in the original language design.

Evaluation Order

A language specification should not specify too much and should give the implementer enough freedom to choose an efficient implementation. Fortunately, our formalism is precise yet flexible enough to express this freedom.

Consider the operator and on Boolean expressions.

Expr and *Expr*

An implementation should have the freedom to test the expressions in either order—that is, it should be able to stop and return `false` if either expression evaluates to `false` without evaluating the other expression, and similarly, it should be able to raise an error if either expression raises an error.

We can easily capture these conditions in our evaluation and error rules. The first two rules for the conjunction (and) operator below yield `false` if either expression yields `false`, and the third rule yields `true` if both expressions yield `true`.

$$\frac{dynEnv \vdash Expr_0 \Rightarrow \texttt{fn:false()}}{dynEnv \vdash Expr_0 \texttt{ and } Expr_1 \Rightarrow \texttt{fn:false()}} \text{ (AND-LEFT-FALSE)}$$

$$\frac{dynEnv \vdash Expr_1 \Rightarrow \texttt{fn:false()}}{dynEnv \vdash Expr_0 \texttt{ and } Expr_1 \Rightarrow \texttt{fn:false()}} \text{ (AND-RIGHT-FALSE)}$$

$$\frac{\begin{array}{c} dynEnv \vdash Expr_0 \Rightarrow \texttt{fn:true()} \\ dynEnv \vdash Expr_1 \Rightarrow \texttt{fn:true()} \end{array}}{dynEnv \vdash Expr_0 \textit{ and } Expr_1 \Rightarrow \texttt{fn:true()}} \text{ (AND-BOTH)}$$

The next two rules for conjunction raise an error if either expression raises an error.

$$\frac{dynEnv \vdash Expr_0 \textbf{ raises } Error}{dynEnv \vdash Expr_0 \texttt{ and } Expr_1 \textbf{ raises } Error} \text{ (AND-LEFT-ERR)}$$

$$\frac{dynEnv \vdash Expr_1 \textbf{ raises } Error}{dynEnv \vdash Expr_0 \texttt{ and } Expr_1 \textbf{ raises } Error} \text{ (AND-RIGHT-ERR)}$$

The rules for conjunction are the first ones we've seen with hypotheses that are not mutually exclusive, which means the result of evaluating a conjunction is non-deterministic. For example, the rules AND-LEFT-ERR and AND-RIGHT-FALSE are both applicable to an expression whose left-hand expression evaluates to false and whose right-hand expression raises an error. This choice means that an expression may either yield a value or raise an error. Consider the expression

```
(1 idiv 0 < 2) and (4 < 3)
```

Here is the proof that this expression may raise an error

$$
\cfrac{
  \cfrac{
    \cfrac{
      \cfrac{
        \cfrac{\Gamma}{0 \Rightarrow 0}\ (\text{VALUE})
      }{\texttt{1 idiv 0 \textbf{raises} dynErr}}\ (\text{IDIV-ERR})
    }{\texttt{(1 idiv 0) < 2 \textbf{raises} dynErr}}\ (\text{LT-LEFT-ERR})
  }{\texttt{(1 idiv 0 < 2) and (4 < 3) \textbf{raises} dynErr}}\ (\text{AND-LEFT-ERR})
}{}
$$

And here is a proof that this expression may return false.

$$
\cfrac{
  \cfrac{
    \cfrac{
      \cfrac{\Gamma}{4 \Rightarrow 4}\ (\text{VALUE}) \quad
      \cfrac{\Gamma}{3 \Rightarrow 3}\ (\text{VALUE})
    }{\texttt{4 < 3 } \Rightarrow \texttt{ fn:false()}}\ (\text{LT})
  }{\texttt{(1 idiv 0 < 2) and (4 < 3) } \Rightarrow \texttt{ fn:false()}}\ (\text{AND-RIGHT-FALSE})
}{}
$$

In such cases, the implementer is free to choose either behavior, but the rules make clear that these are the only two choices!

Note that the non-deterministic semantics for conjunction implies that the following two expressions are not equivalent, because they differ in their evaluation order.

$$Expr_0 \text{ and } Expr_1$$
$$\texttt{if } (Expr_0) \texttt{ then } Expr_1 \texttt{ else false()}$$

The first expression can evaluate $Expr_0$ and $Expr_1$ in either order, but the second always evaluates $Expr_0$ first, and only if it is true does it evaluate $Expr_1$. So the second expression is more constrained in its evaluation than the first; an optimizer might choose to replace the first expression by the second, but not conversely.

Normalization

We have covered the techniques used for the static and dynamic semantics in XQuery. The last step is to explain normalization. Earlier in the chapter, we explained that normalization rules transform full XQuery into a small core language, which is easier to define, implement, and optimize, and that the dynamic and static semantics are defined in terms of the core language.

Normalization is a process that takes an expression in full XQuery and returns an equivalent expression in core XQuery. Here is how we write it:

$$[\textit{FullExpr}]_{\text{Expr}}$$
$$== \textit{Expr}$$

The *Expr* subscript indicates that any full XQuery expression can be normalized by the rule. Later in the chapter, we'll see rules that only normalize path expressions, in which case the subscript will be Path to indicate that restriction.

The subset of XQuery used in this section is so simple that none of the expressions require normalization. So to explain normalization, we add a variant of the `let` expression that includes a `where` clause—this is a warm-up for the semantics of FLWOR, discussed in the section below entitled "FLWOR Expressions."

Here is the grammar for a full XQuery expression. It includes all the expressions we've seen so far, plus the new `let` expression.

$$\textit{FullExpr} ::= \textit{Expr}$$
$$| \quad \texttt{let } \$\textit{Var} \text{ as } \textit{Type} := \textit{Expr} \text{ where } \textit{Expr} \text{ return } \textit{Expr}$$

Here's the normalization rule for the new `let` expression, which rewrites it into a simple `let` expression that returns the value of its `return` clause if the `where` condition is true; otherwise it returns the empty sequence.

$$[\texttt{let } \$\textit{Var} \text{ as } \textit{Type} := \textit{Expr}_0 \text{ where } \textit{Expr}_1 \text{ return } \textit{Expr}_2]_{\text{Expr}}$$
$$== \texttt{let } \$\textit{Var} \text{ as } \textit{Type} := [\textit{Expr}_0]_{\text{Expr}} \texttt{ return if } ([\textit{Expr}_1]_{\text{Expr}}) \texttt{ then } [\textit{Expr}_2]_{\text{Expr}} \texttt{ else } ()$$

Note that the rule above recursively applies normalization to the subexpressions $\textit{Expr}_0$, $\textit{Expr}_1$, and $\textit{Expr}_2$, as these expressions may also contain `let-where` expressions.

The normalization rules for the other expressions are similar. For example, here is the normalization of the sum operator:

$$[Expr_0 + Expr_1]_{\text{Expr}}$$
$$== [Expr_0]_{\text{Expr}} + [Expr_1]_{\text{Expr}}$$

Even though the sum expression itself is a "core" expression (i.e., it's in our little language), its subexpressions might not be, so the rule must recursively normalize the subexpressions as well. The same holds true for the less-than operator and the other `let` and `if-then-else` expressions.

Literals and variables are the only expressions that do not normalize recursively. They simply normalize to themselves. Here's the rule for a variable:

$$[\$Var]_{\text{Expr}}$$
$$== \$Var$$

Normalizing full XQuery into a smaller core allows us to provide useful syntactic constructs (like the `where` clause) without increasing the expressiveness or complexity of the language. It also makes formal specification easier because the dynamic and static semantics are defined on the smaller core language.

Finishing Getting Started

We have seen how to specify precisely the dynamic and static semantics of a tiny subset of XQuery and how to normalize a slightly larger subset. Even the small language covered required a fair bit of work, but in return for this, a number of details of evaluation have been precisely characterized: definition of variables in `let` expressions and lookup of variables in environments; matching of values against types; issues connected with order of evaluation; relating an expression's static type to its dynamic value; and where and what kind of errors may be raised.

The resulting semantics provides a good road-map for implementers; often, a naive implementation can be written as a straightforward transposition of the inference rules (see [PROG-LANG]). Even though most XQuery implementations will be quite complex and sophisticated, implementers can turn to the formal semantics as a good reference that is independent of any particular implementation strategy.

Now that you are familiar with the techniques and notations used in the formal semantics, you can go read *XQuery 1.0 Formal Semantics* [XQ-FS] or simply use it as a reference document. In the next section, we help you become familiar with the semantics of some key XQuery expressions, including FLWOR, path expressions, arithmetic, comparison, and constructor expressions. For the many simple expressions, such as sequences and conditionals, that we don't cover, you can go directly to the XQuery Formal Semantics.

Learning More about XQuery

We start by describing the formal model of XML values and XML Schema types used in XQuery, which is necessary to understand the rest of the chapter. Then the next section, "Matching and Subtyping," expands on our definition of matching to include matching of complex XML values with complex types. Since FLWOR expressions are the workhorse of XQuery, we cover their normalization and static and dynamic semantics in the section entitled "FLWOR Expressions." The normalization of path expressions into FLWOR expressions is covered next in "Path Expressions." The normalization of arithmetic and comparison operators into function calls is covered next, under "Implicit Coercions and Function Calls." We conclude with a section dealing with node identity and element constructors.

Values and Types

In the "Getting Started" section, we only had Boolean and integer values and types. To define XQuery formally, we first need to define XML values and types.

Values

We start with the formal notation for values. Recall from Chapter 4 that a **value** is a sequence of zero or more **items**. Sequences are central to XQuery's semantics—so much so that one item and a sequence containing that item are indistinguishable. We write ( ) for the empty sequence, and *Item*$_1$, . . . , *Item*$_n$ for a sequence of *n* items. An item is either an **atomic value** or a node value.

$$
\begin{aligned}
\textit{Value} \ ::= \ & \ (\,) \\
| \ & \ \textit{Item} \,(,\!\textit{Item})\!\star \\
\textit{Item} \ ::= \ & \ \textit{AtomicValue} \mid \textit{NodeValue}
\end{aligned}
$$

We also write *Value*$_1$, *Value*$_2$ for the value that is the concatenation of two values.

An atomic value is either an integer, Boolean, string, or date.

$$
\begin{aligned}
\textit{AtomicValue} \ ::= \ & \texttt{xs:integer}(\textit{String}) \\
| \ & \texttt{xs:boolean}(\textit{String}) \\
| \ & \texttt{xs:string}(\textit{String}) \\
| \ & \texttt{xs:date}(\textit{String})
\end{aligned}
$$

Here we use the value-constructor functions to be explicit about the type attached to data. The arguments to `xs:integer()`, `xs:boolean()`, and `xs:date()` must be strings in the lexical space of `integer` and `date`, as defined by XML Schema Part 2 [SCHEMA]. (XML Schema specifies nineteen primitive data types. The full XQuery data model has the same, and also gives special status to `integer`, which is derived from `decimal`. Here we consider only the subset above.)

We write unadorned strings and integers as abbreviations for the corresponding cases above. Thus, `"Red bicycle"` is short for `xs:string("Red bicycle")` and `42` is short for `xs:integer("42")`. We also use `fn:true()` and `fn:false()` in lieu of `xs:boolean("true")` and `xs:boolean("false")`.

A node is either an element or text. An element has an element name (which is a qualified name), a type annotation, and a value. A text node has a text string. We do not discuss attributes, as their semantics is largely similar to that of elements.

NodeValue	::=	element *ElementName TypeAnnotation*? { *Value* }
	|	text { *String* }
ElementName	::=	*QName*
TypeAnnotation	::=	of type *TypeName*
TypeName	::=	*QName*

We may omit the type annotation on an element, in which case the annotation xs:anyType is assumed. Thus,

element *ElementName* { *Value* }

is equivalent to

element *ElementName* of type xs:anyType { *Value* }

(The full data model also has document, comment, and processing instruction nodes. Here we consider only the subset above.)

Types

Chapter 4 introduced XML Schema, briefly explained its relationship to the XQuery type system, and presented some examples of XQuery types. Here is an example just to refresh your memory. Suppose that we have the schema shown in Listing 5.1, in which an article element contains a name element and zero or more reserve_price elements, and a reserve_price contains zero or more decimal values:

Listing 5.1   XML Schema for the article Element

```
<xs:element name="article" type="Article"/>
<xs:complexType name="Article">
   <xs:sequence>
      <xs:element name="name" type="xs:string"/>
      <xs:element name="reserve_price" type="PriceList"
                  minOccurs="0" maxOccurs="unbounded"/>
   </xs:sequence>
</xs:complexType>
<xs:simpleType name="PriceList">
   <xs:list itemType="xs:decimal"/>
</xs:simpleType>
```

This schema is represented in the XQuery type notation as shown in Listing 5.2:

Listing 5.2   XQuery Type Definitions for the `article` Element

```
define element article of type Article
define type Article {
  element(name,xs:string),
  element(reserve_price,PriceList) *
}
define type PriceList restricts xs:anySimpleType { xs:decimal * }
```

We refer to this example in the following sections. We refer you to the XQuery Formal Semantics [XQ-FS] for the complete mapping from XML Schema into the XQuery type system.

We start with an **item type**, which is a node type or an atomic type. A **node type** is an element type or a text type. Element types are explained below. All text nodes have the same type, which is `text()`. An atomic type is given by its name.

ItemType	:=	*NodeType* | *AtomicType*
NodeType	:=	*ElementType*
		| `text()`
AtomicType	:=	*AtomicTypeName*
AtomicTypeName	:=	`xs:string` | `xs:integer` | `xs:date`
		| `xs:boolean`

Every *AtomicTypeName* is also a *TypeName*.

An element type gives an optional name, followed by an optional type name. A name alone refers to a global declaration (e.g., `element(article)`). A name followed by a type name is a local declaration (e.g., `element(name,xs:string)`). The wildcard name * can be used to match any name (e.g., `element(*,xs:string)`). The expression `element()` alone refers to any element.

$$\textit{ElementType} := \texttt{element}\,((\textit{ElementName}\,(,\,\textit{TypeName})?)?)$$

A type is either the nil choice (`none()`), the empty type (`empty()`), an item type, or composed by sequence (,), choice (|), or an occurrence indicator—either optional (?), one or more (+), or zero or more (*).

$$
\begin{array}{rcl}
\textit{Type} & ::= & \texttt{none()} \\
& | & \texttt{empty()} \\
& | & \textit{ItemType} \\
& | & \textit{Type}\,,\textit{Type} \\
& | & \textit{Type}\mid\textit{Type} \\
& | & \textit{Type Occurrence} \\
\textit{Occurrence} & ::= & \texttt{?}\mid\texttt{+}\mid\texttt{*}
\end{array}
$$

A *simple type* is composed from atomic types by choice or occurrence. Every simple type is a type.

$$
\begin{array}{rcl}
\textit{SimpleType} & ::= & \textit{AtomicTypeName} \\
& | & \textit{SimpleType}\mid\textit{SimpleType} \\
& | & \textit{SimpleType Occurrence}
\end{array}
$$

At the *top level* one can define elements and types. A global element declaration, like a local element declaration, consists of an element name and a type annotation. A global type declaration consists of a type name and a type derivation. A type derivation either restricts an atomic type or a named type and specifies the restricted type.

$$
\begin{array}{rcl}
\textit{Definition} & ::= & \texttt{define element } \textit{ElementName} \\
\textit{TypeAnnotation} & & \\
& | & \texttt{define type } \textit{TypeName TypeDerivation} \\
\textit{TypeDerivation} & ::= & \texttt{restricts } \textit{AtomicTypeName} \\
& | & \texttt{restricts } \textit{TypeName} \{\ \textit{Type}\ \} \\
& | & \{\textit{Type}\}
\end{array}
$$

All complex types are derived from `xs:anyType`, thus the shorthand definition

$$
\texttt{define type } \textit{TypeName} \{\textit{Type}\}
$$

is equivalent to

$$
\texttt{define type } \textit{TypeName} \texttt{ restricts xs:anyType} \{\ \textit{Type}\ \}.
$$

Remember that all element types are assumed to have a type annotation. In the case of an XML Schema anonymous type, an implementation-defined name is computed. This property is required by the semantics of matching given next.

Matching and Subtyping

Since XQuery is a strongly typed language, matching values to types is central to its dynamic semantics. We have already seen that matching is used in the semantics of type declarations, which occur in `let`, `for`, `some`, and `every` expressions and function signatures. Matching for Boolean and integer values only was defined in the previous section entitled "Matching Values and Types." In this section, we extend the definition of matching to relate complex XML values with complex types. After matching, the next most important judgment on types is subtyping. Subtyping is used during static analysis to check whether a type is a subtype of another type. Both matching and subtyping are used extensively in this section.

Types in XML differ in some ways from types used elsewhere in computing. Traditionally, a value *matches* a type—given a value and a type, either the value belongs to the type or it does not. In XML, a value can also *validate* against a type—given an (external) value and a type, validation produces an (internal) value or it fails. After validation, one can safely talk about type matching.

For instance, consider the simple type `PriceList`, defined in the XML Schema in Listing 5.1, and the following unvalidated element value:

```
<reserve_price> 10.00 20.00 25.00 </reserve_price>
```

Before validation, this element is represented by the following untyped XML value.

```
element reserve_price { text { " 10.00 20.00 25.00 " }}
```

After validation, this element is represented by the following typed XML value:

```
element reserve_price of type PriceList {10.0 20.0 25.0}
```

(As in Chapter 4, we use this formal notation to illustrate the type labels of validated elements and attributes—it is not a valid XQuery expression.) Validation has annotated the element with its type, `PriceList`. If we extract the typed value of this node by applying the `fn:data` function, the result is the sequence of decimals (`10.0, 20.0, 25.0`).

Unvalidated data may not match against a type; therefore, the following *does not hold:*

```
element reserve_price { text { " 10.00 20.00 25.00 " }} matches
element(reserve_price)
```

Recall that the sequence type `element reserve_price` refers to the globally declared `reserve_price` element. After validation, matching succeeds, so the following *does* hold:

```
element reserve_price of type PriceList {10.0 20.0 25.0}
matches
element(reserve_price)
```

In practice, an XQuery processor does not necessarily need to implement validation itself, but can rely on a third-party XML Schema validator. An XQuery processor, however, must implement matching. Thus, we focus on matching in this section and refer the reader to the XML Schema specification [SCHEMA], or to the formal treatment of validation in the XQuery Formal Semantics [XQ-FS], or to the more gentle introduction to validation in *The Essence of XML* [ESSENCE].

Now we are ready to give the rule for matching elements against element types. The rule uses three new judgments **yields, substitutes for,** and **derives from,** which we define next.

$$statEnv \vdash ElementType \text{ \textbf{yields} element } (ElementName_1, TypeName_1)$$

$$statEnv \vdash ElementName \text{ \textbf{substitutes for} } ElementName_1$$

$$statEnv \vdash TypeName \text{ \textbf{derives from} } TypeName_1$$

$$statEnv \vdash Value \text{ \textbf{matches} } TypeName$$

$$statEnv \vdash \frac{}{\text{element } ElementName \text{ of type } TypeName \{ Value \}} \text{ \textbf{matches} } ElementType$$

First the content of the element type is examined to yield a base element name *ElementName*₁ and a base type name *TypeName*₁. Then the given element matches the element type if three things hold: the element name must be able to substitute for the base element name, the type name must derive from the base type name, and the value must match the type. This is a mouthful, but it will make sense once we define the three ancillary judgments.

Yields

The judgment

$$ElementType \; \textbf{yields} \; \texttt{element} \, (ElementName, TypeName)$$

takes an element type and yields an element name and a type name. We assume that the element names include a special wildcard name ⋆, which is returned if the element type does not specify an element name. For example,

```
element(article) yields element(article,Article)
element(reserve_price,PriceList) yields
element(reserve_price,PriceList)
element(*,PriceList) yields element(*,PriceList)
element()yields element(*,xs:anyType)
```

If the element type is a reference to a global element, then it yields the name of the element and the type annotation from the element declaration. The first hypothesis is a global element definition; this is an abbreviation for stating that the given definition appears in the element declarations in the static environment.

$$\frac{statEnv \vdash \texttt{define element} \; ElementName \; \texttt{of type} \; TypeName}{\begin{array}{c} statEnv \vdash \texttt{element} \, (ElementN \\ \texttt{element} \, (ElementName, TypeName) \end{array}}$$

If the element type contains an element name with a type annotation, then it yields the given element name and type name in the type annotation.

$$\frac{}{\begin{array}{c} statEnv \vdash \texttt{element} \, (ElementName, TypeName) \; \textbf{yields} \\ \texttt{element} \, (ElementName, TypeName) \end{array}}$$

If the element type has a wildcard name followed by a type name, then it yields the wildcard name and the type name.

$$\overline{statEnv \vdash \texttt{element(} *, TypeName\texttt{)} \textbf{ yields } \texttt{element(} *, TypeName\texttt{)}}$$

If the element type has no element name and no type name, then it yields the wildcard name and the type name `xs:anyType`.

$$\overline{statEnv \vdash \texttt{element()} \textbf{ yields } \texttt{element(} *, \texttt{xs:anyType)}}$$

Substitution

The judgment

$$ElementName_1 \textbf{ substitutes for } ElementName_2$$

holds when the first element name may substitute for the second element name. This happens when the two names are equal, or when the second name is the wildcard element name `*`. For example `article` **substitutes for** `article` and `article` **substitutes for** `*`. (We do not discuss element substitution groups here, but the judgment generalizes neatly to handle these.)

An element name may substitute for itself.

$$\overline{statEnv \vdash ElementName \textbf{ substitutes for } ElementName}$$

And an element name may substitute for the distinguished element name `*`.

$$\overline{statEnv \vdash ElementName \textbf{ substitutes for } *}$$

Derives

The judgment

$$TypeName_1 \textbf{ derives from } TypeName_2$$

holds when the first type name derives from the second type name. For example, recall our example from Chapter 4:

```
User derives from User

NewUser derives from User

User derives from xs:anyType
```

Every type name derives from the type that it is declared to derive from by restriction.

$$\frac{\texttt{define type }\textit{TypeName}\texttt{ restricts }\textit{TypeName}_1}{\textit{TypeName}\textbf{ derives from }\textit{TypeName}_1}$$

$$\frac{\texttt{define type }\textit{TypeName}\texttt{ restricts }\textit{TypeName}_1 \{ \textit{Type} \}}{\textit{TypeName}\textbf{ derives from }\textit{TypeName}_1}$$

This relation is a partial order: It is reflexive and transitive by the rules below, and it is asymmetric because no cycles are allowed in derivation by restriction.

$$\overline{\textit{TypeName}\textbf{ derives from }\textit{TypeName}}$$

$$\frac{\textit{TypeName}_1\textbf{ derives from }\textit{TypeName}_2 \qquad \textit{TypeName}_2\textbf{ derives from }\textit{TypeName}_3}{\textit{TypeName}_1\textbf{ derives from }\textit{TypeName}_3}$$

Matches

Now we're back to matches again, but this time, we define it for all types, not just for the atomic and element types. The judgment

$$\textit{Value}\textbf{ matches }\textit{Type}$$

holds when the given value matches the given type. For example,

```
(element name of type xs:string { "Tom" },
element name of type xs:string { "Mary" })
matches
element(name,xs:string)+
```

and

```
(10.0, 20.0, 25.0) matches xs:decimal *
```

Here are the rules for matching against any type. The empty sequence matches the empty sequence type.

$$\overline{() \ \mathbf{matches} \ \mathtt{empty()}}$$

An integer value matches an atomic type name if the atomic type name derives from `xs:integer`.

$$\frac{\textit{AtomicTypeName} \ \mathbf{derives \ from} \ \mathtt{xs:integer}}{\textit{Integer} \ \mathbf{matches} \ \textit{AtomicTypeName}}$$

Similar rules apply to all the other atomic types (e.g., strings, dates, and Booleans).

If two values match two types, then their sequence matches the corresponding sequence type.

$$\frac{\textit{Value}_1 \ \mathbf{matches} \ \textit{Type}_1 \\ \textit{Value}_2 \ \mathbf{matches} \ \textit{Type}_2}{\textit{Value}_1 \ , \textit{Value}_2 \ \mathbf{matches} \ \textit{Type}_1 \ , \textit{Type}_2}$$

If a value matches a type, then it also matches a choice type where that type is one of the choices.

$$\frac{\textit{Value} \ \mathbf{matches} \ \textit{Type}_1}{\textit{Value} \ \mathbf{matches} \ \textit{Type}_1 \ | \ \textit{Type}_2}$$

$$\frac{\textit{Value} \ \mathbf{matches} \ \textit{Type}_2}{\textit{Value} \ \mathbf{matches} \ \textit{Type}_1 \ | \ \textit{Type}_2}$$

A value matches an optional occurrence of a type if it matches either the empty sequence or the type.

$$\frac{\textit{Value} \ \mathbf{matches} \ \mathtt{empty()} \ | \ \textit{Type}}{\textit{Value} \ \mathbf{matches} \ \textit{Type}?}$$

A value matches one or more occurrences of a type if it matches a sequence of the type followed by zero or more occurrences of the type.

$$\frac{Value \textbf{ matches } Type \, , \; Type_\star}{Value \textbf{ matches } Type+}$$

Lastly, a value matches zero or more occurrences of a type if it matches an optional one or more occurrences of the type.

$$\frac{Value \textbf{ matches } Type+?}{Value \textbf{ matches } Type_\star}$$

Subtyping

Finally, the judgment

$$Type_1 \textbf{ subtype } Type_2$$

holds if every value that matches the first type also matches the second. For example,

```
element(article) + subtype element(article) *
element(*,NewUser) subtype element(*,User)
```

All the judgments we have seen in this chapter are defined using inference rules over the structure of values and types. Subtyping is the only judgment that we do not define by using inference rules, because it is not possible to give a complete definition in this way. Imagine trying to define rules that prove the following three types are equivalent:

```
(element(), text())*, element(), text()
(element(), text())+
element(), text(), (element(), text())*
```

Instead, subtyping is defined by a logical equivalence. We have

$$Type_1 \textbf{ subtype } Type_2$$

if and only if

$$Value \textbf{ matches } Type_1 \quad \text{implies} \quad Value \textbf{ matches } Type_2$$

for every *Value*.

Subtyping can be checked by straightforward modification of well-known algorithms that check for inclusion between the languages generated by two regular expressions [ALGORITHMS].

FLWOR Expressions

The FLWOR expression is the workhorse of XQuery: It allows a user to iterate over sequences of values, compute intermediate results, conditionally filter values, and construct new values. In essence, it is the XQuery analog of SQL's select-from-where expression, and its syntax was designed so that it looks familiar to database programmers.

In its full generality, the FLWOR expression contains one or more `for` and `let` clauses, followed by optional `where` and `order by` clauses, followed by a `return` clause. Each `for` and `let` clause may bind one or more variables. Listing 5.3 shows the grammar for the FLWR expression (i.e., a FLWOR minus the `order by` clause):

Listing 5.3   Grammar for the FLWR Expression

Expr	:=	. . . previous expressions . . . | *FLWRExpr*
FLWRExpr	:=	*Clause*+ return *Expr*
Clause	:=	*ForExpr* | *LetExpr* | *WhereExpr*
ForExpr	:=	for *ForBinding* (, *ForBinding*)*
LetExpr	:=	let *LetBinding* (, *LetBinding*)*
WhereExpr	:=	where *Expr*
ForBinding	:=	$*Var TypeDeclaration*? *PositionalVar*? in *Expr*
LetBinding	:=	$*Var TypeDeclaration*? := *Expr*
TypeDeclaration	:=	as *SequenceType*
PositionalVar	:=	at $*Var*
SequenceType	:=	*ItemType Occurrence*

The optional type declaration in a `for` or `let` clause refers to the *SequenceType* production, which is used in XQuery to refer to a type. The optional position variable associated with the `for` clause is bound to the integer index of the current item bound to *Var* in the input sequence.

Normalization

It is easier to define the static and dynamic semantics of an expression if it is small and doesn't do too much. Trying to define the semantics of a complete FLWR expression would be difficult, but luckily a FLWR expression can always be defined in terms of multiple, simpler `for`, `let`, and `if` expressions. For example, the FLWR expression

```
for $i in $I, $j in $J
let $k := $i + $j
where $k >= 5
return ($i, $j)
```

normalizes to the following equivalent expression:

```
for $i in $I return
  for $j in $J return
    let $k := $i + $j return
      if ($k >= 5) then ($i, $j)
      else ()
```

Normalization of a FLWR expression with more than one clause turns each clause into a separate nested FLWR expression, and normalizes the result. Here's the rule to normalize two or more clauses:

$$[Clause_1 \ldots Clause_n \; \text{return} \; Expr]_{\text{Expr}}$$
$$== [Clause_1 \; \text{return} \ldots [Clause_n \; \text{return} \; Expr]_{\text{Expr}}]_{\text{Expr}}, \; (n > 1)$$

Normalization of a `for` or `let` clause with more than one binding turns each binding into a separate nested `for` or `let` expression and normalizes the result.

$$[\text{for} \; ForBinding_1 \ldots ForBinding_n \; \text{return} \; Expr]_{\text{Expr}}$$
$$== [\text{for} \; ForBinding_1 \; \text{return} \ldots [\text{for} \; ForBinding_n \; \text{return} \; Expr]_{\text{Expr}}]_{\text{Expr}}, \; (n > 1)$$

$$[\text{let} \; LetBinding_1 \ldots LetBinding_n \; \text{return} \; Expr]_{\text{Expr}}$$
$$== [\text{let} \; LetBinding_1 \; \text{return} \ldots [\text{for} \; LetBinding_n \; \text{return} \; Expr]_{\text{Expr}}]_{\text{Expr}}, \; (n > 1)$$

Normalization of a `for` or `let` clause with a single binding just normalizes the subexpressions.

[`for` $Var TypeDeclaration? PositionalVar?$ `in` $Expr_0$ `return` $Expr_1$]$_{Expr}$

== `for` $Var TypeDeclaration? PositionalVar?$ `in` $[Expr_0]_{Expr}$ `return` $[Expr_1]_{Expr}$

[`let` $Var TypeDeclaration?$:= $Expr_0$ `return` $Expr_1$]$_{Expr}$

== `let` $Var TypeDeclaration?$:= $[Expr_0]_{Expr}$ `return` $[Expr_1]_{Expr}$

Finally, a `where` clause is normalized into an `if` expression that returns the empty sequence if the condition is false, and normalizes the result:

[`where` $Expr_0$ `return` $Expr_1$]$_{Expr}$

== [`if` $(Expr_0)$ `then` $Expr_1$ `else` $()$]$_{Expr}$

(The normalization rule for `if` expressions is discussed in the later section "Implicit Coercions and Function Calls.") After normalization, we are left with only `for` and `let` expressions each with a single variable binding and with `if` expressions.

Dynamic Semantics

We have already seen the dynamic semantics of the `let` expression in the earlier section "Environments." The dynamic rule for a `for` expression is similar to the rule for `let`, except instead of binding the variable to the entire sequence, it is bound once to each item in the sequence and the resulting values are concatenated together.

$$dynEnv \vdash Expr_0 \Rightarrow (Item_1, \ldots, Item_n)$$
$$dynEnv + varValue(Var \Rightarrow Item_1) \vdash Expr_1 \Rightarrow Value_1$$

$$\ldots$$

$$\frac{dynEnv + varValue(Var \Rightarrow Item_n) \vdash Expr_1 \Rightarrow Value_n}{dynEnv \vdash \text{for } \$Var \text{ in } Expr_0 \text{ return } Expr_1 \Rightarrow (Value_1, \ldots, Value_n)}$$

The sequence operator " , " concatenates two item sequences.

Users new to XQuery sometimes expect one evaluation of the body of a `for` expression to affect later evaluations, as is possible in imperative programming languages such as C or Java. This rule makes clear that each evaluation is independent of every other evaluation, that is, the evaluation when *Var* is mapped to *Item$_1$* has no effect on the evaluation when *Var* is mapping to *Item$_n$*.

Unlike the normalization rules of the previous section, there is no restriction $n > 0$ in the above rule. In the case that $n = 0$, the above rule simplifies to the following:

$$\frac{dynEnv \vdash Expr_0 \Rightarrow (\,)}{dynEnv \vdash \texttt{for } \$Var \texttt{ in } Expr_0 \texttt{ return } Expr_1 \Rightarrow (\,)}$$

In this case, there is no need to evaluate the body of the `for` expression, because the input sequence is empty.

For a `for` expression that includes a position variable, the iteration variable is bound to an item in the sequence, and the position variable is bound to the item's position. The body of the `for` expression is evaluated in the environment *dynEnv* extended with these two variable bindings:

$$\frac{\begin{array}{c} dynEnv \vdash Expr_0 \Rightarrow (Item_1, \ldots, Item_n) \\ dynEnv + varValue(Var_0 \Rightarrow Item_1, Var_1 \Rightarrow 1) \vdash Expr_1 \Rightarrow Value_1 \\ \cdots \\ dynEnv + varValue(Var_0 \Rightarrow Item_n, Var_1 \Rightarrow n) \vdash Expr_1 \Rightarrow Value_n \end{array}}{dynEnv \vdash \texttt{for } \$Var_0 \texttt{ at } \$Var_1 \texttt{ in } Expr_0 \texttt{ return } Expr_1 \Rightarrow (Value_1, \ldots, Value_n)}$$

Finally, the dynamic rule for a `for` expression that includes a type declaration is similar to the dynamic for a `let` expression with a type declaration, except that every item must match the declared type. If any $Item_1, \ldots, Item_n$ does not match the declared type, a type error is raised.

We refer you to the XQuery Formal Semantics for the dynamic semantics of the FLWOR expression that includes the `order by` clause [XQ-FS].

Static Semantics and Factored Types

In addition to `for` expressions, many constructs in XQuery iterate over the items in a sequence. If the type iterated over is a **factored type**, that is, it consists of an item type and an occurrence indicator, then the result type can be computed in a way similar to the `let` expression. Here is a static typing rule that assumes the type of the input sequence is already factored:

$$\frac{\begin{array}{c} statEnv \vdash Expr_0 : ItemType \; * \\ statEnv + varType(Var : ItemType) \vdash Expr_1 : Type \end{array}}{statEnv \vdash \texttt{for } \$Var \texttt{ in } Expr_0 \texttt{ return } Expr_1 : Type \; *}$$

In general, the type of the input sequence may not be factored. Here are some examples of types and their factorizations:

```
((xs:integer, xs:string) | xs:integer)*
subtype (xs:integer | xs:string)*
```

and

```
(element(title), element(author)+)
subtype (element(title)| element(author))+
```

Factoring in this way may lose information. In the first example, we lose the fact that a string is always preceded by an integer, and in the second example, we lose the fact that there is only one title and that it precedes all the authors. But for typing iteration, the information yielded by factoring is usually good enough.

Before defining factorization, we define its result type, which is the product of a *prime type* and a quantifier and is written *Prime • Quantifier*. A prime type is a choice among zero or more item types.

$$
\begin{array}{rcl}
Prime & ::= & ItemType \\
 & | & \texttt{none()} \\
 & | & Prime \mid Prime
\end{array}
$$

A quantifier just represents an occurrence indicator. We can combine an arbitrary type with a quantifier, and get the expected type.

$$
\begin{array}{rcll}
Quantifier & ::= & 1 & \text{exactly one} \\
 & | & ? & \text{zero or one} \\
 & | & + & \text{one or more} \\
 & | & * & \text{zero or more}
\end{array}
$$

$$
\begin{array}{l}
Type • 1 = Type \\
Type • ? = Type \; ? \\
Type • + = Type \; + \\
Type • * = Type \; *
\end{array}
$$

Given an arbitrary type *Type*, we want to factor it into a *Prime* and *Quantifier* such that

$$Type \text{ \textbf{subtype} } Prime \cdot Quantifier.$$

Here is how to compute prime types:

$$
\begin{aligned}
prime(ItemType) &= ItemType \\
prime(\texttt{empty()}) &= \texttt{none()} \\
prime(\texttt{none()}) &= \texttt{none()} \\
prime(Type_1 \text{ , } Type_2) &= prime(Type_1) \mid prime(Type_2) \\
prime(Type_1 \mid Type_2) &= prime(Type_1) \mid prime(Type_2) \\
prime(Type \text{ ?}) &= prime(Type) \\
prime(Type +) &= prime(Type) \\
prime(Type *) &= prime(Type)
\end{aligned}
$$

Both sequence types (,) and choice types (|) are converted into the choice type. Similarly, both the empty sequence `empty()` and the nil choice `none()` are converted into the nil choice, since that is identity for choice (that is, *Type* | `none()` = *Type*, for all types). *Occurrence* operators are dropped.

Here is how to compute quantifiers:

$$
\begin{aligned}
quant(ItemType) &= 1 \\
quant(\texttt{empty()}) &= ? \\
quant(\texttt{none()}) &= 1 \\
quant(Type_1 \text{ , } Type_2) &= quant(Type_1) \text{ , } quant(Type_2) \\
quant(Type_1 \mid Type_2) &= quant(Type_1) \mid quant(Type_2) \\
quant(Type?) &= quant(Type) \cdot ? \\
quant(Type+) &= quant(Type) \cdot + \\
quant(Type*) &= quant(Type) \cdot *
\end{aligned}
$$

We combine quantifiers by applying the rules in the following symmetric tables. The tables formalize the approximate arithmetic required to compute occurrence indicators. This will also be used in the section entitled "Path Expressions."

,	1	?	+	*
1	+	+	+	+
?	+	*	+	*
+	+	+	+	+
*	+	*	+	*

|	1	?	+	*
1	1	?	+	*
?	?	?	*	*
+	+	*	+	*
*	*	*	*	*

•	1	?	+	*
1	1	?	+	*
?	?	?	*	*
+	+	*	+	*
*	*	*	*	*

For example, $(?,+) = +$, that is, zero-or-one item followed by one-or-more items is one-or-more items; and $?|+$ yields $*$, that is, zero-or-one item or one-or-more items is zero-or-more items.

If we apply the *prime* and *quant* functions to the types given above, we get the factorings given above:

prime(((xs:integer, xs:string) | xs:integer)*)
= xs:integer | xs:string

prime(element(title), element(author)+)
= element(title) | element(author)

quant(((xs:integer, xs:string) | xs:integer)*)   = *

quant(element(title), element(author) +)   = +

The following theorem states that the above rules always correctly factor a type, and always find the smallest (i.e., most precise) factorization. To characterize smallest, we define a partial ordering $\leq$ on quantifiers as follows: $1 \leq ?$, $1 \leq +$, $? \leq *$, $+ \leq *$.

Theorem 5.3   Factorization

For all types we have

$$\textit{Type } \textbf{subtype } \textit{prime(Type)} \bullet \textit{quant(Type)}$$

Further if

$$\textit{Type } \textbf{subtype } \textit{Prime} \bullet \textit{Quantifier}$$

then

$$\textit{prime(Type)} \textbf{ subtype } \textit{Prime} \quad \text{and} \quad \textit{quant(Type)} \leq \textit{Quantifier}$$

The first part of the theorem guarantees that every value that belongs to the original type also belongs to its factorization, as we require, and the second part guarantees that the factorization is in some sense optimal. This theorem has practical implications: If factorization did not compute the smallest (i.e., most precise) type possible, the user would have to clutter queries with calls to the occurrence functions `one-or-more` and `one`, which would give the more precise type.

Now that we have factorization, it is easy to write the typing rule for `for` when applied to an expression with an arbitrary type. We compute the type of the first subexpression and then factor that type into a prime type and quantifier. We extend the static environment so that *Var* has the prime type and then compute the type of the body of the `for` expression. The result type is the type of the body combined with the quantifier. Here is the rule:

$$\frac{\begin{array}{c} statEnv \vdash Expr_0 : Type_0 \\ statEnv + varType(Var : prime(Type_0)) \vdash Expr_1 : Type_1 \end{array}}{statEnv \vdash \texttt{for } \$Var \texttt{ in } Expr_0 \texttt{ return } Expr_1 : Type_1 \bullet quant(Type_0)} \quad \text{(FOR)}$$

For example, if

```
$kseq : ((xs:integer, xs:string) | xs:integer)*
```

then

```
for $k in $kseq return
typeswitch($k) case xs:integer return $k<1
               case xs:string return $k
: (xs:boolean | xs:string)*
```

It would be sound to give this expression the more precise type `((xs:boolean, xs:string) | xs:boolean)*`, but finding a type algorithm that is so precise is difficult. In practice, the loss of information implied by factoring is usually acceptable, and when it is not, the extra information can be recovered by using a `treat as` expression.

The static semantics of the functions `fn:unordered`, `fn:distinct-nodes`, `fn:distinct-values`, the operators `union`, `except`, and `intersect`, and the expressions `some` and `every` all factor the type of their input sequences. Now that you understand what a factored type is and how it is computed, you should be able to read and understand the static typing rules for all these constructs.

Path Expressions

In this section, we focus on how the implicit and sometimes complex semantics of path expressions is revealed through normalization.

The notion of defining some expressions in terms of others was put to good use in the XPath 1.0 specification, and this has carried over into XPath 2.0 and XQuery. For instance, the expression `book/isbn` is an abbreviation for `child::book/child::isbn`. In general, *QName* is an abbreviation for `child::`*QName*, which returns all element children of the context node with the name *QName*. The context node itself is referred to as ".", which is an abbreviation for `self::node()`. Similarly, the parent of the context node is referred to as "..", which is an abbreviation for `parent::node()`. Finally, the expression *Expr₁ // Expr₂* is an abbreviation for *Expr₁* / `descendant-or-self::node()` / *Expr₂*. Thus, *Expr // QName* translates to *Expr*/`descendant-or-self::node()`/`child::`*QName* rather than (as you might have expected) *Expr*/`descendant::`*QName*, though these last two expressions turn out to be exactly equivalent.

Though simple and uniform, this translation of " // " has consequences that may not be appreciated even by seasoned XPath users (although this trick goes back to XPath 1.0). For example, *Expr // .* translates to *Expr*/`descendant-or-self::node()`/`self::node()` and not to, say, *Expr*/`descendant::*` as one might have guessed. The former includes the nodes in *Expr* itself, the latter does not.

The XQuery formal semantics expresses the translations such as those above by means of normalization rules. Just as in the earlier section "Normalization" we wrote [*Expr*]_Expr_ for the normalization operator on expressions, here we write [*PathExpr*]_Path_ for the normalization operator on path expressions.

Here are the rules corresponding to the cases discussed above:

$$[QName]_{\text{Path}} \quad\quad == \text{child::}QName$$

$$[.]_{\text{Path}} \quad\quad\quad == \text{self::node()}$$

$$[..]_{\text{Path}} \quad\quad\quad == \text{parent::node()}$$

$$[Expr_1 \text{ // } Expr_2]_{\text{Path}} == [Expr_1/\text{descendant-or-self::node()}/Expr_2]_{\text{Path}}$$

A comparison of the text above with the rules above shows that the rules are more compact, which is exactly why we use formal notation. Note that the last rule recursively applies normalization to its right-hand side. This is because the definition of " / " is also expanded out by normalization, as described in the next section.

Although they serve quite different purposes from a user point of view, XPath expressions using " / " and XQuery expressions using `for` have some common semantics: both iterate over sequences. They differ in that " / " binds an implicit focus of iteration known as the context node, written " . ", while `for` binds an explicit iteration variable. Similarly, " / " binds an implicit position for the context node, written `position()`, while `for` permits binding an explicit position variable with an expression such as `for $x at $i`. Finally, " / " returns nodes sorted in document order with duplicates removed, while `for` returns items in the order they are generated with duplicates retained.

This similarity suggests that the " / " connective and "[ ]" predicates of XPath are closely related to the `for` and `if` expressions of XQuery. In fact, the former can be precisely defined in terms of the latter. We show this by giving the normalization rules for the subset of XPath expressions given in Listing 5.4. As usual, the normalization of the complete grammar is in the [XQuery Formal Semantics].

Listing 5.4   Normalization Rules for a Subset of XPath Expressions

Expr	::= ··· previous expressions ··· | *PathExpr*
PathExpr	::= /
	| / *RelativePathExpr*
	| *RelativePathExpr*
RelativePathExpr	::= *StepExpr* / *RelativePathExpr*
StepExpr	::= (*ForwardStep* | *ReverseStep*)*Predicates*
ForwardStep	::= *ForwardAxis* *NodeTest*
ReverseStep	::= *ReverseAxis* *NodeTest*
ForwardAxis	::= `child::` | `descendant::` | `self::`
	| `descendant-or-self::`
ReverseAxis	::= `parent::`
Predicates	::= ([*Expr*])*
NodeTest	::= `text()` | `node()` | `*` | *QName* `:*`

We start with the rule relating normalization of expressions to normalization of path expressions.

$$[PathExpr]_{\text{Expr}} == \texttt{fs:distinct-doc-order}([PathExpr]_{\text{Path}})$$

This rule guarantees that every path expression returns a sequence of nodes sorted in document order with duplicates removed by applying the function `fs:distinct-doc-order`. (The namespace `fs` is defined in the formal semantics and is used by functions defined only within the formal semantics.)

The normalization rules for absolute path expressions are straightforward.

$$[/]_{\text{Path}} \qquad\qquad == \texttt{fn:root(\$fs:dot)}$$
$$[/RelativePathExpr]_{\text{Path}} \quad == [\texttt{fn:root(\$fs:dot)} / RelativePathExpr]_{\text{Path}}$$

Here the built-in variable `$fs:dot` represents the context node. An absolute path expression just refers to the root of the XML tree that contains the context node.

Now things get more interesting, as we consider the rule for composing steps using " / ":

$$[StepExpr / RelativePathExpr]_{\text{Path}}$$

$$==$$

```
let $fs:sequence := fs:distinct-doc-order([StepExpr]_Path) return
   let $fs:last := fn:count($fs:sequence) return
      for $fs:dot at $fs:position in $fs:sequence return
         [RelativePathExpr]_Path
```

This rule binds four built-in variables: `$fs:sequence`, `$fs:last`, `$fs:dot`, and `$fs:position`, which represent, respectively, the context sequence, context size, context node, and context position. The first `let` binds `$fs:sequence` to the context sequence (the value of *StepExpr*), which is sorted in document order with duplicates removed. The second `let` binds `$fs:last` to its length. Given this context, the `for` expression binds `fs:dot` (and `fs:position`) once for each item (and its position) in the context sequence and then evaluates *RelativePathExpr* once for each binding. The bindings of the built-in variables make explicit the implicit semantics of " / ".

The normalization rule for a "[ ]" predicate is similar to the rules above, but a bit more subtle. It defines the `fs:sequence`, `fs:last`, `fs:dot`, and `fs:position` variables, evaluates the predicate expression in this context, and if the predicate expression evaluates to true, returns the context node; otherwise, it returns the empty sequence.

Here is the normalization rule for a *ForwardStep* expression, followed by zero or more intermediate *Predicates*, and then a final predicate expression `[Expr]`. It returns each context node in the forward step expression that satisfies the predicates in *Expr*:

$$[\textit{ForwardStep Predicates } [\textit{Expr}]]_{\text{Path}}$$

```
==

let fs:sequence := [ForwardStep Predicates]Path return
  let $fs:last := fn:count($fs:sequence) return
    for $fs:dot at $fs:position in $fs:sequence return
      if ([Expr]Predicates) then $fs:dot else ()
```

XPath distinguishes between step expressions in the "forward" axes (e.g., child and descendant) and those in the "reverse" axes (e.g., parent and ancestor), because the meaning of the context position depends on the axis direction. For the forward axes, the context position increases with the document order of nodes in the context sequence; for the reverse axes, it decreases with document order. The rule for reverse axes defines `$fs:position` so that it corresponds to reverse document order:

$$[\textit{ReverseStep Predicates } [\textit{Expr}]]_{\text{Path}}$$

```
==

let $fs:sequence := [ReverseStep Predicates]Path return
  let $fs:last := fn:count($fs:sequence) return
    for $fs:dot at $fs:pos in $fs:sequence return
      let $fs:position := $fs:last-$fs:pos + 1 return
        if ([Expr]Predicates) then $fs:dot else ()
```

The meaning of an individual predicate expression depends on the type of its value. If the predicate value is a numeric, the predicate is true if the numeric value is equal to the context position; if the predicate value is not a numeric, the function `fn:boolean` converts the value to a Boolean.

$[Expr]_{\text{Predicates}}$

==

typeswitch $([Expr]_{\text{Expr}})$

```
  case numeric $v return op:numeric-equal(fn:round($v),
  $fs:position)
  default $v return fn:boolean($v)
```

Finally, a simple step expression (an axis and node test expression with no other predicates) just normalizes to itself:

$$[\textit{ForwardAxis::NodeTest}]_{\text{Path}} == \textit{ForwardAxis::NodeTest}$$

The rule for *ReverseAxis* is similar.

Putting this all together, here is the normalization of the expression `$article/child::reserve_price`:

```
[$article/child::reserve_price]Path==
let $fs:sequence := fs:distinct-doc-order($article) return
  let $fs:last := fn:count($fs:sequence) return
    for $fs:dot at $fs:position in $fs:sequence return
      child::reserve_price
```

You may notice that the variables `$fs:last` and `$fs:position` are defined but are not used in the bodies of the `let` and `for` expressions, and therefore are redundant. We can simplify the expression above to the following:

```
for $fs:dot in fs:distinct-doc-order($article) return
              child::reserve_price
```

You might ask why define these variables if they are never used? The answer is that, in general, a relative path expression may refer to `position()` or `last()`, and therefore require `fs:position` and `fs:last` to be defined. An XQuery implementation is free to make the simplification shown above, but the normalization rules are defined for the most general case. Predicate expressions illustrate how these variables are used. Extending the example above, here's the normalization of `($article/child::reserve_price)[1]`:

```
[($article/child::reserve_price)[1]]Path==
let fs:sequence :=
      (for $fs:dot in fs:distinct-doc-order($article)
        return child::reserve_price)
return
  let $fs:last := fn:count($fs:sequence) return
    for $fs:dot at $fs:position in $fs:sequence return
      if ([1]Predicates) then $fs:dot else ()
```

And the normalization of $[1]_{Predicates}$ is

```
typeswitch (1)
  case numeric $v return
    op:numeric-equal(fn:round($v), $fs:position)
  default $v return fn:boolean($v)
```

Note that `$fs:position` is used in the normalization of the predicate expression but defined in the previous rule. These examples illustrate the convenience of XPath's syntax by revealing the complexity of its semantics.

You may have noticed that normalization rules give a *complete*, but not necessarily *minimal*, definition of XQuery expressions.

Some simplifications, such as removing definitions of unused variables, are well known and simple. Others, such as eliminating redundant sorts by document order, may require some query analysis—Chapter 3 discusses some optimizations for XPath. General rules for simplifying core expressions are outside the scope of this chapter, but we note that many techniques for simplifying expressions in functional languages apply to XQuery [FUNC-LANG].

Implicit Coercions and Function Calls

One important characteristic of XML is its ability to represent irregular data. Suppose that we have the schema shown in Listing 5.5, in which an `article` element may contain zero or more `reserve_price` elements, and a `reserve_price` may contain zero or more decimal values:

Listing 5.5   Schema Containing Irregular Data

```
<xs:element name="article" type="Article"/>
<xs:complexType name="Article">
  <xs:sequence>
    <xs:element name="name" type="xs:string"/>
    <xs:element name="reserve_price "type="PriceList"
                minOccurs="0" maxOccurs="unbounded"/>
  </xs:sequence>
</xs:complexType>
<xs:simpleType name="PriceList">
<xs:list itemType="xs:decimal"/>
</xs:simpleType>
```

This schema is represented in the XQuery formal type notation as follows:

```
define element article of type Article
define type Article {
  element(name,xs:string),
  element(reserve_price,PriceList) *,
}
define type PriceList { xs:decimal * }
```

XQuery accommodates this flexibility by introducing certain implicit coercions. An arithmetic expression is well defined on any item sequence that can be coerced to zero or one atomic value. For example, the path expression `$article/reserve_price` evaluates to a sequence of zero or more reserve_price elements, but in the expression `$article/reserve_price * 0.07`, its typed content is extracted automatically. A comparison expression is well defined on any item sequence that can be coerced to a sequence of atomic values. For example, in the expression `$article/reserve_price < 100.00`, the typed context of `$article/reserve_price` is extracted automatically. Finally, XPath's predicate expressions are well defined on any item sequence. For example, the expression `$article[reserve_price]` returns each node in `$article` that has at least one `reserve_price` child. The expression `reserve_price` evaluates to a sequence of zero or more `reserve_price` elements, but in the expression `$article[reserve_price]`, the sequence is treated as a Boolean value.

Such flexibility is permitted in almost *every* XQuery expression: in path expressions, in arithmetic and comparison expressions, in conditional expressions, in function calls and returns, and in cast expressions. The normalization rules for these expressions make this flexibility explicit by coercing the values of subexpressions to values whose types are required by the expression. We describe two such coercions next.

The first coercion is applied to expressions that require a Boolean value (e.g., in `if` expressions, `where` clauses, and XPath predicate expressions). It simply maps the *Expr* argument to a core expression and applies the function `fn:boolean` to the result. The `fn:boolean` function evaluates to `false` if its argument is the empty sequence, the Boolean value `false`, the empty string, the singleton numeric value zero, or the singleton double or float value NaN; otherwise, `fn:boolean` returns `true`. For example, applying `fn:boolean` to `0.0` yields `false`, and applying it to the sequence `(false, true, 0.0)` yields `true`.

Here's the normalization rule for `if`, which applies the `fn:boolean` function to the conditional expression. The `then` and `else` branches are normalized by recursively applying the rule for expression normalization.

$$[\texttt{if } (Expr_0) \texttt{ then } Expr_1 \texttt{ else } Expr_2]_{\mathrm{Expr}}$$

$$==$$

$$\texttt{if } (\texttt{fn:boolean}([Expr_0]_{\mathrm{Expr}})) \texttt{ then } [Expr_1]_{\mathrm{Expr}} \texttt{ else } [Expr_2]_{\mathrm{Expr}}$$

The second coercion is applied to an expression when used in a context that requires a sequence of atomic values. The coercion is known as *atomization*, because it coerces any sequence of items to a sequence of atomic values. It simply maps the *Expr* argument to a core expression then applies the function `fn:data` to the result. The `fn:data` function takes any item sequence, applies the following two rules to each item in the sequence, and concatenates the results:

- If the item is an atomic value, it is returned.
- Otherwise, the item is a node, and its typed value is returned.

For example, applying the function `fn:data` to this sequence of items, each of which is validated as `element reserve_price`,

```
(<reserve_price> 10.00 </reserve_price>,
<reserve_price> 20.00 25.00 </reserve_price>)
```

yields the sequence of decimal values (`10.0, 20.0, 25.0`).

The typed value of every kind of node is defined in the XQuery data model[XQ-DM]. For this discussion, there are only two cases of interest. If the element is validated against a simple type or a complex type with simple content, the typed value is the sequence of atomic values that results from validating the element's content. (The same rule applies to attribute nodes that are validated against a simple type). If the element is validated against a complex type with complex content, `fn:data` raises a type error, because it is not sensible to try to extract atomic values from an element with complex content.

We put atomization to use in the normalization of arithmetic and comparison expressions. Because values are often optional or repeated in XML documents, the arithmetic and comparison operators are well defined on item sequences that can be atomized, that is, coerced to atomic values. This permits users to apply arithmetic and comparison expressions to empty sequences or node sequences. Arithmetic and comparison operators are also overloaded. This permits users to apply them to a variety of value types. Comparison is defined on every XML Schema data type, and arithmetic is defined on numerics, dates, and durations.

We start with the normalization rule for the plus (+) operator. The rules for other arithmetic operators are similar.

$$[Expr_1 + Expr_2]_{\text{Expr}}$$

```
==

let $v1 := fn:data([Expr₁]Expr) return

let $v2 := fn:data([Expr₂]Expr) return

fs:plus($v1, $v2)
```

The normalization rule for plus first atomizes each argument expression and then applies the overloaded internal function `fs:plus` to each atomized argument.

As you can see, much of the semantics of the plus operator boils down to a call to the overloaded function `fs:plus` function, which may be applied to numerics or dates and durations, among others. An overloaded function is resolved to a non-overloaded function based on the types of its arguments. Table 5.2 specifies how `fs:plus` is resolved when applied to the types `empty`, `numeric`, `xs:date`, and `xdt:yearMonthDuration`.

The semantics of a function call raises a type error if the values of arguments do not match one of the permissible combinations of types specified in the function's resolution table. For example, `fs:plus` applied to `numeric` and `string` would raise a type error because `numeric` and `string` is not a permissible combination of types for `fs:plus`. Moreover, if the query is evaluated by a processor that supports static typing, all type errors raised must be detected and reported at query-analysis time; otherwise, they must be detected and reported at query-evaluation time.

When dynamic typing is in effect, function resolution must be handled dynamically—that is, the function's resolution table would be queried at run-time to determine the specific function to call. Implementers should note that when static typing is supported, it is often possible to resolve an overloaded function to a specific function after static analysis. For example, the function call $fs:plus(Expr_1, Expr_2)$ can be resolved to $op:numeric(Expr_1, Expr_2)$ statically under the following assumptions:

$$statEnv \vdash Expr_1 : Type_1$$

$$Type_1 \textbf{ subtype } numeric$$

$$statEnv \vdash Expr_2 : Type_2$$

$$Type_2 \textbf{ subtype } numeric$$

TABLE 5.2 Resolution of Overloaded Function `fs:plus` on `empty`, `numeric`, `xs:date`, and `xdt:yearMonthDuration`

Type of A	Type of B	Resolves to
`empty`	`T`	`()`
`T`	`empty`	`()`
`numeric`	`numeric`	`op:numeric-add(A,B)`
`xs:date`	`xdt:yearMonthDuration`	`op:add-yearMonthDuration-to-date(A,B)`
`xdt:yearMonthDuration`	`xs:date`	`op:add-yearMonthDuration-to-date(B,A)`

Where `T` = `empty` | `numeric` | `xs:date` | `xdt:yearMonthDuration`.

In addition to resolving overloaded functions, the semantics of function calls applies rules to promote values to required types. We refer the reader to the XQuery Formal Semantics [XQ-FS] for the complete semantics of function calls.

Here's an example that illustrates the flexibility of the arithmetic operators. Assume we have the following expression:

```
$article/reserve_price * 0.07
```

Assume also that `$article/reserve_price` may evaluate to one of the following four values, all of which are validated against `element reserve_price`:

```
(<reserve_price/>)
(<reserve_price> 10.00 </reserve_price>)
(<reserve_price> 10.00 </reserve_price>, <reserve_price/>)
(<reserve_price> 10.00 </reserve_price>,
<reserve_price> 20.00 25.00</reserve_price>)
```

When applied to the first value, the expression returns the empty sequence, because `<reserve_price/>` is empty. When applied to the second and third values, the expression returns `0.7`, because in both cases, the atomized value is the decimal `10.0`. When applied to the fourth value, a type error is raised, because the atomized value is the sequence of decimals (`10.0, 20.0, 25.0`), which is neither the empty sequence nor one atomic value.

The general comparison operators (i.e., `=`, `!=`, `<`, `>`, `<=`, `>=`) are existentially quantified over sequences of atomic values, after atomization. This permits general comparison operators to be applied to any item sequence that can be atomized. The normalization rule makes the atomization and existential quantification explicit. We give the rule for the `<` operator:

$$[Expr_1 < Expr_2]_{\text{Expr}}$$

```
==

some $v1 in fn:data([Expr₁]Expr) satisfies
some $v2 in fn:data([Expr₂]Expr) satisfies
fs:less-than($v1, $v2)
```

The `some` expression evaluates to `true` if some value in the atomized value of $Expr_1$ is less than some value in the atomized value of $Expr_2$. The function `fs:less-than`, like `fs:plus`, is overloaded and can be applied to numerics, Booleans, or dates, among others.

Node Identity and Element Constructors

Element constructors are among the most complex expressions in XQuery. In Chapter 4, we saw how elements are constructed, validated, and typed. To review, at evaluation time, an element constructor creates a new element node with a new identity distinct from all other nodes, and it implicitly validates the element using the validation context and mode determined by the lexical scope of the constructor expression. At static-analysis time, an element constructor checks that the type of the element's content is appropriate for the type of element being constructed and raises a type error if it is not. In this way, static typing prevents some validation errors that would occur when the element's content could never be validated successfully.

We begin with the formal definition of node identity and conclude with the dynamic and static semantics of node constructors.

Node Identity

An element constructor always creates new nodes with new identities. For example, consider the following expression:

```
let $name := <name>Red Bicycle</name>
return <article>{$name, $name}</article>
```

This expression first constructs a new `name` element containing one text node with contents `Red Bicycle`. The expression in the `return` clause constructs a new `article` element containing two *copies* of the `name` element—that is, the element bound to the variable `$name` and the two elements contained in the `article` element have distinct identities. For example, the following expression:

```
let $name := <name>Red Bicycle</name>,
    $article := <article>{$name, $name}</article>
return (
    $name is $article/name[1],
    $name is $article/name[2],
    $article/name[1] is $article/name[2])
```

evaluates to the sequence (`false`, `false`, `false`), because each `name` element has a distinct identity. This should not be a surprise, as we know from the study of path expressions that nodes can be distinguished by their order within the document; thus, node identity and document order are closely related.

To capture node identity, we introduce the notion of a **store** into the dynamic environment. The store is a mapping from node identifiers to node values. In our case, the store is *immutable*—the node associated with a node identifier never changes. The same notion of store can also be used for mutable nodes, if one wishes to model an extension of XQuery with update.

We use *NodeId* to range over node identifiers. The syntax of node identifiers is not specified further. The definition of *Item* given earlier is modified to take node identity into account. Instead of

$$Item ::= NodeValue \mid AtomicValue$$

we now have

$$Item ::= NodeId \mid AtomicValue.$$

Before we can see how this affects our semantics, we need to introduce a notation for defining stores. The notation is similar to that used for *varValue* and *varType*, except that we write *dynEnv* ∪ *store(NodeId* ⇒ *NodeValue)*, with ∪ in place of +, to indicate that *dom(dynEnv.store)* may not include *NodeId*. This guarantees that *we never change* the node value associated with a node identifier; that is, the store is immutable.

Here's an example that we first saw in Chapter 4:

```
<article>
  <name>Red Bicycle</name>
  <start_date>1999-01-05</start_date>
  <end_date>1999-01-20</end_date>
  <reserve_price>40</reserve_price>
</article>
```

When we are explicit about node identity, this corresponds to the node identifier N_1 and the store shown in Listing 5.6.

Listing 5.6   The Store for the `<article>` Example

store(

$N_1 \Rightarrow$ element article of type Article { N_2, N_3, N_4, N_5 },

$N_2 \Rightarrow$ element name of type xs:string { "Red Bicycle" },

$N_3 \Rightarrow$ element start_date of type xs:date { "1999-01-05" },

$N_4 \Rightarrow$ element end_date of type xs:date { "1999-02-20" },

$N_5 \Rightarrow$ element reserve_price of type xs:decimal {"40.0"}

)

Evaluation and the Store

Constructor expressions create new nodes in the store, and we need a new evaluation judgment that specifies how evaluation affects the store. Here is how we write it:

$$Store_0; dynEnv \vdash Expr \Rightarrow Value; Store_1$$

This is read, "Given old store $Store_0$ and $dynEnv$, evaluation of expression $Expr$ yields value $Value$ with new store $Store_1$." Note we have separated the store from the dynamic environment. If $Expr$ does not construct new nodes, then $Store_0$ and $Store_1$ will be identical.

The XQuery expressions considered so far, including arithmetic, path expressions, and iteration, do not modify the store. But any of these expressions might include as a subexpression an element constructor that does modify the store. To be rigorous, all of the dynamic inference rules of the preceding sections must be rewritten with the new judgment to make the effect upon the store explicit. But all of these rules treat the store in the same way, so to rewrite them in full would achieve little other than to increase length and decrease clarity.

Instead, we introduce a simple abbreviation, by which a rule that uses the old judgment can be expanded into a rule that uses the new judgment. Every inference rule of the following form:

$$dynEnv_1 \vdash Expr_1 \Rightarrow Value_1$$
$$dynEnv_2 \vdash Expr_2 \Rightarrow Value_2$$
$$\cdots$$
$$\frac{dynEnv_n \vdash Expr_n \Rightarrow Value_n}{dynEnv \vdash Expr \Rightarrow Value}$$

is considered an abbreviation for an expanded rule of the following form:

$$Store_0; dynEnv_1 \vdash Expr_1 \Rightarrow Value_1; Store_1$$
$$Store_1; dynEnv_2 \vdash Expr_2 \Rightarrow Value_2; Store_2$$
$$\cdots$$

$$\frac{Store_{n-1};\ dynEnv_n \vdash Expr_n \Rightarrow Value_n;\ Store_n}{Store_0;\ dynEnv \vdash Expr \Rightarrow Value;\ Store_n}$$

Note that each new store computed through a given judgment is passed as input to the next judgment.

For example, here is the inference rule for dynamic evaluation of `let` expressions:

$$\frac{\begin{array}{c} dynEnv \vdash Expr_0 \Rightarrow Value_0 \\ dynEnv + varValue(Var \Rightarrow Value_0) \vdash Expr_1 \Rightarrow Value_1 \end{array}}{dynEnv \vdash \texttt{let } \$Var := Expr_0 \texttt{ return } Expr_1 \Rightarrow Value_1} \quad \text{(LET)}$$

It is considered as an abbreviation for the following rule:

$$\frac{\begin{array}{c} Store_0;\ dynEnv \vdash Expr_0 \Rightarrow Value_0;\ Store_1 \\ Store_1;\ dynEnv + varValue(Var \Rightarrow Value_0) \vdash Expr_1 \Rightarrow Value_1;\ Store_2 \end{array}}{Store_0;\ dynEnv \vdash \texttt{let } \$Var := Expr_0 \texttt{ return } Expr_1 \Rightarrow Value_1;\ Store_2} \quad \text{(LET)}$$

In this way, most rules treat the store implicitly. We only mention the store explicitly in those rules that depend upon it, such as the rule for element construction considered in the next section.

Dynamic Semantics of Element Construction

Naively, one might expect element construction to look like this:

$$\frac{\begin{array}{c} Store_0;\ dynEnv \vdash Expr \Rightarrow Value;\ Store_1 \\ NodeId \notin dom(Store_1) \\ Store_2 = Store_1 \cup store(NodeId \Rightarrow \texttt{element } ElementName \ \{Value\}) \end{array}}{Store_0;\ dynEnv \vdash \texttt{element } ElementName \ \{Expr\} \Rightarrow NodeId;\ Store_2}$$

One first evaluates the expression for the contents. One then allocates a fresh node identity, not already allocated in the store. Then one extends the store by binding the new node identity to an element node with the given name and contents. Finally, one returns the node identity for the new node with the new store.

This naive form of element construction is too naive, because it ignores key aspects of the XQuery data model. In the XQuery data model, all elements are labeled with a type name, and the content of the element must correspond to that type name. Therefore, in keeping with XML tradition, each element is validated as it is constructed.

XML Schema validation is only defined on unvalidated documents—recall that validation takes an untyped document, validates it against some schema, and produces a new document in which all nodes have an associated type annotation. So to apply validation, we must first erase any type annotations resulting from previous validation.

We introduce two judgments to capture this process. The judgment

$$Store_0; dynEnv \vdash Value \textbf{ erases to } UntypedValue; Store_1$$

holds when erasing the type information in $Value$ yields $UntypedValue$. The judgment

$$Store_0; dynEnv \vdash \textbf{validate } \{UntypedValue\} \Rightarrow Value; Store_1$$

holds when validating the $UntypedValue$ results in $Value$. Formal definitions of erasure and validation can be found in the XQuery Formal Semantics [XQ-FS] and in "The Essence of XML" [ESSENCE]. Note that the second of these judgments is responsible for allocating the new typed element nodes in the store, which is done in much the same way as in the untyped naive element construction rule above.

Given these auxiliary rules, the basic rule for element construction is quite simple.

$$\frac{\begin{array}{c} Store_0; dynEnv \vdash Expr \Rightarrow Value_1; Store_1 \\ Store_1; dynEnv \vdash Value_1 \textbf{ erases to } Value_2; Store_2 \\ NodeId \notin dom(Store_2) \\ Store_3 = Store_2 \cup store(NodeId \Rightarrow \texttt{element } ElementName \{Value_2\}) \\ Store_3; dynEnv \vdash \textbf{validate } \{NodeId\} \Rightarrow Value_3; Store_4 \end{array}}{Store_0; dynEnv \vdash \texttt{element } ElementName \{Expr\} \Rightarrow Value_3; Store_4}$$

This evaluates the expression to yield a value, erases all type information in the value, constructs the untyped element node, and then validates it to yield the final typed value.

These inference rules might suggest a rather expensive implementation that requires erasing type information before validating a new element, but implementers certainly can employ more clever strategies for implementing element constructors that do not erase existing type annotations. Again, the formal rules say what to do, but not how to do it.

Static Semantics of Element Construction

We conclude with the static semantics for element constructors, which is an appropriate place to end, because it stresses one of XQuery's biggest strengths—the ability of the static type system to perform a conservative analysis that catches errors early, during static analysis rather than dynamic evaluation.

In particular, the static semantics of element construction errs on the side of safety, insisting that the type of the data must statically match the type declared for the element. For instance, if the element is declared to have type `xs:integer` then the type of its contents must be `xs:integer` (or one of its subtypes). It cannot be, say, `xs:string`, even though the string might contain only digits, and thus successfully validate as an integer.

We give the rule for globally declared elements; the rule for locally declared elements is similar.

$$\frac{\begin{array}{c} \text{define element } \textit{ElementName} \text{ of type } \textit{TypeName}_1 \\ \text{define type } \textit{TypeName}_1 \text{ restricts } \textit{TypeName}_2 \; \{ \textit{Type}_2 \} \\ \textit{statEnv} \vdash \textit{Expr} : \textit{Type}_1 \\ \textit{statEnv} \vdash \textit{Type}_1 \; \textbf{subtype} \; \textit{Type}_2 \end{array}}{\textit{statEnv} \vdash \text{element } \textit{ElementName} \; \{\textit{Expr}\} : \text{element} \, (\textit{ElementName}, \textit{TypeName}_1)}$$

This rule checks that the type inferred for the element's content is indeed appropriate for the element that is being constructed. In particular, the fourth judgment checks that the content type ($\textit{Type}_1$) is indeed a subtype of the type against which validation is to be performed ($\textit{Type}_2$).

The Forest through the Trees

We have introduced several powerful techniques and formal tools: normalization rules that define a large language in terms of a smaller core; inference rules for defining both the dynamic evaluation of and static typing of expressions; and judgments for relating external values, internal values, and types.

The foundations of the techniques presented in this chapter are in logic and programming language theory. The main technique we use to specify XQuery's semantics is widely used, so much so that it goes by several names, including *natural semantics*, *big-step semantics*, and *evaluation semantics*; it is a special case of what is called *operational semantics*. The technique was originally proposed by Plotkin [STRUCTURAL] and Kahn [SEMANTICS], and used to good effect in the formal semantics of Standard ML [STANDARD-ML]. The notation for inference rules goes back to Frege's seminal work on logic [FORMULA-LANG; see also DDJ]. Natural semantics is covered in numerous introductory texts [PROG-FOUNDATIONS; PROG-LANG; THEORIES; and FS-PROG].

The process of formalizing XQuery gives us confidence in the correctness and completeness of XQuery's informal definition and can serve as the basis for formulating correct and semantics-preserving optimization techniques. Most important, we hope that the formal semantics can inform XQuery implementers in their day-to-day work, and that this chapter provides them the instruction necessary to use the XQuery Formal Semantics effectively.

Part IV
DATABASES

Chapter 6

MAPPING BETWEEN XML AND RELATIONAL DATA

Denise Draper

X Query operates on XML documents—or to be more precise, on instances of an XML data model. Often we assume that these XML documents exist in files or as data in network messages. But in another very common scenario, documents are generated on demand by being translated or created from a different data representation. Relational databases are probably the most important of these different sources of data for XML applications.

This chapter explores the various methods for mapping between XML and relational data models. As of this writing, many relational database vendors have announced various kinds of support for XML, ranging from the ability to transmit results as XML to built-in implementations of XQuery or SQL/XML. In addition, many middleware vendors also provide support for mapping between XML and relational data. In this chapter we do not attempt to cover the specific vendor solutions, since they are in considerable flux. Instead, we focus on the underlying fundamentals: goals and requirements for mapping between XML and relational data; issues that arise when mapping, such as handling of datatypes and order; and when a particular technique can or cannot support **update** operations. We generally present these concepts from the perspective of a middle-tier solution that builds on top of a relational database. The same concepts are often also valid for implementations integrated within a relational database, but that particular perspective is covered in more detail in Chapter 7, "Integrating XQuery and Relational Database Systems."

We begin with some background, establishing the processing model that we assume and distinguishing different kinds of applications and data sources insofar as they affect mapping. Then we introduce the main representational dichotomy: storage of XML data as XML strings (called "**LOB** representation") or as individual fields or data items ("composed representation"). The largest part of the chapter delves into the common techniques for composed representations and their implications for supporting different application types. We take a special look at **shredding**, which is the name for the technique of extracting individual data items from an XML document in such a way that it can be recomposed. Finally, we cover the implementation principles for both LOB and composed representations in just enough detail to suggest the strengths and weaknesses of various approaches.

Our goal is to provide enough information so that readers can gauge their requirements, identify potential pitfalls, and stack these up against the various approaches, whether employed by some commercial software package, custom-built, or a combination of the two.

Framing the Problem

In theory, we could discuss the mapping between XML and relational data without reference to the applications that will use such a mapping or how those applications might be implemented. However, these factors have implications for the type of mapping chosen—one may want or be constrained to choose a different mapping technique based on the actual requirements of a particular application. In particular, we consider XQuery as one particular type of application, one that places certain requirements on how to map between XML and relational data. We also consider other types of applications that have fewer or additional requirements.

Processing Models

We will begin by discussing at a high level the processing models that might be used to implement an XML application on top of a relational database. One straightforward processing model layers an XML application on top of an SQL database. In this case, the SQL database itself remains unchanged, and the XML application is implemented via some combination of SQL statements and additional XML-focused processing. Figure 6.1 shows this processing model schematically.

There are several ways to divide the boxes in Figure 6.1:

- In a completely custom application, the XML Processor functionality might be embedded within the end application, as a library or as custom-written code.
- With a middle-tier (also known as middleware) approach, the XML Processor is the middleware component and sits between an end application and the relational database, providing a **virtual XML view** of data stored in the relational database.
- Part or all of the XML Processor could be implemented as user-defined functions or stored procedures within the database, rather than on a separate tier.

The main alternative to a layered approach is one in which the relational database is extended to provide native XML functionality. In this case, the architecture may still somewhat resemble that shown in Figure 6.1 (except with the XML processor embedded in and accessed from within the overall relational architecture), or we may use an entirely different architecture, in which the XML and relational functionality are mingled together. These alternatives are discussed in Chapter 7.

In this chapter, we generally assume the middle-tier version of the model shown in Figure 6.1. This model is sufficient to cover most issues relating to mapping between XML and relational data; we intend to highlight areas

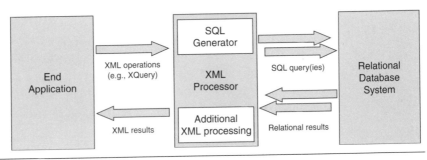

Figure 6.1 Layered Processing Model for XML Applications

where the choice of a processing model affects the mapping. Issues that arise particularly in a native implementation are discussed in Chapter 7.

Application Types

We characterize types of applications by what basic sorts of operations they have to perform on XML data: extract, transform, and so forth. Significant variation may exist within each application type, based on the particular languages (XQuery, XPath, etc.) used and especially on the richness of the set of specific available operations.

Emitting XML Documents

The most basic application type simply returns an XML document or documents. In this case the relational database is merely acting as a repository for some set of XML documents. The emitted XML document might be used directly by some application, or it might be further processed. For example, the document might be further processed with XSL to transform it for display in a web portal.

Selecting and Emitting XML Fragments

The application type that selects and returns **XML fragments** is characterized by the XPath language, which returns nodes from within an XML document that match specified conditions. The key requirements are the ability to "reach into" the document to access individual elements, attributes, and their values, both in order to evaluate predicate conditions and to extract the node contents.

A trivial way to implement this application type would be to emit all XML documents (using the application type above), and then in a post-processing step, evaluate the conditions and output only the requested portion of the document or documents. However, this would generally be inefficient, since it could require emitting all the XML documents in order to ultimately retrieve only one or a few documents or document fragments. Thus our main goal for this type of application is to find a way to *push* the selection and extraction criteria into the database, using the database to perform these operations for us.

This is a common theme throughout this chapter: Whenever possible we want to make the relational database engine perform the kind of work it is good at, rather than repeating this work externally.

Querying or Transforming XML Documents

Querying and transforming are often considered to be different operations, but in terms of the requirements they place on mapping between XML and relational data, they are quite similar. XQuery is the most general example of this kind of application. As we have seen, XQuery has very powerful ways to navigate, select, combine, transform, sort, and aggregate XML data. The output of a query in XQuery may have no structural resemblance to the XML source: elements can be renamed and rearranged, and the data can be transformed by functions. An XQuery query may combine data from multiple XML input documents to create a single output.

XQuery is the most obvious example of a query-and-transform language, but it is not the only one. XSL also performs querying and transformation. And some applications may use their own query or transform definitions; this may especially be appropriate if the needs of the application are much simpler than full XQuery and a general-purpose XQuery implementation is not available. In all cases, the defining characteristic of applications in this class is the ability to both select and combine individual pieces of the XML input in complex ways, creating new XML structures that may not have existed in the input.

As for the "select and extract" application type, it is possible to implement XQuery by first emitting entire XML documents and then post-processing them with a generic XQuery processor. (And similarly for any other query or transform language.) But the more interesting approach is again to push as much of the XQuery processing into the database as possible, in essence translating from XQuery to SQL or an extended language such as SQL/XML.

Updating XML Documents

All of the above application types are read-only: The application processes an XML document and transmits the result of that processing to some other client application. There are fundamental changes when the application must also update the XML document in place.

The most significant new requirement that arises with update is the ability to correctly identify individual nodes within XML documents. For example, if the application needs to change the value of an attribute from `owner='sam'` to `owner='bob'`, it is not sufficient to find some attribute `owner` whose value is `sam` and change the value to `bob`; it must be the specific attribute referenced by the client. In order to implement this requirement, the client application must have some way to name which node it wishes to modify. There are three general approaches:

1. The client always provides a new value for the entire document (in which case the problem goes away).
2. The client must use some form of addressing (e.g., XPath or the tumbler notation of XPointer) to uniquely identify nodes to change.
3. The communication between the client and the XML management system must be an API that directly provides handles on nodes (e.g., **WebDAV** or **DOM**).

The addressing approach tends to increase complexity in the client (which has to generate the addresses), but it still enables the communication channel between the client and the database to consist of serialized XML, which can be easier to implement than a rich API, particularly in a loosely coupled environment. When either the addressing or API approaches are used, update requires the ability to translate either an address or node handle into a location or locations in the database.

Another issue that arises with update is the addition of transactions and locking to the picture, and the need to coordinate these with the underlying SQL engine. Some of the issues involved are addressed in Chapter 7.

Unlike the previous application types, the actual update operations on XML documents must finally be implemented entirely within the database, either directly by the database vendor, or by translation of the update operations to SQL—post-processing cannot help here. The middle tier is used differently in this case: It translates a set of updates against an XML document into a set of update operations on the relational database. The translation process can be quite complex: for example, computing the difference between an updated XML document and its previous version to generate a list of SQL updates, or batching a set of changes into a single update.

Within the class of applications that update XML documents, there is one additional distinction that is very important: Does the application require the ability to change the XML schema of the document? Changing the schema of the document (or equivalent scenarios, such as changing the structure of a document that either has no schema or has a schema that uses the xs:any construct) can greatly increase the complexity of mapping techniques, and rules out some of them altogether.

Sources of XML Data

The other major dimension we must consider is the source of XML data that our applications wish to process.

Relational Sources

In some cases, the original data is actually relational: data stored in tables and columns of the relational database, and generally created and maintained by some relational application. In this situation, we assume that our XML application needs to access this data as if it were XML. We call this general model a virtual XML view of relational data.

XML Sources

XML documents may be the original input data. They might be manually created in an XML editor or created by an XML-based application; for example, they might be received from a B2B (Business-to-Business) application. The originating application might also operate directly on the XML stored within a relational database; for example, an XML editor might store the documents that it manages in a relational database. In this case, we have options to consider regarding how to store the XML within the relational database.

The category of XML sources includes several important subcategories: XML may be structured, semi-structured, or marked-up text, and the XML may either have a given schema (or DTD), variable schemas, or no schema.

Terms like *structured* and *semi-structured* have different definitions in the literature; in this chapter, semi-structured XML may have variant sub-structure (corresponding to the use of union types, `xs:choice`, or repeating groups), while structured XML does not. As a rule of thumb, it is possible to navigate a structured XML document without examining the document content (e.g., the first child element of the second child element of the root will always be an `address` element). Marked-up text uses mixed element content and has the additional challenge that logical units of text (such as sentences) may span multiple elements.

Many applications manipulate documents with only a single given schema or DTD. Other applications require the ability to interchangeably manipulate documents with different schemas or change the schema of a given document from time to time as the document is updated. In general, structured or semi-structured XML with a given schema is the easiest to handle, and the other alternatives all significantly increase the complexity of mapping between XML and relational data.

LOB or Compose?

The most basic dichotomy in mapping between XML and relational data is the choice between representing an XML document in a single column or in multiple columns: LOB representation or composed representation. Additionally, relational databases that have been extended to add XML functionality may implement a native XML type.

In an LOB representation, a column in a database table contains a literal XML string, usually in a **CLOB** (character large object) or similar datatype—hence the name. A single application might store multiple types of XML documents in different columns or even in the same column. Listing 6.1 shows an example of LOB XML. In this example, we have a database table that stores purchase orders as XML documents in one column and includes two other columns: `id` and `receivedate`, that are part of the management of the purchase order document. (Note: in this and all other examples of XML used in this chapter, whitespace has been added for clarity; it is not necessarily part of the actual XML data.)

Listing 6.1   Example of LOB-Encoded XML

id	receivedate	purchaseorder
4023	2001-12-01	`<purchaseOrder`
		`    xmlns="http://po.example.com">`
		`    <originator billId="0013579">`
		`        <contactName>`
		`            Fred Allen`
		`        </contactName>`
		`        <contactAddress>`
		`            <street>123 2nd Ave. NW</street>`
		`            <city>Anytown</city>`
		`            <state>OH</state>`
		`            <zip-four>99999-1234</zip-four>`
		`        </contactAddress>`
		`        <phone>(330) 555-1212</phone>`
		`        <originatorReferenceNumber>`
		`            AS 1132`
		`        </originatorReferenceNumber>`
		`    </originator>`
		`    <order>`
		`        <item code="34xdl 1278 12ct"`
		`              quantity="1"/>`
		`        <item code="57xdl 7789"`
		`              quantity="1"`
		`              colorcode="012"/>`
		`    </order>`
		`    <shipAddress sameAsContact="true"/>`
		`    <shipCode carrier="02"/>`
		`</purchaseOrder>`
5327	2002-04-23	`<purchaseOrder`
		`    xmlns="http://po.example.com">`
		`    <originator`
		`        ...`

The other major approach to mapping between XML and relational data employs a composed representation of XML data. In a composed representation, the XML document does not exist in its XML form in the relational database. Instead, an XML document is composed from individual data items that are stored in many columns, and often in multiple tables, in the relational database. Typically each XML element that has simple data corresponds to the value of some column in some row of the relational data.

For example, the same data that we saw in Listing 6.1 might look as shown in Listing 6.2 in a composed representation. A key observation for the composed representation is that the same relational data could be used to represent many different XML documents by choosing different columns, arranged in different ways, and different corresponding element names. There must be some explicit or implicit mechanism to determine what the XML for a set of relational tables is supposed to look like. We call such a mechanism a **composition technique**. A variety of composition techniques exist, and we explore a few of the variations in the next section.

Listing 6.2 Example of Composed XML

```
purchaseorder table
id          receivedate

4023        2001-12-01
5327        2002-04-23


originator table
poid        billId      contactName     street          . . .

4023        0013579     Fred Allen      123 2nd Ave. NW


order table
poid        code              quant   color   size

4023        34xdl 1278 12ct     1     null    null
4023        57xdl 7789          1     012     null


ship table
poid        carrier     . . .

4023        02
```

An important aspect of the composed representation concerns the use case where the original data is in XML form. In this case, the XML document must be decomposed into values that can be placed into the relational tables—a process often called by the evocative name "shredding." This shredded, or decomposed, representation is then recomposed on the fly to generate the final XML. The shredding, or decomposition, process can also be configurable; ideally it uses the same information that is used in the composition technique that will be used to recompose the data. Shredding creates a variety of additional issues and choices that we discuss in a separate section below.

LOB and composed approaches can coexist, of course: part of an XML document can be (de)composed, while certain subelements are maintained in LOB form. For example, a table that mixes composed and LOB data might look like the one shown in Listing 6.3. In this case, the document data is divided between decomposed, or shredded, elements and XML LOB contents. In other scenarios, the division might be redundant: Certain elements of the LOB information might be duplicated as individual database columns.

Listing 6.3   A Table with Both Composed and LOB Data

```
originator table
poid      billId       contactName      address

4023      0013579      Fred Allen       <contactAddress>
                                          <street>1234 2nd Ave. NW</street>
                                          <city>Anytown</city>
                                          <state>OH</state>
                                          <zip-four>99999-1234</zip-four>
                                        </contactAddress>
```

Finally, when the database itself is extended to include native XML functionality, then another representation option is a native XML type. That is, the SQL language is extended to allow "XML" to be a primitive datatype. If we look behind the implementation of such a type, we will generally find a dichotomy similar to the one we have outlined here: either an LOB data object or some structured representation is used. But of course the SQL database may also have additional options, especially with regard to details like indexing. Options for an XML native datatype are discussed in more detail in Chapter 7.

Different vendors use different approaches to support mapping between XML and relational data: Some use an LOB representation, some use a composed representation, and some allow either, or a mixture of both. (The same holds true when the database supports a native XML datatype: The database designer may have a choice of underlying representations.)

With respect to the kinds of applications supported by each representation, we can make the following observations:

- Clearly if the source data is relational, a composed representation is used.

- LOB representations are the most flexible with respect to wide varieties of XML inputs, including marked-up text and variable- or no-schema documents. Composed representations with shredding can manage structured or semi-structured XML documents with a given schema much more easily than they can the other types of XML sources.

- LOB representations obviously make it easy to implement the "emit documents" application type. All the other application types, however, require some ability to look inside the document, which must be implemented as an additional layer of processing that cannot take advantage of the database's capabilities, unless implemented as part of a native implementation. This is a significant restriction. By comparison, the composed technique exposes the XML data in such a way that it is possible to use the SQL engine's own capabilities to implement important operations such as selection, at the cost of requiring additional complexity to generate XML output.

- Hybrid and redundant representations can help obtain the benefits of both approaches by enabling indexing and easy access to some elements, while preserving complex XML representations. The cost is a more complex representation of the data, essentially requiring that any access or update methods be able to handle both cases. Redundant representations also add the overhead of keeping multiple representations of the same data in sync.

Composition Techniques: Common Concepts

Every composed representation requires some ability to express how an XML document is composed from the rows and columns of an SQL database. Over the last several years, many different approaches have been tried, some as research projects, some commercially. These techniques may look very different, but they have a number of conceptual similarities, which we will examine. In the next section we look at some specific techniques that use these concepts. As usual, we do not attempt to list the different composition techniques currently in use by vendors, concentrating instead on the underlying principles and variations.

Certain concepts are common to most composition techniques. First of all, a composition technique is either implicit or explicit. With an implicit technique, the user or application has no control over how the relational data is translated into XML. An explicit technique allows control (either on the part of the application accessing the XML or, in the case of shredding, during the design of the database representation).

If explicit control is allowed, it may include the following capabilities:

1. Select which tables and columns to use in the XML document. Some techniques allow you to specify a (SQL) query to use as a starting point, which also allows for joins, selections, data transformations, and aggregations to occur over the source data before using it to generate the XML. As we will see, however, this has serious implications for update.

2. Map rows from tables (or queries) onto XML elements. That is, we can create an XML element for every row in a table (or query result).

3. Map columns from tables (or queries) onto XML elements or attributes. The column value is generally the element or attribute value.

4. Choose names for the XML elements or attributes.

5. Allow control over datatype coercions and formatting.

6. Add fixed XML elements, attributes and/or values. This allows the creation of certain kinds of additional structure in the XML. As a simple example, most composition techniques would allow the addition of the fixed address element in the following XML (where the database might have contained columns for name, street, etc.):

```
<name>Francis Smith</name>
<address>
   <street>123 Main St.</street>
   <city>Anytown</city>
   <state>OH</state>
   <zip>88888</zip>
</address>
```

7. Create additional XML structure by allowing the specification of additional XML-producing operations on the relational data. This item is the most significant. Since the output of SQL queries is relational, we need some *non*-SQL way to generate more complex hierarchical data. The main way to do that is to model some relationships in the XML by special XML-generating operations on the relational data. We examine two such operations in detail in the following sections: hierarchical joins and grouping. These operations are very closely related to their normal SQL counterparts, but we must keep in mind that they are different: relational `join with` and `group by` generate relational results, while the operations we introduce generate hierarchical XML results.

8. An additional level of complexity and power is introduced if explicit control is allowed to compute whether or not an element or attribute will be present in the XML document via an arbitrary expression (in contrast with the usual case: An element is present if its content value is non-null) or to compute an element or attribute's name via an expression. Most composition techniques do not support this level of control. Sometimes, however, we need these capabilities in order to generate an XML document according to a certain standard. Usually in this case some form of composition is combined with XQuery or another transformation language to achieve the final XML (we demonstrate this kind of combination when we describe default mappings in the next section).

Here's a scorecard of how these different capabilities match up with different application types: As a general rule, all of them support the application types of selecting from, querying, and transforming XML documents. Update applications are compatible with items 1–5, so long as the values for the XML come from a single SQL table; as soon as joins or many other SQL capabilities are involved, full update capability becomes impossible (though limited update capability may still exist). Items 6 and 7 are also not compatible with full update capability. These are specific examples of a general problem known in the relational database world as "updating through views." The problem stems from the fact that the operations of a powerful query language are not, in general, uniquely reversible. Therefore, if one attempts to update the result of a (nonreversible) query, there is usually no unique way to determine how to update the original data in a corresponding way. A simple example is attempting to update a generated field that has been created by concatenating two source fields: If you change the value of the concatenation, how should you "break" that value across the sources? To preserve update capability, therefore, we must restrict the complexity of the query or transformation operations to those that are reversible.

Generation of XML Structure through Hierarchical Joins

To illustrate generation of XML with a join schematically, suppose that we have two tables, Table A and Table B. If we generate XML structure through a join from A to B, the XML is going to look something like that shown in Listing 6.4. The general idea is that within an element corresponding to a row of Table A, there are subelements that correspond to "matching" rows in Table B—that is, the rows of Table B that join with a particular row of Table A. The relationship is actually most similar to a relational left outer join, because the mapping usually contains all rows of Table A, even those which have no corresponding rows in Table B.

Listing 6.4   Generation of XML Structure from a Join between Two Tables

```
<ElementforRowofA>
    <SubElementFromColumnofA>
    ...
    <SubElementforMatchingRowofB>
        <SubElementFromColumnofB>
        ...
    </SubElementforMatchingRowofB>
    <SubElementforMatchingRowofB>
        <SubElementFromColumnofB>
        ...
    </SubElementforMatchingRowofB>
    ...
</ElementforRowofA>
```

The structure shown in Listing 6.4 may vary, of course. In general, the elements corresponding to data from Table A may be intermixed with those corresponding to data from Table B. Some element may contain all the data from Table B collectively, or the elements shown that contain all the data from a given row of B may be missing.

Most important, there is no limitation on the number of tables that may be joined in this fashion to produce a single XML document. Listing 6.5 shows an example that uses four tables. Note in particular that Table A joins to B, which in turn joins to C, while separately Table A joins to D. We call this arrangement a **nonlinear hierarchy**, because A has more than a single child that has been added through different hierarchical joins. Note that this relationship could not be modeled with standard relational joins (though it could be modeled in a nested-relational representation). Creating XML structure through hierarchical joins is the most widely supported and most commonly used idiom in composition. It is particularly useful with normalized relational data or star schemas.

Listing 6.5   Complex Hierarchy Generated through Multiple Joins

```
<ElementforA>
    <AContents>...
    <ElementsforB>
        <BContents>...
        <ElementsforC>
            <CContents>...
        </ElementsforC>
    </ElementsforB>
    <ElementsforD>
        <DContents>...
    </ElementsforD>
</ElementforA>
```

Generation of XML Structure through Hierarchical Grouping

To illustrate generation of XML with hierarchical grouping, suppose that we generate XML structure through grouping on a single Table A. The resulting XML will look similar to that in Listing 6.6. In this scenario, we create an XML element for every unique value of a set of grouping columns of A, and then within that element occur subelements corresponding to data for nongrouped columns of the individual rows within the group. Generating structure through hierarchical grouping is particularly useful if we want to recreate a "normalized" XML structure from denormalized relational data.

Listing 6.6   Generation of XML Structure from Grouping on a Single Table

```
<ElementforGroupKeyofA>
   <SubElementFromGroupingColumnofA>
   ...
   <SubElementforSingleRowofA>
      <SubElementFromNonGroupedColumnofA>
      ...
   </SubElementforSingleRowofA>
   <SubElementforSingleRowofA>
      <SubElementFromNonGroupedColumnofA>
      ...
   </SubElementforSingleRowofA>
   ...
</ElementforGroupKeyofA>
```

Most composition techniques do not provide direct support for hierarchical grouping. When such support is lacking, the same effect can be generated by joining Table A to itself, where the "outer table" is a query that generates the unique group keys from A, and the inner table retrieves the matching rows. But the self-join technique can be much more expensive than a direct implementation of grouping.

Composition Techniques: Examples

In this section, we consider examples of composition techniques that illustrate the available variety. We divide composition techniques into three fundamental camps: **default mappings,** extended SQL, and annotated schemas. We illustrate each camp with a specific example—but it should be emphasized that these are just three current examples from a much wider selection, offered by commercial vendors, academic research and freeware.

Default Mapping

In the simplest kind of composition technique, a default mapping,[1] the structure of the database is exposed directly, as a fixed form of XML document.

---

[1] The names used for different composition techniques in this chapter are our own characterization; vendors often have many different names for the same concept.

This is an implicit composition technique, in which the user has little or no control over the generated XML. Listing 6.7 shows an example of a default mapping.

Listing 6.7   An Example of a Default Mapping from a Table to XML

```
table customer
name            acctnum    home

Albert Ng       012ab3f    123 Main St.,  Anytown OH 99999
Francis Smith   032cf5d    42 1/2 Seneca, Whositsville, NH 88888
...


<customerSet>
  <customer>
    <name>Albert Ng</name>
    <acctnum>012ab3f</acctnum>
    <home>123 Main St.,  Anytown OH 99999</home>
  </customer>
  <customer>
    <name>Francis Smith</name>
    <acctnum>032cf5d</acctnum>
    <home>42 1/2 Seneca, Whositsville, NH 88888</home>
  </customer>
  ...
```

In a default mapping, the names of the tables and columns become (with escaping of reserved characters) the names of elements and/or attributes. These elements and attributes are arranged in a simple structure—usually some form of the three-level hierarchy you see here, or a simple variation that uses attributes instead of elements for column values. Datatypes follow some fixed conversion (e.g., SQL VARCHAR to XML String), and null values in the database either become missing elements or elements with missing values.

One advantage of default mapping is that it supports update very easily: Operations to update element values and add or delete elements have a very direct translation into update operations on the underlying database. However, default mapping does not by itself support many applications, since applications often need XML data in certain specific formats that don't happen to correspond to default mappings from the database. But if a default mapping is combined with a general-purpose query or transformation language such as XQuery, then XQuery may be used to "reformat" the implicitly mapped XML document into the desired XML form.

Listing 6.8 illustrates a simple example of using XQuery to transform the document from Listing 6.7. This is a very simple example; a more realistic example would probably involve combining data from multiple tables, and so forth.

The combination of default mapping with XQuery is quite powerful in that it re-uses the same transformation capabilities that are supported in XQuery already. It is also generally efficient when the application needs to select from, query, or transform the resulting XML document, which is accomplished by composing the two operations (one query to generate the XML document, the other to select from or transform it). Since XQuery is defined to support query composition, a general XQuery implementation will be able to support this scenario.

Listing 6.8   Using XQuery to Transform a Default-Mapped XML Document

```
<ActiveCustomers xmlns="http://www.example.com/custlist"> {
    for $i in doc("customer")/CustomerSet/Customer
    let $firstname := substring-before($i/name, " ")
        $lastname := substring-after($i/name, " ")
    return
      <customer acct="{$i/acctnum}">
        <name type="full">
            <first>{$firstname}</first>
            <last>{$lastname}</last>
        </name>
      </customer>
    }
</ActiveCustomers>


<ActiveCustomers xmlns="http://www.example.com/custlist">
  <customer acct="012ab3f">
    <name type="full">
      <first>Albert</first>
      <last>Ng</last>
    </name>
  </customer>
  <customer acct="032cf5d">
    <name type="full">
        <first>Francis</first>
        <last>Smith</last>
    </name>
  </customer>
  ...
</ActiveCustomers>
```

One thing to keep in mind is that the advantage of default mapping with respect to update applications is lost when combining default mapping and XQuery. While it is easy to update the directly mapped document itself, it is not usually possible to update an XML document that is the result of a query or transformation, since it suffers from the same "update through views" problem discussed in the previous section.

Extended SQL

Default mapping plus XQuery is one way to create a complex XML structure from relational data. Another is to add the capability to process and generate XML to SQL. An extended SQL language could be directly implemented by a database vendor, or it could be implemented in a layer on top of the database.

This is the approach taken with SQL/XML, which, as of this writing, is in draft form before ISO as an extension to the SQL query language [SQLXML]. SQL/XML could evolve to become a full solution to emitting, querying, transforming, and even updating XML in its own right. We cannot fully cover SQL/XML here, but we can summarize the major points with respect to mapping between XML and relational data.

How does SQL/XML generate XML? SQL/XML consists of a definition of a native XML datatype, as well as definitions of implicit and explicit ways of generating XML from relational data. The native XML datatype allows XML to be manipulated by the SQL query language, which means that XML documents can be treated as relational values (values of columns or procedure parameters, etc.). The language is intended to support both composed and LOB implementations of the native XML datatype.

SQL/XML also defines an implicit default mapping from relational data to XML. The standard defines how SQL identifiers are to be escaped to create legal XML identifiers and vice versa, as well as extensive conversion rules for standard SQL datatypes. The mapping can be applied to individual values, tables, and entire catalogs. Within SQL/XML, the default mapping is used to define the manner in which SQL datatypes are translated to XML when they appear in XML-generating operators.

Finally, SQL/XML defines a set of XML-generating operators that can be used in an SQL expression: XMLELEMENT, XMLFOREST, and XMLGEN. Each of these allows the creation of an XML element (or fixed sequence of elements) with substitution of values from relational data. For example, the XMLELEMENT operator creates an XML element with content mapped from its arguments:

```
SELECT e.id,
    XMLELEMENT ( NAME "Emp",
                 XMLATTRIBUTES ( e.name AS "name" ),
                 e.hire,
                 e.dept ) AS "result"
FROM employees e
WHERE ... ;
```

This SQL statement generates a table that has two columns, one containing e.id, one containing an XML element Emp, with the indicated contents supplied by values from the employee table. The default mapping rules are used to determine how the data values are translated to XML and how the nested elements are named.

Interestingly, these generator functions lack features that directly support the generation of hierarchy through hierarchical joins. Although they allow you to create XML hierarchy, the hierarchy is all fixed and is populated directly from a relational set of values. Instead, the effect of generation of hierarchy through joins is piggybacked on existing object-relational features of SQL, in particular by applying the direct-mapping rules to nested-relational structures, as shown in Listing 6.9:

Listing 6.9   Generating Hierarchical Structure with Object-Relational Features of SQL/XML

```
SELECT XMLELEMENT( NAME "Department",
                   d.deptno,
                   d.dname
                   CAST(MULTISET(
                        select e.empno, e.ename
                        from emp e
                        where e.deptno = d.deptno)
                   AS emplist)))
       AS deptxml
FROM dept d
WHERE d.deptno = 100;
```

Listing 6.9   Generating Hierarchical Structure with Object-Relational Features
of SQL/XML *(continued)*

```
<Department>
  <deptno>100</deptno>
  <dname>Sports</dname>
  <emplist>
    <element>
      <empno>200</empno>
      <ename>John</ename>
    </element>
    <element>
      <ename>Jack</ename>
    </element>
  </emplist>
</Department>
```

SQL/XML does provide a function, XMLAGG, which directly supports
generation of structure through grouping. It is used in collaboration with
the SQL GROUP BY operation as in the example shown in Listing 6.10:

Listing 6.10   Generating Hierarchical Structure through Grouping in SQL/XML

```
SELECT XMLELEMENT
         ( NAME "department"
           XMLELEMENT ( NAME "name" e.dept )
           XMLELEMENT ( NAME "employees"
                        XMLAGG (
                          XMLELEMENT ( NAME "emp", e.lname )
                        )
                      )
         ) AS "dept_list"
FROM employees e
GROUP BY e.dept
```

The XMLAGG function acts like an aggregation operation, generating a list
of XML content (in this case a single nested element): one item for each
row in the group. The output of the query of Listing 6.10 might look like
the example of Listing 6.11:

Listing 6.11   An Example XMLAGG Result

```
<department>
  <name>Physics</name>
  <employees>
    <emp>Smith</emp>
    <emp>Thompson</emp>
    <emp>Johnson</emp>
  </employees>
</department>
<department>
  <name>Computer Science</name>
  <employees>
    <emp>Hinson</emp>
    . . .
```

Extended SQL composition techniques are well-suited for supporting selection and transformation over XML documents. They usually cannot support update applications, unless the SQL expressions are very limited.

Annotated XML Template

Another way to express the construction of XML from relational data is to supply an XML template that is "decorated" with expressions that indicate how to compute corresponding XML. The template could be in the form of the XML document itself, or it could be an annotated DTD or schema. To illustrate this mapping technique, we use the Annotated XSD Schema language defined by Microsoft in Microsoft SQLXML 3.0 [SQLXML-MS]

To begin with, in MS SQLXML a completely unannotated schema has a default interpretation: Every complex element is presumed to correspond to a table (whose name is the same as the name of the element), and every simple-valued element or attribute is presumed to correspond to a column of that table (with the same name). Annotations are required to override this assumption, and to specify the relationships between nested complex elements.

Listing 6.12   An Annotated XML Schema

```
<xs:schema xmlns:xsd="http://www.w3.org/2001/XMLSchema"
           xmlns:sql="urn:schemas-microsoft-com:mapping-schema">
  <xs:element name="Customer" type="CustomerType"
              sql:relation="Customers"/>
  <xs:complexType name="CustomerType">
     <xs:sequence>
        <xs:element name="Order" maxOccurs="unbounded"
                    sql:relation="Orders">
           <xs:annotation>
            <xs:appinfo>
              <sql:relationship
                 parent="Customers"   parent-key="CustomerID"
                 child="Orders"        child-key="CustomerID"/>
            </xs:appinfo>
           </xs:annotation>
           <xs:complexType>
              <xs:attribute name="OrderID" type="xs:integer"
                    sql:field="ID"/>
              <xs:attribute name="Amount" type="xs:integer"/>
           </xs:complexType>
        </xs:element>
     </xs:sequence>
     <xs:attribute name="CustomerID"  type="xs:string" />
     <xs:attribute name="ContactName" type="xs:string"
                   sql:field="Name"/>
  </xs:complexType>
</xs:schema>
```

Listing 6.12 shows an example, slightly modified from the Microsoft documentation. In this example, the outermost element, Customer, is populated from a table named Customers (indicated by the sql:relation annotation). Similarly, the nested element Order is populated from the table named Orders. The relationship between them is expressed by the sql:relationship annotation, which tells us that the Customers and Orders are joined through the indicated values.[2] Multi-attribute joins are indicated by specifying the appropriate attribute names, in order, in the parent-key and child-key fields. The various simple fields (all of which are attributes in this example) either are mapped implicitly from table columns (e.g., CustomerID), or indicate, with the sql:field annotation, the name of the column from which they are derived (e.g., ContactName from Name).

---

[2] While these are called parent-key and child-key, the term *key* is a misnomer. These are simply fields that participate in the join condition. A separate annotation, sql:key-fields, is used to directly name the table keys associated with a complex element.

Note that there are no SQL expressions in this technique. Instead, only names of existing tables and columns are allowed. A very simple variation on this mapping technique would be to allow the `sql:relation` annotation to contain an arbitrary SQL statement, or the `sql:field` annotation to contain an SQL expression. This would make it possible to generate more flexible XML documents from a given relational database.

But the restriction to table names and columns has a very powerful advantage: It enables the use of this mapping "in reverse," to support both update operations and shredding of XML documents. If arbitrary expressions were allowed, it would not be possible to support either update or shredding with the same annotated schema. The same trade-off exists in other composition techniques, which either likewise do not allow arbitrary expressions, or in some cases, come in two varieties, where the user chooses which. For example, Microsoft SQLXML handles this by supporting two mapping techniques: annotated XSD to support update and shredding, and an extended SQL notation (the `FOR XML` clause) for arbitrarily computed XML.

We note below a few more interesting features of the annotated XSD before moving on to our next category:

- The example in Listing 6.12 showed a generation of hierarchy through joins with a single join between a parent table, `Customers`, and a child table, `Orders`. You can also express a parent-child relationship that requires a chain of joins. For example if we wanted XML that contained information about customers and the products they had purchased (but not specifically about their individual orders), that might require a join from `Customers` to `Orders` to `Products` to generate the child elements. This is accomplished by inserting multiple `sql:relationship` annotations, in order, one for each required join.
- While the XSD annotation does not permit general conditional expressions, it does allow one limited form of condition. Annotations `sql:limit-field` and `sql:limit-value` can be added to any element or attribute that specifies the `sql:relation` annotation, to indicate that only those rows of the relation that satisfy `limit-field=limit-value` are to be used. This is useful for selecting rows of a certain type; for instance, in the example shown in Listing 6.13, it selects billing addresses from a generic address table.

Listing 6.13   Generating XML Elements in Certain Conditions in MS SQLXML

```
<xs:element name="BillTo"
            type="xs:string"
            sql:relation="Addresses"
            sql:field="StreetAddress"
            sql:limit-field="AddressType"
            sql:limit-value="billing">
  <xs:annotation>
    <xs:appinfo>
      <sql:relationship
          parent="Customers"  parent-key="CustomerID"
          child="Addresses"   child-key="CustomerID" />
    </xs:appinfo>
  </xs:annotation>
</xs:element>
```

■ If the XML Schema contains xs:any, this can be annotated to indicate an "overflow" column where any extra data encountered during shredding will be stored (in string XML form). The system won't do anything with the information in this field, but it will at least be reproducible when the document is recomposed.

The chain of joins and limit-field features are examples of carefully pushing the limits of expressiveness while still maintaining the ability to update.

Additional Mapping Languages

The previous examples added extensions either to SQL or to existing XML standards to bridge the gap between XML and relational data. Another alternative is to express composition in a new, different, language, whose entire goal is to take relational data as input and generate XML data as output, or vice versa. This approach was initially quite popular, but it has waned because it adds an extra level of complexity—a new language to learn—over the other approaches, without adding much in the way of convenience or expressive power.

Additional languages are still in use by some vendors. They may also be used as an internal compiled form for one of the other mechanisms.

Shredding

The previous discussion concentrated primarily on the composition from relational data to XML data. In the case of shredded XML, we must first solve the opposite problem: How do we take XML data and represent it in a relational database? Stated another way, How do we encode an XML document as a set of relational entities, relations, and attributes?

The issues involved for shredding are very similar to the issues for update for any composed mapping technique, which is not surprising, given that shredding an XML document is essentially an update operation that adds a new instance of the document to the store. Thus it is also not surprising that the same basic approaches that work for composed mapping techniques work for shredding as well—so long as they preserve the ability to update. In this section we explore a few additional issues that are unique to shredding.

Creation of the Database

First, when XML is being composed from relational data, we normally assume that the relational data already exists. That is, either the tables and schemas for the relational data have already been created for some other application, or else some application designer has expressly created tables for storing XML data—but in either case, the act of designing and installing the tables has been accomplished before we consider the details of how to map those tables to XML. With shredding, the opposite is usually the case. Initially we are presented with XML files, a DTD, or an XML schema, and we have to design and install the tables and columns that will hold the corresponding data.

Thus shredding always begins with a "design" or "registration" step, in which the database structures to hold the XML are actually created. Different vendors have different approaches to this. The process can be completely automated and implicit (analogous to a default mapping, but the other way around), or an explicit technique can be used to guide the creation of the table layout. Ideally, but not always, the same composition technique (e.g., annotated template) can be used to accomplish both shredding and (re)composition. An explicit composition technique may include additional content to provide instructions for things like precise mapping of datatypes or definition of table keys, foreign keys, and indices.

Adding Extra Information to the Composition

One difference between shredding and general composition techniques is that a shredding implementation has the opportunity to store extra "hidden" information that it derives while parsing an XML document. For example, it is possible to assign a unique, internal identifier (a GUID or row-id) to some or all nodes in an XML document and then use these identifiers as keys when generating hierarchy through joins, rather than insisting on the existence of some key in the XML itself. This makes it possible to reliably represent, and update, XML data that may contain duplicates, for example. (Note: It might be tempting to use XML ID attributes for this purpose, if they are present, but that is generally a bad idea, because (1) many applications will not validate that IDs are in fact unique within a document, and (2) IDs only need to be unique within a single document, and most applications need to manage multiple XML documents in the same database.)

In addition to identifiers for nodes, ordinal values (the position of a node within its parent) can be extracted and stored. Preserving order in XML documents can be a complex task otherwise and may even be impossible in some cases (e.g., arbitrarily interleaved lists of different types of elements). Care must be taken with the representation of the ordinal value if update is required (while a simple numeric index would work, the computational cost of inserting a new node into the document would be significant).

Inlining and Consolidation

Shredding involves two basic table layout choices: when to break information across multiple tables and when to consolidate tables for different elements. A simple algorithm for defining the database layout starts at the top of the XML document, with a root element (or set of possible root elements). The element is associated with a table, and then, for each of the possible children of that element, a decision is made whether to put them in the same table (**inlining**), or start a new table (and either find in the XML data, or create artificially, a field or fields that will be the join condition between the two tables).

The simplest rule for breaking XML information across multiple tables is to create a new table for every element that can occur multiply (has `maxOccurs > 1`) within its parent element. Elements that occur exactly once within a parent element are placed in the same table as the parent (and any reasonable shredding algorithm should be able to do this through multiple levels of singular elements). But what about optional elements? These could be placed in their own table, or they could be placed in the same table with the parent, using null when the element is not present. Inlining optional elements avoids an extra join at runtime, but can result in larger database sizes, particularly if the optional element is large and does not occur often in the data. Neither choice is optimal in all circumstances.

Consolidation is the process of re-using the same table for data that occurs in multiple locations in the database, most often because a common element type (e.g., something like an address) is re-used multiple times. For consolidation to be possible, a consistent set of fields must be used to join between the consolidated table and various parent tables (either the same fields are used in each case, or at least the entire set of fields is populated consistently). This is an easy condition to satisfy if node-ids are used as join conditions, but can be more difficult otherwise. Consolidation reduces the total number of tables required for a shredded representation.

Support of Full XML

The most important factor that affects shredding applications is that input XML sources can use arbitrary features of XML (and DTDs or XML Schema), including features that do not map well to relational storage. Examples of these features include poor mapping of datatypes (e.g., strings with unbounded length), variability of representation (e.g., `xs:choice`), ordered polymorphic sequences (particularly sequences containing repeating subsequences), mixed content, and arbitrary extensibility (e.g., `xs:any`). DTDs suffer from many of the same problems. XML with variable or no schema is even harder to handle. For variable schemas, if the schemas are known in advance, it may be possible to create a shredded representation that encompasses the union of all the possible structures. When the schema is not known in advance, or doesn't exist at all, it may be possible to guess a "shape" of the XML by looking at sample documents, but there is no guarantee that future documents will share that shape. In general, the more amorphous or varying the structure of the input XML, the more likely it is that a LOB representation will be more appropriate than a composed representation.

Schema-Independent Representation

One possibility for handling the vagaries of full XML is to use a relational representation that is totally independent of the schema of the XML data. An example of such a representation is an **edge table**, in which a single table contains information about the relationship between parent and child elements (using node identifiers), and another column contains simple element content. Listing 6.14 provides an example of an XML fragment and an edge-table representation of it.

Listing 6.14   An Edge Table for an XML Fragment

```
<Department id="A12x" name="Physics">
  <Employee id="555-23-4567">
    <name>Mary Phillips</name>
    <office>21</office>
  </Employee>
  <Employee id="544-12-3456">
    ...

edge table
parentid  childid  name         value
```

parentid	childid	name	value
null	1	Department	null
1	2	@id	A12x
1	3	@name	Physics
1	4	Employee	null
4	5	@id	555-23-4567
4	6	name	Mary Phillips
4	7	office	21
1	8	Employee	null
8	9	@id	544-12-3456

While edge tables or similar structures offer a certain attractive simplicity and can represent almost any XML input, they have not been widely used in layered processing models, since they do not take effective advantage of relational database capabilities: Every single navigation requires an independent join onto the same table or tables, and indexing is not very effective. However, the edge table can be a useful model for a native XML implementation within a relational database, in which the database can add additional crucial indexing information to the table (see Chapter 7 for a discussion).

Implementation Concepts

Generally, details of implementation are hidden within the database or middleware that implements the XML view of relational data. Nevertheless, it is valuable to understand the basic approaches in order to gain insight into performance or for debugging. A thorough discussion of implementing the different kinds of applications introduced in the second section, using different XML representations and different mapping techniques, is beyond the scope of this chapter. Our aim in this section is to outline the basic requirements for implementation. We begin with the simple application type of emitting XML documents, which allows us to introduce several implementation strategies for composed techniques—most important, the varieties of techniques for generating hierarchical structure through joins. We also include a very high-level outline of implementation techniques for the other application types.

Emitting XML Documents

Our simplest application type consisted of emitting XML documents that are stored in a relational database. When the document is stored in LOB form, this is quite simple: The column value is simply accessed and returned. The more interesting case is emitting a composed XML document (an XML view of relational data).

Most aspects of generating an XML document from a composed representation are also not very complex. The basic concept is to create a standard SQL statement (one that does not involve any extended features).

This will, of course, return relational data. Then, in a post-processing step, for each row of the relational data, XML "decoration" is added: XML element tags, additional static content, and so on. Of course if the implementation is directly within the database engine, it need not actually be implemented in these two steps, but conceptually (and often in practice) this is representative of the process.

The basic step is to generate an SQL statement that retrieves content from a single table. This SQL statement simply names the table and whichever columns are needed. If the composition technique only refers to a single table, this is the only step that is required. For example, we can convert the annotated XSD shown in Listing 6.15 into the SQL shown in the last three lines of the listing. All the work of adding element tags is handled by the post-processor.

Listing 6.15   Creating an SQL Statement for an Annotated Schema

```
<xs:element name="Employee" sql:relation="Persons"
            sql:limit-field="Type"
            sql:limit-value="Emp">
  <xs:complexType>
    <xs:sequence>
      <xs:element name="FName" type="xs:string"
                  sql:field="FirstName"/>
      <xs:element name="LName" type="xs:string"
                  sql:field="LastName"/>
    </xs:sequence>
    <xs:attribute name="EmpID" type="xs:integer"
                  sql:field="EmployeeID"/>
  </xs:complexType>
</xs:element>


SELECT e.FirstName, e.LastName, e.EmployeeID
FROM Employees e
WHERE e.Type="Emp";
```

Generation of hierarchy through grouping is also relatively straightforward. Instead of using the SQL GROUP BY construct, we will SORT BY the grouping keys instead. Then, during post-processing, a new grouping-level element is created each time a new value of the group keys is encountered, and new subordinate elements are created for each row of the data, as above. For example, we would convert an SQL/XML statement as shown in Listing 6.16:

Listing 6.16   Translating an SQL/XML XMLAGG Query

```
        SQL/XML
SELECT XMLELEMENT
         ( NAME "department"
           XMLELEMENT ( NAME "name" e.dept )
           XMLELEMENT ( NAME "employees"
                          XMLAGG (
                            XMLELEMENT ( NAME "emp", e.lname )
                          )
                       )
         ) AS "dept_list"
FROM employees e
GROUP BY e.dept;

        SQL
SELECT e.dept, e.lname
FROM employees e
ORDER BY e.dept;
```

The SQL statement often becomes much simpler: All of the XML-oriented tasks are moved to the post-processing step. The part of the post-processing that handles the grouping would look something like the pseudocode shown in Listing 6.17:

Listing 6.17   Pseudocode for Reconstructing Grouped XML Data from SQL

```
groupkey ← null;
cursor ← execute the sql query;
while ( cursor not empty ) {
   newgroupkey ← getgroupkey(cursor);
   if ( groupkey != newgroupkey ) {
       if ( groupkey != null )
          emit close tag for old group element;
       emit open tag for new group element;
       groupkey ← newgroupkey;
   }
   process non-grouping fields in row;
   advance cursor;
}
if ( groupkey != null )
   emit close tag for old group element
}
```

The most complex aspect of emitting XML from composed representations comes from the generation of hierarchy though joins. The basic premise is still the same: We want to create standard SQL, with post-processing that can generate XML from the relational results. Depending on the database vendor, the database might itself already internally support nested tables or some similar concept that can be used for this purpose. But if the database does not provide those capabilities, or if the application is being implemented in middleware that lacks access to those capabilities, then another approach is required. There are three commonly used techniques, which we call simple join, **dependent join**, and **sorted outer union.** We introduce each of these below.

Simple Join

Perhaps the most obvious approach is to try to first compute a join using the ordinary SQL join syntax and then use post-processing to reconstruct the hierarchy from the join results. The idea is similar to the method for reconstructing hierarchy for grouping: First join the appropriate relations together, sort the results so that rows that represent children of the same element will occur consecutively in the results, and use the same "Did the key change?" logic that we used for grouping to control when new container elements are opened and closed. The left outer join must be used in order to accurately reconstruct cases where an element has no children (e.g., a department with no employees).

This approach can work in certain limited cases. The following must be true:

- There must be a key associated with each element that is not a leaf element. If there is no such key, then duplicate elements will look alike and be merged. For example, in the following sample join result, if the employee's name is not a key, then there is no way to tell whether or not this represents a single employee named Mary with two phone numbers, or two people named Mary, each with a single phone number:

deptid	deptname	empname	empphone
21	Physics	Mary	x2017
21	Physics	Mary	x4007

As noted earlier, if the relational data is the result of shredding, it is possible to automatically add node-ids for elements, thereby guaranteeing that the required keys will exist.

■ The XML hierarchy must be linear; that is, the complete set of joins must form a linear path: A left-outer-join B left-outer-join C, and so forth. The hierarchy depicted in Listing 6.5 does not satisfy this condition: in this case Table A is joined to both B and D. The problem with this arrangement is that when a complete join of A, B, C, and D is done, the result will be a full cross-product between B and D. This has two effects: The data size is exploded (consider what can happen if there are more than two nonlinear hierarchies), and the logic required to reconstruct the intended hierarchy becomes considerably more complex.

The second limitation is significant, because it seriously restricts the type of XML that can be generated with the simple join technique.

Dependent Join

This approach works without any restrictions. In this case we do not attempt to create a single SQL query; instead, the "post-processing" step becomes a master control that creates and executes multiple SQL queries. We form one SQL query for the topmost relation, and then, for each row in that relation, invoke a separate SQL query for each related child (and in turn, for each of those rows, a separate SQL query for their children, etc., recursively).

Thus for the structure that was depicted in Listing 6.5, the processing would look something like what is shown in Listing 6.18:

Listing 6.18   Code Structure for a Dependent Join

```
cursorA ← sql for table A
while ( cursorA not empty ) {
    process elements for row in A
    cursorB ← sql for table B
    while ( cursorB not empty ) {
        process elements for row in B
        cursorC ← sql for table C
        while ( cursorC not empty ) {
            process elements for row in C
            advance cursorC
        }
        advance cursorB
    }
}
```

Listing 6.18   Code Structure for a Dependent Join *(continued)*

```
cursorD ← sql for table D
while ( cursorD not empty ) {
    process elements for row in D
    advance cursorD
}
advance cursorA
}
```

In actual practice, of course, we would use a generic recursive algorithm that would operate over any hierarchy, but this way it is easier to see the relationships, both for linear (B, C) and nonlinear (B, D) relationships. Each SQL statement except the outermost will be a parameterized SQL statement (i.e., a prepared statement), and the join condition will be represented by a parameterized condition. For example, the SQL for Table B might contain lines like the following:

```
SELECT ...
FROM B
WHERE B.key = &;
```

At run-time, the parameter will be substituted with the corresponding value from table(s) higher in the hierarchy.

It is easy to see that this technique can create numerous SQL statements and can also have many cursors open simultaneously, even though only one is in use at a time. The algorithm does not use database resources very efficiently. And indeed, while the dependent join is adequate for small or light-load use cases, it does not by itself scale effectively to larger application demands.

The Sorted Outer Union

If the simple join only works in limited cases, and the dependent join does not scale, what are we to do? A very clever, and fairly complicated, technique was introduced by Jayavel Shanmugasundaram et al. [EFFICIENT]. It is known as the Sorted Outer Union (SOU). The Sorted Outer Union is, in effect, an improved version of the simple join approach, but it removes the restriction against nonlinear hierarchy (though keys are still required).

The fundamental question is this: If the simple join technique works for a linear join hierarchy, can we somehow pack together multiple queries, one for each linear hierarchy, in one query, in such a way that the results are neither a cross-product nor ambiguous? This is what the SOU accomplishes.

The output of the SOU contains columns for all of the tables involved—even tables that are "parallel" to each other in the XML (e.g., B and D in the example from Listing 6.5). However, in any one row of the output, only columns from a single table (and the chain of keys from the root to get to that table) will be filled; all other columns will be null. The entire SOU query consists of the union over a set of smaller SQL queries, one for each interesting join path in the XML, where each of these smaller SQL queries is in essence the simple join query for that join path. The effect is to fill the output with "blocks" of data: a set of rows to retrieve values from Table A, then another for Table B (given a key from A), and so forth. In a final bit of magic, the entire result set is sorted by the keys in such a way as to interleave the rows of the data in exactly the same order in which the fields are used in the XML document.

We illustrate this pattern with the structure from Listing 6.5, which involved Tables A, B, C and D. Thus the output of the SOU query will have columns from each of these tables, as shown below:

```
A-key   A-cols   B-key   B-cols   C-key   C-cols   D-key   D-cols
```

According to the SOU algorithm, there are four interesting join paths: A itself, A-B, A-B-C and A-D. If we look at just one of these paths, say A-B, the SQL query for that path will create the join path to B and retrieve the columns of B. All the other columns will be filled with nulls. The pattern of the query, and of its output, appear as shown in Listing 6.19:

Listing 6.19   An Example of an SOU Join Block, and the Result It Generates

```
SELECT A-key, null as A-col1, null as A-col2, ...,
       B-key, B-col1, B-col2, ...,
       null as C-key, null as C-col1, null as C-col2, ...,
       null as D-key, null as D-col1, null as D-col2, ...
FROM   A, B
WHERE  A-key = B-key;
```

A-key	A-cols	B-key	B-cols	C-key	C-cols	D-key	D-cols
a1	*nulls*	b1	*bvals*	*nulls*	*nulls*	*nulls*	*nulls*

Notice the use of null, cast to the appropriate datatype, to fill the unused columns. Also notice that we used an inner join here, not an outer join: the outer join is not required because its effect will be achieved by separate queries for each join path (in this case a separate query to retrieve values from A by itself).

One query of this form is generated for each interesting join path, the individual queries are unioned together, and the results sorted by the table keys:

```
sql-query-for-A
UNION ALL
sql-query-for-A-B
UNION ALL
sql-query-for-A-B-C
UNION ALL
sql-query-for-A-D
ORDER BY A-key, B-key, C-key, D-key;
```

The effect of the sort operation is to interleave the results from the different queries so that all the rows for a particular element appear together, in order. The algorithm assumes that the key order is the same as document order. (If it is not, then separate columns are required to represent the proper ordinal values, and the sort will be on those columns instead.) Also, nulls are assumed to sort low, which assures that the shorter join paths appear before the longer ones; thus, information about A is retrieved before information about A-B, and so on. (If nulls sort high, the algorithm can be modified to sort keys in the opposite order.)

The SOU query relies on the existence of keys for each table for the same reason as the simple join: Without them it is impossible to reliably handle duplicates or to generate the correct ordering. Beyond that, it places no inherent restrictions on the hierarchy of the XML, and can be used to generate single queries that make effective use of database connections. And while the database results are "wide" (containing many columns), many of the columns will be null, so the actual result size is reasonable; if the database driver can compress nulls, it is close to as efficient as possible. By comparison, the simple join technique, even when it is applicable, will replicate values in data columns many times (e.g., the columns from the higher levels of the hierarchy), which can greatly increase the overall size of the data returned.

The SOU may still have problems scaling, however. The SQL queries generated by the SOU technique can be quite large, and large XML structures may push the limits of what databases (or their optimizers) can handle.

Avoiding Unnecessary Dependent Joins or Unions

Both dependent join and SOU pay a price for each "join block." One way to improve their performance is to try to limit the number of join blocks they require. For example, we can improve the performance of the dependent join by using it across larger queries. Analyzing the structure of the XML hierarchy and verifying the existence of keys may allow us to identify when it is legal to join multiple tables in a single query using the simple join technique, and only use the dependent join technique between the resulting query blocks. This approach, when applicable, can reduce the number of SQL statements and cursors required. When the structure of the XML hierarchy is actually linear, it reduces to the simple join technique.

A way to improve the performance of both dependent joins and SOU queries is to recognize situations in which the outer join is from one table (A) to a key in another table (B). We can call this kind of join a "lookup," because that is its effect: Given information about some entity/element in Table A, we are "looking up" the value of some other attribute in Table B. Since the lookup occurs on a key, the join will match exactly once, returning either null or the single matching value. In this situation, it is possible to inline that particular join into a single SQL query (either a query in a dependent join, or a single query within an SOU)—and this is true regardless of the structure of the XML hierarchy. This optimization is easy to apply if the field in B is declared as a key; if it is not declared in the database metadata, then it might be identified by additional information in the mapping directly (e.g., an additional annotation in an XML template).

Querying and Updating XML Documents

Querying and transforming applications require adding the capability to select parts of XML documents and to create new XML structure dynamically. A rich language such as XQuery or XSLT has powerful methods for selection, based on many possible properties of the XML input, and can create essentially any output structure for the results.

Conceptually, we think of implementing a query or transformation using the same approach we have followed for emitting XML documents from composed sources: First translate as much of the query or transformation as possible to one or more SQL statements and then add an extra post-processor to finish any additional necessary processing. When emitting documents, our post-processing step was pretty much limited to translating the SQL results to XML for composed representations (LOB representations required no additional work at all). Now, however, the post-processor may do a lot more than that in order to to handle operations that are not translatable to SQL.

For LOB implementations, we generally must start by extracting the required information from the LOB, using functions that process the XML string content. An entire XML query processor might be implemented within these functions, or the functions might be more limited to extracting field data, using SQL to do the rest of the work. Either way, one challenge that must be surmounted is that many natural operations on XML will return multiple results, which will require the use of arrays, nested tables, or similar structures. The only real alternative is to limit the query functions to those that can only return single results, which is a strong limitation indeed, one that is appropriate only if the structure of the XML and the application happen to satisfy that requirement and are unlikely to change over time.

Performance is also a serious issue for general-purpose query processing of LOB XML data. General querying usually requires complete scans of all the LOB data, which exacts a large performance cost compared to normal query processing in relational databases. Text-indexing or special purpose XML-indexing tools can create indices of particular elements or attributes inside the LOB data, which helps to limit the scanning required. Also, this cost can be reduced if the XML LOB data can reside in memory (in a database cache, or by using an in-memory database processor). Query processing must still stream through all the data, but the dominant cost of reading the data from disk is avoided.

Implementation of querying for composed representations is naturally quite different. In this case the document we are querying is a virtual document that is already computed by a SQL query or queries (plus post-processing). Thus our goal is to merge the application's query or transform with the composition query that generates the document. We illustrate this with a very simple example. The following XQuery

```
for $x in doc("purchases.xml")/PurchaseOrder/originator
where $x/contactAddress/zip-four = "98102-1234"
return $x/contactName
```

translates to SQL such as the following:

```
SELECT contactName
FROM purchaseorder, originator
WHERE purchaseorder.id = originator.poid AND originator.zip4 =
"98102";
```

We can paraphrase an algorithm that would produce this query as follows:

1. Start with the SQL query that would be used to emit the entire PurchaseOrder element list (from the root of the document).
2. Translate the XQuery selection conditions into equivalent SQL selection conditions (if possible).
3. Prune the SQL query so that it will reference only the tables and columns necessary either to evaluate the selection conditions or to return required results.

Of course this merely brushes the surface: We must also recognize and handle joins between multiple documents, and so forth. We will not delve into further details in this chapter.

One issue is worth highlighting because it can be controllable. One of the most significant differences between the XML and relational models is that the order of elements is important in an XML document, so results must be generated in a particular order, and XQuery and other languages can query the document based on that order. Since the relational model is unordered, we cannot guarantee that data will be returned from a relational database in any particular order unless an ORDER BY clause is used in the query. Note that strictly speaking it is not even sufficient to say that "whatever order comes out of the database" is the order of the document, because the order is not guaranteed to be *stable*: changing the query, for example by adding new constraints, could cause the order of the results to be changed (e.g., because the database optimizer changes the join order). We can enforce a stable order by adding ORDER BY clauses to the SQL; in the case of shredded XML, we can add a separate ordinal value to the relational data for this purpose.

But ordering XML is expensive. If the application does not require stable order in the XML, it is very advantageous to avoid the unnecessary sorting steps. This is the motivation for the unordered operator in XQuery, which allows the application to declare that it is not interested in order. As an alternative, the mapping technique could allow the declaration that order of certain elements is *never* meaningful and therefore not supported.

Conclusion

This chapter has presented a variety of concepts pertaining to mapping between XML and relational data. Facilities for accomplishing this mapping are provided by the database vendors and by third-party software manufacturers (either XML specialty vendors or XML-based middleware vendors); in some cases they may be written directly in stored procedures or applications. Vendors, especially database vendors, will also provide facilities for executing XQuery, WebDAV, or other XML processing models directly on top of the relational data model, bypassing translation at the data level.

Which actual features are required for mapping between XML and relational data depends on both the application and on the (possibly evolving) XML schema of the XML data that needs to be supported. The materials in this chapter can be used to assess those requirements and compare them against the capabilities available from various sources.

We have looked at two fundamentally different approaches to storing XML data in relational databases and examined to some degree the approaches used to implement applications on each representation. If we look at both of these representations, we can see some clear contrasts in their applicability, particularly in two areas: support for a wide variety of XML, and support for application types.

LOB representation has some clear advantages in certain situations. If an application requires only a logically accurate view of the data contained in an XML document, in elements and attributes, then both representations are equally applicable. But other applications may require preservation of XML comments, XML processing instructions, or exact preservation of whitespace—or, in general, exact reproduction of an initial XML document. These requirements complicate a composed representation considerably, beyond the capabilities of most commercial applications, whereas they are quite simple for LOB representations.

Certain other kinds of XML structures are possible under composed representations, but may have limited support; these include XML Schema concepts such as substitution groups, recursive schemas, and mixed-content XML (mixed content is easily represented in a composed representation, but may not be so easily queryable). Again, none of these are at all difficult for LOB representations, though they may complicate indexing of LOBs.

Finally, LOB is really the only alternative in situations where the schema of the XML is not known or may evolve in an ad-hoc manner. Because composed representations rely on a fixed relational schema, they are not easily adaptable to changing XML schemas. We did see one example of support for a limited kind of variability (an overflow field to hold any data matching an `xs:any` portion of a schema), but in general composed representations are unable to query or access any XML structure for which they have not been prepared in advance.

So LOBs can represent a wider variety of XML, which is important if the application must handle source XML data that uses any of these features. When it comes to application types, we also have differences.

The most basic form of application, emitting an XML document, is trivial for an LOB representation. The composed representation requires generating potentially complex queries to reproduce output. As a result, the performance for composed representations suffers with document size. Whether or not performance becomes an issue obviously depends on the complexity of the XML documents.

All the above might make it sound like the LOB representation is the obvious choice. However, most complex query operations—selection, extraction, and recombination of data—clearly favor the composed representation. Even with indexes, processing of LOBs can easily require scanning all the data, which cancels out much of the power of the relational database. While the algorithms to support complex query or update operations are themselves quite complex, they can make effective use of the relational database power to make the actual computation efficient.

Update applications show a similar pattern, with the added proviso that update is really only feasible for certain composed representations that permit "reversible" mappings. Update for LOBs is simple in principle, but will often require complete scans, and will always require constructing complete new data values, both of which hamper performance.

It is clear that no single approach, whether LOB or any of the variety of composed representations, is best for all situations. As support for XML data in databases continues to evolve, we can expect improved support for and performance of both representations, and fewer differences between them.

Chapter 7

INTEGRATING XQUERY AND RELATIONAL DATABASE SYSTEMS

Michael Rys

XML allows the combination of highly structured, semi-structured, and **markup data** in one common representation, and thus provides a more flexible data representation model than the existing **relational data model.** On the other hand, relational database systems have a proven track record of providing efficient and cost-effective management of **structured data.** Since most relational database systems have begun to add XML support and features to their relational database engines and are deeply entrenched in the data management arena, one need not be a prophet to predict that relational database systems will most likely capture a large market for both virtual and native XML data storage and processing. Querying XML data will be an integral part of the complete XML support, and XQuery is very likely to become an important component of XML-enabled relational database systems.

This chapter outlines how to integrate XQuery with a relational database system. It shows how to query XML in the context of and in conjunction with relational data and how to provide specific query-hosting environments in the context of relational systems that the XQuery specification assumes but does not describe. In particular, it covers how to apply XQuery over XML views on relational data (using an XML view mechanism such as annotated schemata) and how XQuery can be used on a relational **XML datatype.**

Getting Started

XML and the vocabularies defined with XML have established themselves as the prevalent and most promising lingua franca of business-to-business, business-to-consumer, or generally, any-to-any data interchange and integration. One of the major reasons for the success of XML in this space is that XML is a simple, **Unicode**-based, platform-independent syntax for which simple and efficient parsers are widely available. Another important factor in favor of XML is its ability not only to represent structured data, but also to provide a uniform syntax for structured data, semi-structured data, and markup data. *Structured data* is data that easily fits into a predefined, homogeneous type structure such as relations or nested objects. *Semi-structured data* is data that may change its structure from instance to instance. For example, it may have some components that are one-off annotations that appear only on single instances or it may have components that are of heterogeneous type structure (e.g., one time the address data is a string, another it is a complex object). Finally, *markup data* is data that is mainly free-flowing text with interspersed markup to call out document structure and highlight important aspects of the text. Listing 7.1 gives a short example of each type of data.

Listing 7.1　Examples of Structured, Semi-Structured and Markup Data

```
structured data:
<Customer>
  <ID>C1</ID>
  <FirstName>Janine</FirstName>
  <LastName>Smith</LastName>
  <Address>
    <Street>1 Broadway Way</Street>
    <City>Seattle</City>
    <Zip>WA 98000</Zip>
  </Address>
  <Order>
    <ID>O1</ID>
    <OrderDate>2003-01-21<OrderDate>
    <Amount>7</Amount>
    <ProductID>P1</ProductID>
  </Order>
  <Order>
    <ID>O2</ID>
    <OrderDate>2003-06-24<OrderDate>
    <Amount>3</Amount>
    <ProductID>P3</ProductID>
  </Order>
</Customer>
```

Listing 7.1   Examples of Structured, Semi-Structured and Markup Data *(continued)*

```
semistructured data:
<PatientRecord pid="P1">
  <FirstName>Janine</FirstName>
  <LastName>Smith</LastName>
  <Address>
    <Street>1 Broadway Way</Street>
    <City>Seattle</City>
    <Zip>WA 98000</Zip>
  </Address>
  <Visit date="2002-01-05">
Janine came in with a <symptom>rash</symptom>. We identified a
<diagnosis>antibiotics allergy</diagnosis> and <remedy>changed her
cold prescription</remedy>.
  </Visit>
</PatientRecord>
<PatientRecord>
  <pid>P2</pid>
  <Name>Nils Soerensen</Name>
  <Address>
    23 NE 40th Street, New York
  </Address>
</PatientRecord>

Marked-up data:
  <Visit date="2002-01-05">Janine came in with a
<symptom>rash</symptom>. We identified a <diagnosis>antibiotics
allergy</diagnosis> and <remedy>changed her cold
prescription</remedy>.</Visit>
```

Much of the data interchanged today originates from relational databases and is finally stored again in relational databases. Since relational systems today are predominantly used to manage structured data (an educated guess would be 80 percent or more), most of the XML generated and being consumed at this time in the context of data interchange also fits the relational model of structured data. Therefore most relational database systems have first focused on providing XML capabilities that fit this most common usage scenario and have just recently begun to provide XML capabilities to deal with data that doesn't fit into the structured mold.

By adding the more general capabilities to deal with any form of XML data, relational database systems will be able to extend their efficient and effective processing of structured data to new application areas such as XML-based document management, management of XML messages such as **SOAP** messages, and the processing of audit logs in XML format. By handling XML natively instead of requiring shredding into relational structures, relational database systems will be able to provide seamless support for these applications.

Relational database systems not only store XML data, but also provide query and update support on the relational and XML data they store. While SQL has proven itself as the query language for relational data, it is not suitable in its current form as the direct query language over XML data. Since a query language should have as little impedance mismatch as possible to the data model it queries, the W3C, in cooperation with its member companies, decided to design a new XML query language named XQuery. To provide the necessary support for native XML data storage and processing, XQuery must become an integral part of XML-enabled relational database systems. In order to store and query XML data natively in a relational database, the XML data must be exposed in the relational system as a manageable entity. Relational systems store and expose XML in one of the following forms:

- *Virtual XML view:* a virtual document—also called a virtual XML view—over predominantly relational data
- *LOB (large object) storage:* an LOB-based XML document, either as a character LOB, called a CLOB, a binary LOB, called a **BLOB,** or a native XML datatype (XML)
- *Relational table mappings:* an XML document decomposed into relational data structures, possibly with subtrees mapped to LOBs

Chapter 6, "Mapping between XML and Relational Data," provides the in-depth investigation of the multitude of options for storing and querying virtual XML views over relational and XML documents that have been decomposed into relational data. Each of these options operates as a conceptual mid-tier or client-side component that uses the existing relational interfaces. They all expose an XML view against one or multiple relational databases. XML queries posed against the exposed view are translated into relational queries that are shipped over to the database server. After they have been executed, the result is returned either as XML or relational data for potential further post-processing.

Unlike Chapter 6, this chapter concentrates on the storage and processing of XML data that integrates with the relational system's capabilities, such as the relational query processor and execution environment. We begin with an overview of the XML datatype—the primary mechanism provided by relational systems for native XML data storage—before explaining how XQuery access is provided on the XML data and how XQuery is embedded in the relational query system. Then we outline how the concept of tables as collections of tuples can be generalized and applied to collections of XML documents and how XQuery can be integrated with that approach.

The section on the XML datatype discusses the appearance of the type to the user (its logical model), the physical implementation options, and the relationship to the XML Schema metadata. The section on integrating XQuery and SQL describes how to use XQuery to query an XML datatype instance, how to combine XQuery with SQL, how to correlate relational and XML data. We conclude with an overview on how to physically map XQuery in the context of a relational query engine.

As this is written, many of the features described below are available in one form or another from current or upcoming versions of the major relational database systems such as (in alphabetical order) IBM DB2, Microsoft SQL Server, and Oracle. Since the feature sets of individual database systems are changing from release to release, we do not usually attribute the features described here to any particular database system. Instead, we refer to the SQL/XML part of the **SQL-2003** standard [SQL2003] where appropriate and use a pseudo-notation for anything that is not (yet) described in SQL-2003. For example, we use an abstract functional notation of the form `isvalid(XML, SchemaComponents, 'lax'|'strict')→boolean` for functions on the `XML` datatype. Different implementations may provide different syntax, ranging from method calls on the XML type instance to SQL keywords.

Relational Storage of XML: The XML Type

XQuery processing on XML stored in the database as an LOB depends heavily on the actual physical storage mechanism chosen to store the XML. All LOB-based storage mechanisms have in common that they basically provide a built-in XML datatype. In the following, we use the relational type named `XML` to designate a new SQL built-in datatype that provides the logical abstraction for XML data stored in a relational database.

Listing 7.2 gives an example of a relational table where one column is of type XML. While the example uses an XML document representing structured data that could also be mapped into relational tables, the discussion of the XML datatype below applies equally to any form of XML data (semi-structured and markup data). In what follows, we look first at the logical models for such an XML datatype, discuss the different physical representations, and look into some other important aspects of XML datatypes, such as the relationships of **encodings** and database collations and their association with XML schemata.

Listing 7.2   Example of Relational Table with XML Datatype

```
CREATE TABLE Order(id int, orderdate date, PODetail XML)
```

Example data (using a string representation of the XML datatype instances):

id	orderdate	PODetail

4023	2001-12-01	`<purchaseOrder`
		`    xmlns="http://po.example.com">`
		`  <originator billId="0013579">`
		`    <contactName>`
		`      Fred Allen`
		`    </contactName>`
		`    <contactAddress>`
		`      <street>123 2nd Ave. NW</street>`
		`      <city>Anytown</city>`
		`      <state>OH</state>`
		`      <zip-four>99999-1234</zip-four>`
		`    </contactAddress>`
		`    <phone>(330) 555-1212</phone>`
		`    <originatorReferenceNumber>`
		`      AS 1132`
		`    </originatorReferenceNumber>`
		`  </originator>`
		`  <order>`
		`    <item code="34xdl 1278 12ct"`
		`        quantity="1"/>`
		`    <item code="57xdl 7789"`
		`        quantity="1"`
		`        colorcode="012"/>`
		`  </order>`
		`  <shipAddress sameAsContact="true"/>`
		`  <shipCode carrier="02"/>`
		`</purchaseOrder>`

5327	2002-04-23	`<purchaseOrder`
		`    xmlns="http://po.example.com">`
		`  <originator`
		`        . . .`

Logical Models for the XML Datatype

The SQL-2003 standard defines an XML datatype as part of its XML-related extensions that are commonly referred to as SQL/XML [SQLXML]. The standard does not prescribe the exact storage format as long as the type satisfies the XML datatype requirements. One requirement is that the type must be able to represent not only an XML 1.0 document but any element content, including multiple top-level element nodes and text nodes. Listing 7.3 gives an example of an XML datatype instance that has multiple top-level element nodes. The current logical model of the XML datatype is based on an extended XML Infoset in which the document information item has been extended to allow top-level text nodes and more than one top-level element node.

Listing 7.3   Example of XML Datatype Instance with Multiple Top-Level Elements

```
<Order>
  <ID>O1</ID>
  <OrderDate>2003-01-21<OrderDate>
  <Amount>7</Amount>
  <ProductID>P1</ProductID>
</Order>
<Order>
  <ID>O2</ID>
  <OrderDate>2003-06-24<OrderDate>
  <Amount>3</Amount>
  <ProductID>P3</ProductID>
</Order>
```

This Infoset-based model can easily be mapped to an untyped instance of the XQuery data model by applying the Infoset mapping outlined by [XQ-DM]. The addition of type information is explained below. This model is somewhat more limited than the XQuery data model in the sense that certain components of the XQuery data model, such as top-level attribute nodes, multiple document nodes, top-level typed values and top-level heterogeneous sequences containing such items, cannot be represented. However, these items can still be used inside XQuery expressions. Also, typed values returned by XQuery expressions that cannot be represented as XML datatype instances but must be exposed in the relational model have to be mapped into the relational type system.

A future version of the XML datatype's logical model may be extended to an XQuery data model. However, in what follows, we work with the

Infoset-based model extended with the ability to deal with typed data. As a built-in "scalar" type in the SQL type system, such a type can be cast, for example, from and to the SQL character types using the SQL `cast` expression. Casting from string to XML will parse and casting from XML to string will serialize the XML data.

Physical Models for the XML Datatype

There exist a wide variety of physical representations for XML datatypes (regardless of the exact logical model). In addition, the storage format has some relation to the questions of whether the XQuery processor should integrate with the existing relational query processor or be a separate component that only executes XQuery expressions, and how the storage format affects the update performance. We will examine several possible storage mechanisms and identify the major issues related to the query-processing approaches and updates. Query-processing aspects are discussed in more detail in a later section. All the storage mechanisms assume that the data actually has been verified to be a well-formed instance of the XML datatype.

Users may have different expectations about **XML storage fidelity.** Generally, we can distinguish among *string-level fidelity*, in which the XML datatype instance preserves the original XML document code-point for code-point; *Infoset-level fidelity*, in which the XML datatype instance preserves the XML document structure on the level of the XML Infoset model; and the *relational fidelity level*, which only preserves information important from a relational point of view, such as the property-value association, and disregards XML-specific properties, such as document order. Obviously the XML datatype's logical model requires at least Infoset-level fidelity.

Character LOB

With CLOB, the XML is stored in a character representation. The representation may preserve the original XML data exactly (string-level fidelity), or the data may have been transformed by changing the encoding or by **canonicalizing** the content, while still providing Infoset-level fidelity.

This storage format does not lend itself well to efficient, server-side XQuery processing, since it either requires extensive **indexing** mechanisms or requires every query to parse the data before executing the query in a separate XQuery component. The indexing mechanisms end up replicating one of the other storage mechanisms in order to take advantage of the existing relational query processing. In addition, basic character LOBs are hard to update on a node level, since most LOB update mechanisms are based on positional ranges and not logical subtrees.

Binary LOB

The binary format may represent preprocessed XML in the form of a W3C **Document Object Model** (DOM) tree, which has been shown empirically to increase the storage size by a factor of two to six over the textual representation due to the storage overhead of the DOM nodes. Some other preprocessed binary format is more likely to be used that may provide more efficient index processing, compression, or other benefits to the query processing. While a binary format could provide string-level fidelity, it usually provides only Infoset-level fidelity.

A binary LOB provides an additional level of abstraction over CLOBs at the cost of not being able to read the XML without an access method that reproduces the original textual representation. As with CLOB, XQuery processing often requires additional indexing to take advantage of the relational query processor, or the use of a separate XQuery component such as an embedded XQuery engine written in Java or C#. Propagating node-level updates are often costly since the general BLOB support in relational systems is not designed for logical updates.

User-Defined Type

All the major relational database systems provide (or are going to provide) programmatic extensions inside the database server that allow users to add their own code and datatypes. Of course the database system can also use this mechanism to provide additional, more complex, built-in datatypes such as XML. Such user-defined types may again represent the XML data in many ways, ranging from a string representation over a DOM tree representation to an Infoset object representation. The user-defined type may require the whole instance to be loaded into memory before it can be operated upon, or it may provide some integration into the relational buffers to provide partial loading of the data.

Two major approaches are currently advocated for supporting user-defined types. The deep integration approach provides tight integration into the actual query processor at the cost of complex programming and registration requirements, since, for every user-defined type, code specific to the query processor must be provided through predefined APIs (this approach is often called *data blade*, *extender*, or *cartridge*). The other approach uses a virtual machine such as the **Java Virtual Machine** or the **Common Language Runtime** to add user-defined types (the VM approach). This approach trades off better programmability against tighter integration.

The integration approach can be used to implement most of the other physical designs outlined in this chapter and integrates tightly into the components of the relational database engine's architecture, such as memory management and query processing, at the cost of flexibility and programmability. The VM approach is an alternative that gives great flexibility in processing XML data at the cost of minimal or no integration with the general storage engine and query processing. In this case, the XQuery engine is usually a component separate from the relational engine that can operate on XML datatype instances that are loaded fully into the VM's memory and use a memory-based representation of the data model. Some examples of the latter are query components written in Java or C# that run inside the virtual machines. Eventually, these two approaches may merge and combine the VM's comparable ease of programming and the efficiency of the integration approach.

Updates are provided as another method on the user-defined type. Depending on the internal structure, they may or may not be very efficient.

Relational Table Mappings

If XQuery processing is being integrated with the relational query processor, the actual XML data needs to be mapped to relational data and indices. As with mid-tier mapping strategies, a variety of approaches exist. Some of them hide the generated tables from the relational user and thus serve as purely physical models, while others expose the tables in the relational context.

By mapping the XML into relational structures, we can define additional relational indices on the tables, integrate the XQuery processing with relational query processing, and perform update processing on the node level. Every relational table mapping has to provide Infoset-level fidelity in order to be usable as physical storage of the XML datatype. Note that several XML-to-relational mappings provided outside of the relational database engine often only provide relational fidelity.

Node Tables

The most general approach generates the so-called **node table** (sometimes also called **edge table**) that represents every node in the XML instance as a row in the relational table. It is the most general, since it can represent any XML document structure without loss of information.

Unlike the node table that is normally used in mid-tier mappings (see Chapter 6), such node tables may be combined with additional mechanisms such as clustered keys based on a hierarchical Dewey-decimal numbering system (see Figure 7.1 for an example), tokenization of types and names, and additional path and value indices. The Dewey numbered keys, for example, provide document order and physical nearness of parent nodes and their children; combined with the cluster on the keys, this can provide very efficient tree traversals and subtree retrievals. These mechanisms and the ability to map XQuery directly into physical operations instead of SQL queries overcome many of the disadvantages of the mid-tier node-table approach.

Updates generally encounter no problems, although the keys based on the Dewey-decimal system must be managed carefully to keep them balanced. Thus, some variants on the Dewey numbering provide improved key management in the context of updates. Such node-tables are normally not directly exposed to the relational user but hidden behind the abstraction of the XML datatype.

Table Shredding

If additional structural information is available in the form of a schema, we can use the schema information along with potential annotations to provide *mappings into related tables,* which is colloquially called *shredding* (see Figure 7.2). Chapter 6 provides a more detailed overview of such shredding-based approaches. Such tables can be exposed to relational users for relational processing or remain hidden behind the XML datatype abstraction. However, this approach still requires additional hidden information that encodes the original order information and therefore does not work well with data formats that are not easily mapped into the relational or extended-relational (e.g., nested) tables of the database system.

XML (untyped)

```
<doc>
 <Customer cid="ALFKI">
  <Order oid="01"/>
 </Customer>
 <Customer cid="BONOD"/>
</doc>
```

XML node table

id	parentid	nodetype	localname	ns-uri	datatype	value
1	0	E	doc	NULL	NULL	NULL
1.1	1	E	Customer	NULL	NULL	NULL
1.1.1	1.1	A	cid	NULL	$\frac{xdt}{"xdt"}$: untypedAtomic	ALFKI
1.1.2	1.1	E	Order	NULL	NULL	NULL
1.1.2.1	1.1.2	A	oid	NULL	$\frac{xdt}{"xdt"}$: untypedAtomic	01
1.2	1	E	Customer	NULL	NULL	NULL
1.2.1	1.2	A	cid	NULL	$\frac{xdt}{"xdt"}$: untypedAtomic	BONOD

Figure 7.1   An XML Datatype Node-Table Format with Dewey-Decimal-Numbered Keys

XML with a schema that describes Customer and Order

```
<Customer cid="ALFKI" customername="Alfred's Futterkiste">
  <Order oid="01" orderdate="2002-10-10"/>
</Customer>
<Customer cid="BONOD" customername="Bon Odessa"/>
```

Relational tables

Customer	
cid	customername
ALFKI	Alfred's Futterkiste
BONOD	Bon Odessa

Order	
oid	orderdate
01	2002-10-10

Figure 7.2   An XML Datatype as Virtual Schema-Driven View

Combinations

Of course these different physical models can be combined. For example, a BLOB approach may provide explicit, XML schema-driven indices that map structured XML into relational tables and provide an index based on the node-table approach for unstructured XML.

Encodings and Collations

XML documents normally carry their encodings with them in the XML declaration (or are defaulted to UTF-8 or UTF-16). The XML parser uses that encoding information to map the encoded character stream into the Unicode code points of the character information items of the XML Infoset.

In relational systems, information is available about the character set and collation used by the database system for storing, indexing, and comparing character data. Collation information describes the equivalence of different code points, characters, and glyphs for different languages and uses. Because it indicates what language ordering and other comparison options, such as case-sensitivity, should be applied when comparing character data, it is important for both the query semantics and for indexing.

In relational database systems, collations are attached to data (e.g., to table columns), whereas the XML model does not provide a way to do this. Instead, XQuery attaches collations to individual string operations. For example, it is possible to sort the same data in two different ways, with two different collations, once for case-sensitive order, and once for case-insensitive order. The impedance mismatch between these two approaches leads to some potential confusion. Relational database systems can make different collation information available for storage and indexing, whereas XQuery assumes a default collation and provides overriding capability only in the operational context.

When storing XML, the XML datatype as described in SQL-2003 [SQL2003] translates the given XML encoding into Unicode following the Infoset model. The SQL-2003 standard is currently only concerned with storing and retrieving full instances of XML and does not provide for collation information on the XML datatype. However implementations can associate the relational default collation with the XML data and make it the default collation when executing XQuery expressions on it.

For schema-directed mappings, a relational system may also use schema annotations in the mapping to identify character sets and collations to be used when mapping string data to relational columns. It usually also provides a way to directly associate a collation to the XML datatype that is to be used for indexing and querying as in the following example:

```
CREATE TABLE Order(
        id int,
        orderdate date,
        PODetail XML COLLATION EN-US-CASE-SENSITIVE
)
```

The collation information provided when storing the XML can then be picked up as the default collation used by the XQuery expressions (see below for more details). This enables the queries to use the collation-specific indices.

Typing an XML Datatype

One of the important features of XQuery and its data model is the ability to use XML schema information to operate on typed data. Thus, we must be able not only to validate or physically map a relational XML datatype, but to type its value according to an XML schema.

Several schema languages could be used to perform the typing, as long as they map into the type system expected by XQuery; here we use the W3C XML Schema language as our XML schema language in order to illustrate the necessary capabilities. This also appears to be the primarily supported XML schema format in all the major XML-enabled relational database systems. In order to provide type information from an XML schema, the type-relevant information, such as the attribute, element, and type declarations contained in the schema, must be managed in the metadata component of the database.

W3C XML Schema information is organized and scoped according to target namespace URIs and schema location hints. On the other hand, the naming and scoping of relational database systems components are based on a variant of dot-separated SQL identifiers that identify the catalog, schema, and schema object. For example, the table Customer in the catalog MyCat and the schema MySchema have the three-part name MyCat.MySchema.Customer. Since identifiers fit into the relational naming system but target namespace URIs do not, a relational system usually provides a mechanism to map the target namespaces to SQL identifiers.

For example, a schema could be registered using the data-definition statement given in the following example, which registers the content of the schema under the target namespace http://www.example.com/po-schema and any of its imported schemata and gives it the SQL identifier POSchema.

```
CREATE XML SCHEMA POSchema NAMESPACE
    N'<schema xmlns="http://www.w3.org/2001/XMLSchema"
            targetNamespace = "http://www.example.com/po-schema">
    ...
    </schema>'
```

This identifier is then used in the SQL context to refer to the registered XML schemata, whereas the target namespace URIs continue to be used in the XML contexts such as XML Schema and XQuery. The schema management component must also provide for some schema evolution capability, which is outside of the scope of this discussion.

Once the relational system provides for an XML schema repository, these schemata can be used for validating individual XML datatype instances, constraining the value of XML-typed columns, and providing type information to XQuery. XML Schema validation offers two functions:

- *Basic validation:* verifies conformance to the constraints of the document class described in the schema
- *typing:* identifies the datatypes of the document's information items during the generation of the *Post-Schema-Validation Information Set* (PSVI)

It also offers three validation modes:

- *Skip validation:* performs no validation (and thus does not need to be provided as an explicit option)
- *Lax validation:* validates a subtree only if it finds an applicable schema component
- *Strict validation:* requires that all data conform to the schema

Basic validation provides functionality that is often needed in the context of relational check constraints during table definitions and in relational query predicates. Relational systems therefore usually provide a validation function such as `isvalid(XML, SchemaComponents, 'lax'|'strict')`→`boolean` that takes an `XML` instance, schema component identifiers such as the schema's SQL identifier, and the validation mode, and returns a `true` or `false` result depending on whether the validation succeeded.

Users may want to either validate against the collection of schemata described by the schema's SQL identifier, or restrict it to a single namespace contained in the schema collection or even a single element. Thus the schema-component argument may provide a combination of the SQL identifier with optional indication of a namespace and an element name.

While an instance of type `XML` can be typed via an XML Schema using a dynamic validate operator, it seems more appropriate to make an XML Schema-constrained `XML` datatype a distinct SQL type. Using the validate operation would require a dynamic association and would not provide enough static information for any form of static processing, while the second approach provides a static association that can be used to perform static processing.

The static association allows type information to be used for static constraints of the content of XML columns and variables, to provide additional static hints for storage, and to be used by the static phase of query processing, including XQuery's static typing. We are going to indicate a typed XML type in the following form (as always, the actual syntax may look different): XML TYPED AS SchemaComponents where SchemaComponents denotes a schema collection identifier and, optionally, a namespace or top-level element contained in the schema collection. Listing 7.4 gives an example of a relational table that contains two XML-typed columns. The PurchaseOrders column is statically constrained by an XML Schema, and the OrderForm column is dynamically validated by schema information given in another column using a table-level check constraint.

Listing 7.4   Example of XML-Typed Columns

```
CREATE TABLE Customers (
    CustomerID int PRIMARY KEY,
    CustomerName nvarchar(100),
    PurchaseOrders XML TYPED AS POSchema,
    OrderForm XML,
    OrderFormType nvarchar(1000)
    CHECK isvalid(OrderForm, OrderFormType, 'strict')
)
```

The main difference between the handling of the two columns is that the statically typed column can take advantage of the XML Schema information when mapping to the physical level. It can be used to map the relationally structured parts of the XML document to relational tables, fold simple-typed values into the element nodes instead of keeping them as separate text nodes, or provide additional information to design path or value indices. The dynamically constrained column, on the other hand, cannot provide such static information, and physical designs normally do not take such dynamic information into account. In addition, static and dynamic constraints affect the type information accessible to queries over the XML datatypes (see below).

In order to type and validate an "untyped" XML datatype instance or retype/revalidate an already typed instance, we can use the SQL casting functionality, as shown in the following example, to cast from the unconstrained to the statically constrained XML type:

```
SELECT CAST(OrderForm AS
            XML TYPED AS POSchema)
FROM Customers
```

Other Aspects of the XML Datatype

There are many other aspects of the XML datatype that are not directly related to its queryability and thus outside of the scope of this chapter. Among them are SQL functions defined on the XML datatype such as parsing, serializing or concatenation, the issues of how the database APIs provide access to XML datatype instances and columns, and how to cast to and from the XML datatype. For example, should casting a string to XML be equivalent to parsing the string, and casting from XML to string be equivalent to serializing it?

Integrating XQuery and SQL: Querying XML Datatypes

Once the XML data is safely stored in a relational table, the easiest way to get at the data is to use SQL to query the table and retrieve the XML-typed column, as in the following example:

```
SELECT CustomerName, OrderForm
FROM Customers
WHERE CustomerID = 1
```

However, SQL per se cannot query information inside an XML datatype instance. That is where XQuery comes in. XQuery allows us to query and transform the XML data. What we need to understand now is how to integrate the two, so that we can invoke XQuery functionality from SQL, and also provide information from the relational environment to the XQuery context.

This section introduces three ways to query XML datatype instances in the context of the SQL query language. It explains how the XQuery expressions access both static and dynamic information provided by the SQL context, including data stored in other SQL columns.

To understand how we combine relational queries and XQuery, we must first have a conceptual understanding of how relational queries operate. First, all tables in the FROM clause are combined into a larger relational table using either a Cartesian product (if they are combined using a comma) or the given join operation (using the SQL-92 join syntax [SQL92]). For example, the query shown below produces a table consisting of the Cartesian product of Table A and the left outer join between B and C:

```
SELECT A.*, function(B.b) as b
FROM A, B LEFT OUTER JOIN C ON B.id = C.b
WHERE C.id = 1 AND A.id = B.a
```

Second, the predicate expression given in the WHERE clause is applied to each tuple in the table. Finally, the SELECT clause indicates the columns of the tuples satisfying the predicate filter that will be returned in the final resulting table (potentially after applying a final transformation).

The relational processing model is very close to the conceptual processing model of XQuery. However, there are some fundamental differences such as the typing rules based on a different type system and the handling of order. Unless an explicit order is given in the SQL statement, the SQL query processor is free to neglect the order of the tuples, which enables the query-execution engine to apply algorithms that may reorder the tuples in order to achieve a more efficient execution.

SQL is also a strongly and statically typed language on the relational type system, which means that the inferred relational type of each expression must be known at query compilation (or static analysis) time.

XQuery Functionality in SQL

The SQL query-processing model together with static typing indicate that the following query functionality should be provided in order to support XQuery in the context of SQL:

Transforming XML Datatype Instances

We must be able to transform an XML datatype instance to another XML datatype. This functionality is usually used in the SQL SELECT clause; it makes use of the XQuery construction functionality.

Extracting a Value into the SQL Value Space

We must have a way to extract information from an XML instance that fits into the SQL type system:

- Values that fit into the scalar SQL types, such as character types and numeric types (e.g., integer, decimal, float, etc.)
- XML nodes and subtrees that will be represented with the XML datatype

Testing the XML Structure for Existence

We need a way to test for the presence or absence of nodes and values based on a query expression. While this functionality could be provided using the XQuery function `empty()` and the value-extraction function, having such a function available at the SQL level seems more user-friendly. The following functions provide the functionality specified in the above sections:

- `query(XML, XQueryString)`→`XML`

    This function applies the XQuery expression instance and returns an XML type instance. While the input instance can be statically constrained, the result is always untyped (an additional parameter could provide the expected schema type). Since the result type has to be a valid instance of the XML datatype, XQuery expressions that return attribute nodes at the top level must raise an error, while queries that return values must convert them into top-level text nodes. This function provides the mechanism to return subtrees and to transform the XML instance into a different shape (see Listing 7.5 for an example).

Listing 7.5   Transforming the XML Column

```
SELECT CustomerName, query(PurchaseOrders,
      'declare namespace po = "http://www.example.com/po-schema"
      for $p in /po:purchase-order
      where $p/@orderdate < xs:date("2002-10-31")
      return
        <purchaseorder date="{$p/@orderdate}">{
        $p/*
        }</purchaseorder>')
FROM Customers
WHERE CustomerID = 1
```

- value(XML, XQueryString, SQLType)→SQLType

  This function applies the XQuery expression to the XML type instance and returns a relational value typed according to the SQL type indicated with the third argument SQLType. Since the value's SQL type must be statically known to the SQL compiler, the type must be provided as either an SQL type name or a constant string.

  The XML data model value calculated by the XQuery expression is converted to the SQL value by converting the lexical representation of the XML value to the required SQL type. If the XQuery expression results in a node, the data() function is explicitly applied. If the XQuery result is an empty sequence, the result is the relational NULL value. If the result is a sequence of values and the SQL type is a single-column table type, the result is a table.

  This function provides the mechanism to return values that can then be used in SQL expressions or select clauses. The following example shows how two XQuery expressions are used to extract a calculated integer value and extract the value of an attribute as an SQL date value, which are then used in an SQL query.

```
SELECT CustomerName, value(PurchaseOrders,
       'declare namespace po = "http://www.example.com/po-schema"
       count(/po:purchase-order)', integer) as ordercount
FROM Customers
WHERE value(PurchaseOrders,
       'declare namespace po = "http://www.example.com/po-schema"
       /po:purchase-order[1]/@orderdate', date) < date(2002-10-31)
```

- exists(XML, XQueryString)→boolean

  This function applies the XQuery expression to the XML type instance and returns true if the result of the expression is not the empty sequence and false otherwise, as shown in the following example:

```
SELECT CustomerName,
       CAST(OrderForm AS
            XML TYPED AS 'http://www.example.com/orderform-schema1')
       as OrderForm1
FROM Customers
WHERE exists(OrderForm,
       'declare namespace o ="http://www.example.com/orderform-schema1"
       /o:order')
```

Setting the Dynamic Context Item in the XQuery Functions

Since the XML datatype always provides the extended document information item as the XQuery's context item, there is no need to use the `doc()` or `collection()` functions to refer to data. On the contrary, besides being problematic in the context of the SQL processing model, these two functions would need a URI-based naming scheme for documents and collections that again would need to be integrated with the relational naming framework. Thus, all XPath expressions in these embedded XQuery expressions can start directly with the starting slash.

Compiling the XQuery Expressions

The XQuery expressions could be given dynamically or as constant strings. If the XQuery expression is given as a constant string, then relational systems can compile the XQuery at the same time as the SQL statement.

Augmenting the XQuery Static Context

XQuery has a static context that provides several predefined bindings for such things as mapping namespace prefixes to namespace URIs, built-in functions and variables (such as the XQuery functions), built-in schema types (such as the XML Schema and XQuery built-in types), and the default collation. When integrating XQuery into the relational framework of an XML datatype and SQL, the relational system can add some additional static bindings to simplify the query writer's task.

First, the system can predefine some namespace bindings for SQL-related functions and types. For the purpose of this chapter, we assume that the following prefixes are added to the predefined static namespace context:

- The prefix `sql` is bound to the namespace URI representing the relational database system's built-in functions.
- The prefix `sqltypes` is bound to the namespace URI representing the mapping of the relational types into the XQuery's type model.

In addition, the query writer can provide predefined namespace bindings using the SQL/XML extension to the SQL WITH clause as described in the SQL-2003 standard.

Next, the XQuery's default collation is implicitly set to the relational collation in effect for the XML datatype (either from the database system's default or the collation associated with the XML datatype). The functions belonging to the namespace referenced with the prefix sql are added to the static function context, as are constructor functions for the SQL built-in types. The SQL built-in types are added to the static type context, as are the types of the schema components in case of a statically constrained XML datatype.

Note that for the schema types that are used to constrain the XML datatype, the namespace prefix also needs to be provided. If only one schema is being associated with an XML datatype instance, then the system could associate a predefined prefix such as data or the default namespace with the schema's target namespace URI. If multiple schemata can be used to constrain an XML datatype, the query writers will still need to provide the explicit namespace declarations in the XQuery prolog or use the SQL/XML extension to the SQL WITH clause.

Having the XQuery static context extended implicitly in the way described above removes a large amount of syntactic repetition from the embedded XQuery prologs.

Providing Access to SQL Data inside XQuery

The functions above are capable of extracting XML values into the relational processing context. Sometimes, however, an XQuery expression needs to access data from the relational realm. If the relational database system provides variables, then the XQuery system probably wants to provide access to the variables. In any case, we also need access to the columns of the SELECT statement tuple set. This section presents the mechanisms to access relational data in the context of XQuery and uses the same mechanisms to provide access to other XML datatype instances to allow joining two XML datatype instances.

Access to variables can be provided in XQuery in two ways: either by mapping the relational variables directly into the static variable context (and mapping the relational types into their equivalent XML Schema/XQuery types) or by using a functional approach. In the first case, the variables should belong to the `sql` namespace. However, since SQL names allow more of the Unicode code points as name characters than XML names, such characters need to be encoded. For example, an XML name cannot contain a space (code point 0x20) but an SQL name can. The SQL/XML part of the SQL-2003 standard provides such a mapping by encoding invalid XML name characters into _xHHHH_ , where HHHH denotes the Unicode code point of the invalid XML character (e.g., _x0020_ for a space). Since a user would have to remember to encode such names, a more convenient alternative would be to provide a built-in pseudo-function `sql:variable()` that takes the name of the SQL variable as a string constant argument and returns the variable's value with its type mapped to the XML Schema/XQuery type. This approach requires more typing by the user, but it avoids the name-encoding issues.

Access to a column of an SQL statement during the query execution is very useful for integrating relational values into an XQuery. The access can be provided by a built-in pseudo-function called `sql:column()` that takes an SQL column identifier as a constant string argument and refers to the corresponding cell of the tuple that the SQL statement's iterator is operating on. Listing 7.6 gives an example of a simple XQuery expression and how the column-reference function accesses the relational values. Both `sql:column()` and `sql:variable()` can refer to an instance of the XML datatype. This allows joins across different XML datatype instances in any of the query functions above. The two functions operate equivalent to the built-in XQuery function `fn:doc()` in that they return the document node of the other XML datatype instance.

Listing 7.6 Example of `sql:column()` Usage

| Table A: | | Table B: | |
id:int	v:int	id:int	v:int
1	42	1	1
2	44	2	3
3	46	4	7

Listing 7.6   Example of `sql:column()` Usage *(continued)*

```
Query:
SELECT A.id, query(CAST('' AS XML),
                '<A><v>{sql:column("A.v")}</v></A>,
                if (not(empty(sql:column("B.v"))
                then
                    <B><v>{sql:column("B.v")}</v></B>
                else ()')
        as values
FROM A LEFT OUTER JOIN B ON A.id=B.id

Result:
id:int      values:XML
```

```
    1       <A><v>42</v></A><B><v>1</v></B>
    2       <A><v>44</v></A><B><v>3</v></B>
    3       <A><v>46</v></A>
```

Mapping SQL Types to XML Schema Types

In order to be able to import the relational values into the XQuery context, the SQL types must be mapped to XML Schema types that describe the SQL types for the XQuery type system. Since XML Schema does not allow the addition of new primitive simple types as direct derivations from `xs:anySimpleType`, these types must be added as derivations from the built-in XML Schema simple types. The SQL/XML part of the ISO SQL-2003 standard [SQL2003] provides such a mapping that maps to the most appropriate derivation of the XML Schema simple types by using the type facets to model the range and conditions of the SQL types. Additionally, it allows relational systems to provide additional information about the original SQL type using the XML Schema annotation mechanism. An example of such a mapping follows.

```
Relational Type: INTEGER
                (implementation range is [-2147483648,2147483647])
maps to:
<xs:simpletype name="INTEGER">
  <xs:restriction base="xsd:int"/>
</xs:simpletype>
```

However, given that many relational systems provide additional built-in SQL types, the user must expect relational systems to provide mappings that describe the implementation types; thus, the user should probably provide the types in implementation-specific namespaces. Also, the current ISO SQL/XML mapping has a severe shortcoming in that it maps the character string types into individual XML Schema types, one for each length that is directly derived from `xs:string`. This not only means that there are way too many individual string types, but also that they are not type-compatible with each other since they each belong to a separate subtype tree of `xs:string`. Thus, we should expect built-in functions that return mapped SQL string types to return the main relational character types as simple derivations, such as `sqltypes:nvarchar` being derived from `xs:string`, disregarding the length component.

Once the SQL types are mapped into XML Schema simple types, mapping values in general becomes simple. The SQL/XML part of the ISO SQL-2003 standard provides detailed rules for the value mapping. However, bear in mind that there are still certain SQL character type values that are allowed in SQL but are considered invalid XML characters. For example, most of the low-range ASCII control characters such as ETX (code point 0x3) or BELL (code point 0x7) are not allowed in XML documents. Thus the integration must take them into account and provide correct error handling.

Adding XQuery Function Libraries

XQuery provides a way of importing externally defined XQuery function libraries. The import mechanism follows a model based on namespace URIs and location hints similar to the XML Schema import model. Given this analogy, a relational system can therefore use a similar mechanism to provide storage of XQuery function libraries by extending the metadata to allow them to be stored according to their namespace URI or an SQL identifier. Such libraries would then be loaded and stored in a precompiled format and imported into the XQuery static context when referred to by the user. Listing 7.7 gives an example in which the function library is defined using a target namespace and then used inside a query.

Listing 7.7   Example of an XQuery Function Library

```
CREATE XML FUNCTION NAMESPACE
   N'module "http://www.example.com/myfns"
     declare namespace myf = "http://www.example.com/myfns"
```

Listing 7.7   Example of an XQuery Function Library *(continued)*

```
define function myf:in-King-County-WA
       ($zip as xs:integer)
       as xs:boolean
{$zip < 98100 and $zip>=98000 }

define function myf:King-County-WA-salestax($x as xs:decimal)
       as xs:decimal
{$x * 0.088}
'

SELECT CustomerName, query(PurchaseOrder,
       'import module namespace myf="http://www.example.com/myfns"
       declare namespace po = "http://www.example.com/po-schema"

       for $p in /po:purchase-order, $d in $p/po:details
       let $net as xs:decimal := $d/@qty * $d/@price
       where myf:in-King-County-WA($p/po:shipTo/po:zip)
       return
         <po-detail id="{$p/@id}"
                    total="{$net +
                            myf:King-County-WA-salestax($net)}"/>')
       as po-detail-price
FROM Customers
```

A Note on the XQuery Data Modification Language

XQuery has not yet defined an update language, but it will undoubtedly do so. When that occurs, we will require a way to integrate that update capability with the SQL data modification language. Simply populating a column cell with an XML datatype instance can be performed using the relational insertion (see Listing 7.8, which assumes an implicit cast from string to XML that parses the data). However, updating XML also requires the ability to make finer-grained, node-level changes to an XML column. We assume that this is done via a relational update to the XML datatype instance combined with a new **mutator**: modify(XML, XQueryDMLString), where XQueryDMLString is expressed in the as-yet-undefined update language for XQuery. In the following examples, we use an update language extension to XQuery. Other update languages, such as so-called updategrams [RYS2001], will probably be provided as well in similar fashion.

Listing 7.8 Inserting XML Data

```
INSERT INTO Customers VALUES (42, N'Jane Doe',
    N'<po:purchase-order
        xmlns:po="http://www.example.com/po-schema" id="2000">
      <po:shipTo>
        <po:address>42 Main Street</po:address>
        <po:city>Redmond</po:city>
        <po:state>WA</po:state>
        <po:zip>98052</po:zip>
      </po:shipTo>
      <po:details qty="1" price="23.44"/>
    </po:purchase-order>', NULL, NULL)
```

Since an XML datatype is a relational column type, even a node-level change will have to lock the whole XML datatype either directly or indirectly via the row locks at the isolation level of the relational system's context. Making the concurrency control aware of the tree structure of the XML datatype instances will be certainly an important research area to improve the performance. The following is an example of how po:detail elements may be deleted from the PurchaseOrders XML instances. The concurrency control will not only lock the parent of the deleted subtrees but the whole XML instance of all the rows that satisfy the update statements where clause.

```
UPDATE Customers
SET modify(PurchaseOrders,
    'declare namespace po = "http://www.example.com/po-schema"
     delete /po:purchase-order/po:details'
WHERE exists(PurchaseOrders,
    'declare namespace po = "http://www.example.com/po-schema"
     /po:purchase-order[po:details and po:shipTo/po:zip=98052]'
```

If the XML datatype is constrained by an XML Schema, then updates may fail if they would result in an instance that violates the XML Schema constraints.

Physical Mappings of XQuery

The previous sections have presented the functional description of how to integrate XQuery and XML into the SQL processing model of relational systems. From a performance point of view, another interesting aspect is how such combined queries are being mapped into a physical operator tree. Since this mapping depends on the physical mapping of the XML datatype and also depends heavily on the vendor-specific architectures, this section provides a more general, higher-level discussion of the different mapping strategies of XQuery into physical execution plans.

In the following, we assume that the XQuery expressions are provided as constants; thus, compilation can occur at the same time as the compilation of the SQL expressions. The handling of parameterized queries is left as an exercise for the reader. The general processing model of an SQL statement is as follows (individual steps may vary in actual implementations; e.g., a logical operator tree may contain more or less physical information):

- Static compilation phase:
  1. Parse the statement into an abstract syntax tree (AST).
  2. Normalize the AST (example: perform the implicit conversions of single-cell rowsets into scalar values) and check it for type-correctness.
  3. Convert the AST into a logical operator tree representing the relational algebra of the implementation engine. A logical operator tree may indicate a join operation, but does not indicate, for example, which physical join implementation is used.
  4. Store the operator tree for later dynamic processing after potentially applying some additional static rewrite rules.

- Dynamic execution phase:
  1. Compile the logical operator tree into a physical operator tree using dynamic statistics such as costing information. This transformation may reorder operations and will choose among the different access methods (e.g., scan vs. index) and join methods.
  2. Execute the physical operator tree.

There are two major approaches to compiling and executing XQuery expressions in the context of SQL statements: a *decoupled* and an *integrated* approach. The *decoupled approach* works with a standalone XQuery engine that is added to the relational system. It is usually employed when the XML datatype is being modeled as a user-defined datatype that appears as a binary object to the relational processor. In this case, the `query` function is processed as is any other external function in the SQL compilation: The XQuery expression is passed to the XQuery processor outside of the general SQL processing model, the query is processed, and the result is returned to the SQL environment. If XQuery has been extended with access to the relational processing environment (for example, the `sql:column()` function mentioned above), then the external XQuery engine must be able to call back into the relational processing environment to access the data. Figure 7.3 shows the decoupled approach in form of a block diagram. It uses the Greek symbols σ and Π for selection and projection respectively.

The *integrated approach* maps the XQuery expressions into logical operator trees that are integrated with the logical operator tree of the SQL statement. This approach requires that the physical design of the XML datatype use one of the relational mappings described above. Note that such a relational physical design can occur as the primary storage or as part of an indexing scheme on an LOB-based storage model or even a just-in-time shredding of such an LOB when processing XQueries. The XQuery

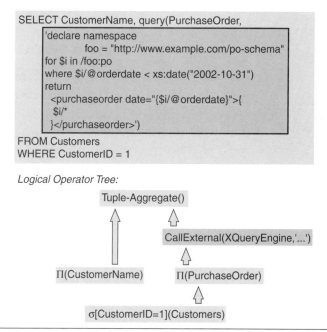

Figure 7.3   Decoupled XQuery Processing Approach

logical operator tree must consist of operations that the relational query processor understands such as projections (Π), selections (σ), and aggregations. Figure 7.4 provides the block diagram of the integrated approach.

Note that the integrated approach is not as simple as it sounds. First, since XQuery has a more complex, nested and sequence-based data model, the relational algebra must be extended with operations that capture the necessary semantics, such as nest/unnest and document-ordering. Furthermore, the XML Schema built-in scalar datatypes and their operations do not normally map one-to-one to the built-in relational scalar datatypes and their operations. For example, relational string comparisons may disregard trailing spaces during string comparisons, whereas XQuery's string compare does not, or the relational expression service that provides the operation semantics may deal only with true scalar types, while the XML Schema types may be not truly scalar, as is true of the XML date and time datatypes that provide a `(value, timezone)` pair. Thus relational systems must extend their expression services to deal with the new datatypes and different operational semantics.

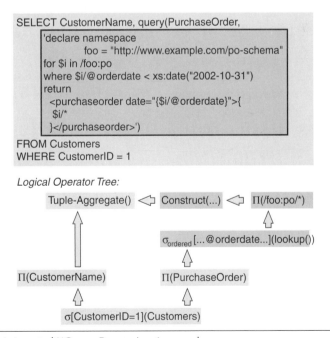

Figure 7.4   Integrated XQuery Processing Approach

Finally, integrating XQuery processing into the SQL processing model also means that the cost-based optimizer will have to choose execution plans that preserve the XQuery semantics and understand potentially additional cost factors. One important aspect that affects the execution plan is the preservation of document and input order. An optimizer must either choose only order-preserving `join` and `set` algorithms or add specific `reorder` operators to allow the use of more efficient algorithms that are not order-aware.

Another area that makes the XQuery evaluation more complex than the evaluation of SQL statements is the execution order. The presence of an index often prompts the optimizer to choose a so-called bottom-up evaluation strategy, where first indices are used to filter the processed tuples before any of the other operations are evaluated. Since the naïve execution strategy of XQuery is described top-down, an optimizer may produce dynamic errors by reordering the evaluation order that the top-down evaluation strategy would have avoided. A simple example of this situation appears in the following XQuery expression:

```
for $i in //A
where $i/@a castable as xs:integer
return
  for $j in $i/B
  where xs:integer($i/@a) > 10
  return
    $j
```

A naive, top-down evaluation of the nested `for` expression would only execute the inner `for` expression if the value of `$i/@a` is really castable to `xs:integer`. However, an optimizer may choose to rewrite the above query to the following equivalent:

```
for $i in //A, $j in $i/B
where $i/@a castable as xs:integer and xs:integer($i/@a) > 10
return
  $j
```

and then choose to execute the comparison before the check for castability. If then there are `a` attributes that are not castable to `xs:integer`, the cast in the comparison will fail with a runtime error that in the naive evaluation would have been avoided.

Note that this type of behavior can already occur in processing normal SQL statements without XQuery—although less frequently. The XQuery language specification also recognizes the benefits of processing optimizations and thus indeed allows these rewrites. However, an XQuery system that integrates with such an optimizer should provide an optimization hint that can force the result of the naive top-down evaluation strategy to provide the query writer with the option to force a correct, error-free evaluation.

Issues of Combining SQL, XML Datatype, and XQuery

Combining XQuery and SQL for querying XML datatype instances is indeed a powerful combination of the two languages. However, some major issues arise with this approach:

- XQuery users interested in querying across multiple documents need to understand and use SQL to iterate over the collection of documents and to use SQL joins to be able to join among two different documents.
- SQL users interested in querying into XML documents need to learn the new XQuery language.

Since the languages are closely related, somebody familiar with one language should be able to learn the other easily. However, the need to know two languages is still an additional level of complexity that future relational systems will need to address. Today's relational database systems address the second problem by shredding the XML data into relational tables that can then be queried relationally, thus replacing the need for a second query language with a simpler mapping approach. However, this mapping approach often only provides relational fidelity and thus does not address order preservation and markup scenarios. Thus either the SQL model itself must be extended to deal with the nonrelational aspects of order and heterogeneity (this still means that a query writer would have to learn and understand these extensions), or the SQL model will eventually be subsumed under the XML and XQuery model (which would mean that a large number of people would have to learn this new model). Relational database systems will probably provide a combination of the two approaches, thus providing both an SQL- and an XQuery-based approach, each addressing a different skill set.

Top-Level XQuery

Top-level XQuery provides a way to query collections of XML documents and forests, and XML views of relational data without the need to use SQL. It becomes the top-level language that is used as the primary query language at the same level as SQL is being used for relational data. It basically subsumes SQL under the XML and XQuery model and enables XML-savvy users to operate on both relational and XML data without having to use SQL. Unlike queries on an XML datatype, XQuery expressions can combine different XML documents and XML views of relational data. Another advantage of having top-level XQuery expressions is the ability to provide finer-grained concurrency control and locking (such as node-level tree locking).

Many relational database systems and tools providers offer this approach as a mid-tier extension, providing views over the relational data and an XQuery data integration engine (see Chapter 6). However, if a relational database system already provides an XML datatype, then it seems straightforward to extend the programming model to provide top-level XQuery support over a collection of XML instances and XML views of relational data. In the following, we use the keyword XQUERY to indicate a top-level XQuery and enclose the XQuery expression in curly braces. Such an expression returns either a single instance of the relational XML datatype or (depending on the relational database system's programming model) a single-column/single-row table or a singleton collection of XML.

XML Document (Fragment) Collections

There are two ways to provide (potentially typed) collections of XML data. One approach simply uses an XQuery function in the top-level XQuery expression to refer to a table column that is typed as XML. The XQuery collection() function could be used to refer to such a column, if the relational system provided a mapping of the relational names into the URI space.

Alternatively, the database could provide a function `sql:collection($c as xs:string) as document*` that refers to the column and returns a sequence of the extended document root nodes. An example based on the table specified in Listing 7.4 is given below. If the column contains typed XML, then the static type information can be used to type the top-level XQuery.

```
XQUERY {
  declare namespace po = "http://www.example.com/po-schema"
  sql:collection('Customers.PurchaseOrders')/po:po/po:details
}
```

Another approach is to extend the notion of a table to allow the creation of a table of `type`, where the type would not be a rowtype but the XML datatype. The example in Listing 7.9 first defines a collection of purchase-order instances statically constrained by the purchase-order schema; then it provides two alternate ways to populate it (one using an SQL INSERT statement and one using a pseudo-XQuery-like syntax), and finally it queries the collection.

Listing 7.9   Example of an XML Collection Using CREATE TABLE OF type and a Top-Level XQuery

```
CREATE TABLE PurchaseOrders OF TYPE XML TYPED AS POSchema

INSERT INTO PurchaseOrders SELECT PurchaseOrders FROM Customers

XQUERY-MODIFY {
  insert
    <po:purchase-order
        xmlns:po="http://www.example.com/po-schema" id="2001">
        <po:shipTo>
          <po:address>42 2nd Avenue</po:address>
          <po:city>Bellevue</po:city>
          <po:state>WA</po:state>
          <po:zip>98006</po:zip>
        </po:shipTo>
        <po:details qty="4" price="3.44"/>
      </po:purchase-order>
  as last into
    sql:collection('PurchaseOrders')
}

XQUERY {
  declare namespace po = "http://www.example.com/po-schema"
  sql:collection('PurchaseOrders')/po:purchase-order/po:details
}
```

XML Views over Relational Data

Besides providing access to collections of XML instances, top-level XQuery expressions should also provide access to XML views over relational data. As described in Chapter 6, there are different view mechanisms.

Since the SQL/XML part of the ISO SQL-2003 standard provides two general forms of default mappings of relational tables to XML [SQLXML], relational systems will most likely provide at least one of them if they provide XQuery access to relational data. They may also provide support for other mappings, such as an annotated schema-driven view mechanism.

The SQL/XML relational-to-XML mapping provides two main mapping approaches: The table-to-doc approach maps every table to an XML document where the root element is named according to the table name. Every row is mapped to an element named `row` underneath that root element and contains the column data of the row as subelements, where the names of the subelements are based on the column names. The table-to-forest approach maps a table into an XML element forest where every row is mapped to an element whose name is based on the table name. As in the other mapping, the column data is mapped to subelements. Both approaches have additional mapping options, such as an option to map columns containing the relational `NULL` values to either absent elements or to elements marked with `xsi:nil="true"`. The table-to-doc approach is well suited for XML-based relational-to-relational data transport, whereas the table-to-forest approach is better suited for querying the relational data with XQuery, since it avoids the additional step expressions introduced by the artificial `row` elements.

Listing 7.10 gives an example of an XML view of the relational table in Listing 7.2 that uses the table-to-forest approach. Whitespace has been added to help in formatting.

Listing 7.10   Example of an XML View of a Relational Table

```
<ORDER>
  <ID>4023</ID>
  <ORDERDATE>2001-12-01</ORDERDATE>
  <PODETAIL>
    <purchaseOrder xmlns=?http://po.example.com?>
      <originator billId=?0013579?>
```

Listing 7.10   Example of an XML View of a Relational Table *(continued)*

```
        <contactName>Fred Allen</contactName>
        <contactAddress>
          <street>123 2nd Ave. NW</street>
          <city>Anytown</city>
          <state>OH</state>
          <zip-four>99999-1234</zip-four>
        </contactAddress>
        <phone>(330) 555-1212</phone>
        <originatorReferenceNumber>AS 1132</originatorReferenceNumber>
      </originator>
      <order>
        <item code=?34xdl 1278 12ct? quantity=?1?/>
        <item code=?57xdl 7789? quantity=?1? colorcode=?012?/>
      </order>
      <shipAddress sameAsContact=?true?/>
      <shipCode carrier=?02?/>
    </purchaseOrder>
  </PODETAIL>
</ORDER>
<ORDER>
  <ID>5327</ID>
  <ORDERDATE>2002-04-23</ORDERDATE>
  <PODETAIL>
    <purchaseOrder xmlns=?http://po.example.com?>
        <originator ...
  </PODETAIL>
</ORDER>
...
```

The top-level XQuery environment can be given access to these views in various ways. Generally this is done either through the existing doc() and collection() functions, where the location and mapping information is encoded in the URI, or possibly through additional built-in functions.

Any of the views can be represented as a single document by making the view's top-level element(s) become the children of a document node. The result will not necessarily correspond to a well-formed XML document, but is allowed by the XQuery data model. In this case, the system must either specify a URI encoding of the view parameters for use with the XQuery doc() function or define a new, built-in XQuery function. For example, top-level XQuery could provide the following built-in XQuery function:

```
sql:table($table as xs:string
          [, $table_map_option as xs:string
          [, $null_map_option as xs:string]]) as element*
```

This function returns the view of the given table `$table` with the optional parameters indicating the preferred table- and null-mapping options. For instance, `sql:table('Order', 'table-to-forest', 'xsinil')` would return the view of Listing 7.10.

Alternatively, the system could also provide access to the views as a collection of individual document nodes, one for each top-level element. In that case, the system would have to provide a function `sql:collection()` or define a URI mapping for use with XQuery's built-in function `fn:collection()`. In any case, the view will probably not guarantee a deterministic order of the top-level elements, because relational tuples have no implicit order. If a relational system provides other relational-to-XML mapping techniques, such as Microsoft SQL Server's annotated schema views [RYS2001], additional functions can be provided to expose them in top-level XQuery expressions.

Turning to implementation, we note that the actual physical mapping of the XQuery expressions against the views—regardless of how they are accomplished—can be done directly against the relational engine's logical algebra operations. This means that an implementation can add new logical operations as needed to express specific semantics not available otherwise. This ability allows an easier mapping than the mid-tier approach, which must either map the query into an SQL statement or ship more data than needed to the mid-tier and post-process the data to get the correct execution semantics.

Any of these view-generation techniques present a major problem for data modification statements. Since they assume a node-based data model, where every node has a unique identification, mapping them into SQL-based update statements on relational tables that may not have such a unique identification requires a careful design of the update propagation through the view.

Conclusion and Issues

This chapter has given an overview of how to integrate relational database systems with XQuery. It introduced the XML datatype and presented both the mixed approach of using XQuery in conjunction with

SQL to query XML datatype instances and the top-level XQuery approach of querying collections of XML instances and XML views of relational data. It also provided an insight into the impact of the actual physical data model of the XML datatype on the processing and mapping of XQuery in the context of relational systems.

Many relational database systems at the time of this writing have just started to add native XML support to their support for bidirectional mapping between relational and XML data, and so far no system ships XQuery as described in this chapter. Before long, however, I believe all major relational database systems will provide functionality of the form described (most vendors have already announced support for a built-in XML datatype).

Many open issues need further investigation and are currently active research topics. Among them are the following:

- Which of the physical mappings of the XML data are the best approaches to support XML inside a relational context? Depending on the data, there may be more than one. In that case the question becomes how to determine the best one and provide support for all the approaches.
- How should the query-processing model be extended? In particular:

    What additions are needed to the logical algebra?

    What additions can be made to the optimizer to improve efficiency?

    What indices help in improving efficiency?

    How is distributed query processing best supported?

- Another area of concern is the area of concurrency control. How can the concurrency control of relational data be extended to deal with tree-structured data and provide fine-grained control? Especially in the context of combined relational and XML queries on relational tables containing XML, the current row-level locking granularity is inadequate if access similar to **online transaction processing** (OLTP) is going to be part of the query mix. Thus, one question is how to improve the parallelism in such queries and how to integrate fine-grained concurrency control of XML data (such as tree-based concurrency control) with the relational concurrency control.

Chapter 8
A NATIVE XML DBMS

Jim Tivy

The term "native XML database" is not a precise technical term, and different people define it in different ways. Essentially, it refers to a database designed specifically for the storage and retrieval of XML documents, and the term is used to contrast such a system with a database that merely provides an XML interface to data whose intrinsic data model is something different. In the early days of relational databases, every database vendor tried to jump on the relational bandwagon by selling their old products with a new relational veneer. The relational purists responded with a set of criteria that distinguished a true relational database from one that was merely dressed up to look like one.

The thinking behind the term "native XML database" is similar, but there is still no definitive set of criteria to distinguish one. In the absence of such a definition, I intend to outline some of the features that users can expect to find in a native XML database, in particular those that distinguish it from a relational or object database that has been given an XML veneer. XML interfaces to relational databases are useful, but the characteristics of a native XML database differ and frequently provide more functionality, and we need to understand the differences.

Database management systems (DBMSs) have long been a central part of computer applications. A database can be defined as being a managed collection of data on which users may perform update and query operations. An XML database is thus a managed collection of XML data. A native XML database, if one interprets the term literally, is a database that was born to handle XML data, as distinct from a database that was originally designed for a different purpose, and was only later adapted to handle XML data.

So how does one recognize a native XML database? One test is to look at the programmer interfaces: A DBMS becomes a native XML database when the most natural way for programmers to manipulate data is in XML form. A native XML database is thus defined in terms of external features apparent to the programmer. An XML database implementation will use special internal indexing and storage strategies to deliver external features in the most effective way, but the internal algorithms do not define whether the database is a native XML database, they are just the special sauce that vendors provide to better serve up the external features. Vendors who decide to store the XML data in a relational database are not therefore excluded from the native XML DBMS club; rather, the "nativeness" of the XML DBMS is judged by the external programmer's experience of working with XML at the database interface.

In this view, the main importance of the word *native* comes down to how the data in the DBMS is modeled to the programmer. The model must respect the structure of XML as defined by the XML data model and, more precisely, the XQuery data model. In addition, the DBMS must work easily with other XML technologies. Alongside this deep respect for the XML data model, an XML database must provide all the features expected of any DBMS, such as transactions, recovery, and multithreading, as well as others described below. A native XML DBMS is thus a blending of features that expose and capitalize on the XML data model, XML technologies, and features generally expected from a DBMS.

One of the best ways to distinguish a native XML database from a database that merely offers an XML veneer is to examine the fidelity with which it can store an XML document—specifically, the extent to which documents can be retrieved in exactly the form in which they were stored. Different systems are surprisingly variable in this respect. Some systems are capable of retaining the exact physical representation of an XML document, down to its use of internal and external entities, character encoding, and details such as the choice of quotation marks or apostrophes around attribute values. A more typical level of fidelity, exhibited by products such as Software AG's Tamino, is at the level of the logical XQuery data model. Such systems do not retain all the lexical details of the original document (they may, for example, reorder attributes and expand XML entities), but they do retain the full textual content of each document. By contrast, systems that provide XML interfaces only as a wrapper to some other data model may well store data internally using normalized representations of values such as dates and numbers. When the document is retrieved, it may then be missing details such as leading zeroes on a number, or comments in the middle of a list of dates. These details may not matter to some applications, but for others they can be crucial. For example, comments in the document might have been used to indicate where the document author was uncertain about the facts.

As well as the interfaces for storage and retrieval of data, a native XML database also uses XML-based interfaces for data description: typically, the structure of the database is defined in terms of a set of XML schemas to which the documents in the database must conform.

This chapter discusses the features of native XML databases in general, illustrating them with examples taken from actual XML DBMS implementations. Many examples come from the XStreamDB database because I am familiar with it inside and out. My aim is to define what the primary features of a native XML DBMS are and then to discuss these features with some reference to internal implementation details. In particular, I suggest that a native XML database is characterized by the pervasive use of the XQuery language and the XQuery data model at all levels of the system.

What Is XML Data?

XML data can be understood at two levels: the textual representation, and the model of this data as a tree of nodes.

XML as Text

XML is often seen in its textual form. As text, XML may be viewed in any text editor and easily passed around the World Wide Web using text-based protocols such as HTTP. The example below shows some XML text. Note the tags `Person` and `FirstName`. Such tags give names to the data.

```
<?xml version="1.0"?>
<Person id="12">
   <FirstName>John</FirstName>
   <LastName>Smith</LastName>
<Person>
```

XML Data Model

In a rough sense, the XML data model (XML Infoset [INFOSET]) describes XML as a tree of data. The XQuery data model is essentially this same tree definition with some important additions, such as sequences and primitive datatypes. As earlier chapters have illustrated, the XQuery data model [XQ-DM] is a central foundation of the XQuery language. In a native XML database, the XQuery data model is also fundamentally important to the architecture of the DBMS. The XQuery data model is used throughout a native XML DBMS to model all XML data as it flows from a stored document collection, through the XQuery system, and out to the client applications via a result set.

The XQuery data model (henceforth called the data model) supports a set of possible values, referred to as the **value space** of the data model. The data values in the value space conform to the data model definition. Often, values in the value space are referred to as "instances of the data model" (more strictly, they are instances of the top-level type defined in the data model, which is the type sequence). By implication, the data model also defines what lies outside the value space: For example, a non-conforming value would be an attribute node that had a child attribute node. Figure 8.1 shows an example data value resulting from the XML in the preceding example of XML text (the `Person` document text). This `Person` document value conforms to the data model diagrammed in Figure 8.2, which is a Unified Modeling Language (UML) diagram that defines the XQuery data model.

Figure 8.2 reflects the set of valid values supported by the data model. Inevitably, it is a simplification. It doesn't specify all the constraints (for example, the fact that an element node cannot contain a document node). It doesn't attempt to show that element nodes and attribute nodes have a typed value, which can be any sequence of atomic values. Further, it shows the constraints that apply to a well-formed document as defined in the XML recommendation [XML] and the XML Infoset [INFOSET] — namely, that a document node contains exactly one element node as a direct child. In fact, the data model relaxes this constraint, largely to allow the temporary trees used by XSLT (remember that the data model is shared between XQuery and XSLT).

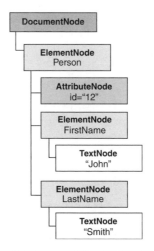

Figure 8.1 `Person` Document Value

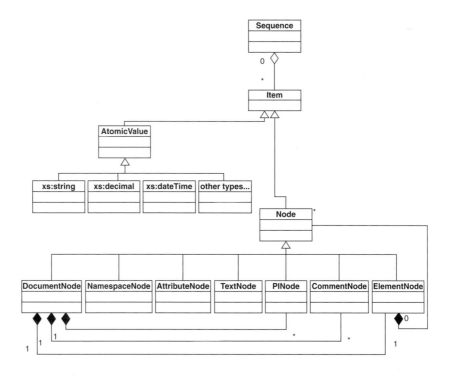

Figure 8.2 The XQuery Data Model

The `Person` document tree in Figure 8.1 conforms to the data model defined in Figure 8.2. In fact, using Figure 8.2 as a UML static class diagram and using Figure 8.1 as an instance diagram, you can see that Figure 8.1 is a conforming instance of the `Sequence` class defined in Figure 8.2. We can describe the correspondence of the `Person` document to the data model definition as follows:

- The `Person` document has a `DocumentNode` at its root. `DocumentNode` is a subclass of `Node`, which is itself a subclass of `Item`. An `Item` may be contained in a `Sequence`, so the top level conforms. Since we only have one document, the `Sequence` is of length one. This `DocumentNode`, in turn, has a child `Element-Node` named `Person`, which has an `AttributeNode` named `id`. An element node is not said to have "child" attribute nodes; rather, it just has attribute nodes. This is consistent with the `child::` and `attribute::` axes in XPath. Following along, the `Person` element has a child element named `FirstName`, which in turn has a child `TextNode` with a value of `"John"`. The other parts of the tree can be similarly described.

- Text nodes containing whitespace only have been ignored in this example. The data model allows insignificant whitespace to be stripped from the tree, and the example assumes that this has been done.

The data model definition above reveals that the value space allows other kinds of values, not only documents. For example, a sequence of `xs:decimal` values without any enclosing node conforms to the data model. A sequence of `DocumentNodes` also conforms. Such values do not correspond directly to any well-formed textual document described by the XML 1.0 Recommendation [XML], and they are not well-formed XML Infoset [INFOSET] instances. Allowing such values, however, makes the XQuery data model more flexible, in that any constituent part or sequence of parts of an XML document can flow through XQuery and the XML DBMS and are conforming values with respect to the XQuery data model.

The most obvious use of the XQuery data model is to describe the persistent documents stored in the database. But in a native XML database, the XQuery data model does more than just describe the persistent documents. For example, it also describes the following:

- *Collections:* Collections, in the terminology of XQuery, are the sets of documents that comprise a persistent database: They are the raw input to a query. A collection itself is modeled as a sequence, typically a sequence of document nodes. This doesn't necessarily mean that order of documents in a database is significant, but it reuses the general-purpose concept of a sequence in the data model and allows persistent collections to be manipulated in the query language in the same way as any other sequence.

- *Working data:* During the processing of XQuery, expression values may be constructed to represent intermediate results, all of which are sequences of nodes and/or atomic values—in other words, they are instances of the data model. This means that any temporary data constructed in the course of query processing can be manipulated using the full power of the XQuery language in exactly the same way as persistent data.

- *Query results:* The result of a query is also a sequence of nodes and/or atomic values—again, a value conforming to the data model. The XQuery specification doesn't say how the results are delivered to a user or to an application; this is up to the implementation to define. Perhaps a standard XQuery client API will emerge in future, but in the meantime, each implementation defines its own. An example of such an API is described later in the chapter. Implementations may also deliver results in other ways: Tamino [TAMINO], for example, allows a query to be submitted in the form of an HTTP request to a web server and returns the results of the query as the response to the HTTP request, serialized as an XML document.

Interfaces to a Native XML Database

As a query language, XQuery is obviously a key interface offered by a native XML database. But it is not the only interface that is required. XQuery does not say how schemas are registered in a database, how data is loaded and updated, or how physical storage features are organized.

Nor does it define how queries are issued by an application program, or how the results are presented. In this section I review some of the other interfaces that a native XML database system needs to offer.

An eventual objective for many of these interfaces is interoperability, so we examine first the extent to which this can currently be achieved. Then we look at some of the key interfaces offered by a DBMS: the data definition (schema) interfaces, the data update interfaces, and the database configuration interfaces.

Interoperability

In a modern DBMS, programmers expect DBMS features to be delivered in a standard way across vendors—an idea often called interoperability. The aim of interoperability is to allow the writing of programs that run on multiple database management systems. This is of great interest to vendors building tools such as report writers and viewers that must run against multiple DBMSs, and it also means that programmers need only learn one command language and one API to use a variety of products.

Interoperability has been addressed for relational DBMSs by organizations such as the International Standards Organization with the SQL specification, and by industry consortia like the SQL Access Group, whose specifications eventually fed into the creation of Microsoft's Open Database Connectivity API (ODBC) and the similar Java JDBC interface. Interoperability and standards have in the past been the challenge for relational and object-oriented database management systems; likewise, interoperability is now the challenge for XML database systems. The World Wide Web Consortium (W3C) has spearheaded the standardization of XML and more recently XQuery, and these two specifications form the cornerstones of an interoperable XML DBMS.

At the time of writing, although XQuery 1.0 is quite stable, its scope is narrow, and several important XML DBMS features are still unspecified. As a result, these features vary across vendors. Although this is clearly not a good end result, it is a reality of this early stage in the XML DBMS standardization process. In the future, standards will emerge for key features such as an update language, full-text search language, API, and others, and vendors will probably follow with implementations of these standards.

Even in the end game of standards compliance, such as in the relational DBMS and SQL standardization process, perfect interoperability has never been totally achieved; it is more of a guiding principle.

In the XML world, expectations for interoperability are high. These expectations arise because of the pervasiveness of the World Wide Web. Database systems in the past, however, have achieved only modest levels of interoperability. It remains to be seen to what extent XML databases will change this.

Data-Definition Interfaces

In the history of database technology, there has always been a separation between data definition and data manipulation. The essence of a database as a shared resource is that the data definition is centrally managed, so that different applications can manipulate the data in different ways while still sharing information.

In a native XML database, data manipulation—at least the retrieval side—is handled using XQuery, while the data-description requirement is handled using a separate schema language. Typically, an XML Schema as defined in the W3C Schema specification [SCHEMA], though other kinds of schemas such as DTDs [XML] or RelaxNG schemas [RELAXNG] might also be accommodated. This section presents an overview, with several examples, of how schemas can be used in a native XML database.

The first role of a schema is to define constraints on what constitutes a valid document: The schema is used for validity checking. An XML document is said to be valid with respect to a schema if that XML document follows the content model, data typing, and other constraints defined by the schema. Some flavors of schema, such as DTD, express fewer constraints on the data than other flavors, such as W3C XML Schema. For example, a DTD cannot specify that a particular attribute must contain a valid date. There are other kinds of integrity constraints, familiar to relational database users, that cannot be expressed even in XML Schema. The best-known example is co-occurrence constraints (e.g., if one attribute has a particular value, another must be absent). Other important integrity constraints that cannot be expressed in a schema are cross-document constraints, such as a constraint that each document in a collection must have a unique reference number, or that all the hyper-links in a document must point to other documents that exist within the collection. So XML Schema doesn't satisfy all the needs for validity checking, but it goes a long way toward this goal.

But data description in a database system is not just about validating the input data: The data description is used to define how the data is organized on disk, for checking the correctness of queries, for optimizing queries by choosing the most efficient access paths, and for constructing the data structures used to contain query results. The datatypes defined in the schema also define the semantics of operations such as comparisons and sorting. So the role of schemas in a native XML database is central.

In a relational DBMS the description of a table, its columns, and their types form the schema for that table, and all rows in that table must comply. In a native XML DBMS there is a similar need to constrain collections of XML documents with respect to schemas. The exact relationship between databases, documents, schemas, and queries is not precisely laid down in the current XQuery specifications: The standards have deliberately tried to steer clear of this. For example, some systems might require that all documents in a collection conform to the same schema, others might permit a range of possible schemas, while some systems may be able to search schema-less documents. The XQuery specification allows an XQuery expression to import a schema, and it must import a schema if it makes explicit use of datatypes defined in that schema, but it isn't required to import every schema that might have been used to validate a document in the collection being searched. The flexibility of the possible relationships between queries, documents, and schemas has caused considerable difficulty in defining the W3C specifications, but in a practical implementation, the relationships are likely to be much simpler. The automatic introduction of schema could be as simple as binding a schema to a collection so that when that collection is used, the schema is also introduced. Currently, XML DBMS vendors must decide for themselves how to manage schemas within the DBMS and how to introduce schema information into the XQuery subsystem.

The XQuery specification describes query processing in terms of two phases: the query-analysis phase and query-evaluation phase. These terms are defined in the *XQuery 1.0 Language* document [XQ-LANG], and I use these terms here. But it is also useful to consider two earlier phases that I will call the database-design phase and the query-authoring phase. These phases occur in the following order:

1. *Database-design phase:* This is the time at which design decisions are made about the logical and physical organization of the database.

2. *Query-authoring phase:* This is the time a query is written by a user or programmer.

3. *Query-analysis phase:* This is the time at which the query processor analyzes the query and prepares the query-execution plan. One of the activities carried out at this time is static type-checking.

4. *Query-evaluation phase*: This is the time at which the query-execution plan is executed: The query is thus evaluated to produce a result, which may be any instance of the data model. This time is often called query run-time, and one of the activities carried out at this time is dynamic type-checking.

Database-Design Phase

Part of the database design task for a native XML database is designing the schemas for the documents that the database will contain. This is an art in itself, and a detailed discussion is beyond the scope of this chapter. There are probably two main scenarios: (1) a schema for the documents already exists, and documents are to be stored in the form in which they arrive; and (2) the schema is custom-designed for the purpose of long-term document storage. The design approach is rather different for each scenario.

Database design, however, is not finished when the schemas are written. Two of the important tasks that remain are the following:

- *Database configuration:* This is the task of defining collections or other database partitions and deciding how different types of documents (represented by different schemas) will be allocated to different collections. For more detailed discussion, see "Collections and Storage" below.

▪ *Index definition:* This is the task of deciding which data should be indexed. As with any other database, this task is essential to achieve satisfactory performance. Systems often provide tools to help. For example, when a value index is defined in the XStreamDB Explorer application, the schema is used to display a tree of all the possible index XPaths, so that the user can make a selection. At that point the index is constructed.

Query-Authoring Phase

Schema information can be very helpful when presented through a graphical user interface in a tool used for building queries or configuring the DBMS. In this case the schema can be used for the following:

▪ *Query building:* A user constructing a query through a graphical user interface often finds it convenient to be able to look up long paths to elements or attributes. If schema information is available, such lookup capability is easily provided, and the corresponding XPath can be inserted into the query under construction. Schema-aided query building is very useful in an XML database explorer or XML report design tool.

▪ *Query explanation:* Systems may provide tools to enable query authors to understand how a query will be executed (e.g., which indexes it will use). Often a query will not be viable unless it can make use of indexes, so this information is vital. In Tamino this tool is called `explain`. In XStreamDB, the query-execution plan is determined at query-execution time and is output to a QueryPlan.html file.

Query-Analysis Time

The task of query analysis is explained in much more detail in other chapters of this book. The main operations carried out at this stage are syntax checking, type checking, and query optimization. Of these, everything except syntax checking makes heavy use of schema information where it is available. The big question here is how flexible the system is in terms of allowing queries against schema-less documents, queries that search documents of more than one type, queries that span multiple versions of the same schema, and so on. Products are likely to vary in such respects.

Query-Evaluation Time

Again, this subject is covered in much more detail elsewhere in this book. Schema information is needed at evaluation time to determine the dynamic types of values (which may be more specific than their statically known types). It may also be needed to validate the result document produced by a query, and perhaps even intermediate working documents. This becomes especially important when update is supported, because the results of a query may produce a new document that is to be stored persistently in the database.

Update Interfaces

Before anyone can run queries against a database, the data must be loaded. A native XML database therefore needs to provide some interface for loading data. This is currently outside the scope of the XQuery specification.

Update commands include the expressions necessary to insert, delete, and update documents in a collection. Commands to insert new documents and delete old documents are fairly easy to implement. The XML document provides a natural unit of granularity for such operations, which may be provided as primitive operations through a client API, quite independently of any query language.

However, document-level update is not sufficient for all applications. It is inefficient to retrieve, delete, and replace a large document just to make one small change, especially if the database is heavily indexed. This becomes even more true when making a small change to every one of a large number of documents (for example, marking a thousand documents with a new attribute, such as a security classification). Performance and storage model considerations make updating of existing documents especially complicated.

In a relational DBMS, updating a row in a table is done as follows:

```
UPDATE table
SET column=expression [, column=expression]*
WHERE predicates
```

In this SQL update, you specify the table, the columns to update, the values to use, and a WHERE clause to select the correct rows to update.

The individual SET clauses allow you to say exactly what needs to change in the underlying table row, which means the row is only partially updated. **Partial update** works well—especially with long binary columns—because you avoid disturbing values in columns that are not changing.

XML update similarly requires a way to introduce the document to be updated and a way to update all or parts of a document. To update parts of a document, we must be able to insert, delete, or replace any subcomponent of a document, including element nodes, text nodes, and attribute values. For example, given a collection of Person documents, similar in structure to the example of Person document text at the beginning of this chapter, I might want to change all the $doc/Person/City values to London. This change operation requires a replacement of the current City element values. If, on the other hand, I wanted to remove the City element from all Person documents, then deleting $doc/Person/City would be necessary. Or suppose I have the text of a play, and I want to insert stage directions into it. In this case I have to find the insertion point and then insert a new StageDirection element as needed.

Any update command syntax should make it easy to optimize a partial update of an underlying document in order to reduce indexing and writes to disk—especially if documents are large. Putting this functionality into XQuery is a challenge. The working group is currently investigating an Update language that will address this challenge. At present, various vendor mechanisms exist for update, some of them based on these proposals. XStreamDB uses XQuery-like syntax; other vendors use a variety of approaches, including an XML-based method called XUpdate [XUPDATE]. For more information, see the upcoming XQuery update language or investigate vendor solutions.

Database Configuration Interfaces

I use the term "database configuration" to describe configuration of a database through the creation of configuration objects such as databases, collections, indexes, stored procedures, **triggers,** schemas, and users.

Although the details of these configuration objects vary from one database system to another, most systems have objects analogous to the ones defined below.

Database

A database is a container for one or more collections. Often a database has a name. In some systems, a database can simply be a collection of collections.

Collection

A collection is a set of XML documents held in persistent storage. In some systems a collection might contain other child collections. Some systems might allow collections to intersect, so that the same document is in several collections. Collections are often associated in some way with schemas. This might be a very simple correspondence (all documents in a collection have the same schema), or something a bit more flexible. See "Collections and Storage" below for further discussion.

Index

An index is concerned with speeding up a certain access path through the data and is used for satisfying conditions in a query. Such conditions typically occur in the `where` clause of a FLWOR expression or in a predicate of an XPath expression. The forms of indexes vary across vendors because, for many vendors, this is the "special sauce" that makes their implementation faster or better than that of a competitor. Some vendors automatically create and maintain indexes either because certain kinds of queries are being repeatedly done or because indexes are an integral part of structuring the storage in the database. More commonly, however, indexes are created on explicit request.

There are different kinds of indexes used in a Native XML database; the details vary from one product to another. A value index is an index of the typed values that exist for attribute and element nodes. For example, if your XML document has element `FirstName` with value `John`, as in

```
<FirstName>John</FirstName>
```

then you may have a value index that contains the entry (`"John"`,`1000`)—where 1000 is a physical or logical address of the corresponding document in the DBMS.

Value indexes are similar to column indexes in SQL databases. They can be selectively created for particular element or attribute values that are often involved in predicates in queries. For example, suppose you have the following query:

```
for $d in collection("foo")
where $d/Book/Author/LastName = "Date"
return $d
```

If a value index is defined on `data(/Book/Author/LastName)`, then it could be used when optimizing the query by replacing the FLWOR expression and its `where` clause with an index access using the key `"Date"`.

One variation among systems is likely to be the granularity of indexing. Does the index entry identify only the document that contains the relevant value, or does it identify the specific node? There is a trade-off here between the cost of indexing, the space occupied by the index, and the value of the index for resolving more complex queries. In the simple case, a value index will index a document with simple (key, document id) pairs. In a more complex case, value indexes may index extents of common fragments. For example, if a bibliography system were to use an aggregated storage strategy, then all the authors for all the books might be stored together and might be indexable. In this case the index entry may be (key, author-id) or even (key, author-id, document-id) triplets. Using such triplets allows either the document or the author node to be returned depending on the query `return` clause. This simple triplet is suggestive of the more general path index used in object-oriented databases.

The structure index of Tamino [TAMINO], a leading XML DBMS, is an example of a second kind of index that indexes the existence of named elements and attributes within the document hierarchy. We can use such an index to locate documents that contain a particular named element type or an element in a particular hierarchic context (e.g., a `footnote` element within a `table` element). This kind of index is especially useful where documents are semi-structured—that is, where the schema is very flexible regarding the structures that it allows to appear in instance documents.

The third type of index that is often encountered in a native XML database is a full-text index, which is used to index words appearing within the content of elements. Such an index is used to optimize queries that search on words using a full-text expression of some sort. Unlike a value index, a full-text index is often applied to all the text in a document, regardless of the element in which it appears. This may be an implementation constraint or it may be done because the user of the full-text index needs to be able to search either the entire document or a particular path in an *ad hoc* fashion. Even when a full-text index is applied to the complete document, the search scope for that document may be restricted to just one path. For example, I may only want to search the `$doc/book/title` for the word "Linux," not the entire book. This path-specific search requirement means full-text indexes will often contain path information along with the words so that path-specific queries can be optimized. Additional discussion on full-text search appears later in the chapter.

Stored Functions

In relational databases, stored procedures are often used in large, complex applications as a way of extending the database command language, so that application logic can be executed within the database system instead of at the application level using another programming language like Java or C++. The idea was first introduced to reduce network traffic in client-server systems, but it also gives more scope for a query optimizer to improve access paths. Historically, stored procedures were often written in proprietary languages invented by each vendor (e.g., PL/SQL in the case of Oracle). Since XQuery is a powerful language with its own function-definition syntax, stored XQuery functions fulfill the same role in the case of a native XML database.

Functions in XQuery are probably more important even than stored procedures in a relational database, because they also perform the role of views in relational systems. Just as relational views allow query authors to interrogate the data without knowing all the intricate details of the schema structures, so functions in XQuery can provide a built-in capability to access derived data. This is especially important for navigating relationships, since relationships can be represented in many different ways in a native XML database, and we can mask these differences by using functions.

The XQuery specifications define a syntax for defining and invoking functions, but they do not say how libraries of functions are managed. A native XML database often has interfaces allowing functions to be compiled and stored within the database.

Triggers

Triggers are a special type of stored procedure. They fire when data in the database is changed or configuration events occur, such as dropping a collection.

Schemas

We have already seen that XML schemas are used to support a broad range of features in a native XML database. Schemas are also configuration objects that need to be managed. The way in which schemas are loaded into the DBMS varies from vendor to vendor.

Access Control and Locking

As with any DBMS, an XML DBMS needs concepts such as users, groups, and permissions on resources in order to manage authentication and access authorization. In the absence of any standard, the ways in which users and permissions are defined differ from one XML database to another. A native XML database may offer access control at the level of individual documents, or it may provide control of parts of a document as a resource. This subcomponent resource may in turn be assigned user permissions. In addition, an XML DBMS may define a long-transaction mechanism that allows users to apply long-duration locks to documents or document subcomponents. Although there is no direct connection between the data model and the type of locking that a database needs to support, the applications that use a native XML database often involve the kind of collaborative workflow that requires long-duration locking, in addition to the more conventional transaction-processing models supported by relational databases.

A Database Command Language

The SQL language first introduced the idea of combining data-definition interfaces, database configuration interfaces, and query/update interfaces into a single language—a concept I will call a database command language. Many modern database management systems have followed this tradition. A native XML database necessarily separates data definition (provided through XML schemas) from data manipulation (XQuery), but there is still scope for unifying multiple functions into a single command language that is processed by the DBMS to query, update, and perform other database configuration tasks. Due to the time it takes to hammer out a standard, the XQuery specification currently defines a command language that is suitable for query only. Other important features of a command language are the following:

- Database configuration
- Update capability
- Full-text search capability

Update and full-text search will probably be addressed within XQuery eventually, though definition of configuration objects may be handled outside the XQuery language. In fact, the XQuery group has currently released working drafts on full-text requirements and full-text use cases.

In XStreamDB we chose to add XQuery command-language extensions for all of the features above. The command syntax and structure in XStreamDB in no way reflect the XQuery working group's direction, but these added commands do serve as an example of such interfaces.

Other native XML databases have implemented this functionality in different ways. Tamino, for example, provides database configuration interfaces through a system management infrastructure designed to provide a single management interface not only for database resources but for other resources such as the networking infrastructure. Tamino implements interfaces for physical database design (e.g., definition of indexes) by means of annotations to XML Schema, using a custom namespace for the annotations to ensure that the schemas remain interoperable.

Database Configuration

The following is a brief sampler of XStreamDB's extensions to XQuery to create, modify, and destroy configuration objects.

Database

A database has 0..n roots. A database can be created and dropped as follows:

- *Create:* CREATE DATABASE DatabaseName
- *Drop:* DROP DATABASE DatabaseName

Root

A root in XStreamDB is a collection of documents. Roots can be bound to a schema, in which case all documents within that root must comply with the schema. As well, this schema and its type information become automatically available for that root.

- *Create:* CREATE ROOT RootName [WITH SCHEMA SchemaName]
- *Alter:* ALTER ROOT RootName [WITH SCHEMA (SchemaName | NONE)]
- *Drop:* DROP ROOT RootName

Index

XStreamDB supports value indexes definable on selected paths and full-text indexes defined across an entire root.

- *Create value:* CREATE [UNIQUE] INDEX IndexName ON RootName PATH PathExpr
- *Create full text:* CREATE FULLTEXT INDEX ON RootName
- *Drop value:* DROP INDEX IndexName ON RootName
- *Drop full text:* DROP FULLTEXT INDEX ON RootName

Trigger

XStreamDB supports triggers that can be set up to fire during operations on documents within a root. These trigger definitions include much of what you would expect.

```
CREATE TRIGGER trigger-name
ON rootname
[PRIORITY integer]
[(BEFORE | AFTER)]
(INSERT | UPDATE | DELETE)
DO TriggerExpr
```

`TriggerExpr` is any valid XQuery expression, including update extensions. In the update trigger case, the special variables `$existingDocument` and `$newDocument` are available for use within the expression `TriggerExpr`.

Collections and Storage

The XML document is a central unit of data in the XML world. For this reason, the XML document is often the unit that is sent, received, edited, and stored by an XML application. It follows that a collection within a native XML database is, most naturally, a collection of XML documents. This also means that a collection is a valid instance of the data model—it is a sequence of document nodes, or at any rate, it is a set of document nodes that can be modeled as a sequence whenever it is accessed.

Given the above definition of a collection, the way collections of XML documents themselves are physically stored may still vary. The size and intended future use of a document may affect the underlying storage model of that XML document in a DBMS. Some applications involve very large documents that may represent, for example, an entire telecommunications network or a procedure manual composed of thousands of pages. Such documents can range from 500KB to many megabytes. In general, as the document becomes larger, queries will tend to drill down into the document to select parts of it, rather than retrieving the whole document.

On the other hand, many applications involve relatively small business documents. The size of an invoice or purchase order like the ones laid out by industry groups may be around 10KB, while other applications may store documents as small as 100 bytes. When relatively small business documents are in use, many queries will probably retrieve the whole document. Indeed, some queries may combine information from many documents into one, or compute aggregate information such as totals over many source documents.

To optimize queries and updates on small portions of large XML documents, a database administrator may be allowed to split a large XML document into fragments—each fragment often rooted on a particular element type. For example, if I have a user guide composed of multiple level-one sections, enclosed by Sect1 tags, I may choose to store each of the Sect1 sections in separate, contiguous parts of the database, even though the database will logically model these sections as one big document. Storing Sect1 sections separately may speed up queries on Sect1/Title when indexes are present, because not all Sect1 data would have to be read from disk, and not all of the document would have to be filtered in order to find only the Sect1 section that met the query conditions.

Such a fragmentation strategy may also interact with locking: A database system might apply locks at the level of a document fragment, in particular the long-duration locks used to support collaborative authoring features in content management systems. This is related to the techniques used for mapping subobjects in object-oriented database systems [OODB], and similar considerations also apply when mapping XML data to relational storage, as discussed in other chapters of this book.

The Tamino database system uses a similar scheme to map parts of an XML document to external databases or web services. This allows the maintenance of "live" documents; for example, the front page of an employee resume (CV) may be generated on-the-fly from an operational personnel database, while the textual content is maintained in native XML storage.

In summary, although at a logical level a collection is a collection of documents, for a large document, a storage strategy that allows multiple subfragments to be mapped to contiguous sections of disk can give advantages in performance and manageability.

XQuery Client APIs

The XQuery specification defines the form that a query takes, but it doesn't define how an application program issues a query, or how it processes the results. A native XML database isn't useful unless client applications have a way of accessing the XML contents. A programmer must be able to write a program that manipulates the XML managed by the DBMS. Programmers demand access that is both easy and powerful.

The basic features of DBMS access follow:

- *Connections* provide the ability to establish a connection from a client program to the database server.
- *Transactions* provide transaction control—begin, commit, rollback, and optionally prepare for two-phase commit.
- *Command execution* allows the execution of queries, updates, and other commands in the DBMS command language, if there is such a language. Many systems also provide the ability to compile a query for repeated execution, though some may rely on stored functions for this capability.
- *Result traversal* enables traversal of collections or result sets from queries. This may include a cursoring mechanism to allow users to scroll backwards and forwards through a large result set.
- *Data extraction* provides a way to move values from DBMS managed data into programming language variables. This is often done through functions that access the query result set, but it can also be done in other ways.
- *Data insertion* provides a way to move values from the programming language variables into the DBMS managed data. This is needed partly for updates, to perform add, delete, or modify operations as driven by a programmer. It is also needed to parameterize queries and other commands, allowing values to be passed from the programming language variables into the command-execution environment.
- *Configuration object access* provides a way to define database, collection, and index objects in the database as well as a way to query this information.

These features are generally made available through an application programmer interface (API), though some operations might be done within the command language rather than through specific API functions. For example, in XStreamDB, a collection is created through the `CREATE ROOT` statement, not through a method such as `collectionManager.create-Collection("mycol")`. In fact, if the database command language is sufficiently powerful, some of the logic of the application can be located in the command language, especially if triggers and stored functions are supported. XQuery is a very powerful language for manipulating XML data, and with the probable addition of stored function libraries, update, and full-text search to XQuery, large applications will rely on XQuery, and XQuery function libraries, to perform some of their application logic.

Over the past ten years the most common and most successful relational database APIs have been Open Database Connectivity (ODBC) and Java JDBC. Both ODBC and JDBC have facilities corresponding to the above list of access features, and they work in tandem with the SQL command language. Since there is no standard XQuery API, and since the central part of the JDBC API is concerned with model-independent concepts such as `Connections`, `Statements`, `PreparedStatements` and `Result-Sets`, it makes sense for a Java-based XQuery API to be designed on similar lines. So, for example, XStreamDB borrows JDBC concepts to provide corresponding `XConnection`, `XStatement`, `XPreparedState-ment` and `XResultSet` interfaces. The method calls in `XConnection`, `XStatement` and `XPreparedStatement` are very similar to methods in JDBC `Connection`, `Statement` and `PreparedStatement`, but the `XRe-sultSet` interface is rather different, reflecting the differences in the data model. Listing 8.1 is a simple program that performs a query using this XStream DB API.

Listing 8.1   Query Using an XStream DB API: Example Query for Persons in Paris

```
import com.bluestream.xdb.*;
import com.bluestream.sys.util.FlexStringBuffer;

public class Example
{
   public static void main(String[] args)
      throws Exception
   {
      SystemManager.init();
      Server server = SystemManager.getServer("MyServer");
      try
      {
         AuthenticationInfo authInfo = new SimpleAuthInfo();
         XConnection xcon = server.getConnection(authInfo);

         xcon.beginTransaction();

         // also valid: Root('PersonDB:Person')[Person/City='Paris']
```

Listing 8.1   Query Using an XStream DB API: Example Query for Persons in Paris
(continued)

```
        String stmtStr =
           "for $doc in Root('PersonDB:Person') "+
           "where $doc/Person/City = 'Paris' "+
           "return $doc";
      // note: the Root function is a vendor addition
      // to the XQuery function library
        XStatement stmt = xcon.createStatement();
        XResultSet rs = stmt.execute(stmtStr,XStatement.SF_DEFAULT);
        FlexStringBuffer fsb = new FlexStringBuffer();

        // traverse result set
        rs.beforeFirst();
        while(rs.nextValue())
        {
           rs.fsbGet(fsb, false);
           System.out.println(fsb.toString());
        }
        xcon.commitTransaction();
    }
    finally
    {
        SystemManager.shutdown();
    }
  }
}
```

The XStreamDB `XResultSet` object allows you to iterate over the items in the sequence returned by an XQuery expression. This iteration is done using the `nextValue()` method. So far this is similar to JDBC, except that JDBC allows you to iterate over a row of column values using `next()`. Since a value returned from `XResultSet` can be either a document, a fragment, or some other data model value, a different approach is required to extract parts of that XML value into programming language variables. In place of the `get{Type}` kind of calls in JDBC, such as `getBigDecimal(String columnName)`, `XResultSet` has `getBigDecimal(String path)` which extracts one or several subvalues using the path parameter to drill into the current result set value. This is useful if you want to return a tree of values in one logical result set value. For example, `getString("/Person/City/text()")` would select the `City` value out of a current result set value of `<Person><City>Paris</City></Person>`.

Other ways of getting values from a result set are discussed below under the heading "Getting the Data." Before discussing this more, let's put the XStreamDB API into perspective by introducing another API. The XStreamDB API described above is essentially a traditional API, in the sense that it follows in the tradition of JDBC and ODBC, and it offloads some of its operations onto the XQuery command language.

Another popular API for an XML database is that defined by the xmldb.org group (http://www.xmldb.org/xapi/xapi-draft.html). This has many similarities, though it provides a larger number of method calls and relies less on having a rich command language (in fact, at the time of this writing, it only supports XPath and not XQuery). This API is supported by both the Tamino DBMS, (though not as its primary API) and by the open-source product XIndice. In the xmldb.org API, data is organized into collections composed of resources. Resources may be either XML or binary resources. Listing 8.2 is an example xmldb program that is a modified version of one from the xmldb.org website.

Listing 8.2   Sample xmldb Program

```
package examples;

import org.xmldb.api.base.*;
import org.xmldb.api.modules.*;
import org.xmldb.api.*;

/**
 * Simple XML:DB API example to query the database.
 */
public class Example1
{
    public static void main(String[] args) throws Exception
    {
        Collection col = null;
        try
        {
            String driver = "org.vendorx.xmldb.DatabaseImpl";
            Class c = Class.forName(driver);

            Database database = (Database) c.newInstance();
            DatabaseManager.registerDatabase(database);
            col = DatabaseManager.getCollection(
                    "xmldb:vendorx://sample.com:2030/Person");
            TransactionService transaction = (TransactionService)
                    col.getService("TransactionService", "1.0");
```

Listing 8.2   Sample xmldb Program *(continued)*

```
        transaction.begin();

        String xpath = "//Person[City='Paris']";
        XPathQueryService service = (XPathQueryService)
            col.getService("XPathQueryService", "1.0");
        ResourceSet resultSet = service.query(xpath);

        ResourceIterator results = resultSet.getIterator();
        while (results.hasMoreResources())
        {
            Resource res = results.nextResource();
            System.out.println((String) res.getContent());
        }
        transaction.commit();
    }
    catch (XMLDBException e)
    {
        System.err.println("XML:DB Exception occured "
            + e.errorCode);
    }
    finally
    {
        if (col != null)
        {
            col.close();
        }
    }
    }
}
```

Here is a comparison of the XStreamDB and xmldb API:

- Both of the examples above contain roughly thirty lines of executable code.

- Although the xmldb API uses an `XPathQueryService`, an `XQueryService` could easily be added.

- Both the XStreamDB API and xmldb.org API expose a set of objects concerned not with the application domain but with the DBMS domain. For example, XStreamDB uses `XConnection`, `XStatement` and `XResultSet`, while xmldb.org uses `DatabaseManager`, `Collection`, `XPathQueryService`, `ResourceSet`, and `Resource`. In contrast, application domain objects might be `Invoice` or `Customer`.

- The xmldb.org API typically uses more objects to perform an operation and is more "object-oriented" in that way. For example, the xmldb API has an object for collection, whereas the XStreamDB API uses collection names right in the XQuery command language. In addition, XStreamDB uses XQuery command-language extensions to INSERT, REPLACE, and DELETE documents, whereas the xmldb.org API performs these operations without using a command language.

- The xmldb.org API is in some ways more conducive to exposing objects to the Internet using a standard mechanism such as WebDAV (Web-based Distributed Authoring and Versioning (http://www.webdav.org), since WebDAV is concerned with collections, possibly nested collections, and resources within those connections, which are constructs similar to those in the xmldb.org API. Making database resources accessible on the Web through HTTP and URI identity is an important option. In fact XStreamDB had to add an additional resource API for this purpose.

- Since the xmldb.org API exposes XML resources as nodes, this resource type is not inclusive with respect to the XQuery data model. Even if the xmldb API did expose other resources to represent other valid XQuery data model instances, it would lead to lots of resource types, and having a resource object for a hundred thousand string data instances could present object-creation performance problems.

- In general, middleware objects such as Connection and Statement are not that interesting to an application. Both the XStreamDB and xmldb.org APIs fail on this level, as did relational APIs. In an object-oriented programming environment, it would be better if the database could return Invoices or Purchase Orders, not resources or string buffers (the difference between the application view of the world and the middleware view is often referred to as the impedance mismatch between database systems and object-oriented programming languages). In a native XML database, as defined at the beginning of this chapter, the defining characteristic of the API should be the pervasive use of the XML data model. This is discussed further below.

Getting the Data

Several mechanisms exist for bringing an XML value into object-oriented programming language variables. Among them are the following:

- *Path extraction*: Use a path to extract atomic data values from the XML into programming language variables.

- *Emit as events*: Emit an XML value as an event stream to an event handler. The event protocol can be the Standard API for XML (SAX) event stream or some other similar event stream.

- *Build a DOM*: Put the returned XML into a Document Object Model (DOM) tree where it can be further manipulated by the programming language.

- *Data binding*: Load the XML into an application domain object such as an `Invoice` object.

Another approach is to avoid handling the result data in the application at all. Sometimes, especially when retrieving whole documents, the only thing the application needs to do with the data is to present it to the user, often via a browser. Such applications are often invoked as servlets running within a web server. A convenient approach in such cases is for the application to pass the query results straight to an XSLT stylesheet (which might be processed either on the server or in the browser) that transforms the results to HTML for display. In this scenario, there is no need to map the query results to the data structures available in the application programming language. The fact that XSLT and XQuery share the same data model makes this a particularly attractive option.

The problem of moving data from a DBMS to a program has been termed an *impedance mismatch* problem. This impedance mismatch occurs between application domain objects, such as an Invoice or Purchase Order, and the XML data values stored in the DBMS. In object-oriented DBMSs this problem was solved by having the database API return application domain objects such as Invoices and by having programming language objects map directly into DBMS managed data using DBMS data identifiers. This close relationship between the programming language and the database was usually called the *binding of the language* to the database, and object databases were the king of this close binding [ODMG].

Binding XML data into object-oriented programming languages can be accomplished, however, by generating objects that can load themselves from XML data and save themselves back as XML data. For instance, Java has a framework called Java Architecture for XML Binding (JAXB) that defines how application domain objects can be generated automatically from XML schemas. These generated objects have no application-oriented methods, but they serve well as pure data objects with load and save capability. Other behavior-rich objects that wrap these generated objects can be used to add the required methods.

Although solving the impedance mismatch problem may seem important to some developers working with data-centric XML, the problem may be entirely unimportant to other developers working with document-centric information. For example, it may not be particularly useful to model text content, such as the content of this book, as an object at all. Indeed, some applications that deal with data-centric content, such as invoices, may only be acting as a repository for those documents and may not need to represent these documents as objects. (While native XML databases can handle both data-centric and document-centric information, as well as the important middle ground called semi-structured information, they face more competition in the area of data-centric applications. This means that in practice, the purely data-centric scenario is less common.) Many applications simply need to extract XML from the database and transform it into other XML grammars for display: such as DocBook to XHTML or GML to SVG. Or perhaps you want to go from DocBook to XSL formatting objects to PDF. None of these scenarios require the XML content to be represented as an object in an object-oriented language; rather, they suggest a need for close integration between a native XML database and an XSLT processor.

Full-Text Search in a Native XML Database

Native XML databases need to handle any kind of XML document, from very rigidly structured, data-centric documents at one end of the spectrum, to very loosely structured, document-centric information at the other end, as well as the semi-structured information that combines both. The less predictable the structure of the data, the more users will rely on the textual content, rather than the structure, to find the information they need. As well as the structured FLWOR and path expressions of XQuery 1.0, therefore, a native XML database needs to provide facilities for text search.

Full-text search is a sophisticated DBMS feature, not a simple bolt-on. Although a task force in the XQuery working group is exploring full-text search features, vendors, as a stopgap, have used their own specifications or borrowed from a past specification such as that in the SQL multimedia specification [SQLMULTI]. In XStreamDB we chose a set of requirements that met a number of simple use cases.

Two techniques have been proposed for adding full-text search to XQuery. One approach is to extend the grammar of the language; the other is to add a function library, perhaps including functions that support a sublanguage oriented to text matching.

In XStreamDB we decided on an approach that embedded match and **rank** expressions directly into the XQuery grammar. We did so to allow other XQuery expressions to be used with our full-text expressions in a freely composable fashion. As a way of illustrating these full-text expressions, consider the following example:

```
Find all books with the word "Linux" in the title
and return those titles.
```

This is a very simple example. In practice, full-text search does not simply look for character strings. It has to break the text intelligently into words, in a way that depends on the natural language in which the text is written. It generally has mechanisms for working out which words are equivalent, either because they are lexical variants (such as plurals) or semantic variants (synonyms). It usually uses algorithms for ranking the significance of a word within the text, based on its frequency of occurrence and on where it appears. The result need not be a Boolean true/false answer; it can be a ranking of how good the match is between the document and the query. The query typically returns the most highly ranked documents, up to some threshold.

The following expression, a word search using a full-text extension, is very similar to standard usage:

```
for $doc in Root("BooksDB:Books")
where match $doc using [/book/title contains "Linux"]
return $doc/book/title
```

Note that the match expression is just a Boolean XQuery expression, and the `for` and `return` clauses are essentially standard XQuery. Adding these additional full-text expression types was natural since XQuery is a functional language composed of nestable expressions. A detailed analysis of the examples above is as follows. The `for` clause introduces a set of bindings for `$doc`; these evaluate according to the `where` clause, which, depending on the data in `$doc`, would reduce the set of `$doc` tuples processed by the `return` clause. The `return` clause evaluates each of the remaining `$doc` bindings to result in a sequence of `title` elements. The only non-XQuery part is the `match` expression. This `match` expression in the `where` clause evaluates to a Boolean for each binding of `$doc`. The `match` applies the predicate in the `using` clause against the `$doc` context to render a Boolean true/false value. The `match` can be read as follows: Match to true in the case where the `$doc` binding has a `/book/title` which contains the word "Linux." The first step in doing this kind of XQuery extension is to use understandable semantics; next in importance is the need to be able to optimize the expression using a full-text index.

Figure 8.3 shows a query-execution plan used to execute the above query at query-execution time. A query-execution plan is a data structure that is traversed and interpreted by a query processor. The plan below is the one that results when no full-text index is present, so no index optimization is possible. In this case, the entire collection of documents is traversed, the words in the `/book/title` path within `$doc` are tokenized, and this set of words is evaluated as to whether it contains the word "Linux." The rectangles in the figure are objects that implement the `next()` and `eval()` methods. The single arrows are invocations of `next()` or `eval()`. The double arrows show the flow of XML through the plan.

To get an idea of the work undertaken by the query processor, consider the steps required to find and return one book title:

1. The user calls `next()` on the `Result Set`.
2. The result set calls `next()` on its child `FLWR` object.

3. The `FLWR` object calls `next()` on the `Root Collection`.

4. `next()` on the `Root Collection` causes an XML document to be referenced by `$d`. `Root Collection` and then returns to `FLWR`.

5. `FLWR` now calls `eval()` on `WHERE`, and `WHERE` calls `eval()` on `CONTAINS`.

6. `CONTAINS` calls `eval()` on `/book/title`, which takes the text in the `/book/title` element and tokenizes it. `CONTAINS` then checks to see if this text contains the word "Linux."

7. If `CONTAINS` returns `true` then the `FLWR` object calls `next()` on the `Filter /book/title`.

8. The filter projects the title out of `$d` and sends that XML to the result set. We now have the first result set return value.

Evaluating this query for a collection of a hundred thousand documents would be time-consuming. Fortunately, the presence of a full-text index optimizes the query. With a full-text index the query plan looks quite different, as shown in Figure 8.4.

The main advantage of the plan in Figure 8.4 is that traversal of the collection and the repeated comparisons are replaced with use of the full-text index. In the optimized plan, the only work that is done, after the

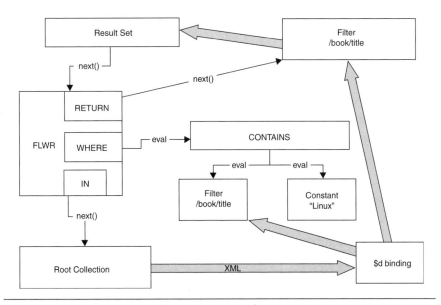

Figure 8.3   A Non-Optimized Query-Execution Plan

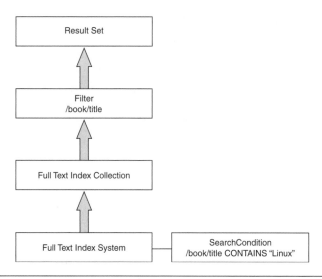

Figure 8.4   An Optimized Query-Execution Plan

full-text index is used, is to project the results using /book/title with the filter node above. Depending on the storage plan, this projection could be optimized as well. Since the full-text index only selects those documents matching /book/title CONTAINS "Linux", this query can be very fast when run on a hundred thousand documents, assuming that only a small percentage of the titles contain the word "Linux." The above match optimization is fairly standard for most types of where-clause optimization in a query, with most of the work being pushed onto the index—in this case a full-text index.

Optimization with document ranking, however is more complicated and is not covered here in any detail. In fact, supporting ranking as an extension to XQuery is more difficult than doing a match. To perform a ranking means to do a match as above, but to return a value as to how relevant the document is with respect to other documents according to the predicates applied against it. For example, the rank expression below returns a value between 0 and 1 inclusive that scores the individual document with respect to how much it has to do with the term "Linux" as compared to all other documents in the collection. A simple ranking algorithm would count "Linux" words contained within a certain document and give those documents with high counts a higher rank. A slightly more sophisticated algorithm takes into consideration how common the term is. A common scoring algorithm developed by Gerard Salton follows:

```
W(d,t) = TF(d,t) * IDF(t)
```

In English, the weight or score of a document for a given term *t* is equal to the term frequency within the current document *d*, times the inverse of the term frequency across all documents in the collection. This is a simple algorithm, but vendors use their own algorithms to improve the precision of their ranking algorithms. (An important consequence of this is that two full-text systems will give different answers to the same query.)

Below is the ranking query used in XStreamDB, which asks for a rank-ordered list of titles from the Books collection which contain the word "Linux":

```
for $doc in Root("BooksDB:Books")
let $rank := rank $doc using [//* contains "Linux"]
where $rank > 0
order by $rank
return $doc/book/title
```

The rank expression `rank $doc using [//* contains "Linux"]` returns the ranking of `$doc` on the word "Linux" relative to other documents in the same collection. Then the documents with `$rank` equal to zero (that is, those where the word does not occur) are dropped by the `where` clause, and remaining documents are ordered by `$rank`. The titles of the books are then returned. Note that the `order by` expression above orders the tuples of the FLWOR expression by `$rank`. Ranking is more complicated than a Boolean match, but it can greatly increase the effectiveness of full-text searching.

In the above extended XQuery expression, the `for`, `let`, `where`, and `order by` expressions are rewritten by the optimizer to use the full-text index. Once this essential optimization is done, the rest of the flow of the documents is similar to the optimized execution plan shown in Figure 8.4.

Obviously, full-text search requires many more features than these examples illustrate. Among the popular features are the following:

- Word proximity and phrase search. For example, "Give me all the titles with the words 'Linux' and 'Database' within five words of each other."
- prefix/suffix and partial word searching using regular expressions.

■ Stemming of words, where similar words are treated the same for comparison purposes. For example, *category* and *categories* are often treated the same if stemming is turned on.

Full-text search is a complex subject. The technology has been under development for forty years, and many books have been written on the subject. Many simple and advanced full-text features will probably find their way into XQuery in one form or another. Full-text search is very compelling for a native XML database—much more so than for a relational DBMS—because for many document-centric XML applications, the only reliable way to find the document you want is a search against the textual content.

Sample Applications

In order to put some of the previous XML DBMS features into context, let's consider two simple applications where an XML database can be used. The two applications are a *data-centric* invoice archive system and a *document-centric* content management system.

Data-centric XML is mostly concerned with data values and less concerned with sections of text written in a natural language like English. In the invoice archive example below, the invoice data is more concerned with data values such as Name, Address, Quantity, and DollarAmount. This kind of data can be summed, referenced to other data, and generally manipulated in a standard data processing fashion. Data-centric XML often represents business documents or business forms—things like invoices, mortgage applications, and purchase orders. Data-centric XML typically has a simple meaning that can be manipulated and understood by either computers or people. Generally, the information in data-centric XML is factual and precise.

Document-centric XML includes text whose meaning depends on all the subtleties of a natural language. It is thus accessible to humans but less accessible to computers because these subtleties are not easily parsed by a computer. The information in document-centric XML is not always factual and not always precise—it is often simply the opinion of the author.

In practice many applications contain a mixture of the two kinds of information. For example, the personnel records in a company contain factual information about salaries, grades, and home addresses, alongside textual information such as the records of employee appraisals. Traditionally these two kinds of information have been handled separately in different applications and different databases, but one of the reasons for the success of XML is the increasing need to handle both kinds of information in an integrated way. However, because the two kinds of information are used in different ways, we will look at two applications that are dominated by one kind or the other.

Applications that use data-centric XML tend to call upon different features of a native XML database than document-centric applications. Data-centric XML is more open to normalization and the kind of data engineering found in relational databases; XML databases therefore find it harder to compete in this territory. Users are reluctant to adopt new technology if old technology can do the job: Why not just normalize the data and store it as tables?

But there are several reasons why a native XML database can provide benefits over a normalized relational database, even for this kind of information, including the following:

- An increasing number of applications use both data-centric and document-centric information in an integrated way. It makes sense to use the same database technology for both.
- Many applications handle data that is small in quantity yet complex in structure. An example might be a web site holding the results of a sports tournament, or a schedule of training courses. The design of a normalized relational database holding this information can be a significant task, which becomes an obstacle when new web applications must be produced in two weeks from start to finish. Designing the data as an XML document structure is often far simpler and more flexible.

■ In some applications, the problem is variability of the data. For example, a telecommunications company managing records of installed equipment may have to handle thousands of different types of equipment, with slightly different data maintained for each kind. Designing a relational database for this situation is notoriously difficult, and managing the frequent changes needed by the design can be a nightmare. Such an application can be vastly simplified if each piece of equipment is recorded as one (semi-) structured XML document containing all the relevant fields.

■ Sometimes the data originates as XML outside the organization, and the recipient company may want to store the information in that same form, knowing that the details may change from time to time as the sending organization changes its business processes. The recipient organization doesn't want to change its relational database design every time the incoming document format has a new field added. Far better to store the XML in its original form. This is the rationale we use for our example of a data-centric application, an archive of incoming invoices.

Invoice Archive

Our invoice archive system uses a native XML database to archive incoming vendor invoices. Vendor invoices are complete documents that contain different values such as customer name, date, item description, item amount, and total. The diagram in Figure 8.5 shows this flow of documents. The vendor's computer sends an invoice for services rendered to the customer. This XML invoice is received by the customer's computer. The customer's computer stores the invoice in a native XML database with a status of "unqualified." Unqualified invoices are viewed by a clerk in accounting and are either rejected or qualified by the accounting department. Rejection of the invoice will trigger its own chain of events. If the accounting department qualifies the invoice, its status is set to "qualified," and the invoice in the database is updated. At this point the company's accounting system, perhaps running on another computer, is updated with the invoice number, date, and vendor payable amount. If questions arise later regarding the invoice, it can be retrieved from the invoice archive database. Finally, when the check run is done, the invoice is marked in the database as "paid."

XML DBMS Features Used

- *Storage as XML.* The incoming invoice is in XML, and it is preferable to maintain the invoice in its original form. To place the invoice in the database requires an XQuery `Insert` command.

- *Schema validation of the incoming XML.* Incoming data must be validated to ensure that it is a valid instance of the invoice schema, which has presumably been agreed upon between vendor and customer.

- *Invoice searching and sorting.* For example, we may need to display the invoice documents in date order by status, or by status alone. It might be necessary to examine all invoices from a particular vendor, or to find the invoices relating to a particular purchase order.

- *Update of the XML.* The invoice document in the XML DBMS requires updating to set the status.

- *Two-phase commit.* Used when the invoice document is updated as "qualified" in the XML DBMS, and the accounting system DBMS is updated with the payable amount.

- *Full-text.* Occasionally, a simple full-text search may be required to find an invoice with a particular word in the description.

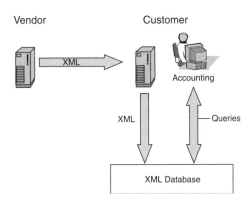

Figure 8.5   The Flow of Invoice Data

A Content Management Application

This scenario involves creating XML content using a full-featured XML editor and publishing the XML content to the web for further browsing and searching by a content reader (consumer). For the purposes of this example, imagine that you need a system for a market research company that wants to publish ten thousand documents on its web site. Consumers visit the web site and want to search on, browse for, and read content online as well as print this content. Figure 8.6 shows the flow of information between author and consumer in this scenario.

A content management scenario involves at least three main roles:

- *Author*: the person who authors the content.
- *Publisher*: the person who makes the content available to the consumer.
- *Consumer*: the person who uses the content.

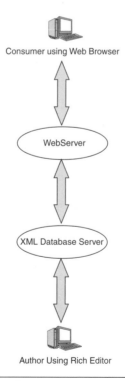

Consumer using Web Browser

WebServer

XML Database Server

Author Using Rich Editor

Figure 8.6   Content Management Flow

In addition, a designer may be required to design the graphic layout of the content, and an administrator may registers consumers as authorized users of the system. The role of author may also be specialized further; for example, there may be researchers, subeditors, and photographers.

Actual content management applications often use not one XML database, but two. One database is typically used to serve online published content, while another is used for material in the course of preparation. It is not uncommon to use a third database as a staging server.

Authors are likely to use a variety of desktop tools for the actual content preparation, using a check-in /check-out mechanism to update the database. Publishers need to manage the workflow, checking on the status of content and releasing it for publication when all the steps in the process are complete.

The web application used by the consumer is likely to support the following features:

- Full-text search on document title with ranking of results
- Full-text search on the full document
- Browsing titles of documents by category
- Option to download a printable PDF of the content

XML DBMS Technology Used

The author of the XML content

- May use a WebDAV interface to the database to enable the remote editing of documents using a rich editor
- Will want some sort of exclusive locking while multiple authors collaborate and work on documents
- Will want to query for documents using XQuery to select them for editing
- May need her own application that uses the database to categorize and organize documents if there are many documents
- May need document or partial document checkout if many authors are working on the document

- Will need a way to categorize documents for the consumer
- May need storage for large documents
- May require document versioning

The consumer of the information

- Will want to access the documents using full-text search. This access may specify different search targets in the XML document such as titles, all text, or abstracts.
- Views the content typically as HTML or PDF, after it has gone through XSL transformation.
- Will want to browse the documents by category. This might be implemented using a predefined set of XQuery stored functions.

In addition, the system is likely to need some kind of replication technology to control the migration of data between one database and another, and it may require integration with a workflow engine to manage the authoring and publication process.

These two sample applications give an idea of the range of XML applications and some of the XML DBMS features that can be brought into play when building such an application. For an application builder who needs to write one of the above applications, well-placed features in a native XML DBMS will greatly ease the task.

Conclusion

The fundamental characteristic of a native XML database is its pervasive use of the XML data model not only at the query language interface to the system, but in all its other interfaces as well. We have reviewed some of these interfaces and seen how XQuery represents only a small part of the facilities that a real system needs to offer.

Because XML is being stored and manipulated in databases, a new set of database features attuned to XML is expected in a native XML DBMS. This is partly because the data is semi-structured—as well as structured data, it may contain loosely structured document-centric information that requires special features not found in relational or object databases.

Even data-centric XML, containing information such as invoices and purchase orders, is very different from relational data because of the tree-based XML data model.

With data definition, update capability, and full-text search added to XQuery, along with other XML technologies integrated into a native XML database, such a DBMS becomes a natural choice for managing XML data, since it can so easily work with XML data. Such systems will initially be used in areas where relational databases are weak, that is, where the data structures are at the same time complex, variable, and flexible. In time, with a flexible data model like XML and a powerful language like XQuery coupled with other capabilities such as searching technologies, native XML database management systems may become useful in areas that are currently the exclusive preserve of the relational database.

REFERENCES

[ALGORITHMS]. Alfred Aho, John Hopcroft, Jeffrey Ullman. *The Design and Analysis of Computer Algorithms.* Addison-Wesley, 1974.

[CODD]. E. F. Codd. "Relational Completeness of Database Sublanguages." In *Data Base Systems, Courant Computer Science Symposia Series 6.* Prentice-Hall, 1972.

[DC]. Website for the Dublin Core: `http://dublincore.org/`.

[DDJ]. Philip Wadler. "New Language, Old Logic." *Dr. Dobb's Journal.* December, 2000.

[EFFICIENT]. Jayavel Shanmugasundaram, Eugene Shekita, Rimon Barr, Michael Carey, Bruce Lindsay, Hamid Pirahesh, and Berthold Reinwald. "Efficiently Publishing Relational Data as XML Documents." *VLDB Journal* 10, nos. 2–3 (2001): 133–54. See `http://citeseer.nj.nec.com/shanmugasundaram00efficiently.html`.

[ESSENCE]. Jérôme Siméon and Philip Wadler. "The Essence of XML." In *Proceedings of the Thirtieth Annual ACM SIGPLAN-SIGACT Symposium on Principles of Programming Languages.* Association for Computing Machinery, January, 2003.

[EXEMPLARS]. Mary Fernández, Jérôme Siméon, and Philip Wadler, eds. "XML Query Languages: Experiences and Exemplars." Draft manuscript, September 1999.

[FORMULA-LANG]. Gottlob Frege. "Begriffsschrift, a Formula Language, Modeled upon That of Arithmetic for Pure Thought." In *From Frege to Godel: A Source Book in Mathematical Logic, 1879— 1931*, ed. Jan van Heijenoort. Harvard University Press, 1967. Originally published in 1879.

[FS-PROG]. Glynn Winskel. *The Formal Semantics of Programming Languages*. MIT Press, 1993.

[FUNC-LANG]. Simon Peyton Jones and David Lester. *Implementing Functional Languages*. Prentice Hall, 1992.

[GALAX]. Galax: An Implementation of XQuery. See `http://db.bell-labs.com/galax`.

[INFOSET]. *XML Information Set*. W3C Recommendation, 24 October 2001. See `http://www.w3.org/TR/xml-infoset`.

[NAMESP]. *Namespaces in XML*. W3C Recommendation, 14 January 1999. See `http://www.w3.org/TR/REC-xml-names`.

[OODB]. Francois Bancilhon, Claude Delobel, and Paris Kanellakis, eds. *Building an Object-Oriented Database System: The Story of O2*. Morgan Kaufmann Publishers, 1992.

[ODMG]. Rick Catell, Douglas Barry, and Dirk Bartels. *The Object Database Standard: ODMG 3.0*. Morgan Kaufmann Publishers, 2000.

[OQL]. T. Atwood, D. Barry, J. Duhl, J. Eastman, G. Ferran, D. Jordan, M. Loomis, and D. Wade. *The Object Database Standard: ODMG-93, Release 1.2*. Ed. R. G. C. Catell. Morgan Kaufmann Publishers, 1996.

[PROG-FOUNDATIONS]. John C. Mitchell. *Foundations of Programming Languages*. MIT Press, 1996.

[PROG-LANG]. Benjamin C. Pierce. *Types and Programming Languages*. MIT Press, 2002.

[QL98]. QL'98: The W3C Query Languages Workshop. See `http://www.w3.org/TandS/QL/QL98`.

[QUILT]. Don Chamberlin, Jonathan Robie, and Daniela Florescu. "Quilt: An XML Query Language for Heterogeneous Data Sources." In *The World Wide Web and Databases*, ed. D. Suciu. Springer-Verlag, 2001. `http://www.almaden.ibm.com/cs/people/chamberlin/quilt.html`.

[RELAXNG]. *RELAX-NG Specification.* OASIS Committee Specification, 3 December 2001. See `http://www.oasis-open.org/ committees/relax-ng/spec-20011203.html`.

[RYS2001]. Michael Rys. "Bringing the Internet to Your Database: Using SQL Server 2000 and XML to Build Loosely Coupled Systems." In *Proceedings of the Seventeenth International Conference on Data Engineering (ICDE)*. IEEE Computer Society, 2001.

[SCHEMA]. *XML Schema, Parts 0, 1, and 2.* W3C Recommendation, 2 May 2001. See `http://www.w3.org/TR/xmlschema-0`, `http://www.w3.org/TR/xmlschema-1`, and `http://www.w3.org/TR/xmlschema-2`.

[SEMANTICS]. Gilles Kahn. "Natural Semantics." In *Proceedings of the Symposium on Theoretical Aspects of Computer Science*. Lecture Notes in Computer Science, vol. 247. Springer-Verlag, 1987.

[SERIAL]. *XSLT 2.0 and XQuery 1.0 Serialization.* W3C Working Draft, 2 May 2003. See `http://http://www.w3.org/TR/xslt-xquery-serialization/`.

[SQL2003]. International Organization for Standardization (ISO). *Information Technology—Database Languages—SQL*. Standard No. ISO/IEC 9075:2003. Ed. Jim Melton. Forthcoming. (ISO publications are available from American National Standards Institute, New York, NY 10036, (212) 642-4900.)

[SQL92]. Jim Melton and Alan R. Simon. *Understanding the New SQL: A Complete Guide*. Morgan Kaufmann Publishers, 1993.

[SQL99]. International Organization for Standardization (ISO). *Information Technology—Database Language—SQL.* Standard No. ISO/IEC 9075:1999. Ed. Jim Melton et al.

[SQLMULTI]. International Organization for Standardization (ISO). *Information Technology—Database languages—SQL—Multimedia and Application Packages—Part 2: Full-Text.* Standard No. ISO/IEC 13249-2:2000, 2000.

[SQLXML]. International Organization for Standardization (ISO). *Information Technology—Database Languages—SQL—Part 14: XML-Related Specifications (SQL/XML).* Standard No. ISO/IEC 9075-14, 2003. Ed. Jim Melton. Forthcoming.

[SQLXML-MS]. Microsoft. *SQLXML and XML Mapping Technologies.* See `http://msdn.microsoft.com/library/default.asp?url=/nhp/default.asp?contentid=28001300`.

[STANDARD-ML]. Robin Milner, Mads Tofte, Robert Harper, and David MacQueen. *The Definition of Standard ML (Revised).* MIT Press, 1997.

[STRUCTURAL]. Gordon Plotkin. *A Structural Approach to Operational Semantics.* Report DAIMI FN-19, Computer Science Department, Aarhus University, Aarhus, Denmark.

[TAMINO]. Tamino XML Server. See `http://www.softwareag.com/tamino/`.

[W3C]. World Wide Web Consortium (W3C). See `http://www.w3.org`.

[THEORIES]. John C. Reynolds. *Theories of Programming Languages.* Cambridge University Press, 1998.

[XML]. *Extensible Markup Language (XML) 1.0 (Second Edition).* W3C Recommendation, 6 October 2000. See `http://www.w3.org/TR/REC-xml`.

[XML-QL]. Alin Deutsch, Mary Fernández, Daniela Florescu, Alon Levy, and Dan Suciu. *A Query Language for XML.* See `http://www.research.att.com/~mff/files/final.html`.

[XPATH1]. *XML Path Language (XPath) Version 1.0.* W3C Recommendation, 16 November 1999. See `http://www.w3.org/ TR/xpath`.

[XPATH2]. *XML Path Language (XPath) 2.0.* W3C Working Draft, 2 May 2003. See `http://www.w3.org/TR/xpath20`.

[XPATH2REQ]. *XPath Requirements, Version 2.0.* W3C Working Draft, 14 February 2001. See `http://www.w3.org/TR/xpath20req`.

[XPTR]. *XML Pointer Language (XPointer).* W3C Working Draft, 16 August 2002. See `http://www.w3.org/TR/xptr`.

[XQ-DM]. *XQuery 1.0 and XPath 2.0 Data Model.* W3C Working Draft, 2 May 2003. See `http://www.w3.org/TR/query-datamodel/`.

[XQ-FO]. *XQuery 1.0 and XPath 2.0 Functions and Operators.* W3C Working Draft, 2 May 2003. See `http://www.w3.org/TR/xquery-operators`.

[XQ-FS]. *XQuery 1.0 Formal Semantics.* W3C Working Draft, 2 May 2003. See `http://www.w3.org/TR/query-semantics/`.

[XQ-FULL-REQ]. *XQuery and XPath Full-Text Requirements.* W3C Working Draft, 2 May 2003. See `http://www.w3.org/ TR/xquery-full-text-requirements/`.

[XQ-LANG]. *XQuery 1.0: An XML Query Language.* W3C Working Draft, 2 May 2003. See `http://www.w3.org/TR/xquery`.

[XQ-REQ]. *XML Query Requirements.* W3C Working Draft, 15 February 2001. See `http://www.w3.org/TR/xmlquery-req`.

[XQ-UC]. *XML Query Use Cases.* W3C Working Draft, 2 May 2003. See `http://www.w3.org/TR/xmlquery-use-cases`.

[XQ-WG]. W3C XML Query Working Group. See `http://www.w3.org/XML/Query`.

[XQ-X]. *XML Syntax for XQuery 1.0 (XQueryX)*. W3C Working Draft, 7 June 2001. See `http://www.w3.org/TR/xqueryx`.

[XSLT]. *XSL Transformations (XSLT) Version 1.0.* W3C Recommendation, 16 November 1999. See `http://www.w3.org/ TR/xslt`.

[XUPDATE]. Andreas Laux and Lars Martin. *XUpdate Working Draft— 2000-09-14*. See `http://www.xmldb.org/xupdate`.

GLOSSARY

abstract syntax. A term for the grammatical description of a language in which precedence relationships between the productions are ignored for the sake of simplicity. Such a description has fewer constraints than those specified by a concrete syntax.

anonymous type. An unnamed type in XML Schema. The scope of the type is limited to the element or attribute within which it is defined. This is convenient for "one-off," in-place type definitions that don't need to be reused.

atomic type. An XML Schema simple type that is not a list type or a union type.

atomic value. The value of an item in the value space of an atomic type.

atomization. A type-conversion process used to convert certain types of expressions to a sequence of atomic values. The main use is to extract atomic values from a node sequence, as in the application of an arithmetic function such as `avg()` or `max()` to an XPath expression yielding nodes. A type error is raised if the attempted conversion is illegal.

attribute. One of two basic mechanisms in XML for partitioning data, the other being the element. The question of which should be used when is under debate. The common wisdom is that elements are used to encapsulate basic information; attributes are used to encapsulate "metadata" about that information.

Basic XQuery. A description of the "core level" features and behavior expected of a conforming XQuery implementation. The optional "Schema Import Feature" and "Static Typing Feature" modify the items in this Basic XQuery description. For example, the use of a `SchemaImport` statement in basic XQuery raises a static error. Specifying that the XQuery processor implements a "Schema Import Feature" removes that limitation (among others).

BLOB. In SQL, a binary large object.

canonicalized XML. XML that has been canonicalized; that is, transformed into a standardized form on application of an agreed-upon set of rules that preserve an equivalence to the original document.

case-sensitive. The property of a language specifying whether the distinction between upper- and lowercase characters is significant. XQuery is a case-sensitive language. All keywords use lowercase characters.

CLOB. In SQL, a character large object.

closure. A desirable property of XQuery; under closure, all expressions in the language return values that conform to those specified in the Query data model.

collection. A sequence of nodes identified by a URI.

collation. A language identifier and its set of character-mapping descriptions, used to determine comparison and sorting order.

Common Language Run-time. A portable language run-time for a variety of Microsoft language environments such as Visual Basic, C#, J#, and C++.

complex type. In XML Schema, an element type that may contain subelements and/or attributes (as opposed to a simple type).

composition technique. As described in Chapter 6, an explicit or implicit mechanism used to determine the appearance of the XML for a set of relational tables.

compositionality. A basic principle of functional languages such as XQuery, in which the output of any expression can be plugged into the input of any other with complete generality (with some possible semantic restrictions).

conclusion. The "below the line" judgment in a formal semantics inference rule. When all the "above the line" judgments, or hypotheses, are true, then the conclusion is true by definition.

concrete syntax. The grammatical description of a language that includes precedence and parentheses. The opposite of abstract syntax.

consolidation. As described in Chapter 6, the process of reusing the same relational table during shredding to store data that occurs in multiple places.

constructor. An XQuery mechanism for creating and returning new XML structures from within a query.

context item. The item currently being processed during evaluation of the expression E1/E2 or E1[E2]. During the processing of E1/E2, for example, E1 is first evaluated to a node sequence. Each node in turn is then set as the context item, and E2 is evaluated in respect to that context item.

data model. For XML in general, this refers to the data model described by the XML Infoset [INFOSET], an abstract specification of the legal contents of an XML document. In this book this more often refers to the XQuery data model, an abstraction of the Infoset (see *Query data model*).

data-oriented (or data-centric) XML. The set of XML vocabularies that represents data that is more tightly structured than in document-oriented (or document-centric) XML, such as an invoice, purchase order, or some other type of business data.

default mapping. As described in Chapter 6, one of three composition techniques. The database is composed to XML based on a fixed mapping between column names and a final XML structure. The user has little or no control over the generated XML.

dependent join. A join algorithm, as described in Chapter 6, in which tuples from one source are scanned, and for each tuple, another source is scanned to retrieve matching tuples.

derivation by extension. In XML Schema, the mechanism of defining new types in terms of an existing base type, in which additional elements or attribute content are added to the base type.

derivation by restriction. In XML Schema, the mechanism of defining new types in terms of an existing base type, in which the original value range is narrowed or further restricted.

derived type. In XML Schema, the definition of a new type in terms of an existing datatype.

document order. The order in which nodes are encountered as an XML file is read, either by a human visually or by an XML parser programatically.

Document Type Definition (DTD). The syntactic unit in the original XML Recommendation for specifying constraints on the names and numbers of elements and attributes allowed in a document. A fairly primitive but simple mechanism, it has been supplanted, where the need for greater specificity exists, by more complex mechanisms such as XML Schema and RELAX-NG.

document-oriented (or document-centric) XML. The set of XML vocabularies that are used when authoring loosely structured natural language documents. DocBook is an example of one such vocabulary.

Document Object Model (DOM). A W3C-specified API for traversing XML documents.

dynamic error. Dynamic errors occur during evaluation of a query when an error other than a static error is encountered. This causes implicit invocation of the `fn:error()` function, which can also be invoked explicitly in a query if desired.

dynamic semantics. Specifies precisely the relationship between input data, an XQuery expression, and output data. Generally contrasted with static semantics. See also *type soundness theorem*.

dynamic type. The type of an operand that is determined at run-time. This is the most specific type that can be determined for the value under consideration. The static type of the operand, on the other hand, is a compile-time property of an expression.

edge table. A construct that represents the structure of a tree or graph in tabular form, in which each row identifies the properties of an edge, such as its name and the source and target vertices. The construct can be used to represent parent-child connections in an XML tree in a tabular, relational format. When representing trees, the edge table is isomorphic to the node table. See *node table*.

Effective Boolean Value (EBV). The result of the process during evaluation of a sequence of items that first reduces the sequence to a single Boolean value. This is required in the evaluation of certain XQuery constructs, such as logical operations and conditionals. The XQuery 1.0 document specifies how EBVs are to be calculated, depending on the expression type. For example, before the logical expression `sequenceA and sequenceB` can be evaluated, each operand needs to be replaced by its equivalent EBV. If either sequence is empty, its EBV is `false`. If either sequence is a single Boolean `false`, its EBV is `false`, and so forth.

element. One of seven node types in the data model, and generally the most important for containing information. Elements can optionally contain attributes, other elements, and text.

element constructor. An XQuery syntactic structure that allows the creation of new XML element nodes directly in a query. The created elements may be specified either as literal "angle bracket" XML, or they may be computed dynamically.

element declaration. The formal declaration of an element's allowable contents (or alternatively, its type), either through a DTD or XML Schema declaration.

encoding. The physical mapping between the representation of characters in an XML document and their underlying Unicode basis.

end tag. The angle-bracket representation in serialized XML that marks the end boundary of an element. In the element, for example, `<elemName>contents</elemName>`, `</elemName>` is the end tag.

environment. Very generally, a mapping from symbols to values, the symbols and values depending on the context in which the environment is used. During static analysis, for example (see the *formal semantics*), an "element name" symbol is mapped to its type definition, and a variable's name is mapped to its type. Dynamic evaluation uses the static environments, as well as mappings from a variable's name to its value, and so forth. Sometimes referred to as a "dictionary" or "context."

evaluation judgment. A statement in the inference language of the formal semantics which states that the evaluation of an expression yields a specified value.

existential quantification. An operation in which certain XQuery evaluations automatically (or implicitly) iterate over a sequence of items in order to evaluate an expression. For example, during evaluation of the path expression, `//book[author = "Mark Twain"]`, a number of author nodes may be present for each book node. Existential quantification occurs during evaluation of each such author sequence, in which the `=` operation will be determined as `true` if *any* of the author nodes have the content `"Mark Twain"`.

Extensible Markup Language (XML). Refers to both the precise syntactic definition of a markup language in which "tags" delimited by angle brackets impose a treelike structure on a document (see [XML]), and an alternative specification (see [INFOSET]) that describes the same structures much more abstractly.

facet. A type of attribute in XML Schema nomenclature that acts to characterize or constrain the properties of a datatype. For example, `minOccurs` and `maxOccurs` facets can be used to constrain repetitions, and a combination of the two can represent the full usage of the occurrence indicators, `*`, `+`, and `?` in DTDs.

factored type. A union of item types and an occurrence indicator. For example, the factored type (element (plumber) | element (surgeon))* denotes zero-or-more `plumber` or `surgeon` elements. Factored types make it easier for the XQuery type system to assign types to any expression that iterates over a sequence or that changes the order of a sequence (e.g., the `for`, `some`, `every` expressions and the function `fn:distinct-nodes()`). Any XQuery type can be re-expressed as a factored type.

FLWOR expression. A powerful and useful XQuery construct that allows both iterative and groupwise processing of sequences. It stands for `for`, `let`, `where`, `order by`, and `return`, which are the various clauses it contains, some optionally.

foreign key. In relational database parlance, a column that represents, after normalization, data whose primary key is found in another table. For example, a university `Class` table might contain a foreign key column containing student IDs. These IDs in turn correspond to the primary student ID key in a separate `Students` table.

formal semantics. The formal mathematical foundations that describe the operations and behavior of XQuery precisely, as described and defined in [XQ-FS].

function overloading. The ability of a language processor (including XQuery) to support multiple functions having the same name but different signatures. The processor determines through function resolution which function to call, depending on the number and types of parameters passed.

function resolution. The process of choosing the best function for a given function call, based on a static analysis of its argument types.

function signature. The combination of function parameters and their types that is unique to each function, even those having the same name (see *function overloading*).

functional language. Somewhat of a misnomer, this has nothing to do with the definition of *function* in standard usage. It refers rather to a language that is primarily expression-based. Expressions can be freely composed together, the output resulting from evaluation of one expression becoming input to another. "Pure" functional languages typically do not have side effects, and every expression/operator can therefore be expressed as a function. XQuery is an "impure" functional language because it does have the side effect of creating new nodes with distinct identity.

general comparison operators. The six XQuery operators =, !=, >, >=, <, and <=. These act on sequences and perform existential quantification on their operands. For example, the comparison `sequenceA > sequenceB` returns `true` if any single item in `sequenceA` is greater than any single item in `sequenceB`.

global element declarations. A form of declaration of an element type in both XML Schema and the XQuery type system in which the element is declared globally, not by reference to a local type declaration, so that the element is globally accessible within the schema and within any schema that imports the schema containing the declaration.

grouping. The process of forming various data into groups, often applying aggregation functions such as `count()` and `avg()` to the assembly. FLWOR expressions are commonly used for this purpose, along with element constructors to wrap the resulting grouped data.

hierarchical join. A query or mapping construct that creates hierarchical data from relational data by nesting matching records within a containing record.

hypotheses. The "above the line" judgments in a formal semantics inference rule. When these are all true, then the conclusion (the "below the line" judgment) is true by definition.

identity. Two nodes have the same identity only if they are exactly the same node.

indexing. The process of adding secondary, "behind the scenes" information on where data is located, so that it can be efficiently found and retrieved at query time.

information item. The Query data model builds on the definitions of the XML Information Set [INFOSET]. Information items are basic constituent units of the latter. For example, each element in a document is defined by an element information item, which in turn is defined by optional child information items and attribute information items, and so on.

Information Set (Infoset). An abstract definition of the constituent pieces of a well-formed XML document (see [INFOSET]), as opposed to the syntactic, angle-bracket definition in the original W3C Recommendation, *Extensible Markup Language (XML)* [XML].

inheritance. In XML Schema, two mechanisms for defining new types in terms of existing types, called derivation by extension and derivation by restriction.

inlining. As described in Chapter 6, a process in which children are placed into the same table as their parent during the process of decomposing (shredding) XML into relational tables.

inner join. The selection of nodes from different documents (more correctly, different sequences of items) in which items are returned only if both sequences contribute a data point.

item. The formal term for the individual members of a sequence in the Query data model, each of which is either a node or an atomic value.

item type. The type of an item in the XQuery data model: either an atomic type, an element type, a comment node type, or a processing instruction type.

Java Virtual Machine. A portable language runtime for the Java language.

join. A concept borrowed from SQL, in which a FLWOR expression is used to combine information, most typically from two different documents. More formally, a join consists of selecting specific portions of the Cartesian cross-product of two or more sequences.

keyword. Fixed terms specific to the XQuery language, such as `if`, `and`, `for`, `where`, and the like. These terms are not reserved, in the sense that elements and attributes, for example, can also use the same names. A query processor is able to distinguish between these usages by context through the structuring of the formal grammar.

lax. One of three validation modes for checking an element against its XML Schema declaration. If a schema declaration is present, `lax` validation is the same as `strict`. If no declaration is present, `lax` acts as `skip` validation does.

list type. One of the three XML Schema datatypes collectively called *simple types*. A list type is a sequence of atomic types.

LOB. In SQL, an acronym for large object. LOBs are more specifically either character LOBs (CLOBs) or binary LOBs (BLOBs).

local element declaration. A form of declaration of an element type in both XML Schema and the XQuery type system in which the element is declared locally, and not by reference to a global type declaration.

markup data. A reference in Chapter 7 to data that is characterized by free-flowing text, with interspersed markup used to call out document structure and highlight important aspects of the text. Also known as loosely structured data; most document-centric usage scenarios refer to instances of this type of data.

matching judgment. A statement in the inference language of the formal semantics that specifies the type of a particular value.

metadata. Information about information, the form of which depends on the context. In a relational database, for example, metadata represents information on column names and types in the form of a catalog or schema. This is opposed to the tabular content itself. In XML, metadata is the structural information imparted by the markup itself, again as opposed to its content. In a slightly different usage, it refers to additional descriptive information about content that is often placed in attributes. In the following example,

```
<lengthOfBody units="feet">42</lengthOfBody>
```

the attribute `units` can be viewed as metadata that further describes the contents of the element.

mutator. A stored procedure or method that changes a data value via a side effect.

namespace. A mechanism described by the W3C Namespace Recommendation [NAMESP] that allows XML vocabulary sets to be reused. They can be imported into and coexist within single documents without collisions between overlapping element and attribute names. Names belonging to a particular namespace are prefixed by a namespace prefix and colon. The namespace prefix in turn is a shorthand for a fuller URL that represents the namespace.

namespace prefix. An optional NCName prefix to an element or attribute name, prepended to it by a colon. The prefix is mapped to a unique namespace URL by a namespace declaration in the document.

nesting. XML imposes a treelike structure on documents, in which elements may in turn contain other elements. These latter are also called *subelements*, or *children*, of their containing parent and are said to be nested within them.

node. Collectively describes the seven types of data that can comprise an XML tree. Node types in the XML Infoset (and by extension the Query data model) are elements, attributes, text, comments, processing instructions, namespace nodes, and a document node representing the document itself.

node hierarchy. The description of positional relationships between nodes in an XML tree. Most commonly, this refers to the superordinate-subordinate relationships between parent nodes and their children.

node table. A construct that represents the structure of a tree in tabular form, in which each row identifies the properties of a node, such as its name, its value, and a reference to its parent node. The construct can be used to represent parent-child connections in an XML tree in a tabular, relational format. Since a node table represents a tree, it is isomorphic to the edge table. See *edge table*.

node type. One of the seven types of XML nodes in the XQuery data model: document node type, element node type, attribute node type, namespace node type, processing-instruction node type, comment node type, and text node type.

nonlinear hierarchy. As described in Chapter 6, the result of a composition technique in which an element has multiple children that have been added to it through different hierarchical joins.

normalization rule. The description in the formal semantics of the rules that specify how to transform the full XQuery language into a smaller core language that is easier to define, implement, and optimize.

null. A special "out of band" value in SQL representing unknown or inapplicable data.

occurrence indicator. A grammatical shorthand for specifying constraints on the allowable numbers of an item (used in a nontechnical sense). The indicator specifies whether the items are optional and/or how many times they're allowed to be repeated. The indicators follow:

?: optional (zero or one only)

*: optional (zero or more)

+: one or more

These can be used to modify `SequenceType` expressions (e.g., `element(*, po:address)+`). They can also be found in the description of function parameters, and several type-related expressions such as `instance of` and `typeswitch`.

online transaction processing (OLTP). A form of data processing in which end-user transactions update databases in real time.

operational semantics. The name in the field of logic and programming language theory for the techniques employed in the formal semantics to define XQuery. These include the normalization rules that define a language in terms of a smaller core, inference rules, and judgments.

optimization. A process in which an XQuery processor will programmatically simplify the form of a query to make data retrieval more efficient.

orderspec. A specification that states how two items are to be compared for the purpose of determining sort order. An `order by` clause may have one or more orderspecs.

outer join. The selection of nodes from different documents (more correctly, different sequences of items) in which items are returned regardless of whether both sequences contributed a data point.

partial updates. Updating only a few data values within a larger set of values in a document.

path expression. The navigational portion of the XPath and XQuery languages, which specifies how to locate various nodes within the XML being queried.

Post-Schema Validation Infoset (PSVI). An extended version of the XML Infoset employed during XML Schema processing both to add type-related information and to normalize certain values.

predicate. A modifier on an XPath step that specifies a filter against which items may be tested. Predicates can be numeric or conditional. Numeric predicates are used as an array index into a sequence to select a particular item; with conditional predicates, a Boolean test is applied against each item in the sequence.

primitive type. The term for one of the nineteen XML Schema "base" datatypes, which are not derived from another type. Primitive types include `xs:string`, `xs:boolean`, `xs:decimal`, `xs:float`, `xs:double`, `xs:QName`, `xs:hexBinary`, `xs:anyURI`, hexadecimal and base 64 encodings for binary data, and nine datatypes representing time- and date-related information.

prolog. The optional frontmost section of a query, which provides information on its context through various types of declarations and definitions. User-defined functions are defined here; for example; they can be referenced in the body of the query. Namespaces are declared in the prolog, as is information on collations and imported schemas to be used.

proof tree. The description of a series of inference rules applied to an expression, each of which is true, which demonstrates the corresponding conclusion.

qualified name (QName). Taken from the XML Recommendation [XML], a `QName` represents a valid name type for several different XQuery constructs. Most commonly used to denote legal element and attribute names with optional namespace prefixes, QNames are also used to specify the names of datatypes, variables, and functions.

Query (or XQuery) data model. The form of data model specific to XQuery. It's an abstraction of the Infoset [INFOSET], which ignores some detail, such as individual character information items and entity references, while adding type information supplied by XML Schema and the notion of multiple documents.

query language. A language used to interrogate the contents of a data store.

Quilt. A precursor to XQuery that provided much of its present functionality and syntax.

rank. A numeric value assigned to the individual results of a full-text search. Usually provides some measure of the weight of the result with respect to the original query.

recursive function. A function that calls itself. The canonical example is the definition of factorial as a recursive function: $f(n) = n*f(n - 1)$, where $n > 0$ and $f(1) = 1$. XQuery supports recursive functions.

relational database. The most common form of database, in which information is placed in tables, where rows hold multiple values, one value per column. The most common language for specifying queries against such data is SQL.

relational data model. The data model underlying relational databases, introduced by E. F. Codd in 1970. Data is described as a sequence of tuples, or rows.

reserved word. A keyword that can only be used in very specific syntactic contexts. XQuery has keywords (for, where, etc.), but they're not reserved.

root node. The topmost node of an XML tree: the document node in a full XQuery document; otherwise the single, topmost node of a fragment.

schema. In general, a formal description of the names, types, and allowed patterns of occurrence of elements and attributes in a document.

DTDs are a simple form of schema, as are the catalogs in a relational database. In the context of XQuery, the term generally refers to a schema as defined in the XML Schema Recommendation [SCHEMA].

schema import. An optional XQuery feature that allows an XML Schema to be imported so that its definitions are available to a query.

schema validation. The process in which information contained in an XML Schema is compared to data nodes to determine their type. If the node conforms to a schema declaration, it is considered valid, and its data model information item is "annotated," or marked, with the type information. Otherwise validation fails, and an error is reported.

semantic constraints. Syntactically, the operands of any XQuery expression can be any other expression. This doesn't always make sense semantically, however. For example, while the XQuery grammar allows two node sequences to be added together (as a consequence of the principle of compositionality), this will actually produce an error at runtime.

semi-structured. XML data in which the structure provided by the markup is not totally regular and has some variation in substructure between instances. In practice, such substructure can be denoted by the use of XML Schema union types, `xs:choice` annotations, or repeating groups. In general, the term *semi-structured* refers to any data model that is self-describing and may have arbitrary structure.

sequence type. The XQuery syntax used to describe the type of a sequence. For example, a function parameter might be described as type `node()+`, meaning one or more nodes (of any of the allowable seven node types), or `element(LastName, nameType)?`, meaning an optional Last-Name element conforming to a schema definition for `nameType`.

shredding. The name for the process in which XML data is decomposed into values suitable for storage in relational tables.

simple type. An XML Schema primitive type, or a type derived from an XML Schema primitive type, by restriction, list, or union.

skip. One of three validation modes for XML Schema. The element being validated must be well-formed. It and all subordinate elements are labeled as `xs:anyType`, and any attributes are labeled `xs:anySimple-Type`.

SOAP. An acronym for Simple Object Access Protocol, an XML-based protocol for web services.

sort keys. The operands of an `order by` expression that optionally modifies a FLWOR expression. The key or keys specify the ordering mechanism by which the output of the FLWOR is sorted.

Sorted Outer Union. A query or data-mapping construct that creates hierarchical data from relational data by grouping the relational data on common keys.

SQL. Originally an acronym for Structured Query Language, SQL is a language for defining, modifying, and controlling the data in a relational database. Pronounced officially with the individual letters sounded out, as S-Q-L; frequently as "sequel" informally.

SQL-2003. The most recent ISO Standard version of SQL.

SQL/XML. An ISO proposal that adds standard XML extensions to SQL. It adds the definition of a native XML datatype to the language, which allows XML documents to be treated as relational values in columns. It also provides implicit mappings from relational data to XML.

start tag. The angle-bracketed portion of XML markup that denotes the point in a serialized document where an element begins. Start tags can optionally contain attributes.

static environment. All the information that is available during static analysis of a query, prior to its evaluation. This information comes from the query prolog and from the host environment.

static semantics. The portion of the formal semantics that describes how static types are associated with expressions in XQuery.

static type. The type of an expression as determined by the static typing rules applied during static analysis. Static analysis examines only the query and types used in the query (as specified by imported XML schemas) and is independent of any input data.

static type-checking. The process of checking during static analysis that an inferred static type is a subtype of an expected type. This guarantees type soundness during dynamic execution since all type errors are deleted statically.

step. The part of an XPath expression that generates a sequence of nodes, optionally filtered by a predicate. A step always returns a sequence of nodes in document order and eliminates duplicate nodes based on node identity.

store. A mapping in the formal semantics relating node identifiers to node values.

strict. One of the three validation modes under XML Schema. A schema declaration must be present, and the element must validate with respect to that declaration. The element and all subordinate content are labeled with the appropriate type annotation.

string value. The content of a node displayed as a single string. The `string-value()` accessor (see the *data model*) determines how this is derived for each specific node type. For example, the string value of a document node is defined as the concatenation of the string values of all the text node descendants of the document in document order. The string value of an element is similarly the concatenation of the string values of all the text node descendants of the element, and the string value of an attribute is simply its value.

structured data. Data that fits easily into a predefined, homogenous model. See *semi-structured*.

subelement. An element contained within another, superordinate element.

substitution group. A mechanism in XML Schema that allows elements of one name to be substituted for elements of another name.

tag. The angle-bracket-enclosed section of XML markup that denotes either the start or the end point of an element. Can be one and the same for an empty element.

three-valued logic. A form of logic in SQL that specifies the results of logical operations on operands having the standard binary values of `true` and `false`, as well as on operands representing the special null value. Not used in XQuery.

transitivity. A mathematical property of an operator that states, given that `operandA op operandB` and `operandB op operandC` are both true, that `operandA op operandC` is also true. XQuery's value comparisons are transitive (because `$var1 eq $var2` and `$var2 eq $var3` implies `$var1 eq $var3`), while general comparisons are not (since `$book1/author = $book2/author` and `$book2/author = $book3/author` does not imply that `$book1/author = $book3/author`). The latter fails transitivity because existential quantification is applied to the operands of general comparisons and may affect each pair differently.

trigger. A procedure that is automatically executed in a DBMS in response to certain operations, such as update of a particular column.

two-valued logic. Standard binary logic in which a Boolean operation performed on its operands returns either `true` or `false`.

type. A set of constraints, as specified in an XML schema, that denotes a set of values in the XML data model.

type annotation. The property of element and attribute nodes in the Query data model that describes the type of the node, as determined by the schema-validation process.

type error. A type error is raised by XQuery when the type of an expression does not match the type required by the context in which it appears. For example, passing a string as a function argument where an integer is expected would raise a type error. How type errors are reported is implementation-dependent.

type promotion. A process in which atomic values are promoted from one type to another, both during the resolution of function calls and the processing of operators that require numeric operands. For example, if a function parameter is declared to be of type `xs:float`, the function can actually be passed an argument of type `xs:decimal`, which will be promoted to type `xs:float`.

type soundness. The property of a type system that guarantees that evaluation of a type-correct expression will never raise a type error.

type soundness theorem. Expressed in two parts, this theorem provides the mapping between static and dynamic semantics in the formal semantics. The first part states that static analysis and dynamic evaluation in matching static and dynamic environments yield matching results. The second states that if an expression has a particular static type, dynamic evaluation of that expression will never yield a type error, and if the expression yields a value, then the value matches the specified static type.

type system. The XQuery type system consists of the set of XML Schema primitive and node types, the set of operators for combining and comparing types, the rules for associating types with values in the XQuery data model, and the rules for associating types with XQuery expressions.

typed value. The simple-valued content of an attribute or element node whose type annotation denotes a well-formed node, a node with simple content, or a node with mixed content.

typing judgment. The formal description, in the nomenclature of the formal semantics, that states the type of a particular expression in a static environment.

Unicode. A unified system for representing international character sets. Standardized by both the ISO and the Unicode Consortium.

union type. A type that denotes a choice of XML Schema datatypes. The value space and lexical space of the new type are the union of the value space and the lexical space of the types being unioned.

universal quantification. Derived from the field of predicate logic, a form of existential semantics that posits that every member of a sequence meets a specified condition. More concretely in XQuery, a quantified expression of the form, `every ... satisfies`.

Universal Resource Identifier (URI). A standard mechanism for addressing Web-based resources. Primarily used in XQuery to identify namespaces, as well as the targets of the `doc()` and `collection()` input functions.

untyped data. Data whose type is unknown because it's not described by a schema. XQuery associates special type annotations with untyped values, and operators apply special conversion rules to untyped data, depending on the context in which it is used.

update. The ability to change the value of nodes and write the updated value back to the underlying data store from which it was selected in the first place. Not a part of XQuery Version 1.

use case. A hypothetical usage scenario, specifying a specific query, its input data, and its expected results. Discussion of proposed new features within the Query working group has centered around such scenarios, which are formalized in the Use Cases document [XQ-UC].

validation. In XML generally, the process of determining whether a document instance complies with the definitions and constraints specified by a DTD or schema. In XQuery, which uses XML Schema, a major by-product of the validation process is determination of the type of each node being validated.

validation context. Controls how the name of a given element is matched against declarations in the imported schemas. For example, a `validate` expression can specify a context for locally declared elements or attributes.

validation mode. Specified in the prolog, this can be one of the following: `lax`, `strict`, or `skip`.

value. The contents of an actual data instance, as opposed to its type.

value comparison operators. XQuery operators that are used to compare two single, non-node values. The general comparison operators, which are used to compare sequences of items, add the concept of existential semantics to build on this base.

value space. The set of allowable values for a given datatype. For example, the value space for the built-in type `xs:boolean` consists of {`true`, `false`}. See `http://www.w3.org/TR/xmlschema-2/#value-space`.

virtual XML view. A view of non-XML data that is presented in an XML format without actually materializing the view (or caching it for later reuse).

WebDAV. An acronym for Web-based Distributed Authoring and Versioning. It is an IETF Proposed Standard, a set of extensions to the HTTP protocol that allows users to edit and manage files collaboratively on remote web servers.

whitespace. Defined in the XML Recommendation [XML] as one or more spaces (#x20), carriage returns, line feeds, or tabs. Whitespace is meaningful in an XML document if it is not being validated against a DTD or schema. If it is being validated, its significance depends on the schema definition.

World Wide Web Consortium (W3C). The organization in charge of developing and maintaining the common protocols that define and govern the World Wide Web. Member companies sit on working groups that work by consensus to develop W3C Recommendations. Some of the technical areas under W3C purview are HTTP, HTML, PNG, and the rapidly growing umbrella of XML-related technologies.

xdt:dayTimeDuration. An XQuery-specific specialization of XML Schema's `duration` datatype. Its lexical space contains only day, hour, minute, and second components, and its value space is the set of fractional second values.

xdt:untypedAtomic. An atomic value for which no type information is available. An atomic value inside an untyped node, such as `<answer>47</answer>` is of type `xdt:untypedAtomic`.

xdt:yearMonthDuration. An XQuery-specific specialization of XML Schema's `duration` datatype. Its lexical space contains only year and month components, and its value space is the set of integer months.

XML datatype. A relational datatype in SQL for representing XML data.

XML fragment. An XML tree whose root node is not a document node. A partial tree.

XML Schema. The W3C specification that provides a more complete mechanism for specifying validity constraints on XML documents than that provided by the original XML mechanism of Document Type Definitions (DTDs).

XML storage fidelity. A term used in Chapter 7 to describe the degree to which the storage of XML documents maintains properties of the original format. There are three variations: (1) string-level fidelity, in which storage preserves the original XML document, code-point for code-point; (2) Infoset-level fidelity, in which storage preserves the document structure on the level of the XML Infoset model; and (3) relational fidelity, in which storage preserves relationally important information and discards XML-specific properties such as document order.

XPath. The W3C specification that acts as an enabling technology for other W3C technologies, such as XSLT and XQuery, in which it's embedded. It provides a mechanism for searching for specific nodes within an XML document, in which both structural and content constraints can be specified.

XQuery data model. See *Query data model.*

xsi:nil. A special attribute defined in XML Schema that permits the element to be accepted as valid with no content during the process of Schema validation, even though the element has a declared type requiring content.

XSLT. A competing and complementary mechanism to XQuery for locating and transforming XML from one format to another. XSLT uses a stylesheet mechanism to drive a transformation from an XML input tree to an output tree that can be either XML, HTML, or text.

INDEX

Symbols

- (minus) operator, 8, 40
<< (node precedes) operator, 45
>> (node follows) operator, 45
$fs:dot, 289–292
$fs:last, 289–292
$fs:position, 289–292
$fs:sequence, 289–292
(: :) (begin/end comments), 8
* (multiply) operator, 40
* (wildcard) operator, 14, 221
' ' (apostrophe), delimiting string literals, 8
. (decimal), 8
" " (quotation marks), delimiting string
    literals, 8
// (double slash), 10, 13
/ (slash), 10, 99, 288
[ ] (brackets), 10–11
{ } (curly brackets), 15, 93, 123
+ (plus) operator. *See* plus (+) operator
= (equals) operator, 43–45

A

Abstract syntax, 241, 381, 443
Access control
    configuring, 410
    DBMSs and, 415
Accessor functions, built-in to XQuery, 49
Analysis-time. *See* Query-analysis phase
Annotated XSD Schema language, 331–334,
    340
Anonymous types
    defined, 443
    use of, 69
    XML Schema, 117

APIs (application programming interfaces), 415
apostrophe (' '), delimiting string literals, 8
Application programming interfaces (APIs), 415
Arithmetic operators, 40–41
    atomization and, 113
    flexibility of, 297–298
    kinds of, 40
    normalizing, 295–296
    untyped data, 41
    XPath and, 105
At (positional variable), 28–30
Atomic types
    conversion rules, 48
    defined, 443
    referencing, 119
    XQuery data model, 90
Atomic values
    comparison operators and, 41–43
    defined, 443
    formal semantics, 267–269
    items and, 90, 207
    matching to types, 248–250
    XQuery data model, 6
Atomization
    comparison operators and, 41–43, 298
    conversion of arguments, 113, 217
    defined, 443
    value extraction and, 40, 104
    as XPath implicit coercion, 294–296
Attributes
    defined, 443
    document order of, 7
    importing types and, 66
    node attributes, 208
Auction use case
    converting input (XML) to output
        (XHTML), 196–197

Also Available from Addison-Wesley

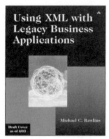
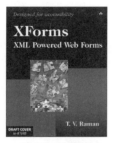

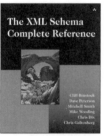
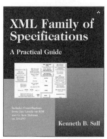

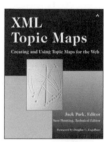
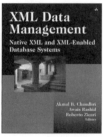
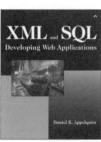

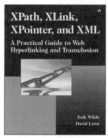
www.awprofessional.com